Contemporary Museum Architecture and Design

Contemporary Museum Architecture and Design showcases 18 diverse essays written by people who design, work in, and study museums, offering a variety of perspectives on this complex building type. Throughout, the authors emphasize the new kinds of experiences that museum architecture helps create, connecting ideas about design at various levels of analysis, from thinking about how the building sits in the city to exploring the details of technology.

With sections focusing on museums as architectural icons, community engagement through design, the role of gallery spaces in the experience of museums, disability experiences, and sustainable design for museums, the collected chapters cover topics both familiar and fresh to those interested in museum architecture. Featuring over 150 color illustrations, this book celebrates successful museum architecture while the critical analysis sheds light on important issues to consider in museum design.

Written by an international range of museum administrators, architects, and researchers this collection is an essential resource for understanding the social impacts of museum architecture and design for professionals, students, and museum-lovers alike.

Georgia Lindsay is a Senior Lecturer in Architecture and Design at the University of Tasmania. Her research focuses on the human experience of architecture, with a special interest in museums. She is author of *The User Perspective on Twenty-First-Century Art Museums* (2016) and co-editor with Lusi Morhayim of *Revisiting "Social Factors": Advancing Research into People and Place* (2015). She earned her PhD at the University of California, Berkeley.

"Georgia Lindsay has charted a course of self-discovery for the reader in her latest book, *Contemporary Museum Architecture and Design: Theory and Practice of Place*. Her assemblage of relevant case studies, categorized in a logical order, offers a diverse and unique perspective into architectural museum design. Her ability to inform and challenge, affords us the opportunity to reshape the museums of the future."

Kathleen Fitzpatrick, MBA, Senior Associate, DLR Group

Contemporary Museum Architecture and Design

Theory and Practice of Place

Edited by Georgia Lindsay

NEW YORK AND LONDON

First published 2020
by Routledge
52 Vanderbilt Avenue, New York, NY 10017

and by Routledge
2 Park Square, Milton Park, Abingdon, Oxon, OX14 4RN

Routledge is an imprint of the Taylor & Francis Group, an informa business

© 2020 selection and editorial matter, Georgia Lindsay; individual chapters, the contributors

The right of Georgia Lindsay to be identified as the author of the editorial material, and of the authors for their individual chapters, has been asserted in accordance with sections 77 and 78 of the Copyright, Designs and Patents Act 1988.

All rights reserved. No part of this book may be reprinted or reproduced or utilized in any form or by any electronic, mechanical, or other means, now known or hereafter invented, including photocopying and recording, or in any information storage or retrieval system, without permission in writing from the publishers.

Trademark notice: Product or corporate names may be trademarks or registered trademarks, and are used only for identification and explanation without intent to infringe.

Library of Congress Cataloging-in-Publication Data
Names: Lindsay, Georgia, editor.
Title: Contemporary museum architecture and design : theory and practice of place / edited by Georgia Lindsay.
Description: New York, NY : Routledge, 2020. |
Includes bibliographical references and index.
Identifiers: LCCN 2019044285 (print) | LCCN 2019044286 (ebook) |
ISBN 9780367075231 (hbk) | ISBN 9780367075248 (pbk) |
ISBN 9780429021176 (ebk)
Subjects: LCSH: Museum architecture.
Classification: LCC NA6690 .C66 2020 (print) | LCC NA6690 (ebook) |
DDC 727/.6--dc23
LC record available at https://lccn.loc.gov/2019044285
LC ebook record available at https://lccn.loc.gov/2019044286

ISBN: 978-0-367-07523-1 (hbk)
ISBN: 978-0-367-07524-8 (pbk)
ISBN: 978-0-429-02117-6 (ebk)

Typeset in Minion Pro
by Swales & Willis, Exeter, Devon, UK

Contents

Acknowledgments   *vii*
List of contributors   *ix*

   Introduction – Georgia Lindsay   1

PART 1: ICONS: Interrogating Spectacle and Design   7

1. *Iconic or Engaging? Beyond the Spectacle* – Elizabeth Ann Macgregor   9
2. *The Power of Star Architecture and Iconic Design: Kunsthaus Graz, Austria* – Johannes Dreher, Nadia Alaily-Mattar, and Alain Thierstein   23
3. *Transformational Architecture as Urban Catalyst: Toronto's Royal Ontario Museum, Municipal Policy, and the Cultural Renaissance* – Shoshanah B.D. Goldberg-Miller   43

PART 2: INVITATIONS: Design with Communities in Mind   63

4. *Designing with Community for Revitalization: A Creative Hub at the Denver Art Museum in Colorado, US* – Ann Baier Lambson   65
5. *Making an Urban Living Room: Museum of Contemporary Art Cleveland, Ohio, US* – Megan Lykins Reich   86
6. *Museum as Place-maker* – Kerstin Thompson   105
7. *Design for Citizenship: North Carolina Museum of Art in Raleigh, US* – Daniel P. Gottlieb   119

PART 3: EXPERIENCES: Understanding and Reimagining Design Inside   135

8. *The Open and Integrated Museum* – William Smart   137

9	*Building Citizens by Building Museums: Royal Ontario Museum & Art Gallery of Ontario* – Matt Patterson	155
10	*Experience and Meaning in Museums* – Helen Norrie	178
11	*Planning Art Museums from Inside-out: Design for Visitor Experiences* – İpek Kaynar Rohloff	195
12	*Illuminating History: The Mosegaard Museum in Aarhus, Denmark* – Jade Polizzi	215

PART 4: BODIES AND MINDS: Designing for Inclusion — 229

13	*A Sensory Place for All* – Meredith Banasiak	231
14	*Understanding Museum Architecture from Disability Experience: Pavilion of Knowledge in Lisbon, Portugal* – Caroline Van Doren, Peter-Willem Vermeersch, and Ann Heylighen	246
15	*Body Conscious Design in Museums* – Galen Cranz and Chelsea Rushton	260

PART 5: SUSTAINABILITIES: Green Design for New Museums — 277

16	*Triple Bottom Line Sustainable Design: Western Spirit: Scottsdale's Museum of the West in Arizona, US* – Christiana Moss and Christopher Alt	279
17	*Less Energy, More Stability: Passive Building Principles for Collection- and Visitor-Friendly Net-Zero and Net-Positive Buildings, and a Proposal for the Museum of Energy* – Jonathan Bean	297
18	*Bringing Nature into Place: Green Roofs as Place Makers in Museum Architecture* – Angela Loder	314

Index — 333

Acknowledgments

Support for this book was provided by the Program in Environmental Design at the University of Colorado Boulder and by the Undergraduate Research Opportunities Program at the University of Colorado Boulder. Humble thanks are due to all the chapter authors—assembling the materials required for your contributions took a dedication to detail and patience with deadlines not of your own making. I appreciate your willingness to explore ideas in writing. Thank you to Abby Clark for your work organizing the material, and to the editorial team at Routledge for your patience. Special thanks to my writing group members: Shawhin Roudbari, Stacey Schulte, Angela Loder, and Danielle Rivera at CU-Boulder and Mark Sawyer and Ceridwen Owen at the University of Tasmania. Finally, thank you to Micah Schwartz for being my team.

Contributors

Nadia Alaily-Mattar is Research Associate and Lecturer and the Chair of Urban Development of the Department of Architecture, Technische Universität München (TUM). Nadia is a trained architect and graduate of the American University of Beirut (AUB). She received her Masters degree in Housing and Urban Regeneration form the London School of Economics and Political Science and her PhD degree in Planning Studies from the University College London (UCL). She has worked at the United Nations Economic and Social Commission of Western Asia. Her research interests revolve around star architecture and its media effects, futures-oriented urban planning, urban planning methods, and the role of architecture in urban development.

Meredith Banasiak, M.Arch., EDAC, Assoc. AIA, cultivates multi-disciplinary research, knowledge sharing, and application to inform design innovation which optimizes health, performance, and access. Her experience in research, practice, and pedagogy supports the transformational shift in design towards an evidence-based, person-centered culture. As a design researcher, she is responsible for cultivating research partnerships with healthcare organizations, exploring novels methods for conducting real-time research, and translating evidence with designers. A former faculty member in architecture, Meredith brings experience of academic and community-based research. Meredith is an advisory council member for the Academy of Neuroscience for Architecture (ANFA).

Jonathan Bean is an interdisciplinary scholar and Assistant Professor in the School of Architecture at the University of Arizona. His current research focuses on the emergence of high-performance building. He is co-editor of the book *Taste, Consumption, and Markets: An Interdisciplinary Volume* and he is recognized in the field of marketing for his pioneering work on taste regimes, which was published in the Journal of Consumer Research. Bean also contributes a column on consumer culture and technology in the human–computer interaction magazine *Interactions*. He has been the faculty advisor to University of Arizona student teams in the Race to Zero and Solar Decathlon Design Challenge competitions.

Galen Cranz is Professor of the Graduate School in Architecture at the University of California at Berkeley, a PhD sociologist from the University of Chicago, and a certified teacher of the Alexander Technique. She is author of *The Chair: Rethinking Culture, Body, and Design* (W.W. Norton 1998), which received EDRA's 2004 Achievement Award. In 2011 she also received the EDRA Career Award, its highest award. Galen has taught "body conscious design" since 1989. She currently studies vision (EyeBody) with Peter Grunwald of New Zealand, and Body-Mind Centering with Bonnie Bainbridge Cohen in California. She swims and practices Tai chi daily.

Johannes Dreher is a research associate at HafenCity University Hamburg (HCU). He was previously research associate at the Chair of Urban Development at Technical University of Munich (TUM). Johannes was part of an interdisciplinary research project funded by the German Research Fund (DFG), titled "Star architecture and its role in re-positioning small and medium sized cities." Currently he investigates the role of large-scale construction projects as drivers for innovations in the construction industry in an interdisciplinary research project. Johannes holds a Diplom degree in geography from the Goethe-University Frankfurt and has worked as a research analyst at CBRE GmbH in Frankfurt.

Shoshanah B.D. Goldberg-Miller specializes in creative economic development, cultural policy, arts entrepreneurship, and nonprofit management. She examines how cities use arts and culture in planning, fostering livable communities and creating economic development strategies to build their brand, attract residents and tourists, and distinguish themselves from other urban centers worldwide. Her book, *Planning for a City of Culture: Creative Urbanism in Toronto and New York* (Routledge 2017) brings a fresh perspective to the study of creative cities by using policy theory as an underlying construct to understand the role of arts and culture in both the transformation of Toronto and the revitalization of New York during the 2000s. Goldberg-Miller is Assistant Professor at The Ohio State University.

Daniel P. Gottlieb directs the transformation of NCMA's 164-acre campus from prison site into a cultural destination, integrating art, recreation, and sustainable design and oversees architecture, landscape, environmental design. He co-curates the Museum Park sculpture program. He has received the following awards and distinctions: Honorary ASLA; AIA *Honor Award*; North Carolina's *Order of the Longleaf Pine*; NCSU College of Design *Lifetime Achievement Award*; numerous awards for environmental design and leadership; Delegate to *Summit on Fostering Universal Ethics Through Museums with His Holiness the Dalai Lama*, Dharamsala India. He also works as an exhibiting artist in photo-generated mixed media, exploring human relationships to nature and time.

Ann Heylighen is Research Professor at KU Leuven, Department of Architecture. She co-chairs the Research[x]Design group, and teaches design theory and inclusive design. Her research examines the relationship between how space is designed and how space is experienced. Ann holds an MSc and PhD in Engineering: Architecture from KU Leuven. She also studied at ETH Zürich and conducted postdoctoral research at Harvard and UC Berkeley. She was awarded several fellowships, including two grants of the European Research Council for her work on architectural design and disability. She is a Fellow of the Design Research Society and Associate Editor of Design Studies.

Ann Lambson joined the Denver Art Museum (DAM) in 2015 as the interpretive specialist for Architecture, Design, and Graphics, where she creates engaging experiences with architecture and design for visitors of all ages. Ann has been a consultant for the Smithsonian Institution and National Young Scholars Program. Prior to joining the DAM, Ann was the Head of Education at the Brigham Young University Museum of Art in Provo, UT and the former Director of Youth Education at the National Building Museum in Washington, D.C. She holds an MA in Art History and Curatorial Studies from Brigham Young University.

Georgia Lindsay is a Senior Lecturer in Architecture and Design at the University of Tasmania. Her research focuses on the human experience of architecture, with a special interest in museums. She is author of *The User Perspective on Twenty-First-Century Art Museums* (Routledge, 2016) and co-editor with Lusi Morhayim of *Revisiting "Social Factors": Advancing Research into People and Place* (Cambridge Scholars Publishing, 2015). She earned her PhD at the University of California, Berkeley.

Angela Loder is Vice President of Research for the International WELL Building Institute. As a research scientist, strategic planner, and educator, Dr. Loder brings over a decade of experience in interdisciplinary research and partnerships around occupant health, well-being, and the built and natural environment. Prior to joining

IWBI, Dr. Loder ran her own consulting firm, working with governments on urban planning, sustainability, and health. She is a Canada-US Fulbright Scholar and holds a collaborative PhD from the University of Toronto in Health Geography and Centre for the Environment. Her book *Small-Scale Urban Greening: Creating Places of Health, Creativity, and Ecological Sustainability* is forthcoming with Routledge.

Elizabeth Ann Macgregor, OBE, began her career as curator/driver of the Scottish Arts Council's travelling gallery, taking exhibitions around Scotland on a converted bus. In 1989 she was appointed director of the Ikon Gallery, where she championed cultural diversity in programing and connecting artists with the local community. In 1999, she became Director of Australia's Museum of Contemporary Art where she negotiated a new funding model, focused the Museum on supporting Australian artists in an international context, and developed innovative programs for engaging with broad audiences. In 2012 she was awarded an OBE. She was included in ArtReview's 2019 Power 100 list.

Christiana Moss and **Christopher Alt** are principals of Studio Ma, which has risen to national prominence for emotionally resonant and intellectually taut architecture. They practice performative design: Studio Ma consistently pushes the limits of energy-and resource-efficiency in their projects, yet their buildings' expressiveness is what you remember. Alt and Moss studied architecture at Cornell and with the Pritzker award winner, Sverre Fehn. After working in New York, they moved to Phoenix and founded Studio Ma in 2003. Living in the Desert Southwest has profoundly shaped their practice. Studio Ma's name comes from the Japanese concept of *ma*, the dynamic relationship between objects and the surrounding environment, which Moss and Alt experience daily in Phoenix, a city surrounded by jagged mountains, and where the play of light and shadow offers an ever-changing backdrop.

Helen Norrie is a design academic working across scales from the curation of ideas through text and exhibitions, to the design of buildings and urban environments. Helen teaches Architecture & Design at the University of Tasmania (UTAS). She is the founder of the Regional Urban Studies Laboratory (RUSL), a collaborative urban design research project that engages directly with local councils and communities to examine urban spatial, temporal and social issues in small towns and cities. Her research explores the intersection of development, planning and urban design, examining the agency of architecture to engage with broader urban and cultural narratives.

Matt Patterson is an Assistant Professor in Sociology at the University of Calgary. His research concerns the role of culture and the cultural industries in urban life and has appeared in journals such as *Urban Studies*, *City & Community*, *Poetics*, and *Qualitative Sociology*.

Jade Polizzi is a licensed architect and faculty member at the University of Colorado's Program in Environmental Design. Jade's primary research focus is in design-build and service learning. However, after spending a year traveling the world and visiting countless museums and historical attractions in dozens of countries, she has developed her eye for public structures and exhibit design. Jade also teaches studio classes, history and construction methods.

Megan Lykins Reich is Deputy Director at the Museum of Contemporary Art (moCa) Cleveland where she has worked since 2004. Reich manages and evaluates the implementation of the museum's strategic plan, which she co-authored in 2015, and oversees the Engagement department. Reich has organized or coordinated over 30 exhibitions for moCa and she has written, edited, and contributed to 13 catalogs and publications. She graduated from Pennsylvania State University's School of Visual Arts in Art History and Studio Art, and received her MA in Art History/Museum Studies from Case Western Reserve University, where she also conducted doctoral studies.

İpek Kaynar Rohloff is a design consultant, researcher, and educator working independently in the New York metropolitan area, USA. Her consultancy integrates human-behavior insights with planning and design by decoding behavior-environment interactions and by formulating strategies for human experience. Her work serves public and private organizations in place-making with social and economic viability. Previously she taught architectural design in Boston and Amherst in Massachusetts and advanced her research in sustainable urban development during her role as Mellon Post-doctoral Fellow at Mount Holyoke College and Five Colleges Inc. She earned her professional degrees in architecture from Middle East Technical University (Ankara, Turkey), and received her PhD in Architecture along with Museum Studies Certificate from the University of Michigan, Ann Arbor.

Chelsea Rushton is a practicing visual artist, a 500-hour certified yoga teacher, and a technical writer at the University of California at Berkeley's Architecture Department. Her creative production and scholarly research focus on the intersections of art, spirituality, and somatics in the 20th and 21st centuries, and the ways in which creative process can document and facilitate personal and collective growth and evolution. Rushton's work has been supported by the British Columbia Arts Council, the Alberta Foundation for the Arts, the University of Calgary's Centre for Research in the Fine Arts, and Calgary Arts Development.

William Smart is the founder and Creative Director of Smart Design Studio. Directly involved in every project, his buildings have received critical acclaim, won prestigious awards and have been widely published in architectural and other publications. William initially worked for Gersau Architecture in France followed by Foster & Partners in London, where he contributed to various award-winning projects. In 20 years of directing his own multi-disciplinary practice his enthusiasm and passionate attention to detail is fundamental to the Studio's success, motivating a highly dedicated team of architects and interior designers to realize projects of the highest quality and innovation.

Alain Thierstein is Professor for Urban Development at the Department of Architecture, Technische Universität München (TUM). He also is affiliated with the consultancy of EBP Schweiz AG, Zurich, as partner and senior consultant in the area of urban and regional economic development. He received his MA degree as well as his PhD in Economics from the University of St. Gallen, Switzerland. Thierstein is involved in research on urban and metropolitan development; spatial impact of the knowledge economy, in particular the visualization of non-physical firm relationships; spatial interaction of locational choices for residence, work and mobility; and the role of star architecture for repositioning medium-sized cities. His work is extensively published internationally.

Kerstin Thompson is Principal of KTA. Located in Melbourne, Australia and founded by Kerstin in 1994, KTA has established itself as a significant reference point in Australian architecture and urban design, and has been widely awarded, published and exhibited. The practice focus is on architecture as a civic endeavour with an emphasis on user experience and enjoyment of place. A committed design educator Kerstin is an Adjunct Professor at RMIT and Monash Universities. She regularly lectures and leads studios at various schools across Australia and New Zealand and was Professor of Design in Architecture at VUW from 2011 to 2018. In recognition for the work of her practice, contribution to the profession and its education, Kerstin was elevated to Life Fellow by the Australian Institute of Architects in 2017.

Caroline Van Doren combines her job as an engineer-architect at NMBS (Belgian Railways) with freelancing as journalist and studying Conservation at the University of Antwerp, Belgium. She studied architecture at the University of Leuven (KU

Leuven), Belgium, and at the Instituto Superior Técnico in Lisbon, Portugal, where she conducted the research that lies at the basis of this chapter. She holds an MSc in Engineering: Architecture and an MA in Journalism from the University of Leuven (KU Leuven), Belgium. Before joining NMBS, she was an architect at Verdickt & Verdickt Architecten and an assistant-project lead at Verstraete & Vanhecke, a contractor specialized in building conservation.

Peter-Willem Vermeersch works as a postdoctoral researcher at KU Leuven, and as an engineer-architect at (Full) Scale Architecten in Leuven, Belgium. He obtained his MSc and PhD degree in Engineering: Architecture from KU Leuven, and did his internship at osar architecten in Antwerp. At KU Leuven, he is part of the Research[x]Design group, a multidisciplinary group at the interface of design research and social sciences/humanities which conducts research on how space is designed, how space is experienced, and the relation between both. His research focuses on how the lived experience of disabled people can inform architectural design practice.

Introduction

Georgia Lindsay

Are museums the cathedrals of our age? Like cathedrals, they represent the ideals society holds, gathering objects and people together in service of knowledge and beauty. In creating collections, they delineate whose culture, history, and art is important (Cuno, 2009). In defining audiences, museums articulate which communities are worthy of connecting to that culture and history. Additionally, museums represent the worldly concerns of the people who lead the institutions and the cities that so often support the museums in a symbiotic relationship.

As with cathedrals, the architecture of museums is an intrinsic part of the entire project. With the explosion of new museum buildings—one critic called the turn of the millennium an "age of museum madness" (West, 2006, 220)—*architecture* has become a defining aspect of the museum experience and an entry point into how the general public thinks about museums. For example, the undulating, titanium-clad façade of Guggenheim Museum in Bilbao made a regional business center into a global tourist destination, turning a small town into a household name. The Bilbao Effect emerged after the highly visible opening of the building and the economic boost the city received from the spectacular architecture—and is now shorthand to explain any iconic building inserted into a regional city. It brings to the fore the many issues that are important to museum architecture besides just a building's ability to shelter art and welcome visitors. Museums are often a vital part of the cityscape, iconic landmarks that can help define an area of town and indicate a node of culture and learning. They protect and preserve collections while simultaneously welcoming, entertaining, and enlightening visitors. They are places of leisure and of work. They are integral parts of the local economy, with an ability to draw visitors and increase overnight stays, while needing to draw on the generosity of donors and sometimes the voting public for funding and capital campaigns.

As such a "prominent and important building type" (Self, 2014, vii), museums help articulate how to design for this variety of functions. Museum architecture "surprises us with its heterogeneity and innovation" (Tzortzi, 2015, 1), but it also encapsulates the deeply important issues that architects contend with in a variety of projects. For example, institutions and designers continue to grapple with accessibility and universal design, and museums wrestle with how to address the needs of a variety of communities. In democratic countries especially, there is an ongoing design question of how public buildings remain metaphorically and literally open while still protecting their contents—libraries struggle with this, as well as federal buildings. Architecture is often a symbol or even used as synecdoche for the institution held in a space: think of Apple stores with their glass fronts and lack of cash registers drawing people in to see what the fuss is about, or the California Academy of Science, which uses its green roof to symbolize a connection to its surroundings, as a draw to entice visitors, and as part of their scientific data collection.

In these cases, as in the museums in this book, the design is about so much more than walls and a roof. This book addresses fundamental issues of architecture, using museums as the focal point.

As buildings, museums represent three different paradigms of what buildings are: containers for collections, places for people, and symbols for ideas and values.

MUSEUMS AS CONTAINERS

The museum as we know it today originated in practice in collections of art, ethnographic, or other interesting objects gathered together and then presented for viewers. At first, these cabinets of curiosities might be seen only by royalty and their invited guests, but as "the people" took control of governance, royal collections became public goods, and private galleries were opened to the public.

Galleries are where architecture interacts with objects most visibly. Contemporary gallery space is a unique experience and understanding the space can help clarify the meaning of the objects in it (Carrier and Jones, 2016). The arrangement of objects within galleries affects the meanings visitors draw from the objects, just as the arrangement of galleries helps create messages about the collection as a whole (Carrier and Jones, 2016; Duncan, 1995; Tzortzi, 2015). Some institutions prioritize visitor experience, such as in the North Building of the Denver Art Museum. While the exterior was designed by international architect Gio Ponti and has been compared to a fortress, symbolizing in the designer's mind the safety with which the museum was preserving the public collections, the interior was designed by local architect James Sudler Associates, with significant input from Otto Bach, the director at the time. Bach wanted a visitor to be able to access any of the galleries over lunch—so each of the nine floors is divided into two smaller galleries with a small lounge in between. Visitors can take the elevator to a given floor, spend

45 minutes seeing an exhibition, and leave the museum without much hassle. In this instance, an idea about the gallery space, about how the museum was supposed to contain and display objects, changed the footprint of the building.

MUSEUMS AS PLACES FOR PEOPLE

The Denver Art Museum example is a good reminder that museums are not only visual experiences, but embodied ones as well. Early museums often had galleries arranged enfilade, as a series of rooms that a visitor walked through slowly, stopping and standing in front of pieces of art, a potentially exhausting march through the collection. Increasingly, though, museums focus less on objects and more on experiences, with spaces for active learning and for leisure.

The cafes, views, and gift shops that are now incorporated into museums represent an opening up of the museum, a democratization in usage and an acknowledgment that a variety of people might want a variety of experiences in a museum. Historically, architecture was enrolled in fostering a sense of decorum and imparting middle-class values to those who visited (Bennett, 1995). Now, the architecture signals excitement. As cultural production, the architecture itself has the power to tell the stories of social relations and power structures (Macleod, 2013), speaking to audiences beyond the elites who tend to fund and frequent art museums, or the artists whose work fills them (Harris, 1990).

MUSEUMS IN CONTEXT

A century ago, museum buildings usually resembled the European palaces they had evolved from, with colonnaded fronts and grand stairs (McClellan, 2008). Moreover, the buildings were often removed from the hustle of the city street in some way, taking advantage of what scholar Amir Ameri calls the "illusive distance" (2015) to imply cultivation and high ideals. The Philadelphia Art Museum, for example, sits on a hill, separated from the downtown by a parkway laid at a diagonal to the street grid. Now, museums are increasingly part of the city, both physically and economically as part of revitalization efforts, with the arts considered a vital part of an economic development agenda (Goldberg-Miller, 2017; Grodach, 2008).

Museums are, thus, stewards of the ideals of a city, whether those ideals are about economics or about communities. Museums also increasingly think of themselves as stewards of the environment, as more and more museums embrace green building practices and even pursue LEED certification. The stewardship of the environment moves beyond designing for energy efficiency to designing for biophilia—that is, some museum buildings implicitly impart a connection to ecosystems.

Museum Architecture Considered

This book offers diverse perspectives on each of the above issues, from architects, museum administrators, and scholars. In response to Suzanne MacLeod's challenge to move beyond "the obfuscating focus on surface and the genius of the architect" (2013, 7), the chapters of this book strive to understand museum architecture at a variety of scales and from a variety of analytical frameworks. Part 1: ICONS begins the discussion at a high level of analysis, thinking about star architecture for containing museum functions. The authors interrogate spectacular architecture contextualizing it with economic ideas and curatorial practices. In Part 2: INVITATIONS, the authors discuss how architecture can metaphorically and physically open the museum to diverse audiences. Moving to more internal architecture, Part 3: EXPERIENCES explores the way that the gallery spaces impact visitor experience, with two authors proposing new ways of approaching architecture to cater to new museum practices. The authors in Part 4: BODIES and MINDS remind readers that all experience is embodied, and design should respond to difference and create room for delight. Finally, Part 5: SUSTAINABILITIES is at once the most detailed and the broadest section, with authors analyzing the ways in which "green" design works for museums—at the technical and at the social level.

Throughout the book, regardless of the topic of the chapter, the authors emphasize the experience that the architecture of museums creates. While architecture cannot determine behavior, it does subtly influence the experience of a space, and thus the experience of art and other museum objects. It can also influence perception of an institution or of a city. Bringing together these issues in a single volume means that the chapters begin to speak to each other across scales. While one way to read this book would be to focus on a part to read about a theme, another way might be to read across parts to look at buildings of interest. Or, a reader might be interested in how different stakeholders think about museum design. The strength of this book is in its contributions from architects, museum professionals, and scholars, all groups who are interested in museum design but who do not often get to publish together. Readers who are interested in the architectural perspective can read Chapters 6, 8, 11, 12, 13, and 16; those who want to hear from museum professionals can begin with Chapters 1, 4, 5, and 7; and those who would like to begin with scholars can turn to Chapters 2, 3, 9, 14, 15, 17, and 18. Many of the authors, though, straddle multiple roles. Research into design reaches beyond any one field, and this book offers perspectives from across fields to help readers form a complete picture of museum architecture.

Museums have the power to communicate the identities and values of individuals, institutions, and cultures, and to create a sense of community among disparate members of a city. Museum architecture is often iconic, breaking away from design conventions to create unusual, creative, and startling spaces—spaces to "delight, inspire, and transcend" (McClellan, 2008, 106). It must also create spaces for contemplation and reflection, while simultaneously being responsible to the objects being protected and displayed. Often, museum buildings represent not only the institution they house, but also the very notion of who we are as citizens and what we want from society. This book is intended to uncover the ways that architecture affects museums, to inspire designers to create inclusive, engaging, sustainable spaces, and to encourage museum administrators to inhabit their spaces in creative ways.

REFERENCES

Ameri, Amir H. 2015. *The Architecture of the Illusive Distance.* Farnham, Surrey: Ashgate.
Bennett, Tony. 1995. *The Birth of the Museum: History, Theory, Politics.* New York: Routledge.
Carrier, David, and Darren Jones. 2016. *The Contemporary Art Gallery: Display, Power and Privilege.* Newcastle upon Tyne: Cambridge Scholars Publishing.
Cuno, James (ed.) 2009. *Whose Culture?: The Promise of Museums and the Debate Over Antiquities.* Princeton, NJ: Princeton University Press.
Duncan, Carol. 1995. *Civilizing Rituals: Inside Public Art Museums.* New York: Routledge.
Goldberg-Miller, Shoshanah B.D. 2017. *Planning for a City of Culture: Creative Urbanism in Toronto and New York.* New York: Routledge.
Grodach, Carl. 2008. "Museums as Urban Catalysts: The Role of Urban Design in Flagship Cultural Development." *Journal of Urban Design* 13 (2): 195–212.
Harris, Neil. 1990. *Cultural Excursions: Marketing Appetites and Cultural Tastes in Modern America.* Chicago: University of Chicago Press.
Macleod, Suzanne. 2013. *Museum Architecture: A New Biography.* New York: Routledge.
McClellan, Andrew. 2008. *The Art Museum from Boullée to Bilbao.* Berkeley, CA: University of California Press.
Self, Ronnie. 2014. *The Architecture of Art Museums: A Decade of Design: 2000–2010.* New York: Routledge.
Tzortzi, Kali. 2015. *Museum Space: Where Architecture Meets Museology.* Farnham, Surrey: Ashgate.
West, Mark. 2006. "Edifice Complex: Museums Spend Fortunes on Trophy Buildings, but Are They Really Worth It?" *W Magazine*, November 2006.

PART 1

ICONS
Interrogating Spectacle and Design

Museum architecture is often called upon to do more than just hold objects and people—additionally buildings are asked to be works of art in and of themselves. Buildings serve to identify not just the museum but also the city surrounding it. This section takes seriously the signaling role that museum architecture is asked to take on and interrogate the results of iconic design. Macgregor draws on her experience in commissioning new buildings for two institutions to conclude that instead of starchitecture, what makes museum buildings great is the ability to engage the public and to provide enough flexibility to accommodate evolving art forms. Dreher, Alaily-Mattar, and Thierstein investigate how the decision to build an iconic building has affected the Kunsthaus Graz in Austria. And Goldberg-Miller opens the black box of policy to identify the policy-makers and administrators who make a project happen. Taken together, these authors demonstrate that decisions made at one level of analysis—in this case, choosing starchitecture to benefit the city—have implications for the other functions inside museums.

CHAPTER 1

Iconic or Engaging?

Beyond the Spectacle

Elizabeth Ann Macgregor

As the director of two contemporary art galleries that have undergone a major architectural conversion – one in Birmingham, United Kingdom; the other in Sydney, Australia – my main motivation has been to deepen audience engagement with contemporary art and artists.

While the exterior of a new building captures public attention initially, it is the gallery's programs and the success of the visitor experience in the building that leads to long-term audience engagement. The potential benefits of reusing old buildings to exhibit contemporary art can be overlooked in the temptation to build new, iconic structures.

In 1993 the UK Government passed the *National Lotteries etc. Act*. It was a new and somewhat controversial initiative that had a significant impact on the ecology of the arts, with 25% of the profits after costs allocated to 'good causes', one of which in the initial years was capital funding for the arts via the Arts Council of England. The timing was fortuitous for one gallery in the Midlands: the Ikon Gallery.

The Ikon was founded in Birmingham in 1963 by a small group of artists. In its programming, Ikon was a pioneer in responding to the issues of the 1990s, when artists from different cultural backgrounds were challenging the white (male) bias of the art world. There was an increasing awareness of the breadth of exciting contemporary work being produced around the world, not just in the so-called major centres of London and New York. Ikon's program reflected this broadening of the international agenda as well as including artists from different backgrounds living in Britain.

As director since 1989, I had been seeking permanent premises for the gallery as the lease on the existing warehouse conversion was due to expire. Following a discussion with the Board, we made the decision not to renew the lease but to seek new premises for several reasons. Foremost was the desire for long-term stability and financial certainty that a building owned by the gallery would provide. A close second was the imperative to place the gallery nearer to the city center. Central to the gallery's mission was the objective to broaden its visitor base and find an easily accessible location where people could 'drop in' rather than make a special trip. For Ikon, with its commitment to access, finding a location that encouraged new audiences was of paramount importance.

This mission dictated the kind of location appropriate for the new gallery. Contemporary art then had few household names – even now there are probably only a handful. Strategies to broaden audiences, therefore, had to go beyond hosting blockbuster shows by celebrity artists. Moreover, the perceived elitism of arts institutions and in particular contemporary art galleries was a challenge to reaching new audiences. The derision in the media that greeted the annual announcement of the Tate's Turner Prize, including kneejerk references to the 'man in the street' (whoever he might be), reveals the popular attitude of the times – and not just in the tabloid press. There was also increased pressure from funding bodies for the arts to be more accessible and attract broader audiences, and rightly so.

Eventually a building was identified, on a development site in the middle of the city, on the canal, right behind a new convention centre that houses the wonderful home of the Birmingham Symphony Orchestra. The building was a derelict 19th-century school, built in 1877, with Grade 2 heritage listing – an important remnant of the Victorian architecture of Birmingham in its heyday.

The Ikon Board discussed the merits and challenges of such a project. As a listed building, there would be restrictions on what renovations could be done and the gallery would need to work sensitively with the heritage bodies. The interior had fallen into great disrepair, but the Board and I felt that a sensitive conversion could utilize the high volume of the old classrooms. The building would not offer the neutral warehouse spaces so often synonymous with contemporary art galleries, which we perceived to be an asset – the building could provide spaces that were good for exhibiting art, but were also user-friendly. One of the barriers to attracting visitors who were not already art aficionados was the stark and unwelcoming architecture of many contemporary art spaces. The very fact that the building was historic in a city where much of the heritage had been destroyed meant that it was much loved. It had a history with the immediate community as a school building and sat in one of the most deprived areas of the city, right next to the city center. The public's affection for the building was an advantage that the gallery would be able to build on when seeking to engage new audiences.

Levitt Bernstein Associates, which had undertaken the adaptive reuse of a historic building into the Royal Exchange Theatre in Manchester and initial conversion of an old building on the water into the magical Pier Arts Centre in Orkney, was appointed by the Board to explore options for adaptive reuse of the former school into an art gallery. As we began our deliberations, lead architect Axel Burroughs and I undertook a research trip, visiting several important museum buildings to see what we could learn. We chose some of the most obvious and lauded buildings, but our findings were not what we expected.

We were surprised by the level of dysfunction of these buildings experienced by museum staff and exhibiting artists. In many cases, the staff had not been closely involved in the drawing up of the brief nor in its interpretation. What was seen to be successful (iconic) in architectural terms fell far short in terms of museum operations. We therefore set ourselves the task of designing a user-friendly building appropriate for showing contemporary art in its many forms. The designs were prepared and submitted for lottery funding along with the required business plans.

Here the project hit a roadblock. The Ikon was one of the first applicants for lottery funding. The proposal met all the criteria for funding with one exception – the architecture was deemed 'inappropriate' for a contemporary gallery. This initial rejection led to a (somewhat nerve-wracking) debate with the Arts Council and its assessors about who should decide what kind of architecture was appropriate for a contemporary gallery. It became clear in subsequent meetings that the architectural assessors were seeking an iconic building, not a conversion of a pre-existing historical building. One assessor commented that we should have found a greenfield site in order to commission a 'great building'. The assessors also had objections to the internal layout of the building, in particular the cafe and museum shop being situated on the ground floor rather than galleries, something which had been decided by the architect after a long process of trying out different solutions with the staff and which answered the need to generate revenue.

In the end, the Ikon won the argument; the project got the funding, the building was completed in 1998, and, to our delight, it went on to win the RIBA Award 1999 and Royal Fine Art Commission Trust Building of the Year Award (Figure 1.1).

The opening night proved correct the predictions made about increased audience engagement; local people queued to get in, many of whom had never visited a contemporary art gallery before. While the building was being constructed, an extensive outreach program of artists working with the local community included a project about people's memories of the school. Artists also responded to the renovated building with enthusiasm (Figure 1.2).

Interestingly, when Tate was considering adapting the former Bankside power station into Tate Modern, there was also criticism from some within the

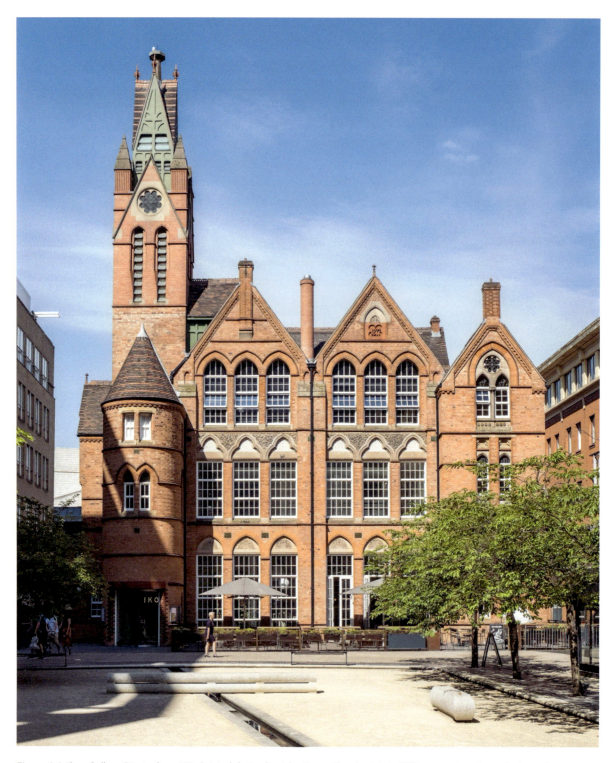

Figure 1.1 Ikon Gallery, Birmingham, UK. Original design by John Henry Chamberlain in 1877; restoration design by Levitt Bernstein Associates and completed in 1998. Photograph: Greg Jones, courtesy The Handover Agency.

Figure 1.2 Installation view of *Nancy Spero: Parade*, Ikon Gallery, Birmingham, 1998. Opening exhibition in the new Ikon. Photograph: Greg Jones, courtesy The Handover Agency.

architectural community for not commissioning a new building. In its deliberations, Tate undertook a survey of artists that revealed an overwhelming preference for the adaptive reuse of an old building. It is interesting to note that a number of 'iconic' buildings supported by the national lottery in the early years failed to achieve the results predicted in their business plans. The Public in West Bromwich and the National Centre for Popular Music in Sheffield for example did not survive, demonstrating that spectacular new buildings do not always lead to success.

Not long after the new Ikon Gallery opened, I moved to Sydney to run another gallery in an old building – the Museum of Contemporary Art (MCA). The Museum had opened in 1991, in an adaptive reuse by architect Andrew Andersons of Peddle Thorp/John Holland Interiors of the old Maritime Services Board building. It is situated on one of Australia's most important sites: the location of First Contact between Indigenous and European peoples, which marks the beginning of the country's colonial history. It is also one of the most beautiful sites in the world, right opposite the Sydney Opera House, a structure that contradicts the above thesis about the inadequacies of iconic buildings (Figure 1.3).

Figure 1.3 Site view of the Museum of Contemporary Art housed in the distinctive former Maritime Services Board building, clad with sandstone, on Sydney Harbour opposite the Sydney Opera House, Australia, 2015. Image: of the Museum of Contemporary Art Australia. Photograph: Anna Kucera.

The Opera House has functional issues, many of which stem from the controversies and difficulties that arose during its construction – not least the sacking of architect Jørn Utzon before it was completed – but its symbolic importance for the nation as one of the world's great monuments surpasses these issues. The Sydney Opera House is first and foremost a work of art.

The juxtaposition of the MCA, housed in an old government building, and the iconic Opera House posed a dilemma when the question arose of how to respond to the problems generated by the growing number of visitors. This increase in visitors exacerbated the problems of poor circulation, multiple entrances on different levels, and the difficulty of access for people with special needs. As interest in the MCA's learning programs also grew, the need for dedicated education spaces became crucial. Should the Museum commission an extension that would try, as one architect put it, to 'wave at the Opera House'? The situation was further complicated by the two previous attempts to expand the Museum, which involved two international competitions: the first won by Japanese studio SANAA in 1997 and the second won by German/English practice Sauerbruch Hutton in 2001, neither of which had progressed beyond the competition stage. In addition to being adjacent to the Opera House, which was inscribed on the UNESCO World Heritage List in 2005, the MCA site also includes historic docks underneath the Maritime Services building and the adjacent car park. There was a moment when the suggestion of moving sites was raised, something that the MCA team regarded with consternation. The MCA's funding model, which requires it to raise over 75% of its income from non-government sources, meant that the site was critical to its capacity to generate income from venue hire. Moreover, a move to a new site would inevitably have led to another competition and the likelihood of loss of control of the process by the Museum staff.

Because of the history of competitions and the complexity of the site, the Board decided to appoint a local architect to work with the museum to address the key issues. Six architects were interviewed and Sam Marshall of Architect Marshall was appointed.

The design brief was developed further by Marshall over a period of time, working closely with senior staff, initially the director and the Chief Operating Officer. A number of options were put to the Board, whose members agreed that a more extensive redevelopment than originally conceived would be necessary to solve all the problems. Alongside the design, a sound business plan outlining ways to increase income after the expansion to underpin the increased running costs was critical to the Board giving the go-ahead.

The preferred scheme was developed following a series of extensive consultation meetings across the MCA, from managers to front-of-house staff, to 'road test' the proposals. This rigorous process of consultation and collaboration between architect and client was critical to the success of the expansion. The architect himself made it clear that, notwithstanding one of the key issues being lack of visibility of the Museum as a contemporary institution, he regarded his task as creating a frame for the art and the other activities of the Museum, saying, 'The most important thing is the art. In the perfect gallery there would be no architecture visible'. His solution to one of the complexities of the site – a sharp difference in levels between the two sides of the building – was a sweeping foyer, with views out over the harbor (Figures 1.4 and 1.5). This grand entrance unequivocally signified 'contemporary' and left the old building intact, as required by the Heritage Council (Figure 1.6).

The circulation issues were resolved by this new addition that also included a major new spacious gallery. Views from the building at key points – on the stair landings and in public spaces – helped to orient visitors. Making the most of the views afforded by the location, the creative learning facilities (Figure 1.7) and the cafe (Figure 1.8) on the top level of the new wing were given a prime position, with large windows and a terrace. In contrast, the galleries were designed to focus on the art, not the views (Figure 1.9).

The new building opened in 2012 and within a year had achieved all the desired outcomes, from financial targets to visitor numbers, which far exceeded expectations (over 1 million visits – double the number prior to the expansion). The National Centre for Creative Learning, (Figure 1.10) where the Museum offers innovative creative programs led by a team of artist educators, has proved to be a huge success, attracting over 95,000 users in 2018. Featuring a range of spaces including

Figure 1.4 MCA ARTBAR event, curated by Caroline Garcia, Museum of Contemporary Art Australia, 2017. Dance performance by Sanggar Tari Bali Saraswati. Artwork by Khadim Ali, *The Arrival of Demons* (detail), 2017, Circular Quay Foyer Wall Commission. Image: the artist and the Museum of Contemporary Art Australia © the artist. Photograph: Leslie Liu.

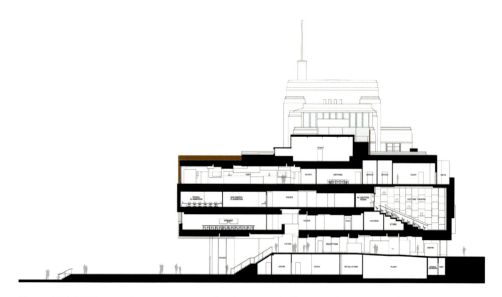

Figure 1.5 MCA Section, Drawing courtesy of Architect Marshall. Image: the Museum of Contemporary Art Australia.

Figure 1.6 View of the MCA showing the juxtaposition of the old building and the new wing designed by architect Sam Marshall, Sydney, Australia, 2015. Photograph: Brett Boardman courtesy the Museum of Contemporary Art Australia.

Figure 1.7 Children working with Artist Educators, school holiday program, National Centre for Creative Learning, 2017. Photograph: Anna Kucera courtesy the Museum of Contemporary Art Australia.

Figure 1.8 The MCA Cafe with views to the Sydney Opera House, 2017. Photograph: Oneill Photographics courtesy the Museum of Contemporary Art Australia.

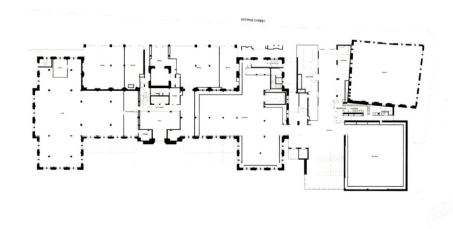

Figure 1.9 MCA map, level 2, Drawing courtesy of Architect Marshall. Image: the Museum of Contemporary Art Australia.

a multimedia studio, the quality and position of this suite of rooms demonstrates the MCA's commitment to access and diversity, which encompasses programs for refugee and immigrant children and their families from western Sydney; a world-first early learning research program; a partnership with the University of Sydney on art and dementia; as well as a room with a commissioned artwork devised for children with special needs.

However, the operation of the center also shows how new buildings need to be adaptable. Initially, there were plans for opening up engagement with regional schools through digital excursions where schools could connect remotely with the center's team of artist educators. However, it became clear after a year or so that schools simply could not keep up with the required investment in the technology and that real-time engagement was very difficult to fit into the tight curriculum. The digital classrooms were reconfigured as it became clear that the delivery of these programs was preferable online. This led to the highly innovative and successful online course for 14–16 year olds *Hello Big Institution* (HBI), devised with artist Lara Thoms.

The second factor that required rethinking was the previously untapped desire for drop-in programs. The center had been designed for booked groups, essentially behind closed doors. The huge success of an open weekend with thousands of

Figure 1.10 Visitors to the Bella Program at the National Centre for Creative Learning, showing the location of the Centre opposite the galleries, 2016. Photograph: Daniel Boud, courtesy the Museum of Contemporary Art Australia.

families taking part required a shift in thinking about how to respond to this exciting potential, both physically and structurally. The spaces were sufficiently flexible to be reconfigured; the key issue now is how to meet the demand from a financial point of view. The Centre's success is due to the employment and training of a large group of dedicated artist educators whose approach to creative learning makes the MCA experience so special and highly regarded.

Two shortcomings of the galleries in the old building were the columns and the low ceiling heights. However, by a clever reorganization of the floors and an addition to the old building on the street side away from Sydney Harbour, the architect created two 4-meter-high galleries with no columns and one more spacious gallery with 6-meter walls in the new wing (Figure 1.11). The expansion did not considerably increase the amount of gallery space, but it improved the quality of gallery space significantly. Moreover, the lower-height galleries (Figure 1.12) are advantageous when dealing with more intimate work and the variations in scale between galleries contribute to a more interesting visitor experience. Again, artists are the final arbiter: since reopening, the MCA has worked with a diverse range of artists, all of whom have given very positive feedback. From Anish Kapoor's sculptures (which required the roof of the new extension to be removed and the works craned in!)

Figure 1.11 Kader Attia, *J'Accuse*, 2016. New galleries, installation view *Kader Attia*, Museum of Contemporary Art Australia, Sydney, 2017. Image: of the artist, Galerie Nagel Draxler, Berlin/Cologne, and Museum of Contemporary Art Australia © the artist. Photograph: Jacquie Manning.

Figure 1.12
Renovated galleries in the old building. Installation view *MCA Collection: Yesterday Today Tomorrow*, Museum of Contemporary Art Australia, Sydney, 2017. Photograph: Jessica Maurer courtesy the Museum of Contemporary Art Australia.

to Pipilotti Rist's immersive installations, the new spaces have proved to be highly adaptable and the older spaces have provided no impediment to showing the range and diversity of art today.

When trying to raise funds for the redevelopment (the MCA raised 50% of the $53 million price tag from private individuals – including chairman Simon Mordant and his wife Catriona after whose family the new wing is named) many supporters wanted to know how much more gallery space would be provided, the assumption being that bigger equals better. Overcoming this expectation was a key challenge in the fundraising campaign. Others thought the museum should have fought to knock down the old building and start again. Given the public outcry when this was revealed as one of the possibilities presented by Sauerbruch Hutton competition winner in 2001, this was not a viable option, nor one that the NSW Government – the ultimate landlord – would have approved.

Given the MCA's low level of government funding (and the fact that it had come close to bankruptcy in the late 1990s), creating more galleries was not a high priority. Improving the visitor experience and providing facilities for the MCA's groundbreaking creative learning programs were the principal reasons for the development.

The MCA attracts over 1 million visitors annually – significantly more than the business plan had projected. With one floor dedicated to the MCA Collection and

Figure 1.13 GENEXT, a free event for young people aged 12–18 years, which attracts over 600 to each event, featuring the harborside entrance to the MCA, 2015. Photograph: Maja Baska courtesy the Museum of Contemporary Art Australia.

two more to temporary exhibitions, visitors tend to spread out across the three floors, a scale that does not feel daunting. As with the Ikon Gallery, the human scale of the spaces is an asset at the MCA.

With many of the major state-funded galleries in Australia planning major extensions, the subject of more space is sometimes raised with the MCA. As collections grow, so does the pressure for more gallery space; whether this is sustainable is a topic for another occasion. The relentless fundraising that all directors face is exacerbated by larger buildings. The MCA has been able to expand its programs by looking at how the space is used and developing programming to drive visitor experience. For example ARTBAR is a late-night program curated by artists that takes over the MCA's four levels, activating spaces throughout the building not accessible to the public during standard operating hours. It provides a late-night experience with art at its core and is a programming strand for more performative work. To encourage new audiences, the MCA also looks beyond its physical walls. The museum runs a significant program in Western Sydney, C3West, which brings artists to consider issues of local concern and engages communities in new ways. A more recent project is the co-acquisition program with Tate, supported by Qantas, a partnership that will increase exposure for Australian art across the globe.

For the Museum of Contemporary Art Australia, with its focus on artists and its commitment to deepening engagement with its audiences, the building and the programming are in harmony, with the fundraising at an appropriate level (Figure 1.13). In the words of the artist Ian Hamilton Finlay, 'Small is quite beautiful'.

CHAPTER 2

The Power of Star Architecture and Iconic Design

Kunsthaus Graz, Austria

Johannes Dreher, Nadia Alaily-Mattar, and Alain Thierstein

The discussion about flagship, iconic, or star architecture has been dominated by the "Bilbao effect" narrative for the last 20 years. It is mostly related to the successful structural change that the city of Bilbao has experienced (Haarich and Plaza, 2010, 5). The most common definition of the Bilbao effect refers to the use of flagship buildings such as a museum, an opera house, a concert hall, or a theater characterized by iconic architecture and designed by a leading star architect, combined with culture-driven revitalization in a depressed city or region with the aim to turn it into an attractive, international, and industrially visible location for tourism, businesses, or the cultural and creative industries (see Heidenreich and Plaza, 2015, 1441; Ponzini, 2011, 5).

The fact that the construction of the Guggenheim Museum in Bilbao (GMB) was only one element in a comprehensive strategic plan for a structural change and a new urban renewal in the city of Bilbao is often overlooked. The supposed success and the seemingly simple formula have aroused worldwide covetousness for the replication of the Bilbao effect (Jencks, 2006, 8; Klingmann, 2007, 247–248), so much that some would argue it became an "urban policy in motion" (González, 2011). The Bilbao effect dominated the discourse on museums architecture and heightened expectations of politicians and city officials, that a museum can play a crucial role in urban economy and urban regeneration. By commissioning star architects, politicians hope for iconic, flagship museums to bring a positive impact on urban development. While the expectations of the Bilbao effect rely on the capacity to be a "flagship" and an "icon", it is important to differentiate between those terms for a better understanding how these projects work. Weidenfeld (2010, 851–853) points to the distinction between flagshipness and iconicity. He argues that flagships are buildings and institutions that are must-see attractions, attracting many visitors into the building with corresponding economic implications for the institution and the city (for example, Euro Disney or LEGOLAND). On the other hand, iconic buildings are authentic, representative symbols of a place that affect both tourists and locals. They can give a place an image and identity and are often the result of a long marketing process. Hence, iconic buildings attract visitors to the city and not necessarily into the building itself (such as the London Eye or the Sydney Opera House). Weidenfeld notes that buildings can be both a flagship and an iconic building – to a greater or lesser degree – and that this can also change over time (Weidenfeld, 2010, 851–853).

Similar to Weidenfeld, Shoval and Strom (2009) use the term "Values Museum" to draw attention to the difference between the significance of an exhibition and the significance of the building and its architecture. They note that museums are increasingly being used in strategic urban settings as urban development measures to achieve investments and to set off economic effects. The location of museums and the packaging of cultural content has gained importance whereas the objects on display at "Values Museum" play a secondary role (ibid., 2009, 157–158). Complementary "Values Museums" are characterized by the fact that they are not built to show an existing collection. Therefore, they do not have a permanent collection, only temporary exhibitions. Thus, the construction of these museums is unbound from existing place-based collections (ibid., 145–158).

Another widely used term is "Star Architecture" or "Starchitecture," underlining the idea that the star fame of the architects and/or the architecture plays an important role in the scale and scope of the impacts of these buildings, particularly as they support the media exposure of the projects (Foster, 2008; Ponzini, 2011). However, it is questionable if such projects eventually become flagships or icons or whether they trigger any impacts (Heidenreich and Plaza, 2015; Klingmann, 2007, 248; Ponzini, 2011, 252). Hence, this chapter uses the term star architecture, because it leaves open whether and, if so, what kind of impact sets in.

Most of the academic literature that discusses iconic or flagship or star-architectural projects treats these projects as a single entity and ignores their complex socio-material nature. Alaily-Mattar, Dreher, and Thierstein (2018, 175) argue that the outputs of star-architectural projects are complex and dynamic bundled offerings. Following this idea, we propose to investigate the effects and impacts of star-architectural projects, while taking into consideration the project development process, the star architecture as a physical building, the location of the property, the institution, and the function. Drawing plausible linkages between these elements of star architectural projects and observed impacts help the examination of a more differentiated understanding of "how star architectural projects work." By doing so we reveal effects of star architectural projects. We understand effects in a non-deterministic way and impacts as a multidimensional, multi-scalar process (Thierstein, Alaily-Mattar, Dreher, forthcoming). Even if it is not possible to clearly trace back impacts to a single element of a project in the sense of a causal relationship, because of possible overlapping contributions of different elements to these impacts and external influences, uncovering the contribution of the different elements of a star architectural project improve our understanding of such star architectural projects. Although star architectural projects produce a wide range of effects, this chapter will focus on effects that can be related to the star architecture as a physical building. Based on our case study of the Kunsthaus Graz in Austria, we discuss the effects of the star architecture on 1) the function, that is, the program of the exhibition house, 2) on the operating institution, and 3) on the city.

The research that this chapter draws from is based on interviews, document analyses, and statistical data. The interviews were conducted with project proponents and documents were analyzed to examine the intended objectives of the Kunsthaus Graz project. This helped us to understand the context from which this project emerged and to develop an impact analysis. Additionally, we conducted interviews with local experts to uncover and evaluate the impact of the Kunsthaus Graz, whether intentional or not. Based on their experience and expectations the local experts helped us to understand how the project works, especially with regard to the effect of the architecture. Our interviewees are cited as a standard reference; details about the interviews can be found in the reference list. In addition, we analyzed socio-economic longitudinal data of the city of Graz and the Kunsthaus Graz in order to examine and evaluate socio-economic effects. Finally, an analysis of print media and social media – Flickr – helped us to uncover the media effects of the architecture.

EFFECT OF STAR ARCHITECTURE ON FUNCTION AND PROGRAM

The origin of the Kunsthaus Graz is strongly connected with a progressive contemporary art scene that arose in the city of Graz in the late 1960s, with expanding exposure at a super-regional scale. In the 1980s the idea to support the local art scene with a Kunsthaus (German for art house) was born. Two competitions were held but due to political changes neither of these two projects were realized. When in 1999, the city of Graz won the application for the European Capital of Culture Year (ECOC) the city officials saw the opportunity to realize the Kunsthaus Graz within this framework. The Kunsthaus Graz had a special position within the event of European Capital of Culture Year, also named Graz 2003. It was the major architectural project, which was envisaged to become a permanent symbol or legacy for this event with a Europe-wide presence. This was to be accomplished by a spectacle of star architecture, which should meet the objective of capturing attention at a European scale. Schrempf who was then the Managing Director and Deputy Director of Graz 2003, and is at the time of writing director of Creative Industries Styria (CIS), states, "like Bilbao, we wanted to be a city which receives an extended radius of perception through a new, special architecture that was surely quite essential" (Schrempf, 2016, interview).

Peter Cook and Colin Fournier won the architectural competition in 2000 and three years later, at the end of 2003, the Kunsthaus Graz was inaugurated. The decision for a star-architectural project had consequences for the program of Kunsthaus Graz (Figure 2.1). First, it led to changes in the requirements on the program and objectives. The spectacularity of the star architectural project and the success of its international outreach fed the ambitions and expectations of those in charge of the Kunsthaus Graz, who began to favor exhibiting the works of international artists rather than the local art scene. After fighting for over two decades for a house for contemporary art, the local artists were expecting to exhibit their works in the Kunsthaus Graz. The spectacular architecture made the project more prominent and extraordinary and therefore reinforced the desire of local artists to use the Kunsthaus Graz as their exhibition site. Conflicts thus surfaced due to this shift of the program's focus from local to international contemporary art. Rückert, the former councilor in Graz responsible for cultural affairs, describes it in the interview as follows "(It is) an old discussion … you want to shine internationally, but everyone wants to do exhibitions in it, all local artists. And that does not work" (Rückert, 2016, interview). The conflicts were accompanied by diverse expectations by different politicians: "Actually, they didn't know what they want" according to Pakesch, Director and Curator of the Kunsthaus Graz from 2003 to 2015 (2016, interview). Schnitzler, the Public Relations Manager of the Kunsthaus Graz, summarizes these ambiguous political goals: "There is also the expectation of being regional and international […] and regional politicians often expect something regional." The desire of local artists to exhibit at the Kunsthaus Graz, as well as the politically divided, unstable, and ambivalent goals of positioning the Kunsthaus Graz as a local and/or international exhibition house, is a challenge for the management (Schnitzler, 2016, interview).

Figure 2.1 Kunsthaus Graz, view from the historic center. Photograph by Universalmuseum Joanneum/N. Lackner.

Figure 2.2 The exhibition Space 01 has no intersection or straight walls to hang pictures. The spiral lighting is a significant feature of the room. Photograph: Universalmuseum Joanneum/J. J. Kucek.

The second consequence for the program pertains to the opportunities and challenges that the extraordinary exhibition space presents to the artists and the management of the Kunsthaus Graz (Figure 2.2). The exhibition spaces of the Kunsthaus Graz are not typical white boxes. This is acknowledged in the mission statement of the Kunsthaus Graz, the particular architecture has implications for the aspect of the artistic program. The two large exhibition spaces (Space 01 and Space 02) represent a very different character. The international, challenging and open – Space 01 – is ideal for large scale sculptural or architectural interventions […] The dark room – Space 02 – allows a special presentation of media works and photography.

(Universalmuseum Joanneum, 2017)

Schrempf confirms that the special architecture requires not only special contents, but also the openness and willingness of the artists to deal with this challenge, because "much of the interior fights against the dominance of architecture […] in the Kunsthaus Graz every exhibition has to be staged in the context of architecture, that's the difficulty" (Schrempf, 2016, interview). This difficulty combined with irregular walls, no separating inside walls and few possibilities to place paintings, led to a rejection of the exhibition spaces by some regional artists (Strobl, former Councilor of Graz, 2016, interview). More challenging for the Kunsthaus Graz was the criticism of regional art critics who denied the exhibition space its expected capability, due to the interior design. As the former director of the Kunsthaus explains:

In the same way the external form and the urban development situation were always seen as positive, so the people, especially the art critics, had a hard time with the inside of the Kunsthaus Graz. […] Certain public interest groups have not understood that.

(Pakesch, 2016, interview)

This attitude of art critics is captured by an article in the newspaper *Der Standard*:

The blue bubble fails as white cube […] The spiral lighting in the pimples is so dominant that almost every painting goes down. […] Only those (artists) who react to the coupled space can compete with it […] Michael Kienzler subordinated, Sol LeWitt built a wall. However, in general the upper level is not suitable as an exhibition venue.

(Trenkler, 2014)

While some artists had difficulties dealing with the challenges, other artists as well as the curators and critics were fascinated and attracted by the exhibition spaces and the new possibilities opened by the special exhibition space. In an interview Pakesch describes his experience as curator of the Kunsthaus Graz and expressed that this enthusiasm, commitment, and innovative approach to space in art can be traced back to its special architecture:

> We have always worked systematically with space at the Kunsthaus (Graz) and considered it as an important task. […] We have also created new spaces […] that was an enormous but exciting challenge […] I made exhibitions that have worked completely different than any previous exhibitions […]. The artists were completely enthusiastic. […] It has always been a great honor for artists to be invited. That was not necessarily due to my person or the program, but to the architecture […] in principle, curiosity and the contributions of the artists were great
>
> (Pakesch, 2016, interview)

The extraordinariness of the exhibition space and the possibility to do new things there is also seen as positive, as a "unique selling position" according to the public relations manager of the Kunsthaus Graz, Schnitzler:

> These productions are not available anywhere else in the world […] And that has the consequence that the international media also write more about it, because it is a unique effect […]. This is a chance for us. A white cube would not attract so much attention when you realize projects there. […] So for us it is also an advertising and editorial advantage that it is not a white cube. A project that does not exist anywhere else.
>
> (Schnitzler, 2016, interview)

A third consequence that is fostered through the special interior design is in the field of education. According to the curator and director of the Kunsthaus Graz, the extraordinary interior architecture – namely the open space, the strange and dark atmosphere – that is not only different to other buildings but also to other museums or exhibition spaces, is helpful to put the visitors of the Kunsthaus Graz in an exceptional state of mind, which makes them more open and receptive to contemporary art, to prevent the emergence of the typically recurrent question, "Is that art?" "Due to the architecture there is a certain willingness to accept a kind of emergency state in which interaction takes place […] in terms of reception, another level has been reached" (Pakesch, 2016, interview).

SUFFERING AND BENEFITTING FROM STAR ARCHITECTURE: EFFECT OF STAR ARCHITECTURE ON THE INSTITUTION

The special star architecture of the Kunsthaus Graz and the related objectives of capturing international attention and being the major attraction of the ECOC event resulted in high expectations which put the operating institution of the Kunsthaus Graz under pressure. High visitor numbers were expected. "Exciting architecture should make more people curious about what's inside" (Schrempf, 2016, interview). Especially because the architecture was perceived so positively – both by the citizens (HLW, 2014) who identify with the Kunsthaus Graz and by positive international media coverage such as in the *Guardian* (Sayej, 2016) – this expectation of success was transferred onto the expectations of the institution. The fact that the Kunsthaus Graz did indeed become a new landmark of the city of Graz, as for example supported by the Flickr analysis of Alaily-Mattar, Büren, Thierstein (2019, 42), and the continuous use of images of the Kunsthaus Graz in the tourist marketing brochures of Graz, fostered the expectations of politicians and the media of the Kunsthaus Graz's capacity to attract exhibition visitors. "But while the Kunsthaus Graz is one of the most popular photo motifs from the Schlossberg, the run on the exhibitions is limited" (Hecke, 2014) and "the visitor numbers are not as exciting as the architecture" (Kramar, 2014). The visitor numbers are lower than the expected 100,000 visitors each year (Fritz et al., 2001), decreasing from 81,000 in 2004 to 59,000 in 2014 (Universalmuseum Joanneum 2016, Figure 2.3, top). The disappointing visitor numbers has resulted in criticism, political discussions, and fierce debate regarding the future of the Kunsthaus Graz (Kramar, 2014). Local stakeholders, including our interviewees, talked about a conversion, reorganization, or even closure of the Kunsthaus Graz (Hecke, 2014; Trenkler, 2014). Referring to the nickname of the Kunsthaus Graz the newspaper *der Standard* even titled an article on the museum "Blue bubbles burst too" (Trenkler, 2014). The discussion about closure or conversion of the Kunsthaus Graz shaped international protest in the art scene. A famous example is the Chinese artist Ai Weiwei, who took sides with his poster "Protect Kunsthaus" for the Kunsthaus Graz (Figure 2.3, bottom).

The institution faced two problems: high expectations regarding visitor numbers from the politicians and the media on the one hand, and a small budget to cover the running costs of the institution on the other hand. In our interview the former director of the Kunsthaus Graz summarizes "they wanted blockbusters with big names, but they did not understand that you need different conditions for that" (Pakesch, 2016, interview). The expectations and the financial possibilities have diverged, as the public relations manager of the Kunsthaus Graz puts it: "There is less and less money, but you always should do more catchpenny exhibitions, there are many contradictions that cannot be solved" (Schnitzler, 2016, interview). In terms of financing the Kunsthaus Graz the challenges are related to fixed budgets and high running costs because of the special architecture, according to the finance director of the Kunsthaus Graz, Enzinger. "A difficulty we are faced with, is that we have incredibly high maintenance costs, since the Kunsthaus was partly not built from an energy-efficiency point of view"

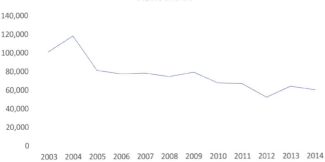

Figure 2.3 (top) The number of visitors to Kunsthaus Graz (data source: Universalmuseum Joanneum 2016). (bottom) Chinese artist Ai Weiwei, who pleads for the protection of the Kunsthaus Graz from closure or rededication. Photograph: Ai Weiwei Studio.

(Enzinger, 2016, interview). For instance, the glass surface of the Kunsthaus Graz causes high energy costs (Figure 2.4) and the preparation of exhibitions is often costly, because, as Enzinger states,

> there are no straight walls, the bubble continues inside. That means relatively high costs for exhibition design. You always have to rebuild the architecture and you cannot reuse much. You have to hang pictures on walls, the walls have to be built first.

The challenge with the running costs is gaining momentum because energy and personnel costs are increasing over time, while the budget for the Kunsthaus Graz is fixed. That means the budget for exhibitions and marketing is effectively decreasing over time. "The budget for the program and marketing has almost halved over the last twelve years, because it is simply consumed by the running costs," Enzinger

Figure 2.4 (top) The characteristic glass façade of the Kunsthaus Graz. (bottom) The individual preparation of space 01 for an exhibition causes high running costs. Photographs: Universalmuseum Joanneum/N. Lackner.

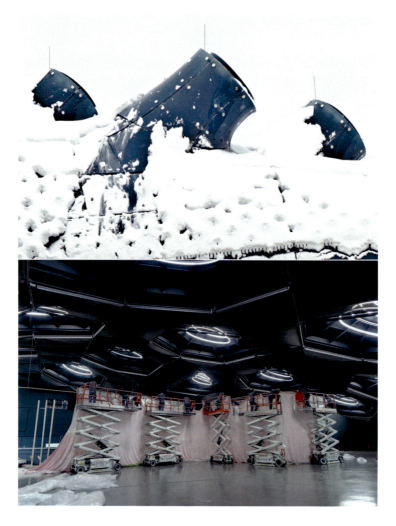

explained during our interview. He elaborated that the Kunsthaus Graz has the "lowest exhibition rental costs and marketing costs of all Art Exhibition Houses in Austria."

On the other hand, the institution was able to benefit from its star architecture by attracting sponsors. The Kunsthaus Graz is sponsored by companies, which like to be associated with it. According to Schnitzler, the public relations manager of the Kunsthaus Graz, "They [the sponsors] want to be associated explicitly with the Kunsthaus Graz. They want to appear as the sponsor of the Kunsthaus Graz because of the innovative and young image" (Schnitzler, 2016, interview). The former director and curator of the Kunsthaus Graz, Pakesch confirms this:

> the Raiffeisen Bank wanted to have a more progressive image, they want to associate with the Kunsthaus Graz. They used it for advertising purposes as

they wanted to modernize their traditional farmer bank image with the help of the Kunsthaus Graz.

(Pakesch, 2016, interview)

Schnitzler concludes that the architecture acts as an advertising medium. Also, the renting of the conference and event space (Figure 2.5) benefits from the architecture and the perception that is associated with it. The rooms are in high demand by companies because "the Kunsthaus Graz is future-oriented, technological, innovative, transparent, and embodies high-tech" (Filzwieser, 2016, interview). Our interviewees Pakesch and Schnitzler emphasize that technological firms especially like to hold events in the Kunsthaus Graz because of its technologically advanced image and the innovative perception of the conference room – Space 04. Filzwieser states that the event spaces have a high occupancy rate because external customers like to use the Kunsthaus Graz as venue and every renowned firms hold events there.

Figure 2.5 Space 04 is highly demanded as a conference and event space because of its modern design. Photograph: Universalmuseum Joanneum/N. Lackner.

EFFECT OF STAR ARCHITECTURE ON THE CITY

The Kunsthaus Graz has not only promoted global connections with the international art scene due to its program, but its architecture was also used to gain access to the global network of the United Nations Educational, Scientific, and Cultural Organization (UNESCO) Creative Cities. According to Schrempf the design of the Kunsthaus Graz was an important argument in the successful application for the title UNESCO City of Design (Figure 2.6). He describes the role the Kunsthaus Graz has for the creative economy in Graz:

> The building and its architecture make a decisive contribution to the city's special role in the network of Creative Cities in the World Heritage Network. We are City of Design […] so, the Kunsthaus Graz becomes an icon, a design object of great importance, especially in its external presentation. The Kunsthaus Graz thus expresses the attitude of a whole city: forward-looking, looking ahead, courageous.

As a UNESCO City of Design, Graz belongs to the global network of similarly labeled cities. Annual meetings, conferences, and other events foster global linkages and exchange between 31 cities around the world. Five years after becoming a City of Design, the strong connection to the Kunsthaus Graz and its importance

Figure 2.6 (right) The Kunsthaus Graz was used on the cover for the application for the title UNESCO City of Design. Photograph by Graz Tourismus/H. Schiffer, edited by M. Reiner, Managerie. (left) Picture used in the program of celebrating the five-year anniversary of the designation of UNESCO City of Design. The Kunsthaus Graz is featured prominently in the center of the picture. The German lettering in the photo means: Graz celebrates five years UNESCO City of Design. Photograph: Graz Tourismus/H. Schiffer, edited by moodley brand identity.

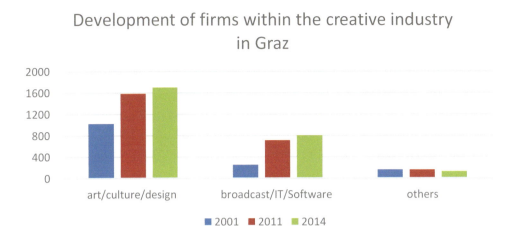

Figure 2.7
Development of firms within the creative economy in Graz (data provided by Statistik Austria, 2016, analyzed by Dreher).

for being a city of design was emphasized through the picture with the title "Graz celebrates five years City of Design" (Figure 2.6). The Kunsthaus Graz is in the center of the picture; it is the symbol for the City of Design.

Schrempf emphasizes the importance of the creative economy the Kunsthaus Graz is contributing to: "Design and creative industries are important for innovation and further development and thus important location factors when creative industries contribute to added value." An analysis of the development of the creative sector in Graz confirms the growth of this sector. The number of firms in the creative sector from 2001 to 2014 increased 24% points more than the average of Graz (data source: Statistik Austria, 2016, analyzed by Dreher). A more detailed analysis of the development of firms within the creative industry in Graz reveals, that those with a strong relationship to the Kunsthaus Graz, namely the sectors: art, culture, and design grew more strongly in absolute terms than those with no direct relationship to the Kunsthaus Graz (Figure 2.7).

Even if we cannot measure exactly the effect of the Kunsthaus Graz´s architecture on the expanding creative sector, the architecture was an essential factor in the initial phase which helped the city of Graz to pave the way to become a creative design city, integrated in the international economy. Events like the "Design Month Graz" or the founding of the networking association Creative Industries Styria (CIS) are further examples of this development. And in this context the Kunsthaus Graz also plays an important role as an event location.

The star architecture of the Kunsthaus Graz coupled with the strategic choice of the plot in which the Kunsthaus Graz was built supported the connection of two sides of Graz exerted by the river Mur that had until then been insurmountable. The Kunsthaus Graz was deliberately developed on the less privileged side of the town. Nevertheless, its architecture is oriented to the historic center and communicates with it, even literally, due to the ability to display text messages on the facade, the so-called media front, with the help of integrated bulbs. The architecture and the strategically chosen plot of the Kunsthaus Graz on the river front, next to a bridge forms a passage and gateway between Murvorstadt and the historic center. According to Ablasser, head of the Executive Office for Urban Planning, Development and Construction in the city Graz, the Kunsthaus Graz at this strategic location has helped to "overcome the barrier" of the river which had a strong spatial separating effect on the city.

In line with the reduced spatial barrier, the previously perceived functional and social separation was also diminished. The Kunsthaus Graz helped to revitalize the run-down district. Rückert, the former councilor in Graz responsible for cultural affairs, confirms, that through the spectacular and modern architecture, the Kunsthaus Graz contributed to the emergence of an urban, not provincial flair, which was an addition to the historic buildings of the old town (Rückert, 2016, interview). The revival of the district with shops, restaurants, social intermingling of residents and other building activities were promoted, among other measures, by the Kunsthaus Graz. This was confirmed by several interviewees such as Schnitzler, Rückert and Strobl. The role of the Kunsthaus Graz was important for the whole regeneration, it is described as a "starting point" (by one of our interviewees) and even as "essential" for the rise of the art and creative cluster by Schnitzler. An analysis by Sedlmeier (2016) reveals that indeed the district where the Kunsthaus Graz is located has a relatively high share of creative enterprises of 27% in comparison to only 7% in the historic center of Graz. Furthermore, the analysis of the founding dates of these businesses has shown a higher dynamic of businesses founded in the district where the Kunsthaus is located compared to the old town – the share of businesses that settled there after 2004 was 15% points higher.

The modern architecture of the Kunsthaus Graz restages the old heritage buildings and creates a contrast – an architectural tension. Schnitzler emphasizes the importance of the architecture for the marketing to tourists:

> Well, the important thing was the marketing, the tourist marketing of the city of Graz. The tension between old and new. The old town is protected and there is the Kunsthaus Graz in-between. The view from above of this blue bubble in the middle is a unique selling point for Graz for tourism, to market Graz. Surprisingly modern but also traditional, and the resultant field of tension is interesting. Accordingly, the building is important as architecture and the exhibition is for tourists often secondary.
>
> (Schnitzler, 2016)

The tension the Kunsthaus Graz creates is exposed by the relation of the Kunsthaus Graz, the new landmark of Graz with the former landmark, the historic clock tower (Figure 2.8). The roof of the Kunsthaus Graz is characterized by these so-called

Figure 2.8 (left) The Kunsthaus Graz surrounded by historical buildings. The modern architecture of the Kunsthaus Graz creates an architectural tension with the historical buildings (Photograph: Universalmuseum Joanneum/E. Martinez). (right – top) The characteristic roof windows, the so-called nozzles. One nozzle in the front is oriented in a different direction than the others. (right – bottom) Through this nozzle you see the old landmark of Graz, the clock tower. Photographs: Universalmuseum Joanneum/N. Lackner.

nozzles, one of which is directed to the clock tower. Figure 2.8 shows how the view through the nozzle frames the clock tower and how these two landmarks act together. The perception that the Kunsthaus Graz has replaced the clock tower as landmark number one, is confirmed by the Flickr analysis (Alaily-Mattar, Büren, Thierstein, 2019, 42), which reveals that in January 2017, 2.2% of all pictures of Graz uploaded on Flickr are tagged Kunsthaus Graz, while the tag of Graz's iconic clock tower accounts only for 0.7%. The Kunsthaus Graz is used in the tourism sector's marketing brochures for Graz and images appear frequently, especially with its historical surroundings as a contrast (Figure 2.9).

However, many citizens struggle with the exhibitions of the Kunsthaus Graz and have a predominantly negative attitude to it. This is confirmed by a survey (HLW Schrödinger, 2014) and was shown by some of our interviewees. The exhibitions and their low visitor numbers were often the reason for negative media coverage. All the more remarkable is the effect of the architecture. Despite dissatisfaction with the exhibitions, the residents are proud of their exhibition house, they like it, identify with it, and see it as their common representative – their new landmark (according to our interviews with Rückert, Pakesch, and Ablasser). This example

Figure 2.9 Images of the Kunsthaus Graz are frequently used in the tourism sector's marketing brochures of the city of Graz. Photograph: Graz Tourismus/L. M. Schweinzger.

impressively demonstrates the power of iconic design and shows how architecture can increase the acceptance and agreement of the citizens despite difficult circumstances.

DISCUSSION: THE WIDE RANGE OF EFFECTS OF STAR ARCHITECTURE

The case of the Kunsthaus Graz demonstrates the wide range of effects of star architecture that go far beyond visitor and tourism numbers; this chapter reveals the effects that star architecture can have on an exhibition site and its respective city. We found that star architecture has an impact on cultural offerings. The architecture changed the original programing of the Kunsthaus Graz and the special interior design influences the exhibitions. We also see many economic effects at different levels. On the one hand, the operating institution is burdened with increased operating costs due to the architecture, but on the other, it also benefits from the star architecture as sponsors want to be associated with it and therefore financially support the Kunsthaus Graz. The architecture, which is perceived as modern, technical, and innovative, also ensures high demand as a venue and generates rental income. The economic effects of the Kunsthaus Graz's star architecture are not limited to the operating institutions but can also be observed on the city scale. The star architecture of the Kunsthaus Graz helped the city of Graz to gain recognition as a UNESCO City of Design and thus promoted the creative industry of the city. Moreover, the extraordinary star architecture of the Kunsthaus Graz, embedded in the historic, traditionally built environment creates a modern flair and is an important driver for the regeneration of the district. The architectural tension created by the "old" environment and the "new" architecture of the Kunsthaus Graz also serves as marketing for the city's tourism. This case study reveals that star architecture awakens special desires and expectations. Many artists would like to exhibit in the Kunsthaus Graz and local politicians expect high visitor numbers. Unclear, diverse, and changing objectives of various stakeholders over time led to disappointment and conflicts. In addition to common and continuous goals, the management of expectations and the integration of the needs of the local scene are important to reduce disappointments and potential conflicts early in the process. The case of the Kunsthaus Graz also highlights that the provision of financial resources must be aligned with the objectives and expectations related to the project. In particular, the long-term operating and maintenance costs have to be taken into account.

A special feature of the Kunsthaus Graz is the strong difference between the function as an exhibition house and the architecture faced by other "Value Museums" (Shoval and Strom, 2009). This facilitates the analysis of the effect

Figure 2.10 The friendly alien: A different building whose friendliness found its space between the existing, historic surrounding buildings. Photograph: Kunsthaus Graz/Zapp-Cam.

of the architecture but creates conflicts. While the exhibitions and visitor numbers are often criticized, the architecture is perceived positively and represents citizens and city as landmark (Figure 2.10). Because the Kunsthaus Graz acts as an icon it raises the expectations to function as a flagship. These expectations are linked to the over simplistic Bilbao narrative, which a) treat projects as an entity, ignoring their complex socio-material nature and b) seems to promise that iconic museums designed by star architects automatically become flagships. The important differentiation between iconicity and flagshipness and the awareness that an icon is not necessarily a flagship and vice versa helps to manage expectations. The finding that the positive effects of the Kunsthaus Graz can be traced back to its star architecture, but less to its exhibitions, fits in with findings by Shoval and Strom (2009), who observe an increased significance of the architecture in contrast to the exhibition at museums without a permanent exhibition.

The unpacking of star-architectural projects into their essential elements facilitates an understanding of the impact of such projects and to capture the effects of the respective elements, as in this case study of star architecture. The investigation of the effects of star architecture in this one example has shown that effects emerge in different disciplinary fields. In addition to economic effects for the operating institution and the city, urban morphological effects have also been observed such as the strengthening of the connection between the spatially separated city halves, as well as socio-cultural effects such as the identification of the citizens with the Kunsthaus Graz. This demonstrates that an interdisciplinary analysis of star architectural projects is important to be able to perceive the breadth of the generated effects and impacts. A task for future research is to investigate the effects of other important components of star architectural projects, such as the project development process, the location of the property, the institution and the function. This provides a more comprehensive picture of the effects of star-architecture projects. And by investigating more star architecture projects with such a methodology one would then be able to extract from a large enough sample any common principles of the impacts of star architecture. Politicians and other promotors of such projects could better understand how such projects "work" and therefore investments in star architecture can be achieved more effectively.

ACKNOWLEDGMENT

The authors would like to thank Diane Arvanitakis for her proofreading and editorial support.

REFERENCES

Alaily-Mattar, N., N. Büren, A. Thierstein 2019. "Transforming the media exposure of a city through star architecture projects?" *DisP – The Planning Review* 55 (2): 36–48.

Alaily-Mattar, N., J. Dreher, A. Thierstein 2018. "Repositioning cities through star architecture: How does it work?." *Journal of Urban Design* 23 (2): 169–192. doi: 10.1080/13574809.2017.1408401.

Enzinger, M. 2016. Interview with Johannes Dreher and Nadia Alaily-Mattar. Graz, February 5, 2016.

Filzwieser, G. 2016. Interview with Johannes Dreher. Graz, August 16, 2016.

Foster, H. 2008. "Image building." In *Architecture between spectacle and use*, edited by Vidler, A., 164–179. Williamstown and Massachusetts: Sterling and Francine Clark Art Institute.

Fritz, O., W. Pointner, M. Steiner, G. Streicher, G. Zakarias 2001. "*Analyse Regionalwirtschaftlicher Effekte der Errichtung und Betreibung des Grazer Kunsthauses.*" Vienna/Graz Joanneum Research Institut für Technologie- und Regionalpolitik.

González, S. 2011. "Bilbao and Barcelona 'in Motion'. How Urban Regeneration 'Models' Travel and Mutate in the Global Flows of Policy Tourism." *Urban Studies* 7 (48): 1397–1418. doi: 10.1177/0042098010374510.

Haarich, S.N., B. Plaza 2010. "Das Guggenheim-Museum von Bilbao als Symbol für erfolgreichen Wandel - Legende und Wirklichkeit in Symbolische Orte. Planerische (De-) Konstruktionen." *Reihe Planungsrundschau* 19: 1–14.

Hecke, B. 2014. "Nagl will das Kunsthaus "wachküssen"." *Kleine Zeitung*, 26.04.2014. Accessed 17.12.2018. www.kleinezeitung.at/steiermark/graz/4148656/Friendly-Alien_Nagl-will-das-Kunsthaus-wachkuessen.

Heidenreich, M., B. Plaza 2015. "Renewal through culture? The role of museums in the renewal of industrial regions in Europe." *European Planning Studies* 23 (8): 1441–1455. doi: 10.1080/09654313.2013.817544.

HLW Schrödinger, Höhere Lehranstalt für wirtschaftliche Berufe. 2014. Steig ein - red'mit! Zum Beispiel Kunsthaus. Unpublished survey. Graz.

Jencks, C. 2006. "The iconic building is here to stay." *CITY* 10 (1): 3–20. doi: 10.1080/13604810600594605.

Klingmann, A. 2007. "Beyond Bilbao." In *Brandscapes, architecture in the experience economy*, edited by Klingmann, A., 237–255. Massachusetts: The MIT Press.

Kramar, T. 2014. "Heftige Debatte über das Kunsthaus Graz." *Die Presse*, 01.05.2014. Accessed 17.12.2018. https://diepresse.com/home/kultur/kunst/1600748/Heftige-Debatte-ueber-das-Kunsthaus-Graz#.

Pakesch, P. 2016. Interview with Johannes Dreher and Nadia Alaily-Mattar. Munich, February 15, 2016.

Ponzini, D. 2011. "Large scale development projects and star architecture in the absence of democratic politics: The case of Abu Dhabi, UAE." *Cities* 28 (3): 251–259.

Sayej, N. 2016. "Why avant garde Graz is Vienna's cooler little sister." *The Guardian* October 04, 2016. Accessed October 28, 2019. https://www.theguardian.com/travel/2016/oct/04/graz-austria-avant-garde-art-festivals-bars

Schnitzler, A. 2016. Interview with Johannes Dreher and Nadia Alaily-Mattar. Graz, February 5, 2016.

Schrempf, E. 2016. Interview with Johannes Dreher and Nadia Alaily-Mattar. Graz, February 5, 2016.

Strobl, H. 2016. Interview with Johannes Dreher and Nadia Alaily-Mattar. Spielfeld, February 5, 2016.

Sedlmeier, F. 2016. *Das Kunsthaus Graz und seine Wirkungskraft. Eine Gewerbeanalyse.* Munich: Technische Universität München.

Shoval, N., E. Strom 2009. "Inscribing universal values into the urban landscape: New York, Jerusalem, and Winnipeg as case studies." *Urban Geography* 30 (2): 143–161. doi: 10.2747/0272-3638.30.2.143.

Statistik Austria 2016. *Statistische Datenerhebungen*. Vienna: Bundesanstalt Statistik Österreich.

Rückert, L. 2016. Interview with Dominik Bartmanski. Graz, March 1, 2016.

Thierstein, A., N. Alaily-Mattar, and J. Dreher 2020. "Star architecture´s interplays and effects on cities." In *About Star Architecture. Reflecting on Cities in Europe*, edited by N. Alaily-Mattar, D. Ponzini, A. Thierstein, 156–171. Cham: Springer International.

Trenkler, T. 2014. "Auch blaue Blasen platzen."*Der Standard*, 04.05.2014. Accessed 17.12.2018. https://derstandard.at/1397522419766/Auch-blaue-Blasen-platzen.

Universalmuseum Joanneum. 2016. Origin and number of visitors of the Kunsthaus. Email from Schauer, R. Received 13.01.2016.

Universalmuseum Joanneum. 2017. "About Kunsthaus Graz. Mission statement." Accessed 13.02.2017. www.museum-joanneum.at/en/kunsthaus-graz/about-us.

Weidenfeld, A. 2010. "Iconicity and 'flagshipness' of tourist attractions." *Annals of Tourism Research* 37 (3): 851–854.

CHAPTER 3

Transformational Architecture as Urban Catalyst

Toronto's Royal Ontario Museum, Municipal Policy, and the Cultural Renaissance

Shoshanah B.D. Goldberg-Miller

INTRODUCTION

After the City of Toronto underwent the amalgamation of surrounding municipalities with the center city in the late 1990s, its leadership aspired to becoming an active participant in the burgeoning knowledge economy. As an urban center with relatively little municipal power, the city's leaders needed an innovative way to accomplish this goal. The heads of Toronto's anchor cultural institutions called for the refurbishment of their aging infrastructure, and among those entities was the Royal Ontario Museum. Through provincial and federal government funding, together with private sector support, an architectural wonder designed by architect Daniel Libeskind was added to the heart of the city's landscape (Figure 3.1).

The Michael Lee-Chin Crystal became a defining addition to the museum, rebranding it as innovative and edgy. As a symbol of the "big build" that propelled Toronto to international renown as a creative city, the museum served as a visual

Figure 3.1 Detail of facade of Michael Lee-Chin Crystal and the ROM Plaza, June 2007. Courtesy of the Royal Ontario Museum © ROM. Photo Credit: Brian Boyle, MPA, FPPO.

Figure 3.2 Detail of C5 Restaurant Lounge, Michael Lee Chin Crystal and Philosopher's Walk Building, June 2007. Courtesy of the Royal Ontario Museum © ROM. Photo Credit: Brian Boyle, MPA, FPPO.

icon of the aspirations of a once-stodgy urban center, which now was comfortably competing with Montreal as the country's cultural mecca (Figure 3.2).

Through historical and archival data as well as interviews with 21 key stakeholders from Toronto's public, private, and nonprofit sectors, this chapter discusses the policy entrepreneurs who fostered this transition and the strategic engines that drove change. I explore how creative economic development, arts leadership, urban cultural policy, and a sense of shared optimism fueled this transformation during the decade of the 2000s.

AGENDA SETTING AND PUBLIC POLICY: TOWARD THE CREATIVE CITY

This research involved semi-structured, in-depth interviews of up to two hours with 21 individuals in Toronto who were representative of a number of key stakeholder groups. Among those interviewed, I selected from two overarching areas: those that worked for the government, including the City of Toronto and the Province of Ontario; and those outside of the government, representing artists, real estate developers, museum managers, arts organizations, and philanthropists. By category, I interviewed six individuals who worked in policy or planning for the City of Toronto, two who worked in the cultural policy area for the Province of Ontario, seven arts administrators from Toronto organizations, three respondents affiliated with businesses in Toronto's creative sector, one real estate developer, one philanthropist, and one academic (Goldberg-Miller 2017, p. 11). This process revealed interviewees' thoughts on the role of arts and culture in the city's economic development and public good realms in the 2000s, in addition to eliciting their opinions about the leadership and stakeholder partnerships that contributed to Toronto's cultural renaissance during the decade.

Together with substantive archival and historical research into documents such as Toronto's cultural plans, relevant literature, and municipal policy documents and reports, I was able to develop a comprehensive understanding of the perceptions of and facts concerning the decade of the 2000s in Toronto regarding the tremendous growth and opportunities provided by the creative economy in that city. Although this group of respondents cannot be thought of as a generalizable sample, the data gleaned from these interviews, together with the historical and archival materials gathered can inform an understanding of the case of Toronto's Royal Ontario Museum and the context in which it became a symbol of a burgeoning city.

The investigation is grounded in a policy theory called agenda setting, which is useful in analyzing the take-up of policy interventions in cities, which could include how decisions are made about granting building permits, allowing height restrictions to be expanded, or the repurposing of city owned properties. This theoretical framework assists us in understanding how arts and culture options gain a foothold on a crowded municipal agenda. Policymakers are bombarded with numerous issues competing for their time, attention, and funding. How do creative economy interventions capture the interest of these important thought leaders?

The theory known as agenda setting is part of a larger policy framework called Multiple Streams (Kingdon 2011), which focuses on the alignment of municipal problems, policies, and politics. This framework posits that it is only when these three are aligned through the opening of what is known as a policy "window" that significant change can occur. For Toronto, the open policy window was the amalgamation of the center city with outlying smaller municipalities at the end of the 1990s. Understanding the context of policy opportunity and adaptation is relevant in the study of museums and architecture because many of these cases involve the building of new cultural anchors or the refurbishment/expansion of existing ones. These entities, often located in urban areas, are part of a web of municipal decision-making and policy take up.

Since elected officials and career government workers often are overwhelmed by special interest groups and lobbyists, many of whom focus on issues such as housing, homelessness, workforce development, transportation, and infrastructure, the creative sector can get lost among these other topic areas. While the creative economy has developed a more robust profile among municipal policymakers, it is only through inclusion on a government agenda that this sector can receive the benefit of urban opportunity from the State. Public opinion can play a vital role in shaping decisions made regarding legislation and options for a variety of stakeholders (McCombs & Shaw 1972). Among those shaping the attitudes of the public are both the media and what are known as "policy entrepreneurs." These are individuals, usually operating outside of the government sphere, who have ideas about policy interventions, and often propose them to municipal actors when the opportunity presents itself (Kingdon 2011). They formulate succinct "punchlines," which serve to focus public attention on issues, thereby hopefully gaining the buy-in of leaders in city government (Ingram et al., 2007, p. 100). In the case of Toronto in the 2000s, the policy entrepreneurs were the heads of the major cultural institutions, including the Royal Ontario Museum. This study looks at how a museum uses architecture as a focusing point in gaining a prominent place on a municipal agenda in order to further the development of a burgeoning cultural renaissance.

ARTS AND CULTURE IN THE CITY

There are several aspects of the creative economy and the arts and culture context that are important in developing an understanding of the role of museums and their architecture in urban settings. These areas include: the creative class theory;

the recognition of the role of hard and soft factors; delineating the economic benefit of the creative sector and arts entities; and the importance of brand building. In addition, it is essential to unpack the public good aspect of creative entities, which assists in justifying government support.

The role of cultural districts, creative clusters, and temporal entities such as festivals and fairs all are a part of cultural urban planning, which includes such disparate aspects of citybuilding as tourism, public art, clustering facets of the cultural industries, the repurposing of city-owned buildings, and community development. These and other interventions have become globally institutionalized, thanks to what is known as "policy mobility," that is, when actors travel the world both physically and electronically to tout their ideas and municipal policy successes. Cultural municipal planning has offered a powerful platform for this kind of policy learning and transfer, which is why one can see similar creative economy interventions worldwide.

Understanding the inner workings of urban economic agglomeration effects is not new within the study of world cities; however, as cities compete globally to attract an intellectual elite with specific cultural amenities, the importance of understanding creative class clustering becomes pivotal in realizing this type of urban revitalization strategy (Currid 2007; Friedmann and Wolff 1982; Mitra 2014; Scott and Storper 2015). Museums, traditionally seen as cultural amenities, can themselves act as policy entrepreneurs by promoting creative clustering through the development of innovative spaces and meaningful programing (Ceballos 2004; Lanir et al., 2017). This concept is in alignment with data showing that creatives prefer, and are better sustained, in areas which are immersive innovation districts, rich in cultural amenities (Grodach et al., 2014).

Arts and culture entities can serve as the champions of the creative sector brand by capitalizing on policies that protect and enhance the agglomeration of creatives within a particular city (Currid 2007; Jenkins 2006). By having a recognizable brand within the creative sector, arts and culture entities are able to bridge both the established sphere of policymakers and the innovative sphere of the creatives (Holt 2016). This allows these entities to provide a public service to the creative class. However, it is difficult to demonstrate the intangible cultural positives museums create, meaning that governmental expenditure often is questioned, and in addition, the private sector may be reluctant to subsidize these organizations (Selwood 2003). It is up to museums themselves to provide the case for support of this particular form of public good.

As a source of inspiration and pride, arts and cultural entities can serve a vital role in promoting cultural offerings. Many times, the economic cost of providing these opportunities in the free market would be too much of a burden to both the private and government sectors. Here, governmental and quasi-governmental entities need to step in to protect cultural literacy and promote the arts, using the public good argument to justify their participation (Friedmann & Wolff 1982). It has been observed that the proximity of other urban amenities to one's residence increases the evaluation of the urban space, as well as showing an increase in wages. Therefore, there may be a direct role that museums can play in vitalizing the urban fabric (Schmidt and Courant 2006).

The complexity of actors, institutions, and contexts that surrounds cultural planning creates coordination concerns, and there is debate within the literature as to whether cultural industries themselves can surmount this challenge (Gray 2004; Mulcahy, 2006; Pratt 2005) Arguably, such complexity is best managed by established, publicly backed institutions that are recognizable by creatives as a valued asset. Additionally, as cities embrace this form of urban revitalization in a post-industrial world, cultural planning must include these types of institutions in order to be both publically responsible and nimble (Stevenson 2004).

Instituting substantive change within an organization requires the successful integration both of hard and soft factors (Sirkin et al., 2005). Museums have increasingly been seen as using soft power to successfully change their immediate environment; yet harnessing such persuasive change internally requires taking stock of hard project parameters and soft branding factors that could successfully position a museum's urban presence in a 21st-century world (Lord 2015). Correct positioning is key to drawing creative-sector individuals to a global city (Murphy and Redmond 2009).

Creative cities have a combination of tangible and intangible elements which come together to promote economic and cultural agglomeration (Goldberg-Miller 2017). Hard factors within cities include municipal offerings and infrastructure, such as arts and culture venues, housing, and transportation which support the creative milieu (Musterd and Murie 2010). Soft factors in these urban settings include elements such as proximity to amenities such as temporal events, entertainment venues, and "coffee culture" that add to the authenticity and urban allure of an area (Crossa et al., 2010; Goldberg-Miller and Heimlich 2017; Murphy and Redmond 2009).

Museums increasingly have been seen as using their political position to successfully change their immediate environment; however, instituting successful change within an organization requires the deliberate integration of both hard and soft factors. Projects that speak to urban revitalization through creative class planning require collaboration among policymakers, developers, planners, and fellow arts and cultural entrepreneurs to strategize this kind of cultural destination planning (Goldberg-Miller and Heimlich 2017; Sirkin et al., 2005). Fostering alignment between the three sectors is the key to drawing creative sector people to a global city (Murphy and Redmond 2009). These institutions can effect change as policy entrepreneurs; that is, actors outside of the State who come forward with their own ideas and strategies that they hope will be implemented by government (Ceballos 2004; Mintrom and Luetjens 2017). Museum leaders can influence policies globally, due to the rise of international idea exchange, both through the Internet and as seen in specialty conferences, literature, and cross-country collaboration (Clarke 2012; Peck 2012; Sabatier & Weible 2007).

The literature regarding arts and cultural policymaking toward economic renewal stresses the need to recenter culture as the primary focus of these policies (Caust 2003). This is indicative of the need of authenticity within cultural brand-building. Without such authenticity, cultural policies and their institutional boosters will be seen as insincere, negatively impacting creative agglomeration impacts (Benz 2016). Without well-planned branding and subsequent policy-making, cultural amenities could, at best, fail to connect with the population and, at worst, emphasize schisms within the population that divide the creative class from the rest of the city (Friedmann and Wolff 1982).

Successful creative cities rely upon a multitude of stakeholders to create and execute the process of cultural policy ideation and implementation. These range from policy actors such as the mayor, city council, provincial, state, or federal employees or elected officials, to the cultural community's nonprofit organizations, arts intermediaries, and individual artists. Additionally, the private sector plays an important role through their participation, including contributing corporate sponsorship, fostering real estate development, and providing philanthropic leadership. It is when these disparate actors come together that impactful policy change can occur.

There are multiple options available, requiring stakeholders to engage in what is known as policy learning and adaptation tailored to their specific challenges and assets (Goldberg-Miller 2018). Such changes are affected by networks within municipal communities, through the adaptation of research and case studies from other cities to their own. This process, called lesson-drawing, fosters the mobility of relatable policies to a bespoke creative sector strategy (Bennett & Howlett 1992; Goldberg-Miller, 2018; Rose 1991; Stone 2004). As cities compete globally for the creative class and strive to draw in its contribution to their economic development, the successful commitment to arts and culture interventions becomes a valued economic and branding tool in meeting the goal of finding a place on the global stage (Phillips 2005).

TORONTO AND THE KNOWLEDGE ECONOMY

Formerly known as Metro Toronto, the transition to what became the mega "City of Toronto" took place in the late 1990s. That is when five other municipalities, including Scarborough, Etobicoke, North York, York, and the borough of East

York amalgamated with Toronto proper to create this larger, more powerful municipality (Gertler, Tesolin, and Weinstock 2006). This newly formed metropolis of 2.5 million residents now needed to decide how they wanted to move forward as a united entity. The city's policy actors, recognizing emergent global options for economic growth, chose the burgeoning knowledge economy as a focal point. Including the fields of biotechnology, information systems, and other technology-focused areas, this aggregation counted the creative economy within its context. The newly minted City of Toronto wanted to take its place on the world stage, and one of the pillars of the knowledge economy was the creative community.

The cultural sector was a tool used by municipal policymakers to brand this as a creative city. A key aspect of this aspirational journey was the creation of a ten-year municipal cultural plan – something not done previously to that extent in any urban locale. As a component of a larger strategic plan for the city, Toronto's cultural plan incorporated campaigns focusing on heritage and culture, with the goal of building a strong public face to the creative economy (Table 3.1).

Given that the creative economy includes numerous for-profit sectors, including design, the performing in fine arts, writing and journalism, photography, filmmaking, interior design, and television production as well as architecture, the strength of these multivariate fields served to provide a springboard for the ambitious recasting of Toronto as a magnet for culture (Statistics Canada, 2006).

City leaders wanted to shift their focus from competing in Canada or North America to a platform that included the global stage – but how to do this? In order to be competitive, strategic planning and the city's cultural plan offered the opportunity to utilize existing cultural assets with the goal of drawing in businesses, tourism, and new residents to the city. However, many of the main cultural anchor institutions were in dire need of refurbishment, which galvanized their leadership into proposing a mega-project that would include the revitalization and, often, the

Table 3.1 Economic Development Incorporating Arts and Culture in Toronto

Majority of Toronto Study Respondents' Opinions about Economic Development incorporating Arts & Culture
Iconic architecture a key in fostering global identity for Toronto
Municipal cultural policy actors built a collegial atmosphere integrating economic development and cultural planning goals
Tactics used involved revitalization of neighbourhood building stock
Funding from the corporate community played an important role in the success of the Cultural Renaissance
Temporal events, such as fairs and festivals, built the brand
City recognized the value of arts and culture in economic growth
Private sector is strengthened through the creative economy

expansion of these key entities. An important aspect of this process was the conflation of a number of public, private, and nonprofit sector actors. These included the then Mayor of Toronto, David Miller, who was an avid proponent of arts and culture. Mayor Miller explains:

> Toronto is creative – this is where the arts are. One key element is that we support innovation and creativity. A creative Toronto was at the heart of the economic strategy – it was the number one priority for the arts. My goal was to make Toronto more prosperous, more livable, and to have more opportunities. Arts and culture have helped on all levels. As it became accepted wisdom that arts and culture had an economic value, it became easier to succeed in bringing it in. My administration was championing the arts. We were free to do that. We have increased the funding every year; we made it a part of the conversation from the "bully pulpit" of the Mayor's office.
> (D. Miller, personal communication, January 20, 2011)

An additional factor was the presence of author and academic Richard Florida, who, at the University of Toronto's Martin Prosperity Institute, was becoming a global phenomenon with his "creative class" theory. A third key player was the alignment of the provincial and federal governments who realized, through the studies and reports generated by Toronto, that there was a public good as well as an economic development case to be made in supporting this transformation (Table 3.2).

In addition to the key leadership of Toronto's cultural institutions, the private sector became a partner with these other entities in providing financial support for many of these efforts. In particular, Michael Lee-Chin was the main figure who underwrote the expansion of the Royal Ontario Museum, securing the naming

Table 3.2 Understanding Arts and Culture in Public Good in Toronto

Majority of Toronto Study Respondents' Opinions on the role of Arts & Culture in Public Good
The concept of Diversity is embedded in Toronto's core identity
National dedication to public good a hallmark of the Canadian ethos
Youth in the city incorporate facets of arts and culture in their sense of self
Messaging about Toronto's creative sector options a positive media story
Increased opportunities available for residents to take up arts and culture offerings
Public recognition of the value of the creative sector has increased
Challenges to accessibility, both physical and cultural, remain

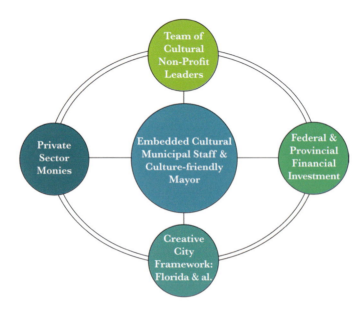

Figure 3.3
Understanding Toronto's Cultural Policy Landscape in the 2000s.

rights to that process. Together, these organizations, policymakers, and private sector actors created a kind of "Cultural Camelot" with aspirations of transforming the City of Toronto into a magnet for creativity (Figure 3.3).

This process was important in understanding how the leaders of cultural institutions, in particular museums, can foster significant change and play important roles in city building. As a senior executive at the Royal Ontario Museum declared:

> Led by the Royal Ontario Museum, individual institutions themselves decided to embark on an ambitious track that has worked and transformed the level of public demand. These changes have not been public driven, more by internal priorities. Think of arts and culture as the "soul of the city." We haven't just rebuilt these institutions – they have been revitalized. This adds to the public good.
> (M. Engstrom, personal communication, January 13, 2011)

While the ROM assumed a pivotal role in this process, they were able to collaborate with the Canadian Opera Company, the Art Gallery of Ontario, the National Ballet School, and Roy Thompson Hall to formulate this idea about the renovation and refurbishment of these key anchor institutions (Table 3.3).

This case illustrates the importance of stakeholder partnerships, strategic planning, and presenting economic development and the concept that includes financial well-being as well as public good. It is this last pillar that allowed the federal and provincial governments to contribute substantially to this process. This is because government entities need to rationalize how they spend taxpayer money,

Table 3.3 Stakeholder Partnerships and Toronto's Cultural Renaissance

Majority of Toronto Study Respondents' Opinions on the Value of Stakeholder Partnerships
Building and maintaining effective partnerships is essential
Toronto Mayor David Miller a visible advocate for the creative economy
Leadership by the arts community was a key pillar of the initiative's success
Emerging and younger artists had an important voice in the citybuilding process
Building stakeholder partnerships was a core aspect of the strategic planning
Toronto's Cultural Renaissance was bolstered by substantive research

and acknowledging that public access, municipal pride of place, and quality of life for residents, tourists, and businesses all are within the purview of governmental support adds to a more traditional State focus on financial growth.

THE MUSEUM AS ICON

Museums themselves compete globally, requiring the constant rethinking both of brand and content. As the marketplace for museum content and presence is dynamic, the act of programming for the public has become an art in and of itself, with the goal of staying relevant (Bertacchini and Morando 2013; Lanir et al., 2017). Museums now have to consider new exhibitions, publications, and educational opportunities in order to diversify their revenues and attract funders. These organizations often adopt entrepreneurial mindsets through risk-taking, the deployment of financial and human capital assets, and collaborative strategies (Christensen 1997; Rentschler 2001). Successful entrepreneurship in this context can manifest as the blending of financial gain with innovative institutional advancement.

The term arts entrepreneur has been debated in the literature, but ultimately it is recognized as business-related and follows the same principles toward success (Beckman 2007; White 2015; Wyszomirski and Goldberg-Miller 2015). Value, within such cultural anchors, is a balance between immediate monetary gain and the totality of cultural production value for sustainable growth (Frey 2005). Pursuing pioneering initiatives often necessitates moving away from the familiar to experiment with the novel in art as well as in industry – and museums are no different (Ahuja & Morris 2001).

Toronto's commitment to the knowledge economy, with a specific emphasis upon the creative sector, resulted in the "Billion Dollar Cultural Renaissance" initiative (Goldberg-Miller 2017). This initiative pledged 1 billion dollars to update cultural anchors in Toronto, including the Royal Ontario Museum (ROM). Arguably part of Zukin's first stage in the Artistic Mode of Production, the initiative set about to revitalize the city through physical reinvestment in these cultural entities (Jenkins 2005; Zukin 2001). Toronto's cultural renaissance, with its related investment by private-sector actors together with the province of Ontario and the Canadian government, was recognized as a vital step for sustaining the ROM.

ROM's Entry onto the World Architecture Stage
Global competition between museums has fueled an interest in "starchitect" builds, in which signature architects are commissioned to build new, or more commonly re-envision, a museum space for the 21st-century visitor (Klimek 2014). The well-known contemporary precedent is the "Bilbao Effect" regarding the Guggenheim Museum at Bilbao (Economist, 2013). However, starchitects often come with their own international style, which if not properly managed, can led to a flagship cultural build competing with, instead of supporting, the local creative class identity (Grodach, 2008). The hope starchitecture builds is that new physical environments will become cultural icons. However, as scholars have noted, authentic branding can be tricky. Without proper management, branding attempts can actually harm the authenticity of an institutional anchor and stifle future innovation (Evans 2003; Lee 2015). This is especially the case in a post-digital world, where consumers are hyper-aware of how cheap and easy it is to tout one's own brand; consumers increasingly look for deeper authenticity imbedded within an institution's mission (Holt 2016).

The ROM's reduced attendance leading into the 2000s was blamed on its aged, gloomy galleries. Caused by a lack of financial resources, the museum's ability to sustain engaging exhibits was in question (McCracken 2003a). A cultural planning focus by the municipal government after the amalgamation in the early 2000s allowed the museum to play a role in policy ideation and subsequently undertake an innovative architectural revitalization plan (Turi and Brunet 2009). At the outset, a series of ROM patron surveys were initiated in order to better understand the local perspective on the museum. ROM's leadership capitalized on the results, together with other research findings concerning patron perspectives and used these data to plan for an innovative built environment with goal of revitalizing both the building and the museum programing (McCracken 2003a, 2003b).

A focusing opportunity that would spur innovation was still needed to shepherd the ROM's physical infrastructure redevelopment. The museum's commitment to community engagement via programing for all ages, with a special emphasis on increasing their adult programing while sustaining their world-renown children's educational programing, became the marketing cornerstone of its revitalization efforts (Turi and Brunet 2009). ROM's leadership began planning for a signature museum design that would increase foot traffic into the building while also creating dynamic interior museum spaces for exhibits (Hume 2017; Plaza 2016).

Figure 3.4 View of J.F. Driscroll Family Gallery of the Stair of Wonders, Michael Lee-Chin Crystal, May 2007. Courtesy of the Royal Ontario Museum © ROM. Photo Credit: Brian Boyle, MPA, FPPO.

Securing an innovative "starchitect" design was identified as a way both to engage residents, reinvigorate the local creative sector, and drive tourist visits to the ROM (Lanir et al., 2017). The ROM's leadership, while acknowledging that that Gehry's previous architectural design had contributed to the creation of Bilbao's own cultural renaissance by increasing tourism, emphasized the importance of connecting strategic planning to a localized creative-class economic agenda (Boddy, 2004; Plaza, 2016).

The quality of Daniel Libeskind's post-modernist ROM design for the Michael Lee-Chin Crystal has been noted in multiple architecture publications, and is part of a larger renovation history of the ROM from 1914 to present (Boake 2006; Browne

Figure 3.5 View of the Hyacinth Gloria Chen Crystal Court, Michael Lee-Chin Crystal, August 2007. Courtesy of the Royal Ontario Museum © ROM. Photo Credit: Brian Boyle, MPA, FPPO.

2008; Chodikoff 2007; Kim 2014). This resulted in the museum's renewed physical brand becoming the visual touchstone and icon of Toronto's cultural renaissance (Figure 3.6).

The delicate act of creating a museum which is a notable cultural icon also requires treading a thin line of style, in which it must be thought-provoking, publicly acceptable, and functional. At the Royal Ontario Museum, this balance is still being finessed, with current entrance redesigns underway to better connect the ROM the cityscape (Patch 2017; Star Editorial; Board 2018). Under the continual guidance of a multi-sector team that included ROM's leadership, Toronto's Billion Dollar Cultural Renaissance brought with it an opportunity

for cultural destination planning through architectural placemaking, showcasing a commitment to the power of Toronto's creative economy (Jenkins 2005; Phillips 2005).

Figure 3.6 Southwest view of the Michael Lee-Chin Crystal, January 2008. Courtesy of the Royal Ontario Museum © ROM. Photo Credit: Brian Boyle, MPA, FPPO.

CONCLUSION

The exploration of the context within which the ROM served as a catalyst for the City of Toronto's cultural renaissance provides a number of valuable observations. The museum community worldwide can look to this case as offering three key pillars with which to ensure successful campaigns in the urban milieu. First, it is important to foster the creation of opportunities within the policy context, specifically focusing on ways to gain access to the city agenda. This can be bolstered through careful and substantive research and strategic planning, and Toronto is an excellent example of the dedication to cultural plans as a policy tool. Second, stakeholder partnerships and knowledgeable leadership are essential components of any project that involves urban planning and design. It is important to have actors from the three sectors who will bring ideas, political will, and public buy-in,

Figure 3.7 Urban Ecosystem for fostering Municipal Cultural Policy.

as well as all-important financial resources to the table. Third, museum leadership, the architectural community, and city planners must recognize the value of public good components to any campaign that focuses on economic development and urban revitalization using arts and culture by understanding that healthy and sustainable creative cities must be physically, culturally and financially accessible (Ramsey 2017; Todes 2011). This blending of the goals of economic wellbeing with those of social justice and cultural inclusion offers a more powerful tool with which to ensure that our global cities will not only survive, but thrive (Figure 3.7).

Understanding that there is a complex web of variables contributing to the success of ambitious museum design or redesign, it is important to recognize the role that municipal policy plays in the success of any project. Policy theories and frameworks offer a way to navigate these networks, which often lie outside of the scope of the architect's practice. On a crowded urban agenda, gaining traction in the minds of policymakers overwhelmed by policy entrepreneurs can be challenging. It is only through the study of successful processes, such as that of Toronto, that coalitions of planners, community members, museum leaders, and architects can forge powerful alliances in order to meet their ambitious goals for fostering impactful museum architecture. These kinds of stakeholder partnerships, fueled by municipal and private sector monies and interest, can contribute to the growth, community development, and brand value of cities and regions worldwide.

REFERENCES

Ahuja, G., & Morris, L.C. "Entrepreneurship in the Large Corporation: A Longitudinal Study of How Established Firms Create Breakthrough Inventions." *Strategic Management Journal 22*, (June 01, 2001): 521–543.

Beckman, G.D. "Adventuring" Arts Entrepreneurship Curricula in Higher Education: An Examination of Present Efforts, Obstacles, and Best Practices. *The Journal of Arts Management, Law, and Society 37*, 2, (2007): 25.

Bennett, C and Howlett, M. The lessons of learning: reconciling theories of policy learning and policy change. *Policy Sciences 25*, (1992): 275–294.

Benz, T.A. "Urban Mascots and Poverty Fetishism: Authenticity in the Postindustrial City." *Sociological Perspectives 59*, 2, (2016): 460–478.

Bertacchini, E., & Morando, F. "The Future of Museums in the Digital Age: New Models for Access to and Use of Digital Collections." *International Journal of Arts Management 15*, 2, (2013): 60–72.

Zukin, S. "How to create a culture capital: Reflections on urban markets and places." In *Century City: Art and Culture in the Modern Metropolis, edited by* Blazwick, I., pp. 258–265. London: Tate Publishing, 2001.

Boake, T.M. "Ordering chaos. (Royal Ontario Museum)." *Canadian Architect 51*, 1, (2006): 54–57.

Board, S.E. "Finally, the Royal Ontario Museum wisens up." *The Star*. (Toronto), April 18, 2018. Retrieved from www.thestar.com/opinion/editorials/2018/04/18/finally-the-royal-ontario-museum-wisens-up.html

Boddy, M., & Parkinson, M. *City matters: Competitiveness, Cohesion and Urban Governance* (1st ed.). Bristol: Policy Press at the University of Bristol, 2004.

Browne, K. *Bold Visions: The Architecture of the Royal Ontario Museum* Toronto: Royal Ontario Museum, 2008.

Caust, J. "Putting the 'Art' Back into Arts Policy Making: How Arts Policy has been 'Captured' By the Economists and the Marketers." *International Journal of Cultural Policy 9*, 1, (January 01, 2003): 51–63.

Ceballos, S.G. "The Role of the Guggenheim Museum in the Development of Urban Entrepreneurial Practices in Bilbao." *International Journal of Iberian Studies 16*, 3, (2004): 177–186.

Chodikoff, I. "Viewpoint." *Canadian Architect 52*, 7, (2007): 6.

Christensen, C. *The Innovator's Dilemma: When New Technologies Cause Great Firms to Fail*. Cambridge: Harvard Business Review Press, 1997.

Clarke, N. "Urban Policy Mobility, Anti-Politics, and Histories of the Transnational Municipal Movement." *Progress in Human Geography 36*, 1, (2012): 25–43.

Crossa, V., Pareja-Eastaway, M., & Barber, A. "Reinventing the city: Barcelona, Birmingham and Dublin." In *Competitive Cities Making, edited by* Musterd, S., & A. Murie, Chichester: Wiley-Blackwell, 2010.

Currid, E. "How Art and Culture Happen in New York: Implications for Urban Economic Development." *Journal of the American Planning Association 73*, 4, (December 31, 2007): 454–467.

Engstrom, M. (2011, January 13). Personal Interview with S.B.D. Goldberg-Miller.

Evans, G. Hard-Branding The Cultural City - From Prado to Prada. *International Journal of Urban and Regional Research 27*, 2, (2003): 417–440.

Frey, B.S. "What Values Should Count in the Arts? : The Tension Between Economic Effects and Cultural Value." Working Paper Series (pp. 1–11), Zurich: Center for Research in Economics, Management and the Arts (CREMA) & University of Zurich, 2005.

Friedmann, J., & Wolff, G. "World City Formation: An Agenda for Research and Action." *International Journal of Urban and Regional Research 6*, 3, (1982): 309–344.

Gertler, M.S., Tesolin, L., & Weinstock, S. *Toronto Case Study, Strategies for Creative Cities Project*. Toronto: University of Toronto, Munk Centre for International Studies, 2006.

Goldberg-Miller, S.B.D. *Planning for a City of Culture: Creative Urbanism in Toronto and New York*. New York: Routledge, 2017.

Goldberg-Miller, S.B.D. "Keeping Creativity Downtown: Policy Learning from San Francisco, Seattle, and Vancouver for Municipal Cultural Planning in Toronto." *The Journal of Arts Management, Law, and Society 2*, (February 02, 2018): 1–21.

Goldberg-Miller, S.B.D., & Heimlich, J.E. "Creatives' Expectations: The Role of Supercreatives in Cultural District Development." *Cities 62*, (February 01, 2017): 120–130.

Gray, C. "Joining-Up or Tagging On? The Arts, Cultural Planning and the View From Below." *Public Policy 19*, 2, (2004): 38–49.

Grodach, C. "Looking Beyond Image and Tourism: The Role of Flagship Cultural Projects in Local Arts Development." *Planning Practice & Research 23*, 4, (2008): 495–516.

Grodach, C., Currid-Halkett, E., Foster, N., & Murdoch, J. "The Location Patterns of Artistic Clusters: A Metro- And Neighborhood-Level Analysis." *Urban Studies 51*, 13 (2014): 2822–2843.

Holt, D. "Branding in the Age of Social Media." *Harvard Business Review* (March 2016): 41–50.

Hume, C. "How the ROM's New (old) Entrance Opens the Museum to the City." *The Star*. (Toronto), December 12, 2017. Retrieved from www.thestar.com/opinion/star-columnists/2017/12/12/how-the-roms-new-old-entrance-opens-the-museum-to-the-city.html.

Ingram, H., Schneider, A., & deLeon, P. "Social Construction and Policy Design." In *Theories of the Policy Process* (2nd ed.), *edited by* P.A. Sabatier, 93–126. Boulder, CO: Westview Press, 2007.

Jenkins, B. "The Dialectics of Design." *Space and Culture*, 9, 2, (2006): 195–209.

Jenkins, B.L. "Toronto's Cultural Renaissance." *Canadian Journal of Communication 30*, 2, (2005): 169.

Kim, S. "Royal Ontario Museum Washrooms. Superkül." *Architectural Record 202*, 9, (2014): 122.

Kingdon, J. *Agendas, Alternatives and Public Policies*. Longman: Glenview, 2011.

Klimek, A. "Museum Projects of the Star-Architects." *Challenges of Modern Technology 5*, 4, (2014): 44–48.

Lanir, J., Kuflik, T., Sheidin, J., Yavin, N., Leiderman, K., & Segal, M. "Visualizing Museum Visitors' Behavior." *Personal and Ubiquitous Computing 21*, (2017): 313–326.

Lee, H. "Branding the Design City: Cultural Policy and Creative Events in Seoul." *International Journal of Cultural Policy 21*, 1, (2015): 1–19.

Lord, G. D. "Soft Power & Museums with Gail Dexter." *MuseumNext Geneva [Video]*, 2015. www.museumnext.com/insight/soft-power-and-museums-gail-dexter-lord/.

McCombs, M.E., & Shaw, D.L. "The Agenda-Setting Function of Mass Media." *Public Opinion Quarterly 36*, 2, (1972): 176–187.

McCracken, G. "CULTURE and culture at the Royal Ontario Museum: Anthropology Meets Marketing, Part 1." *Curator: The Museum Journal 46*, 2, (2003a): 136–157.

McCracken, G. "CULTURE and culture at the Royal Ontario Museum: Anthropology meets marketing, Part 2." *Curator: The Museum Journal 46*, 4, (2003b): 421–432.

Miller, D. (2011, January 20). Personal interview with S.B.D. Goldberg-Miller.

Mintrom, M., & Luetjens, J. "Policy Entrepreneurs and Problem Framing: The Case of Climate Change." *Environment and Planning C: Politics and Space 35*, 8 (2017): 1362–1377.

Mitra, S. "Anchoring Transnational Flows: Hypermodern Spaces in the Global South." In *Cities of the Global South Reader, edited by* Kudva, N., & F. Miraftab, 106–114. London: Routledge, 2015.

Mulcahy, K.V. "Cultural Policy: Definitions and Theoretical Approaches." *The Journal of Arts Management, Law, and Society 35*, 4, (2006): 319–330.

Murphy, E., & Redmond, D. "The Role of 'Hard' and 'Soft' Factors for Accommodating Creative Knowledge: Insights from Dublin's 'Creative Class.'" *Irish Geography 42*, 1, (2009): 69–84.

Musterd, S., & Murie, A. "The Idea of the Creative or Knowledge-Based City." In *Making Competitive Cities, edited by* Musterd, S., & A. Murie. Chichester: Wiley-Blackwell, 2010.

Patch, N. "Toronto Still can't Decide if it Likes the ROM Crystal." *The Star.* (Toronto), June 26, 2017. Retrieved from www.thestar.com/entertainment/visualarts/2017/06/26/toronto-still-cant-decide-if-it-likes-the-rom-crystal.html.

Peck, J. "Geographies of Policy: From Transfer-Diffusion to Mobility-Mutation." *Progress in Human Geography 35*, 6, (2012): 773–797.

Phillips, R. B. "Re-placing Objects: Historical Practices for the Second Museum Age." *Canadian Historical Review 86*, 1, (2005): 83–110.

Plaza, B. "Evaluating the Influence of a Large Cultural Artifact in the Attraction of Tourism." *Urban Affairs Review 36*, 2, (2016): 264–274.

Pratt, A. C. "Cultural Industries and Public Policy: An Oxymoron?" *International Journal of Cultural Policy, 11*, 1, (2005): 31–44.

Ramsey, B. "Arts Boards Still Don't Represent Toronto's Diversity." *The Star* (Toronto), August 9, 2017. Retrieved from www.thestar.com/opinion/commentary/2017/08/09/arts-boards-still-dont-represent-torontos-diversity.html

Rentschler, R., & Queensland University of Technology. "Entrepreneurship: From Denial to Discovery in Nonprofit Art Museums?" Presentation, Brisbane: Program on Nonprofit Corporations, Queensland University of Technology, 2001.

Rose, R. "What is Lesson Drawing?" *Journal of Public Policy 11*, 1, (1991): 3–30.

Sabatier, P.A., & Weible, C.M. "Chapter 7: The Advocacy Coalition Framework: Innovations and Clarifications." In *Theories of the Policy Process, edited by* P.A. Sabatier, 189–220. Boulder: Westview Press, 2007.

Schmidt, L., & Courant, P.N. "Sometimes Close is Good Enough: The Value of Nearby Environmental Amenities." *Journal of Regional Science 46*, 5, (2006): 931–951.

Scott, A.J., & Storper, M. "The Nature of Cities: The Scope and Limits of Urban Theory". *International Journal of Urban and Regional Research 39*, 1, (2015): 1–15.

Selwood, S. "What Difference Do Museums Make? Producing Evidence on the Impact of Museums." *Critical Quarterly 44*, 4, (2003): 65–81.

Sirkin, H.L., Keenan, P., & Jackson, A. "The Hard Side of Change Management." *Harvard Business Review* (October 2005): 1–19.

Staff Writer. "The Bilbao Effect." *Economist 409*, (December 21, 2013): 8867.

Statistics Canada. "Standard Occupational Classification (SOC): statistics(NOC-S) 2006 data." *Canadian Federal Government*, 2006. Retrieved from www.statcan.ca.

Stevenson, D. "Civic "Gold Rush": Cultural Planning and the Politics of the Third Way." *International Journal of Cultural Policy 10*, 1(2004): 119–131.

Stone, D. "Transfer Agents and Global Networks in the 'Transnationalization' of Policy". *Journal of European Public Policy. 11*, 3 (2004): 545–566.

Todes, A. "Reinventing Planning: Critical Perspectives" *Urban Forum* vol. *22* (2011): 115–133.

Turi, A., & Brunet, J. "Company Profile: The Renaissance of the Royal Ontario Museum: Architecture Meets Experiential Marketing." *International Journal of Arts Management 11*, 3 (2009): 74–82.

White, J.C. "Toward a Theory of Arts Entrepreneurship." *Journal of Arts Entrepreneurship Education 1*, 1 (2015): 1–12.

Wyszomirski, M.J., & Goldberg-Miller, S.B.D. "Adapting the Promethean Fire of Business for Arts and Cultural Entrepreneurship." In *Creating Cultural Capital: Cultural Entrepreneurship in Theory, Pedagogy and Practice, edited by* Kooyman, R., 1–12. Delft: Eburon Publishers, 2015.

PART 2

INVITATIONS
Design with Communities in Mind

Architecture can be a fortress, or it can invite people in. In this section, the authors reflect on how architecture can define audiences and engage communities for the museum. Museums often speak about "audiences," while in marketing the same idea might be encapsulated in the term "market segments." Here, I use the term "communities" to broaden the idea beyond any one field and to reinforce the idea that the authors are considering *who* museum architecture serves. Lambson explores how renovations to an existing building can work with stakeholders to respond to community needs. Reich reflects on the impact of a new building, underscoring the importance of architecture that supports the social mission of the museum as a center of the community. Thompson draws on museum projects she designed to demonstrate how buildings can be instrumental in the formation of place and the strengthening of community to reinforce the aspiration of museum as place-maker. Finally, Gottlieb demonstrates how the inspired design of landscape can invite diverse users and uses to museum campuses, linking social and ecological sustainability. Taken together, these chapters offer a call to action and a practical guide for inviting communities into museum spaces at a variety of scales through museum and landscape design.

CHAPTER 4

Designing with Community for Revitalization

A Creative Hub at the Denver Art Museum in Colorado, US

Ann Baier Lambson

Twenty-first-century art museums have evolved into public institutions that give greater emphasis to sharing authority and responsibility. At the Denver Art Museum (DAM), we place people at the heart of our work that is human centered and community focused. This chapter explores the process of working in partnership with communities to define the vision for the DAM's Morgridge Creative Hub, a new learning and engagement space that is part of the J. Landis & Sharon Martin Building revitalization project with a planned completion of fall 2021. With this project, we have both inherited a bold building, whose architecture frames how the space is experienced, and been given the opportunity to create new educational spaces informed by programmatic needs and audience involvement. To ensure we do this thoughtfully, we partnered with our community to envision the Creative Hub. What does collaborating to create a shared vision look like? How are we doing it? What are we learning from this process? What are our creative partners saying, and how is this shaping the design? This chapter explores these questions, laying out the conceptual and physical frameworks for the Creative Hub followed by an explanation of the current process of listening with lessons learned and next steps outlined.

CO-VISIONING WITH COMMUNITY

> The best cultural institutions are those most devoted to thinking *with* their publics—where thinking, as in the idea of the forum, is an inviting mutual event of language and feeling, self-presentation, and the incompleteness of mutual questioning.
>
> (Carr 2003, 66)

Public spaces in museums have changed over the past 50 years since the Denver Art Museum's Martin (formally North) Building (Figure 4.1) opened in 1971.

There is an increased desire for museums to be places of connection and conversation. 21st-century museum audiences expect to experience spaces that are welcoming and provide equitable access to the arts, that invite participation in personal learning and discovery, that give opportunity to be part of something bigger than oneself, and that reflect multiple perspectives and points of relevance.[1] Museum director and author Nina Simon underscores,

Figure 4.1 North and west façades of the former North Building, now the J. Landis & Sharon Martin Building, designed by Gio Ponti and James Sudler Associates, Denver Art Museum. Denver, Colorado, USA, 1971. Image: Denver Art Museum.

Visitors expect access to a broad spectrum of information sources and cultural perspectives. They expect the ability to respond and be taken seriously. They expect the ability to discuss, share, and remix what they consume. When people can actively participate with cultural institutions, those places become central to cultural and community life.

(Simon 2010, ii)

The ethos at the Denver Art Museum relies on tuning into our audiences and communities when creating and refining programs and exhibitions. DAM Learning and Engagement Chief Officer Heather Nielsen explains, "We've taken a visitor panel/focus group model and moved it into a community conversation model that both gives us the evaluative and feedback piece, and it gives us the relationships to implement the programs at a later date" (Nielsen 2018). Our creative partners are essential in the planning process and the programming phase.

We recognize that *community* is a multi-faceted concept that holds varied, and even debated, meanings. Community finds its roots in the Greek κοινός and the Latin *communitas,* or the idea of togetherness or "with-ness" (Tremblay 2016). Community can be understood as interdependence; it creates a sense of belonging and can satisfy the need for connection. Community-management consultant Carrie Melissa Jones describes a particular interpretation that resonates with the way we are approaching the Creative Hub. She explains, "Communities require that every member can contribute, not just consume" (Jones 2015). Therefore, with the Creative Hub, we hope to create a space that convenes and connects people including visitors, artists, and the broader public, and that encourages them to contribute to and share in a larger vision.

As an art museum, we are multi-pronged in our mission: collect and preserve art, present thought-provoking and timely exhibitions, and engage and serve our community. In truth, we do not exist without our community. We do this for and with our public; otherwise, we would be only a repository of objects. We work alongside the community to create more relevant and authentic programmed spaces. Nielsen explains, "I think that community building is essential for our work because it's what makes the work relevant and real. If we really want to be a place for and embedded in Denver's creative ecosystem, then the people who are in that realm have to be our partners. If we want to be a truly accessible and inclusive institution, then we need more of those voices at the table when we are planning our program" (Nielsen 2018).

Community-building consultant and previous DAM Access and Adult Programs Manager Laura Baxter and I were set as the leads for the new Creative Hub. Laura's background in community conversations and mine in architecture and design education made for a logical pairing to begin setting the vision and design parameters for the space. We quickly narrowed in on how essential it was to involve the community in developing and programming this space. Laura Baxter explains, "What the DAM has really attempted as they develop the Creative Hub is to adopt a co-inquiry approach, a key feature of which is the value given to everyone's experience, expertise, and participation. What has emerged is a two-way conversation between community partners and the DAM around an important new civic space—not just for the DAM itself but for the city and its communities. Active participation, mutual respect, and valuing all contributions, including expertise by lived experience, are the core principles this work is based on and are shaping both the development of DAM's Creative Hub space as well as the experience the space will ultimately deliver" (Laura Baxter, email message to author, May 31, 2018).

Those that have joined us on this journey have expressed appreciation that the DAM cares about community/visitors' needs and wants for the space, and were grateful to see the egalitarian mission. One participant said, "If the Hub space can depict all of these aspects, it is really exciting for the Denver community." Another partner, Denver-based artist Emily Przekwas, shared her experience, "With the Creative Hub process, I felt I was able to transfer some of my experiential knowledge of the artistic community to the museum so that it can better serve the needs of the community that uses it and reflect the surrounding cultural values and traditions. Participating in the planning process made me feel valued, respected, and energized and that I was making a contribution to a legacy of inclusion and diversity that will benefit the community of Denver and the region for years to come" (Emily Przekwas, email message to author, June 20, 2018).

THE MARTIN BUILDING PROJECT

The Denver Art Museum is underway with a major architectural endeavor building the new Anna & John J. Sie Welcome Center and revitalizing its historic and admired North Building (now Martin Building) designed by Gio Ponti with Denver architect James Sudler Associates (Figure 4.2). As part of the Martin Building project, we are creating the new Learning and Engagement Center anchored by the Creative Hub and including four workshops, a community art gallery, a sensory garden, and outdoor terraces. As part of the plan to reinstall the permanent collections and create new educational spaces, such as the Creative Hub, we are working with a number of designers to shape spaces that aim to nurture meaningful and varied art experiences for visitors.

When Gio Ponti designed the North Building (Figure 4.3), which opened in 1971, there was a clear intention to create a castle-like structure that could serve

Figure 4.2 Rendering showing aerial view of the Denver Art Museum's new elliptical-shaped Anna and John J. Sie Welcome Center and the revitalized J. Landis & Sharon Martin Building in Denver, Colorado, USA. Image created by Machado Silvetti, Denver Art Museum. Denver, Colorado, USA, 2018. Image: Denver Art Museum

Figure 4.3 North façade of the J. Landis & Sharon Martin Building with the original wall surrounding the west, north, and portions of the east sides of the building. The former North Building was often referred to as a castle or fortress, and the high surrounding walls reinforced this reading. Image: Denver Art Museum.

as a protection for the gems of art inside. Speaking of the North Building design, Ponti said "Art is a treasure, and these thin but jealous walls defend it" (Ponti 1972). Ponti's vision for this exciting new building was to create a safe place to protect the precious art. When it opened, the community noted that it looked like a "Medieval fortress," "a brilliantly stylized Medieval castle," "a super-gingerbread-fortress" (all three descriptions are found in various printed newspapers when the North Building opened in 1971. These press clippings are archived in the *Denver Art Museum Scrapbook, 1971*, vol. 1. DAM staff and volunteers began keeping and archiving the press clippings since 1924 to present. Quotes from: Ray 1971; Coleman 1971; Herald 1971). Although a recognizably imposing structure, the building was also understood as forward thinking. One journalist wrote at that time, " … look at the Denver Art Museum with pride that it dares to dispense with classicism, that it welcomes new ideas, new forms, new outlooks" (Young 1971).

The striking design of the North Building echoes the spirit of Denver, a frontier town having emerged over the decades into a vibrant and international cultural center. Frederick and Jan Mayer Director Christoph Heinrich has led the charge in developing the DAM's strategic plan for the revitalization project called Vision 2021. He describes, "Vision 2021 is driven by the desire to create an enduring world-class institution in the heart of Denver that embodies the creativity, the beauty, the openness, and the boldness of the city itself" (Heinrich 2018). The North Building has served its purpose of protecting the DAM's collection over the years. Now, as we examine where we are and where we would like to go in the future, continued and deepened collaboration with our community is paramount. Under the direction of architects Jorge Silvetti of Boston-based Machado Silvetti and Curtis Fentress of Denver-based Fentress Architects, the intention of the revitalization project is to open our arms more boldly, serving as a beacon and vital part of the community.

THE CREATIVE HUB

The remainder of this chapter addresses the development of the Creative Hub's vision and programming. It describes what the space is, the listening methods we utilized to collaborate with community, and what we heard. The chapter concludes with lessons learned and steps for moving forward.

As the beating heart of the new Learning and Engagement Center (Figure 4.4), the Creative Hub (Figure 4.5) will be an active space for all museum visitors, particularly adults, and Denver's creative community. It is meant to serve as a linking point to spark and inspire creativity through interactive opportunities that foster connection, exchange of ideas, and celebration of local creativity. Situated in the Martin Building's former Ponti Hall, the Creative Hub will be an approximately 5,500-square-foot space with soaring 22´-high ceilings (Figure 4.6).

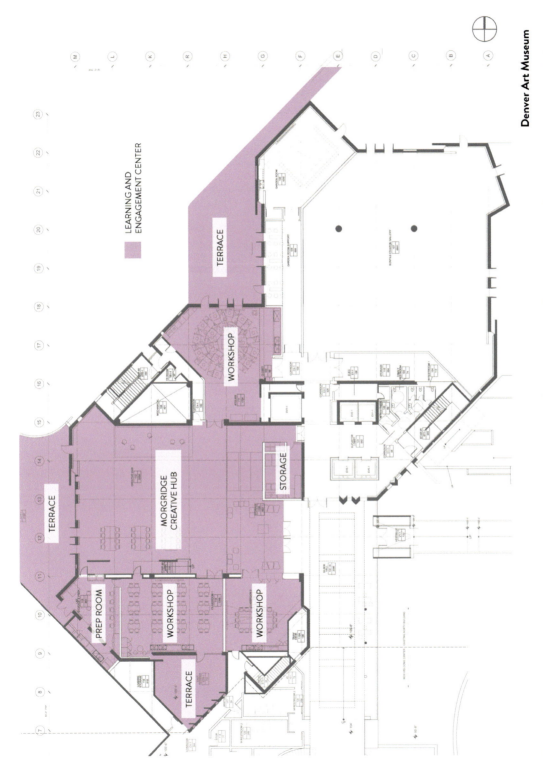

Figure 4.4 Plan of the first floor of the J. Landis & Sharon Martin Building of the Denver Art Museum. The new Learning and Engagement Center is highlighted in purple. Drawing created by Fentress Architects and Machado Silvetti, 2018. Image: Denver Art Museum.

Figure 4.5 Rendering of the Morgridge Creative Hub, an interactive space that will foster connection, exchange of ideas, and celebration of local creativity. The Creative Hub will anchor the new Learning and Engagement Center with workshops and outdoor terraces radiating from it. Image created by Machado Silvetti. Denver Art Museum. Denver, Colorado, USA, 2018. Image: Denver Art Museum.

Denver Art Museum: North Building, 1st Floor　　　　　　　　　　　　　　　　Ponti Hall: Public and special event space view 2 (2007)

Figure 4.6 The former Ponti Hall will become the Morgridge Creative Hub, which will be approximately 5,500 square feet with a 22′-tall ceiling. Image: Denver Art Museum.

The Martin Building comprises two towers joined by a hinge space and enclosed "spine" housing the building's mechanical functions and vertical transportation. The original Ponti Hall, on the main floor of the south tower, served as a public gathering space in the museum where one could relax in café seating or browse the gift shop.

The new Sie Welcome Center, centrally located on the DAM's campus, and the nearby Creative Hub signal openness. A promenade naturally lit with large skylights above and an exterior wall of glass to the northeast channel visitors to the elevator core, carrying them to different gallery floors (Figure 4.7).

Because of climate-control needs, it was necessary to glaze the Creative Hub's entrance; however, in the same spirit of openness and transparency, one has a clear view into the space, feeling invited to come in (Figure 4.8).

This gathering space will be transformed from a place of resting to an active one of connection and interaction with art and our creative community, illuminating the importance of local contributions and of exploring the creative process. Our learning and engagement spaces will be front and center with elevated ceilings and natural light filtering in from Ponti's slot windows.

In thinking about a space that could serve as the heart of the DAM's new Learning and Engagement Center, creativity quickly emerged as an organizing principle as this had been at the core of our work for the past several years.[2] In considering what to call this space, we honed in on the concept of a hub. A hub is the central part of a wheel, with spokes radiating to the outer rim. It is the center around which other elements revolve, a focus of activity. The Creative Hub is a physical linking point for the surrounding Learning and Engagement interior spaces and outdoor terraces. It is also a programmatic locus launching visitors into the greater museum galleries and serving as a place for reconvening after gallery visits. Finally, it plays a pivotal networking role in Denver's creative ecosystem.

METHOD

With our significant building project at the fore, we relied on listening as a primary approach. We hosted and facilitated a series of public conversations at the DAM and the neighboring central public library, casting a wide net throughout Denver's creative community and expressing the aspiration to co-vision a new community space at the Denver Art Museum (Figure 4.9). At the DAM, we define *creative community* as an ecosystem of artists, creatives, leaders, and thinkers in and around Denver with interest and contributions in creating, sustaining, and sharing the arts. These are advisors and thought-partners who are helping us shape the vision and program. In the early sessions, we heard questions

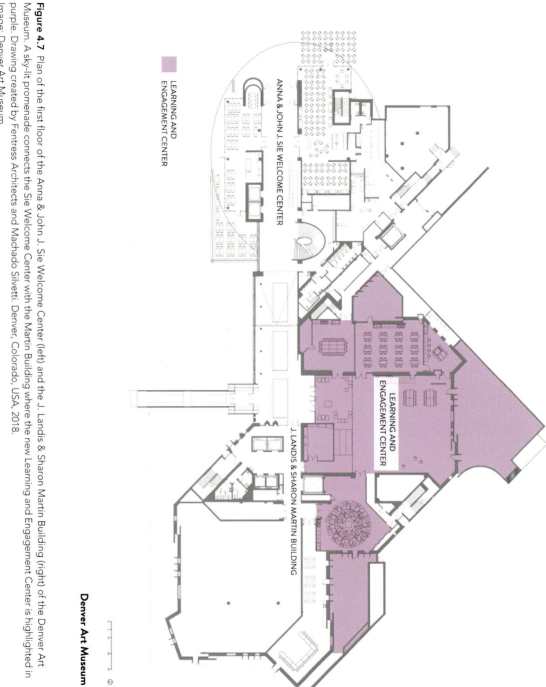

Figure 4.7 Plan of the first floor of the Anna & John J. Sie Welcome Center (left) and the J. Landis & Sharon Martin Building (right) of the Denver Art Museum. A sky-lit promenade connects the Sie Welcome Center with the Martin Building where the new Learning and Engagement Center is highlighted in purple. Drawing created by Fentress Architects and Machado Silvetti. Denver, Colorado, USA, 2018. Image: Denver Art Museum.

DESIGNING WITH COMMUNITY FOR REVITALIZATION   75

Figure 4.8 Rendering of the entrance to the Morgridge Creative Hub. The transparent glass invites visitors to look and come into the interactive space. Rendering created by Machado Silvetti. Denver Art Museum Martin Building. Denver, Colorado, USA, 2018.
Image: Denver Art Museum.

Figure 4.9 Creative community brainstorm session in Ponti Hall of the North Building at the Denver Art Museum, October 2017.
Image: Denver Art Museum.

like, "Will the space be free?," "Who is welcome here?," "Who is going to set the rules?," "What is the ultimate goal of this space?," and "How can it balance the DAM's mission with community needs?" The open invitation quickly became a catalyst for examining our true intentions. We found a steadfast group that was eager to work with us—to have us listen and respond to them, and to listen and respond to us.

During these daylong or half-day sessions, we put forth questions that we were grappling with at that moment, such as "Who is this space for?," "What is the vision?," "How do we design a shared space for multiple audiences?" We then worked together as a group to think through the challenges and propose solutions. We synthesized what we were learning and shared it back with the group. Our goal has been to be in contact with the group regularly throughout the project as we understand and value these conversations as ongoing.

Damon McLeese, Director of the Access Gallery located in the heart of Denver's Art District on Santa Fe, participated in a number of these creative community-brainstorming sessions centered on the Creative Hub. He underscores the importance of being included in the conversation: "It is a rare thing to have the perspective of disability at the table during the planning process. It was refreshing to interject the viewpoints of people who too often are only thought of after the fact. By thinking of accessibility and inclusion as opportunities rather than from a regulatory standpoint, I believe the Creative Hub and the Denver Art Museum will ultimately be a richer and more welcoming environment for all of our citizens" (Damon McLeese, email message to author, July 9, 2018).

DAM's Manager of Studio and Artist Programs Jodie Gorochow joined the Creative Hub endeavor as one of the project co-leads, and she shared the fundamental understanding that successful and impactful collaborative work relies on an open dialogue. Through her extensive work with the museum's network of artists and creative community leaders, Jodie explains, "I've learned that successful dialogue can only happen when you are open to a two-way exchange. This understanding has been important in my work with the creative community because in order to stay relevant and to provide meaningful opportunities, we need to hear directly from the community. We need to continue to find ways to have community conversations to learn more about Denver's creative landscape and thus understand what the DAM can offer and what artists can offer. We want to be in dialogue" (Gorochow 2018).

In our practice, we continue to dedicate resources and efforts to community building, research, and staff training to further develop skills in facilitation, empathy interviews, evaluative visitor panels/focus groups, surveys, organizing expert advisory groups, and creating prototyping structures. Based on visitor feedback, we continue to explore and factor into our work ideas of creativity, co-creation, wellbeing, choice, relevance, multi-sensory experiences, and how artists can serve as bridges between art and community. We also seek more understanding of audience needs by learning from our peers through conversations and experiencing their work in person. And, we continue to work with thought partners, who through consistent check-ins, guide our practice with clarifying and alternative perspectives.

Another method in seeking community partnership has been with the Denver campus of the University of Colorado. We have met with design and architecture faculty who have built assignments into their syllabi that give their students real world experience and application while helping us answer questions we are wrestling with as we conceive the Creative Hub and other learning spaces. For example, one design course spent four sessions with us—being introduced to design process and empathic research methods, touring the museum and experiencing the North Building and future location of the Creative Hub, giving mid-semester presentations sharing their research about a refined topic centered around "welcome," and then giving their final presentations to DAM staff—sharing their research and proposed solutions. It was enlightening and immensely helpful to hear firsthand millennial perspectives with ideas about how we could be more accessible to this audience.

WHAT WE HEARD

Through many different listening sessions and conversations, we consistently heard these important needs: agency, access, inclusion, cross pollination through collaboration, connection, and flexible space for programming. We also heard appreciation for being invited to participate in the conversation, in addition to a communicated desire for greater clarification around the purpose of the space, the audiences we intend to serve, and the degree to which agency would be shared. These convenings gave us the ability to articulate more fully the vision for the space, helping us construct internal conversations to foster understanding and support. Some of the questions consistently posed were: "What is the vision and mission of the museum around community and social engagement?," "How is the DAM truly being inclusive of under-served populations?," "Is this space free?," "Can it be multi-use?," "Will there be curation by community?," "Who is going to set the rules?," and "How can the Creative Hub drive/develop a paradigm shift in the Museum?"

These are powerful questions, many of which were bigger than the Creative Hub. Invitation and welcome are critical, not only for the Creative Hub, but for the whole museum. People who attended wanted validation that we were listening to them. We also needed to dig in to the definition and exploration of the Creative Hub. Moreover, we needed greater clarity around who we meant by "community."

Our conversations led us to explore further a more wide-reaching community engagement direction for the Learning and Engagement Department. We are now forming a Creative Hub programming collective of external creative partners and internal stakeholders that will help develop community-driven programming. There was also great interest in knowing the parameters and constraints we had for the space. Consequently, we worked internally to define some of those, as we understood them in that moment. We were transparent with consistent communication through the entire process, taking ideas and issues back to the larger group for brainstorm and working with smaller groups on focused issues. Finally, with a more defined community engagement direction and a set of spatial and conceptual parameters, we worked together to identify potential uses/programming for the Creative Hub. We explored "What does inclusive and accessible look like in the Creative Hub?," "How can the Creative Hub be a shared and flexible space enabling collaboration and cross-pollination?," and "What does community-driven programming look like?"

In our discussions, we heard that the Creative Hub should create a sense of community; be accessible to everyone; spark creativity, ideas, moments of surprise; nurture connection: collaboration, mentoring, displaying community/local art; be for learning (experiential, exploration, discovery) rather than for teaching; be dynamic, adaptable, flexible with a shared responsibility for programming; and have a clearly communicated intention. There should be a shared responsibility between the DAM and the creative community, which celebrates local creativity in a dynamic, changing environment while transforming those that participate in the space. We recognized that we needed to continue in this work of asking and listening to further refine the vision for the space.

A SHARED VISION

These sessions with members from Denver's creative community led to a shared vision of the new Creative Hub in which its purpose will be multifold:

- On one level, it will feel like a comfortable place for convening. We envision, like a coffee shop or living room, the space and furnishings will have a welcoming, communal buzz with a warm and vibrant atmosphere, but also a place where an individual can feel comfortable on his or her own.

- We see the Creative Hub as a platform for exchange. It will be a place for diverse and changing community-driven programming and convenings, partner meetings and events, and pre- and post-gallery experiences. It should be a place where visitors can connect with Denver's greater creative ecosystem and where Denver's creatives can connect with visitors.
- We also see it as a place for celebrating local creative contributions. We imagine an adjustable display system to exhibit art from varied community groups, as well as a space for our local Creatives-in-Residence to work with the public on new interactive installations.
- Finally, we envision this as a place for creative experiences. The Creative Hub will provide hands-on, self-directed learning opportunities where visitors can spark their creativity through participatory projects and experiences.

IMPACTS ON DESIGN

How have these conversations affected the design of the Creative Hub? How is our physical space responding to community vision and needs? We are beginning to engage with a design team, and have used these visioning sessions to aid in articulating the needs of the space. With our communities, we have co-visioned a space that is multi-functional, where it can be easily converted from one purpose to the next with moveable, modular furnishings. We see the space and furnishings as warm, welcoming, and inclusive. We plan to take greater advantage of the natural lighting filtering in through the originally designed windows, creating a connection between the interior and exterior. We envision the Creative Hub balancing a degree of familiarity with moments of surprise and serendipity. It will be dynamic and flexible in its space and programming. The Hub will support a variety of ways of engaging, from individual, contemplative experiences to more collaborative and community-focused events. We also envision that the space will provide a place to gather, participate, and share through a diverse range of participatory programming, including drop-in activities, convenings, and performances. Finally, we see the Creative Hub as a place that creates methods for displaying and integrating DAM collection art objects in unusual, unique, and unexpected ways.

We dedicated one brainstorm session to working through four design challenges. Exploring these as a group shifted the focus and helped us become more concrete in articulating the tangible and intangible characteristics of welcoming and flexible environments that would reflect a town hall culture while balancing social/collaborative and personal/restorative needs. With our partners, we explored these challenges (Figure 4.10):

Figure 4.10 During a community brainstorm session, creative partners were given four design challenges to consider and illustrate solutions. This group created a poster about fostering a town hall culture in the Morgridge Creative Hub. The session was held at the Denver Central Public Library in February 2018. Image: Denver Art Museum

DESIGNING WITH COMMUNITY FOR REVITALIZATION 81

1) Define a town hall culture and record ideas and characteristics for how the Creative Hub can reflect this ethos. Visually illustrate potential solutions.
   - Characteristics: open, warm, light-filled, equitable, valued, democratic.
   - Potential Solutions:
     - Facilitate a change of perspective. Foster the ability to affect the space for participants in the Creative Hub—artists and visitors creating art right there.
     - Set the space as a frame to conversation, facilitating confrontation with provocative ideas.
     - Consider going beyond the walls and into the community, potentially with an online component. Connect what happens in the Creative Hub with online audiences as well as with the DAM's neighbors.
2) Consider the tangible and intangible qualities of a welcoming space that orients visitors and builds community. Record ideas and characteristics for how the space can reflect this feeling and purpose.
   - Characteristics: color, sounds, light, water feature, warm, vibrant, fun—atmosphere is important.
   - Potential Solutions:
     - Make connections to Colorado and outdoor spaces/terraces, permeability with outdoors (birds, rocks, etc.).
     - Be a space for invited participation with active and participatory art.
     - Create a metaphor as the heart of the museum through the space's design.
3) Define social/collaborative and personal/restorative environments in the Creative Hub, and record ideas and characteristics for how the space can address and balance these needs.
   - Characteristics: tactile, rounded spaces for individuals that give a unique sensory experience of music, light, and scent. Be circular, not square, in terms of space philosophy and program.
   - Potential Solutions:
     - Emphasize the heart metaphor: central role and functions as a circulatory system, flowing in and out.
     - Encourage engagement from the outside, drawing people in and out.
     - Be a space to spontaneously exhibit work that fosters discussion and community. Bring in new audiences, mix audiences, and have mashups. Include engagement and participatory experiences as part of this space. Design for all abilities.
4) Consider the tangible and intangible qualities of a dynamic, flexible space, and record ideas and characteristics for the Creative Hub that could embody this energetic and changing purpose.
   - Characteristics: flexible, modular, open, comfortable.
   - Potential Solutions:

- Create pockets of convening spaces or semi-permanent mini lounges.
- Utilize modular and easily moved furnishings.
- Invite anyone to hang artwork spontaneously that they create in the space.
- Consider an online display component to encourage ideas and contributions from beyond the museum's walls.

We recalibrated and shifted our thinking as each conversation created emphasis and direction for the next. We increasingly felt that we needed a space for adults to explore creativity—their own and that of others. We heard through multiple sources the need to develop a holistic view of celebrating and embracing creative output from the community, while not being redundant with what was already out there. Although there was an interest in illustrating artistic process, this space did not necessarily need to function as a studio. In fact, in keeping in mind the hub concept, it was better to create steady flow in and out of the DAM and into the local creative community. We had in many cases been using similar language, but found that the series of brainstorm and listening sessions grounded us. They helped us articulate in more richness the intention for programming in the Creative Hub, as it truly became a reflection of our communities' needs and wants dovetailed with the DAM's mission and program.

OTHER LEARNING AND ENGAGEMENT SPACES: DESIGN STUDIO

There are several spaces in the Learning and Engagement Center and the art collection galleries where similar community conversations have guided our work in developing the program. For example, the Ellen Bruss Design Studio will be an approximately 2,000-square-foot space adjoining the new Amanda J. Precourt Galleries and the Joanne Posner-Mayer Gallery for the Architecture and Design collection. Here visitors will able to dive more deeply into the world of design, exploring designers' processes by trying their hand solving various design challenges. Like the Creative Hub planning process, we facilitated visitor panels with external evaluators, formed a local Design Studio advisory group, and participated in creative community brainstorm sessions such as the DAM's "Meet Here" program that pulls together many from Denver's creative networks to generate programming ideas. We have also sought guidance from area design and architecture faculty. Our travels to other museums and meetings with colleagues have expanded our vision for this space. Additionally, we have prototyped activities with visitors through a temporary pop-up Design Lab, giving us a place to test ideas, observe, and talk with visitors.

Through these many measures, we have adapted and fine-tuned our plan for the Design Studio. The space should feel like a studio, where you can work and design.

We should have activities that include crowd-sourced problems, sharing ideas in the studio and online. We should make connections between the collection objects and design projects. Talking with colleagues has encouraged us to consider including designers to help us create interactives for visitors to explore design thinking and process. Our next steps are to test ideas and further develop the vision for the studio while strengthening relationships with Denver's design community. Like the Creative Hub, we have utilized similar listening methods to learn from our creative partners in order to create a space that is relevant for our visitors and communities.

LESSONS LEARNED AND NEXT STEPS

Through these conversations, we have amplified existing community relationships while building new ones that we plan to sustain through continued collaboration once the Creative Hub opens. We have learned many important lessons:

- Keep community at the fore—extend an invitation to participate in the planning.
- Regularly loop-in the community, even when plans change. Some might lose interest if the parameters adjust. Recognize that it has to be beneficial and realistic for both the community partner and the institution. There must be give and take from all.
- Creative partners want to see evidence of how their contributions are affecting the overall project.
- Be willing to risk and have patience. This type of work takes time, try not to jump to conclusions, and take issues back and rework with the group. They are allies.
- Anticipate challenges and set-backs and accept them as necessary to the process. For example, we lost some creative partners along the way as either the process was too slow or our visions did not align. Sometimes we had to temporarily halt external conversations while we worked through internal ones, all the while keeping the momentum moving forward. Embrace this work as both sharing a vision and compromising at points to reach it. This is not all/nothing, either/or work. Collaborating with diverse communities is a complex and nuanced endeavor with results that are richer and more dynamic.
- Identify and utilize external and internal thought partners who can guide the work, provide encouragement and perspective, while helping to build new skills in staff. This work is challenging—trying to carry a vision and build consensus while providing a structure that gives voice to all involved.

For both the Creative Hub and overall Learning and Engagement program, the key to what we have heard is connection, access, shared responsibility, and welcome. We will continue to meet in a variety of sessions, particularly listening, brainstorming, and design-thinking sessions, while also utilizing local university and high-school design programs to help us refine our thinking. We will also take ideas out to the floor and test with our general museum audience. We are now forming a collective with a clear purpose to co-develop some of the programming in the Creative Hub. The process is iterative, and we will continue our efforts, refining each step of the way.

CONCLUSION

Reflective practice anchors our work at the Denver Art Museum. The intent of this chapter has been to share some of our plans, considerations, adaptations, and lessons we are learning as we are still in process. As we consider how the architecture and design shape our new installations of the permanent collection and informal learning spaces of the museum, and even our simultaneous role in influencing the architecture and design of these spaces, our hope is that others may find value in learning from our work.

Designing with community has been a vital process—one with risk, action, and reflection. Rooted in risk is vulnerability, or opening oneself to that which could be uncomfortable and uncertain. It has been extraordinarily valuable to meet often with our communities and envision together the purpose and design of these spaces and programs. Vulnerability is shared in this work, both by the DAM and by our community partners, as we have embarked and continue on an open-ended journey to co-vision spaces and programming that are relevant and authentic in accomplishing a key part of the DAM's mission to spark creativity and facilitate transformative experiences with art.

Dr. Brené Brown, a researcher of human connections, speaks of the essential nature of vulnerability as the birthplace of creativity and connection: "Vulnerability [is] uncertainty, risk, and emotional exposure … Vulnerability is the birthplace of love, belonging, joy, courage, and creativity. It is the source of hope, empathy, accountability, and authenticity" (Brown 2012, 34). We take this to heart: to do truly impactful work that reflects our communities and embraces them as authentic partners, we must open up ourselves and walk a path together that needs frequent recalibration and fluid adaptability from all involved. Ultimately, we trust that our shared responsibility and work will result in spaces and experiences that are community-oriented and driven, because we envisioned with a courage and purpose that aimed for belonging, connection, and creativity. We look forward to the next phase of engaging design teams to help us bring to fruition tangible spaces from the vision that we have created together.

NOTES

1. These are understandings gained at the Denver Art Museum over many years of conducting formal and informal visitor studies.
2. For the past several years, the DAM's Learning and Engagement Department has been involved in work specifically investigating how to foster creativity among visitors and how the museum can be a platform for community creativity. The DAM received and implemented two major, multi-year Institute of Museums and Library Services-funded projects examining the role of creativity in museum visitors' experiences: "Down the Rabbit Hole: Adventures in Creativity and Collaboration" in 2017 and "Tapping into Creativity and Becoming Part of Something Bigger" in 2014. https://denverartmuseum.org/about/research-reports.

REFERENCES

Brown, B. 2012. *Daring Greatly: How the Courage to Be Vulnerable Transforms the Way We Live, Love, Parent, and Lead*. New York: Avery.

Carr, D. 2003. *The Promise of Cultural Institutions*. Lanham, Maryland: AltaMira Press.

Coleman, A. 1971. "Mingling with Mink." Alice in Wonderland. *Aurora Sentinel*. October 7. p. 2.

Denver Art Museum. 2014. "Tapping into Creativity and Becoming Part of Something Bigger." https://denverartmuseum.org/about/research-reports

Denver Art Museum. 2017. "Down the Rabbit Hole: Adventures in Creativity and Collaboration." https://denverartmuseum.org/about/research-reports

Denver Art Museum Scrapbook. 1971. Vol 1.

Gorochow, J. 2018. Interview by Ann Lambson. Denver Art Museum, June 4.

Heinrich, C. 2018. Frederick and Jan Mayer Director of the Denver Art Museum, Groundbreaking: North Building Renovation Project at the Denver Art Museum, *Recorded remarks*. January 11.

Herald, C. 1971. "Ideas and Comments." *Rocky Mountain News*. September 19.

Jones, C. M. 2015. "You're Using the Word Community Wrong, and You're Costing People Their Jobs." Accessed May 23, 2018. https://carriemelissa.com/2015/06/10/youre-using-the-word-community-wrong-and-youre-costing-people-their-jobs/.

Nielsen, H. 2018. Interview by Ann Lambson. *Denver Art Museum*, May 23, 2018.

Ponti, G. 1972. "A Denver." *Domus*. June. p. 3.

Ray, G. 1971. "Six Floors of Treasure." Scratch Pad. *Arapahoe Herald*. August 24. p. 2.

Simon, N. 2010. *The Participatory Museum*. Santa Cruz, California: Museum 2.0.

Tremblay, T. 2016. "Senses of Community – Making Sense of the Word Community in European Languages." *Presentation delivered at Birkbeck* (University of London) in November 2016. Accessed 5.23.18. https://communautedeschercheurssurlacommunaute.wordpress.com/senses-of-community-making-sense-of-the-word-community-in-european-languages/.

Young, A. 1971. "Art Museum May Turn Denver into the City of Its Aspirations." My Side of the Street. *The Daily Journal*. September 29. p. 1.

CHAPTER 5

Making an Urban Living Room

Museum of Contemporary Art Cleveland, Ohio, US

Megan Lykins Reich

Welcome to moCa! Feel free to sit and relax at one of the café tables, check email on your laptop, or just take in the marvelous architectural features. After you're done seeing the exhibitions upstairs, grab a bite at our café kiosk or buy something special at the moCa store. Remember to come back this weekend for our special event—the space will be totally transformed! This is the Urban Living Room, a free and flexible place for you to connect with others and recharge your creativity.

This pretend script describes the Museum of Contemporary Art (moCa) Cleveland's early and untested vision for the "Urban Living Room," the ground floor space of our iconic building that opened in October 2012 (Figure 5.1). As Director of Programs and Associate Curator during the design of the building (now Deputy Director), I remember how we envisioned this roughly 5,000 square foot public environment as the welcome mat for our visitors. In addition to serving gallery-driven audiences, we wanted the space to be a comfortable hangout and study lounge for nearby university students, a lunch spot for local professionals, and a shopping destination for design enthusiasts. It also was to be the hub for our new earned income businesses including an expanded space rental program and large store, which were significant to our financial sustainability models.

Looking outside the building itself, we intended the Urban Living Room to be the dynamic lounge for Uptown—an ambitious new, mixed-use commercial and

Figure 5.1 The exterior of the Museum of Contemporary Art, designed by architect Farshid Moussavi, Cleveland, Ohio, 2012. Sharp angles create a geometric form clad in primarily mirror-finish black stainless steel. Photograph: Dean Kaufman.

retail district that moCa was positioned to anchor. Uptown was a high-priority economic revitalization project that included converting 8.2 acres of formerly vacant land into a mixed-use space and gateway to cultural, educational, and healthcare institutions. Costing more than $200 million and consisting of over 223,500 square feet of new development, the redevelopment project involved Case Western Reserve University (CWRU), Cleveland Institute of Art (CIA), University Circle, Inc. (UCI), moCa Cleveland, the Regional Transit Authority (RTA) and developers MRN Ltd./Zaremba. Planning for the district began in 2005. The majority of construction was completed in 2016, including a renovation and expansion of CIA by MVRDV. In 2015, Uptown received the Rudy Bruner silver medal for urban excellence. moCa is the cultural anchor for Uptown, which continues to evolve.

Overall, we intended for the ground floor to help realize one of moCa's primary goals with the new building: be a catalyst for creativity and engagement. But intentions are not always results. Even with a deeply reflective process and highly responsive designers, moCa's ground floor, once opened, did not achieve most of these goals. Although it saw varying degrees of success—particularly in the realm of events—daily experience ranked low. It was not an Urban Living Room. Instead, the ground floor was one of the most consistently cited problems for staff and visitors alike. Why?

moCa's ground floor is architecturally astonishing. The reflective exterior of the entrance's glass curtain wall performs as a mirror for passers-by. Inside, the ground floor creates the hexagonal base that supports eight, deep blue, triangular and trapezoidal steel walls that lean in or out, rising up to a square ceiling 67 feet above. It houses the dramatic Kohl Family Monumental Staircase; an engineering feat that envelopes a bright-yellow fire stair within a white, meandering, steel-sheet exterior stair in an Escher-like tangle (Figure 5.2). The ground floor offers views of many essential architectural elements throughout the building, like full-height glass walls in unusual places such as the store that expose the museum's back-of-house (in this

Figure 5.2 The Kohl Family Monumental Staircase at the Museum of Contemporary Art, designed by architect Farshid Moussavi, Cleveland, Ohio, 2012. The "floating" exterior stair has an interior fire stair embedded within it. Photograph: Dean Kaufman.

case, revealing the loading dock). The 25 to 35 foot-high walls in Gund Commons and the Kohl Atrium lighten the building's tent-like steel shell while providing desirable real estate for artists working in large scale.

These assets all are attributed to moCa's designer, London-based architect Farshid Moussavi and Foreign Office Architects (FOA).[1] From a competitive international search of over 30 firms, Moussavi emerged as the choice innovator whose interest in affect and holistic design matched our desire for an iconic yet responsive space for art and audiences alike. This was Moussavi's first museum and first major project in the United States. moCa provided Moussavi with a compelling new model for her practice.

Founded in 1968 by Marjorie Talalay, Nina Sundell, and Agnes Gund, moCa is a non-collecting, mid-scale contemporary art museum with a respected legacy of advancing contemporary culture in Cleveland and beyond. Our mission is to push the boundaries of innovation, creativity, and exploration through exhibitions, programs, and publications. Since our founding, we have presented works by more than 4,000 artists in five different locations ranging from a small storefront (as The New Gallery) to a retrofitted Sears department store. Our programs range from toddler tours to performance art, all modeled on supporting encounters with the new and deepening public value through customized, meaningful engagement. With an enduring focus on firsts, moCa is a leader in anticipating an emerging generation of influential artists and movements.

Moussavi and her team worked with our staff, board, and executive architecture firm, Westlake Reed Leskosky (WRL) to produce a design concept that challenged expectations and drove new thinking.[2] I was a central team member, working with the architects, construction team, and subcontractors on design elements that would influence audience experience, education, public programing, technology, and exhibitions. To achieve success, I, along with my fellow team members, had to acquire new skills, learn quickly about areas outside our normal expertise (like emerging technologies), tackle macro- and micro-issues with equal attention, reflect and project simultaneously, and continually reinforce our mission and vision. Our goal was to ensure that the building's extraordinary design matched its intended function. We wanted it not only to support, but elevate and even influence our program, and to push us and the artists and audiences we serve beyond expectations. We wanted a space that would inspire new kinds of experiences and expressions.

The move was imperative to our growth and success. In 1999, we commissioned Lord Cultural Services to do a study in consideration of a future move. Lord's research determined that our former (then current) location at 8501 Carnegie Avenue was "not conducive to the achievement of moCa's goal of impacting the community by exposing more potential visitors to contemporary art." Nearby University Circle, with its concentration of cultural, educational, and medical organizations, provided moCa with greater proximity to potential visitors, and thus the greatest likelihood for success.

This formerly rented location within the Cleveland Playhouse Complex was beneficial in many ways, however. We had expanded and professionalized our practices over 20 years there, particularly in exhibition production and program design. To maintain these proficiencies, we kept a similar gallery scale (approximately 10,000 square feet) in the new design, while also addressing the old location's problems of limited wall flexibility, restricted exhibition support spaces, and inadequate environmental controls. The non-gallery public and event spaces needed the most change to support our ambitious engagement goals. In addition to expanding earned income amenities to include a store and cafe, we sought to create program and learning environments for discovery, reflection, and thoughtful exchange.

Understanding how to translate these goals into space required deep internal reflection. Our new location in University Circle, Cleveland's high-density cultural hub, would provide unprecedented visibility and increased visitation. Further, the new Uptown district aimed to become the social nucleus of University Circle—moCa's success would be linked to Uptown's ability to realize its goals. But what kind of visitor experience did we want inside, and how would the building design help achieve it? To answer these questions, we examined both our current and potential audiences and related programing. In addition to hiring expert consultants, we worked with Case Western Reserve University's Weatherhead School of Management to better understand the University Circle landscape and constituency. We evaluated our program and worked with partners to update initiatives such as the ArtSquad—moCa's vehicle for family learning—which we redesigned with American Greetings. We envisioned ambitious new experiences through thought-leader convenings such as "moCamentum," an appreciative inquiry summit in 2010. We participated in a Cleveland Foundation sponsored program to explore adaptive change and engagement with new audiences.

What emerged was a desire to maintain engagement with our then-current audience (approximately 15,000 people annually, all destination-driven) as well as to connect with new audiences, both intentional visitors and casual drop-ins. To do this, we scaffolded program strategies from captivation to cultivation, developing approaches to match various demographics, user types, and interests. This helped inform the new building's design, particularly the ground floor. In addition to answering key questions about the amount of people our new environment could hold for public and private events, auxiliary details—wall plates, embedded speak-

MAKING AN URBAN LIVING ROOM 91

Figure 5.3 The Gund Commons at the Museum of Contemporary Art, designed by architect Farshid Moussavi, Cleveland, Ohio, 2012. Event chairs are set up facing an angled structural wall. Photograph: Dean Kaufman.

ers, ceiling anchors, fiber runs, projector mounts—were fundamentally linked with our engagement goals and were studied and determined as intensely as all other components.

Flexibility is a key attribute of the building design. Our ability to change the space regularly was imperative to our success—with only 34,000 square feet, every inch had to be functional on many levels. The ground floor embodies numerous examples of creative solutions on this front. Gund Commons (Figure 5.3), our two-story high, 1,400-square-foot event space, has a massive garage door that can be lowered to seal it off from the nearby Cleveland Foundation Lobby for private or smaller events. The moCa store has mobile cabinetry that can dock beneath a long wall of shelves to create an open, 1,200 square foot environment for events (Figures 5.4 and 5.5).

Figure 5.4 The moCa store at the Museum of Contemporary Art, designed by architect Farshid Moussavi, Cleveland, Ohio, 2012. Products are displayed on white shelves on the floor and along the wall. Photograph: Justin Hustle.

Figure 5.5 The moCa store at the Museum of Contemporary Art, designed by architect Farshid Moussavi, Cleveland, Ohio, 2012. For special events, the moCa store can be entirely closed and stored inside wall cabinetry. Photograph: David Williams, DWill Photography.

MAKING AN URBAN LIVING ROOM   93

Floor and wall plates located throughout the space allow for atypically-staged events and audio-visual approaches, while multiple mounted projectors and digital screens provide simple, adaptable support for visual presentations and promotions.

There were two architectural components that greatly influence visitor behavior on the ground floor—the location of the main entrance, and the design of the related welcome desk. Moussavi positioned the museum's main entrance facing east onto a new, paved urban park called Toby's Plaza beside moCa, property that was designed by James Corner Field Operations in consultation with Farshid Moussavi/FMA and that moCa shares with Case Western Reserve University. The location for the main entrance was surprising; most assumed that it would look onto the bustling west intersection of Euclid Avenue and Mayfield Road (Figure 5.6).

Instead, one of the building's two large, trapezoidal-mirrored steel facets abuts this intersection, allowing narrow views into the museum through thin diagonal windows that slice through the wall. Just inside the main entrance, the Jack, Joseph, and Morton Mandel Welcome Center desk was positioned mere steps from a mirrored revolving

Figure 5.6 West facing façade of the Museum of Contemporary Art, designed by architect Farshid Moussavi, Cleveland, Ohio, 2012. Although designed as a secondary entrance, 50% of audiences enter from this side of the Museum. Image: moCa.

Figure 5.7 The Jack + Joseph + Morton Mandel Welcome Center at the Museum of Contemporary Art, designed by architect Farshid Moussavi, Cleveland, Ohio, 2012. An illuminated reception area is tucked into a white wall. Image: moCa.

door. Originally featuring a long, bar-high, white counter that blended into the walls around it, the Mandel Welcome Center looked like a perforation in the larger wall, with three bays for Visitor Services Associates just behind, at a lower level (Figure 5.7). The ADA-compliant counter for people using mobility devices was around the corner, closer to the alternative west side entrance of the building but disconnected from the main desk. It was placed here because the main counter was too high for people who use wheelchairs, but its location proved too far and technologically challenging for active use. In practice, it became a space for materials and storage.

Once the architectural elements were confirmed, it was time for furnishings. For the ground floor, moCa required a cafe kiosk that could display and refrigerate take-away food and beverage offerings—but this too needed to be flexible so it could be repositioned, repurposed, or removed for larger events. We customized a steel hot-dog trolley into a mobile cart for this purpose. Among the programmatic furniture, we selected Vitra HAL Tube Stackable black chairs with thin chrome legs and Symphony Zoey white round tables and high tops with white metal bases that matched the architectural color palette and commitment to clean, continuous lines and geometries. We also commissioned a new, interactive furnishing

Figure 5.8 *Floorscape* by Dave Picket at the Museum of Contemporary Art, designed by architect Farshid Moussavi, Cleveland, Ohio, 2012. Triangular black cushions are angled to create a seating area. Image: moCa.

from an exceptional industrial design student, David Pickett, at nearby Cleveland Institute of Art (CIA) (Figure 5.8). Inspired by the building's materials and forms, Pickett created a black, undulating steel and leather furnishing that provided a delightful topography for youth and adults alike to sit and play on. Based on the success of Pickett's furnishing, we turned this opportunity into an annual competition among junior ID students at CIA for two more years. Our budget precluded additional soft furnishings for the ground floor, although we acquired three black couches and three black Alivar Cartisiano soft benches for other areas of the museum.

Over approximately four years, the building was planned, designed, built, and detailed. By September 2012, our curatorial team was finalizing the exhibitions while our program managers were confirming tours, events, and learning experiences. Our caterer was preparing menus for the cafe; our store manager was stocking the store. The opening parties were scheduled. Toby's Plaza was nearly complete. New Uptown businesses and spaces were opening. Everything was in motion and we were racing to the finish line. Concepts were giving way to realities.

On Friday, October 8, 2012, we opened the building to the public for the first time. For four days, we hosted various events welcoming our diverse audiences. During that time, nearly 5,000 people came to see moCa's new home—almost one third of our normal *annual* audience in our previous site. It was incredible, and we were exhilarated—and exhausted.

A hallucinatory shock occurs soon after you open a new museum building, when the inaugural fanfare has started to dissolve into hazy memories. It is the moment when you realize that you now have to *run the museum*. All that planning, all that time, all that stress were not just for a philosophical or ephemeral project. You have created a space that people are now going to visit, experience, and *judge*.

And judge they did, as do all audiences of new, unusual places. The building received broad critical praise. Prestigious journals such as *The New York Times* and *Architecture Digest* hailed the building as a triumph for both Moussavi and Cleveland, while regional papers like *The Plain Dealer* celebrated its presence as a new icon for the city (Cochran 2012; Litt 2012; Miller Brouchet 2013). With a focus on sustainability, moCa was the first museum in Ohio to receive LEED Silver status. The Museum received the Dominion Community Impact Award (2014) for its role in vitalizing the neighborhood, and we were a key asset in helping Uptown earn a 2015 Rudy Bruner Silver Medal for Urban Excellence.

The general public was interested as well. We saw record numbers of visitors in the first year, nearly tripling our attendance from our old location. Aware that feedback was essential, we designed a visitor evaluation process that included methodical surveying and anecdotal conversations. The response was strong; nearly 90% of those surveyed reported that the visit met or exceeded their expectations. Almost the same number went on to do other things in the neighborhood, confirming our economic and cultural impact. However, these studies also revealed some key issues influencing visitor experience and satisfaction.

With a predominantly first-time audience—it remains today around 50% but was even higher that first year—visitors were not attuned to moCa's mission or nature as a mid-scaled, non-collecting art museum. Thus, questions like "Where is the collection," "Where is all the art," and "Is that all?" occurred regularly. This was, in many ways, a communications issue. While we had created a thoughtful promotional campaign announcing the new building, we had not focused as strongly on the nature of our program. We needed to better articulate our approach (rotating exhibitions, no permanent collection) in order to set expectations before visitors arrived. Furthermore, because the artists we show are not "household names," we needed to consider how to use other aspects of the program—the art, but also the events and the visitors—to show potential audiences the kinds of experiences and people they could expect at the museum.

Another problem influencing this perception among repeat visitors, however, was the increased size of our public and event spaces, in comparison to our former location. While we were featuring the same amount of art as before, the environments supporting non-art experiences were far larger now and the galleries were more "hidden." For instance, audiences now had to take the elevator or stairs to reach the galleries, whereas before the galleries were visible upon arrival. Consequently, it felt like there was less art, even though this was not the case. This concern married with the free ground floor's tepid performance. It seemed that, in contrast to our goals, we had produced an urban *waiting* room rather than the living room we were striving to create. While the exterior was a beguiling experience, the interior ground floor, for most audiences, felt cold (physically and emotionally), austere, and unwelcoming. In part, this was a product of the materials—mostly steel, glass, and concrete—and color palette of primarily white, black, and blue. Natural light was low in most spaces; although it poured in through a massive window wall at the museum's entrance, it was far less present in the lobby or Gund Commons where most guests gathered. The furnishings were ideal for events, but inappropriate for encouraging audiences to linger and enjoy the space. Virtually everything was hard and nothing was organic—there was no intimate nook or cozy chair for a visitor to sink in and exhale. Even Katharina Grosse's incredible site-specific painting, *Third Man Begins Digging Through Her Pockets* (2012), which drenched the Kohl Atrium's pristine white walls with pelt-like sprays of violet and orange, made the space feel severe, even angry.

We responded quickly to these concerns within the constraints of budget and time. Yet, we as a staff were somewhat frozen by the architecture's pristine and unique character. All the supple, gritty elasticity of our previous environment—where we readily would nail-in a new sign or install a quick interactive to improve audience experience—had been replaced by a proud but unyielding steel chapel. Its purity was forceful and intimidating. We were nervous to do anything structural or even decorative that might upset the architectural integrity of the space. So we tried programatic solutions instead.

We had intended the Kohl Atrium to serve as a site for art, but had not considered Gund Commons as an alternative gallery space. Yet, it could easily support video art with a few changes. Four, full-height, inset diagonal windows sliced through the west wall of the space, each with a 6-inch mirrored inlay around its perimeter. On a sunny afternoon, these mirrors cast wavy veins of light onto the 60-foot long south wall (where the projector faced), making it impossible to see any projection. Because custom blinds were not an option given the tilt of the wall, we commissioned two large curtains for the space that could be closed to create a light-locked environment. We also swapped the projector lens and stopped using the retractable screen, which allowed us to show larger-scale video art on the wall. In September 2014, we began showing Jennifer Steinkamp's *Judy Crook, 4* (2014), a mesmerizing array of whirling trees that progress through the four seasons. We continued to program Gund Commons with video art every 14 weeks until January 2018, when we introduced a new, bold approach.

The video program improved the perception of "not enough art" in moCa's public spaces, and provided curatorial opportunities for new commissions and special projects that expanded our reach. For instance, in 2015, we commissioned Nevet Yitzhak to create a new work specifically for this environment. The first project to take advantage double-projection, Yitzhak's related works OFF THE RULING CLASS (2015) and THE ANTITHINKERS (2015) drew inspiration from the bombed Auguste Rodin sculpture, *The Thinker* (ca. 1880) at the nearby Cleveland Museum of Art.

In terms of set-up, we experimented with the Gund Commons' garage door down (sealing the space to become a proper video gallery) and up (making the work visible from other spaces). Both had their advantages, and in general, we preferred the open-floor plan. Yet, there was tension when artworks required close listening and the open orientation allowed sound from other locations to bleed in. Further, because the videos required a dim space, the darkness throughout the ground floor was more pronounced, and more inhospitable. This solution was good, but not great. There was more to be done.

Furnishings were critical to our goals, but we were not financially or mentally prepared to do a full overhaul yet. So, we moved the Alivar Cartisiano benches and black couches from other museum areas to the ground floor to offer soft seating options. We commissioned a second furnishing from CIA Industrial Design student, Katelyn Petronick, which aimed to create an interactive experience through illuminated sails of plexiglass that visitors could write on. All black, these furnishings suggested alternative behavior in the space, but maintained the serious, gloomy tone. It was not enough.

Food service also had been a key element of our Urban Living Room concept. Yet, from the start, our cafe was low performer (Figure 5.9). The large rolling cart, while functional, blended into the space too much and did not entice the senses. Offerings were limited and generally predictable based on the cart's required scale and the lack of an onsite cooking kitchen. The museum's open hours did not correspond to early morning coffee or early evening cocktails, and so relied heavily on lunch traffic for revenue. Lunch traffic was anticipated among the thousands of employees and visitors in university circle daily. Uptown capitalized on this likelihood, quickly opening many fast-food and fast-casual franchises alongside a few locally owned restaurants, creating a "food court" experience during the day and early evening. More visible and better promoted, these restaurants were too much competition for moCa's cafe. After scaling down to coffee and snacks, we discontinued its presence in winter 2016 and moved packaged snacks and non-alcoholic beverages to the store for sale.

Uptown's food service success was evident, and its walkable environment increased pedestrian volume considerably from the parking lots and empty strip malls that preceded it. Yet, Uptown's original goals for tenant diversity and cus-

Figure 5.9 Cafe kiosk at the Museum of Contemporary Art, designed by architect Farshid Moussavi, Cleveland, Ohio, 2012. The mobile steel kiosk was meant to provide light lunch, snack, and beverage service. Image: moCa.

tomer size consistently fell short. While audiences swelled around lunchtime, they were short-lived and single-minded, not the kind of curious explorers who might walk into an art museum. Nightlife was spare, and relied heavily on university students with limited resources and time. Retail boutique stores opened and eventually closed. In terms of brand, Uptown lacked the gritty eclecticism of popular redeveloped Cleveland districts like East 4th, Gordon Square, or Ohio City that draw people specifically to their distinctive businesses. Other than The Cinematheque at the Cleveland Institute of Art, which relocated in moCa's same block in 2015, the museum was the primary cultural activity at Uptown.

This strongly influenced the success of moCa's Urban Living Room. Its concept was based on the notion of a revolving door of both intentional *and* casual visitors, sharing and using the space to various ends. But in reality, most moCa visitors were deliberate, specifically coming to the museum to experience the exhibitions or programs. A few came to shop. Yet, although our store is praised consistently for its unique design items, the lack of other retail opportunities at Uptown reduced the amount of ambling shoppers in the district. University students who we had hoped would use our space for studying and convening found more sympathetic sites on campus and in familiar branded environments, such as Starbucks, and our free Wi-Fi did not override the lack of tables with power and readily available coffee that such constituents desired and could find elsewhere.

After three years of testing the ground floor, and informed by a new strategic plan, we began to make significant changes in 2016. The most important was not in relation to the building, but rather the staff. Given the experimental nature of the art we show, we know that guided experiences provide the most satisfaction to our visitors. We also understand that our ever-changing content requires strategic preparation and skilled communication by our staff. When we opened the building, we enhanced our operations staff significantly to include a new group of Visitor Services Associates, overseen by a director of Operations. We found, however, that these staff members were disconnected from the content and not prepared answer rich questions from our guests. In spring 2016, we moved the department to Education and renamed it Visitor Engagement. Overseen by the curator of Education and Engagement, these key audience-facing staffers (VEAs) are now trained like gallery educators, regularly convening to discuss and develop skills ranging from customer service to art interpretation. We expanded our hiring practices to prioritize "people skills" above all else, assuring that our Welcome Center is filled with individuals with a passion for engagement. We began regular inclusion workshops to build compassion for audiences of all abilities and demographics; we changed signage and integrated new technologies to support audiences with disabilities throughout the space.

These human resource changes spurred a shift in visitor response. More and more frequently, visitors were commenting on the thoughtful, welcoming exchanges they were having with a VEA. This was the first step in creating the welcoming Urban Living Room we desired. The second, however, was more difficult—we had to address the ground floor design of the building itself.

The spark occurred in the form of a simple but mind-boggling recommendation made by architect Jonathan Kurtz (JKURTZ Architects) during a 2015 brainstorm. We hired Guide Studio (then PlaceHolder) to conduct a "space audit" about the museum's public spaces including but not limited to the ground floor. As we reflected on ways in which we could make the ground floor more inviting and user-friendly, Kurtz said we should move the welcome desk. I was stunned by the suggestion. Up to that point, every idea had been additive—what could go on top of the architecture? What kinds of workarounds are possible? How could we embellish the space? But *changing* the architecture had not occurred to us.

The Mandel Welcome Center desk was indeed a problem. Its close proximity to the door did not allow visitors time to acclimate in the space before stumbling upon a staff person. Its height was challenging for young children and people who use mobility devices. For standing audiences, it was awkward: the VEAs, sitting lower than the bar-high counter, were not eye-to-eye with visitors unless they stood up from their chairs. It also was poorly placed in relation to the auxiliary west entrance—too far forward, so visitors only saw the backs of the VEAs. This was a real problem as we discovered that 50% of visitors were using that door to enter.

But it was built into the architecture, unchangeable from our vantage point. Not so, said Kurtz. He noted that the locker room and coat closet in the area behind the desk was generally unused, and that we could probably "push" the desk back in order to provide much needed space for our visitors to enter and familiarize. Receding the welcome desk also would open up visibility to the Gund Commons, allowing greater orientation to the ground floor. He and fellow architect John Williams (from Process Creative) further suggested reorienting the store and adding a long community table near the glass entrance wall to encourage visitors to linger and work at moCa.

In 2017, we developed a new action platform for our strategic plan called moCa 5.0. Among its five key initiatives, ground floor improvement was the most time-sensitive and critical. Coming upon the building's fifth anniversary (October 2017) and the Museum's 50th (2019), we knew that we had to solve the remaining problems and transform the space in order to activate our other goals. In addition to structural changes to the welcome desk, we sought to improve the lighting, add diverse furnishings to create zones of intimacy, and engage art in a bolder, more delightful way. Several board members and donors responded with support for this initiative, and we reengaged both WRL for the redesign and Donley's (our original general contractor for the new building project) for construction. In January 2018, we closed the museum for three weeks to renovate the ground floor.

In February 2018, the first week after the redesign, a visitor entered the museum and commented to a VEA, "This is the most beautiful museum entrance I have ever seen!" That was the first such positive observation of its kind about moCa's ground floor since we had opened the building. Today, the Mandel Welcome Center is an intimate, warmly lit space tucked away from the front door and easily visible from the west entrance, with a lower ceiling and smaller, single height desk that has an embedded bay for wheelchairs (Figure 5.10). New furnishings punctuate the space throughout—a long, white steel table near the reoriented store features counter-high stools and embedded power for computer or phone charging; vibrant orange, blue, and lime green Knoll Bertoia chairs create comfortable seating areas in the Kohl Atrium and Cleveland Foundation Lobby; round and rectangular K-Lounge couches with the same bright colors play throughout Gund Commons (Figure 5.11). Lighting has been increased, particularly in

Figure 5.10 The new Welcome Center at the Museum of Contemporary Art, designed by architect Farshid Moussavi, Cleveland, Ohio, 2012. The design created a new enclosed space for a recessed and lowered reception desk. Image: moCa.

Figure 5.11 New furniture creates an interactive environment at the Museum of Contemporary Art, designed by architect Farshid Moussavi, Cleveland, Ohio, 2012. Photo: David Williams, DWill Photography.

Figure 5.12 Claudio Comte, *Zigzags and Diagonals* (2018) wall mural at the Museum of Contemporary Art, designed by architect Farshid Moussavi, Cleveland, Ohio, 2012. Comte's geometric painting created an optical illusion that expanded across an entire wall. Photograph: Jerry Birchfield.

Gund Commons and around the Kohl Monumental Staircase, where Claudia Comte's largest US mural, *Zigzags and Diagonals* (2018) drew and deceived the eye through its pulsating composition (Figure 5.12). Comte's mural was the first in a new series of commissioned projects on the ground floor designed to seduce and engage visitors.

We married this redesign with a new approach to communication, and saw record number of audiences in the first few months of its unveiling. Our next step is broader promotion. In tandem with a 2019 rebrand led by designer Michael Aberman that will change moCa's voice, graphic identity, and logo, we will extend regular communications and invitations to our local neighbors to enjoy and use the space. We are amending and adding exterior signage near both entrances to increase awareness, while exploring artist-driven pop-ups inside and just outside to pique curiosity and increase delight. We are continuing the Gund Commons mural project and exploring how technology can provide additional engagement opportunities. As always, we are programing dynamic, uncommon events on the ground floor—from town halls on mass incarceration to performative panels on sneaker culture—that welcome and nurture diverse audiences and provide memorable moments inside the museum. And, perhaps most importantly, we are going free for all. Lowering this financial barrier will introduce new audiences to our space, who will receive expanded support through new engagement and spatial strategies. With all of these changes, the Urban Living Room continues to evolve.

Contemporary museum architecture is some of the most experimental and unusual, and moCa's building is no exception. Yet, that innovation can lead to spaces that do not favor or sympathize with certain audiences or experiences. Because of their unconventional designs, these buildings also are often harder to change. While we registered the problems with our ground floor within months of opening the building, it took us six years to create effective solutions. These included adapting both the architecture itself along with our creative use of the space. Listening to your audience and taking seriously their concerns is a first and important step, and piloting small solutions to see what sticks is useful. Ultimately, however, there are times when you must make substantial changes in order to maximize the responsiveness and impact of your museum. The work does not stop, and like contemporary art and its audiences, contemporary museum buildings are living entities that should change over time.

NOTES

1 Farshid Moussavi was a principal at Foreign Office Architects (FOA) until June 2011, when she opened her own firm, Farshid Moussavi Architects (FMA).
2 In fall 2016, Westlake Reed Leskosky merged with DRL Group to form DLR/Westlake Reed Leskosky.

REFERENCES

Cochran, S. 2012. "Farshid Moussavi's Museum of Contemporary Art Cleveland." *Architecture Digest*, October 31, 2012. www.architecturaldigest.com/story/cleveland-museum-contemporary-art-farshid-moussavi.

Litt, S. 2012. "From Every Angle, the New MOCA Cleveland Will Surprise and Delight visitors." *The Plain Dealer*, October 6, 2012. www.cleveland.com/arts/index.ssf/2012/10/from_every_angle_the_new_moca.html.

Miller Brouchet, C. 2013. "Culture Blooms in Cleveland." *The New York Times*, July 18, 2013. www.nytimes.com/2013/07/21/travel/culture-blooms-in-cleveland.html?mtrref=undefined&gwh=31D0501F52F306C9FFAA57975937CAAA&gwt=pay.

CHAPTER 6

Museum as Place-maker

Kerstin Thompson

In her writing, Elaine Heumann Gurian imagines the museum as "the new town square" (2006). It is a place of community and gathering, a place where connections are forged, skills acquired, a love of art nurtured, history and culture celebrated. The museum embraces its traditional role but also exceeds it, with wide-ranging initiatives that include research, education and artists-in-residence programs, as well as commercial purposes such as retail and food and beverage services. If these are programing initiatives, what spatial devices might reinforce the aspiration of museum as place-maker or "new town square"?

Kerstin Thompson Architects (KTA) has designed several museums. Each has attempted to use the architecture and landscape as the blueprint for forming place that not only invites congregation for the purpose of museum-going, but also extends the museum beyond the walls of its official domain, weaving it into the life of the community so that it becomes incidental to everyday experience and enjoyment of place. The following four case studies elucidate our thinking on the role of museum architecture and illustrate our design approach (both built form and landscape) in the formation of place and the strengthening of community. They use spatial devices that attempt to overcome the physical and operational barriers to some user groups, described as "Threshold Fear" by Gurian, and therefore support these museums in their quest to be perceived and experienced as inclusive, relevant and welcoming to all members of their communities.

CAMPUS REPAIR: MONASH UNIVERSITY MUSEUM OF ART

Monash University Museum of Art (MUMA), with its associated Ian Potter Sculpture Forecourt, exemplifies how architecture can be a catalyst for urban repair and can expand the reach of the museum by bringing art into the adjacent

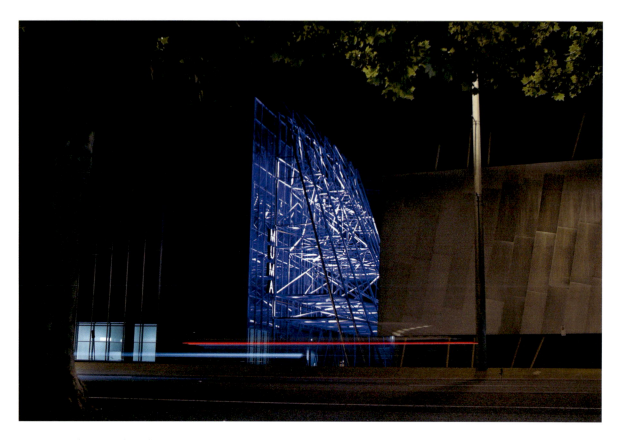

Figure 6.1 *Silverscreen* by Callum Morton, 2010. On the exterior of the Monash University Campus. Photo Greg Ford.

public realm. MUMA occupies the ground floor of a 1960s modernist building on Dandenong Road, Melbourne, at Monash University's Caulfield campus. Completed in 2010, this project presented opportunities to revitalise the campus, with various elements establishing an exchange between the typically internal program of the museum and the daily life of the campus and broader community. Bringing the inside out, art now infiltrates and activates the surrounding landscape, providing a cultural and social focus.

From the adjacent highway, *Silverscreen*, a commissioned roadside art installation by Callum Morton, heralds MUMA and marks the entry into the art-and-design precinct of the campus (Figure 6.1). Exploiting the museum's pivotal location in the precinct, this project bridges the Art and Design and Fine Arts departments. The landscape of the forecourt and other external elements stitch together the disparate campus buildings, transforming what was previously the back of the university into a focal point. One such element is the canopy along the southern edge of MUMA (Figure 6.2). This contains the bulk of the mechanical services essential to achieving climate control in the galleries. By externalising the

Figure 6.2 Services canopy as threshold and link at the Monash University Museum of Art (MUMA), designed by KTA, opened 2010. Photo Trevor Mein.

services in the canopy, we have maximised internal floor area while also providing a threshold between inside and outside, which defines the entry and creates a generous verandah space for outdoor gatherings and events, including after-hours museum openings. It also reinforces and shelters a key pedestrian link between the departments. The canopy's linearity amplifies the gentle curve of the existing building, which is further dramatised by an inky-black glass façade that reflects and refracts the landscaped surroundings. The façade incorporates seats, functioning as adjunct entry foyer, and several picture windows, which allow natural light into the southern galleries and vistas out to the forecourt. Perhaps most importantly, the windows also provide passers-by with direct views into the museum, so that the treats inside are informally revealed to even the most reluctant of visitors.

The sculpture forecourt, previously a dumpster area and car park, has been designed as an extension of the museum. Their relationship is reinforced through a shared geometry; the radial geometry of the existing building is extended out to the center of the campus and coupled with a new geometry of parallel lines running east–west. In combination, these order the galleries, the internal and external circulation, and the landscape's concrete plates, which define a series of major and

Figure 6.3 Ian Potter Sculpture Forecourt at MUMA with WSUD and habitable elements designed by KTA with Simon Ellis and Fiona Harrison. Photo: Derek Swalwell.

minor gathering and exhibition spaces. A layer of timber plinths, platforms and seats – materially reminiscent of the museum interior circulation spine – create more intimate spaces for an array of uses, such as sitting or lying around, gathering or retreating, tutorials or performances (Figure 6.3). Water-sensitive urban design incorporates rain gardens in the forecourt and intensifies the site's remnant native landscape. From the upper-level concourse, the gum forest's canopy provides a treetop walk, while from below it provides welcome shade and a calm retreat, quite distinct from other open spaces on the campus.

This project at MUMA demonstrates how an integrated vision for art, architecture, and landscape can enhance the public realm and make the experience of art more accessible and incidental.

TO LIFE: JEWISH HOLOCAUST CENTER

Located in Elsternwick, the suburban epicenter of Melbourne's Jewish community, the Jewish Holocaust Center (JHC) has been identified in Glen Eira City Council's strategic plan as key to the cultural life of this community. Due for completion in 2021, it will combine museum, research, education and administration functions in a new, five-story purpose-built facility that will incorporate the heritage building that housed the center's earliest incarnation.

The redevelopment of the center will dramatically change the existing interface with the street, addressing the tension between the center's security demands and its need for a welcoming facility. Holocaust museums are notoriously "closed" buildings, their high-risk profile commonly figuring them as bunkers and uniting an associative imperative with a pragmatic one of everyday defence. Overcoming threshold fear, the new JHC strategically uses architecture to balance the desire for security with that of openness. In line with local government's precinct renewal strategy, it will celebrate the Jewish culture of Melbourne while contributing to the formation of a safe, activated pedestrian zone and reinvigorated street life. The arrangement of the internal functions and the treatment of the façade are central to delivering on this intention.

The façade reinforces JHC's role as cultural repository by integrating the original heritage building within it and treating it as an important artefact of the museum (Figure 6.4). Embedded in the south-eastern corner, the heritage building forms the cornerstone for the future JHC and is a potent bearer of cultural memory – of the center's beginnings. Materially and tectonically integrated with the brickwork façade of the new building that encompasses it, it reads as inseparable from and essential to the center's cultural heritage, intrinsically linking the past and future. The distinctive corner turret remains a defining feature of the streetscape,

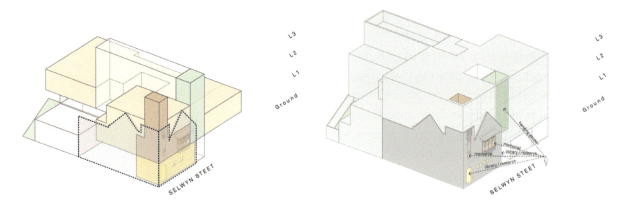

Figure 6.4 The original heritage building at the Jewish Holocaust Centre (JHC) is embedded within the new façade and treated as an artefact of the museum. Diagram: KTA.

a shadowline reinforcing its silhouette on the new skin; internally, its significance is reinforced through its transformation into a dramatic three-storey lightwell that illuminates the memorial space. It is arguably the symbolic heart of the museum, in which the lives lost during the Holocaust are remembered.

In order to establish a visual connection between the museum interior and the street, the facade is variegated through the use of opaque, translucent, and transparent materials. A combination of clay and solid glass bricks allows the façade to be calibrated according to light sensitivity and the nature of internal activities and spaces it encloses. Views into and out of the building are enabled to and from less light sensitive zones such as administration and classrooms, and withheld from gallery and museum spaces. The visually most open parts, formed by glass bricks in a hit and miss formation, are adjacent to the elevated memorial garden and associated central public circulation areas. The November Pogrom of 1938 became known as *Kristallnacht*, "night of broken glass", where the fragility of glazed facades became synonymous with the pogram itself. The incorporation of significant glazed areas in the façade of the JHC indexes the relative freedom to express cultural identity in Melbourne in 2019, and the JHC's desire to be visually and physically connected to the public realm (Figure 6.5).

Other breaches of the wall include the generous door from the street, leading into the main arrival hall; the glazed infill of the arched doorway on the heritage facade. Beyond activating the street, these architectural strategies also reveal and reposition some of the crucial but previously back-of-house activities, such as research, making them legible to passers-by. Importantly glimpses of greenery show and celebrate life within the center (Figure 6.6). At night, glowing from within, the JHC will act as a beacon.

MUSEUM AS PLACE-MAKER 111

Figure 6.5 The façade of JHC is calibrated according to light sensitivity and the nature of internal uses. At night it will act as a beacon. Image: KTA.

Figure 6.6 Glimpses of greenery and people behind the JHC façade show and celebrate life within the center. Image: KTA.

Architecture's role as a spatial language in forming the Holocaust museum is fraught. Can or should architecture be deployed to speak of the Holocaust? At one end of the spectrum, the use of a figurative and associative language attempts to somehow render the horror by reproducing forms and materials extracted from the most notorious sites of trauma; for example, brickwork and wire from Auschwitz. At the other end of the spectrum, our use of a decidedly abstract language recognises that for many people the Holocaust remains outside of representation. Arguably, reproducing material aspects of the Holocaust trivialises rather than encourages understanding of the history. It is the content – the artefacts and museum programs – and in the case of Melbourne's JHC its people (particularly the survivors), which are best placed to attempt to speak of the unspeakable.

GO WITH THE FLOW: SHEPPARTON ART MUSEUM

Shepparton Art Museum (SAM) is the main cultural offering in a regional Victorian town that has a high Indigenous and multicultural population. The setting for the museum's redevelopment is a parkland prone to flooding, due to its being part of a major river system. Our 2017 competition-shortlisted design was underpinned by an ecological response that would integrate people, place, and culture, and intended the museum to perform as a community asset for incidental, informal, and formal use.

Flood landscapes are dynamic and know no boundaries; they extend over vast distances and are subject to torrential downpours and inundation, to periods of both drenching and dryness. So, the concept of "flow" drove our approach to the architecture and landscape design in this limited competition. Rather than quarantine the museum within its official boundary, we envisaged SAM in a greatly extended geographic, ecological, and cultural flow – part of a continuum (Figure 6.7). And rather than resist the climatic and environmental forces, our design responded with resilient buildings and landscapes that would work in productive ways with a dynamic landscape.

The brief required a multi-storey building with a small footprint, to minimise obstructing the flow of water in times of inundation. This "constraint" presented a major opportunity for creating an accessible and welcoming museum. By elevating the bulk of the built fabric, much of the ground plane could be left as a free, democratic and accessible space for everyday enjoyment, incidental use, and pedestrian and bicycle flow, both day and night. Rather than stack the museum's requirements into several levels, our approach was to spread them out at the first-floor level to form a substantial protective canopy over high-quality open, public space below and around the building. This would integrate recreational and functional space,

Figure 6.7 The site of the Shepparton Art Museum (SAM) is conceptually extended beyond its official boundary as part of a broader ecological and cultural continuum. Diagram: KTA.

as well as transportation facilities. The design acknowledged the extremes of local weather, especially summer heat, by creating a civic canopy that would provide a generous amount of shade for ground-floor elements, such as the cafe (located at the northern end, adjacent to the northern park) and places for recreational uses, such as farmers markets, swap meets, and other community events. Aspects that required the highest degree of public interface – the information center, toilets, Kaiela Gallery, and community workshops – were made part of the ground activity, each distinguished with its own mini-building. Situating the workshops on this level would increase visibility and reinforce their vital role as incubators for new ideas and hubs of learning. It would also signal the active, ongoing contribution they make to the township and region. The treatment of the ground plane was designed to alleviate "threshold fear," to make Shepparton's community feel welcome to use the space, whether for arts-related activities or for formal and informal recreation (Figure 6.8).

The building's form was less about object making and more about public-realm formation and definition. So, the canopy was scalloped to create three distinctive territories that embrace and reinforce adjacent conditions: the play park to the north, the Lake Victoria wetland to the west and the approach to the museum from the car park to the south. Each territory could be occupied by specific user groups for various purposes. For instance, the wetland might function as a tool for educating visitors about native flora and fauna, while also doubling as a sculpture park or a site for storytelling or reflection; to the north, a civic space, which includes the amphitheatre, could accommodate kids' parties or cultural events and activities; and the car park area, imagined as an extension of the garden, could double as a site for a farmers market or for festivals.

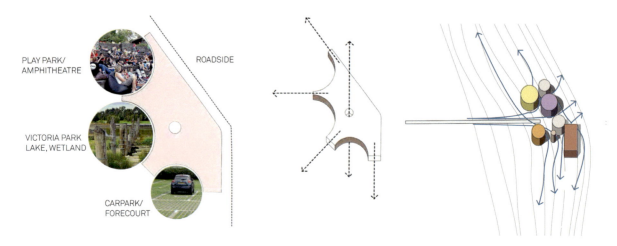

Figure 6.8 The SAM building's form was less about object making and more about public-realm formation the scallops creating a series of territories to its perimeter. Diagram: KTA.

Figure 6.9 An open and accessible ground plane at the SAM imagined as a landscape of peaks and troughs, the design created islands above the projected flood level, and between these wetlands appropriate to the Indigenous ecology of this river system. Image: KTA.

Our intention was to integrate built form, landscape, and infrastructure within a site-wide strategy and shared formal language. Car parking was treated as a landscape opportunity that would enrich rather than detract from the arrival experience, and when not in use become an extension of the parklands for recreational use. Its permeable surface would incorporate vegetation and perform as a water-catchment and filtration system. Imagined as a landscape of peaks and troughs, highs and lows, the design created islands above the projected flood level, and between these wetland and other plantings appropriate to the Indigenous ecology of this river system (Figure 6.9).

IMAGINARY LANDSCAPES: ARTHUR BOYD GALLERY AND CREATIVE LEARNING CENTER

The Arthur Boyd Gallery and Creative Learning Center, due for completion in 2021, will showcase the Bundanon Trust's extensive collection of twentieth-century Australian art. It will use architecture to reinforce an appreciation for art and landscape through an ecological approach to place-making.

The story of "Riversdale" is captured as much by the paintings of Arthur Boyd and the writing about his work as it is through the existing cluster of buildings and their setting on the Shoalhaven site in New South Wales. In a pastoral clearing, under threat of flood from the river below and fire from the dense bushland above, is Boyd's studio, the family's library and former residence, and the much-revered architecture of the Boyd Education Center (BEC) by Murcutt, Lewin, Lark. Acknowledging the cultural significance of these buildings, our design underscores this heritage as the heart of Riversdale and continues the established conversation between art and environment, the interplay between the natural and imagined. It works to foster visitor understanding of landscape and culture through art and architecture.

The KTA masterplan seeks to accommodate increased visitation in ways that preserve the estate's cherished qualities as a remote cultural retreat, rich with ecological, artistic and cultural history. It both preserves and transforms, in equal parts subtle and dramatic. Renowned aspects of Riversdale's setting are maintained, their presence enhanced with an array of new and compelling visitor experiences. The core of the new visitor facilities is collocated adjacent to the historic cluster of buildings to maintain a centralised "heart" (Figure 6.10). New and existing buildings are united by a forecourt, the culmination of the stepped arrival terraces, which also make fully accessible the site's considerable level changes.

The brief proposed facilities larger in scale than those existing. Our design negotiates this in two ways: bunker and bridge (Figure 6.11). The Arthur Boyd Gallery and collection store are buried, a subterranean building as a "reinstated hill." This maintains the BEC setting and provides it with breathing space. The remaining program – creative learning center, dining and accommodation – is figured as a dramatic spanning structure, "The Bridge," which straddles the gully from ridge to ridge (Figure 6.12). Imagined as a piece of infrastructure, its singularity of form highlights the distinctive, undulating topography of Shoalhaven. Recalling the trestle bridges endemic to flood landscapes such as this, the new structure allows the sporadic waters to flow beneath it and, importantly, for the reinstatement of the wet-gully ecology. Along its length, a north–south link is provided, with a series of interior and exterior spaces, small and large, for group or individual activities centerd on learning.

Figure 6.10 The core of the new Riversdale visitor facilities is collocated adjacent to the historic cluster forming a centralised "heart". Image: KTA.

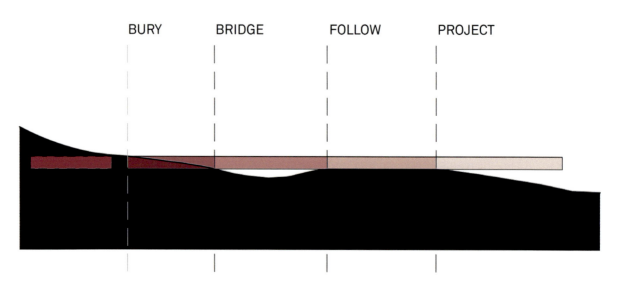

Figure 6.11 The new elements establish alternative relationships with the site's sloping ground, from the buried subterranean collection store and gallery through to the elevated bridge over the gully. Image: KTA.

Figure 6.12 The "Bridge" straddles the gully from ridge to ridge highlighting the undulating topography of Shoalhaven. Image: KTA.

The Bridge forms a beautiful counterpoint to the existing architecture, as well as to the subterranean Arthur Boyd Gallery. If on the Bridge we are dramatically suspended over the land, in the gallery we feel the weight of the hill above us. The drama will be in the engagement with artworks and in the occasional architectural framings of the site (sky or forest) through which visitors will be able to compare Boyd's imaginary landscape with the living landscape around them.

The resolution of the new works through these two very different buildings also aligns with the Environmentally Sustainable Design ambitions for the project. The most thermally sensitive aspect of the building program – the Arthur Boyd Gallery and collection store – is subterranean to achieve passive thermal stability and reduced need for mechanical systems. It can also double as a bushfire refuge. By contrast the Bridge is in the spirit of *en plein air* practice – where one is exposed to environmental conditions. Far more permeable than the gallery, it will have reduced climate control, as is appropriate to its use for workshops, accommodation, a cafe, and dining area – where indoor–outdoor flow and some exposure to the elements is desirable.

In addition to a picturesque appraisal of Riversdale, the future planning in this masterplan is underpinned by an ecological appraisal. In this approach, the design of buildings, landscapes, and site infrastructure support the ecology. They are part of an integrated, site-wide system supporting Boyd's vision for Bundanon Trust as a place dedicated to fostering an appreciation of art and environment.

CONCLUSION

Although these four projects are markedly different from one another – each are distinguished by an architectural approach tailored to the specific local conditions and the cultural and functional aspirations of their briefs – they share some design intentions. First, they establish a public interface and point of entry that is welcoming and relatively open, visually if not physically, to overcome the notion of threshold fear. Second, the setting of the built form and associated landscape of each is designed for continuous purposeful and casual use; that is, it is designed as much for the incidental and everyday enjoyment of those who regularly pass by or through it as it is for those making specific museum visits. Third, planning and development is exploited as catalyst for repair or regeneration of the immediate and extended site, whether an urban street, suburban neighbourhood, university campus or bush wonderland. And fourth, the inclusion and visibility of related programs, such as research and education, combined with some commercial elements, particularly food and beverage facilities, extend the museum's potential reach through social activities. As repositories of cultural production and history, they not only protect, preserve, and store artifacts and other forms of cultural memory and knowledge, but increasingly they use architecture to reveal the larger shape of a collection by bringing what was once back of house to the front, ripe for greater public engagement.

In each of these projects the museum is a critical part of a community's cultural infrastructure. Something of a counter-argument to the reduction of architecture to merely "iconic" forms, these examples demonstrate that the architecture of the museum is a powerful force in both enabling an institution to expand its vision and in connecting communities of citizens with each other through the enjoyment and appreciation of place.

REFERENCES

Gurian, E.H. 2006. *Civilizing the Museum: The Collected Writings of Elaine Heumann Gurian.* New York: Routledge.

CHAPTER 7

Design for Citizenship

North Carolina Museum of Art, Raleigh, US

Daniel P. Gottlieb

The North Carolina Museum of Art (NCMA) is one of a few art museums to have large sites and to embrace land stewardship parallel to collection care: to preserve, conserve, and interpret. For more than two decades, NCMA has evolved from a traditional art museum to a multifaceted campus—one of the largest in the world. The transformation of its 164 acres, guided by strategies to broaden and diversify the museum's audience, is the Ann and Jim Goodnight Museum Park. The first state-supported art museum in the United States, NCMA is located in the economically thriving Research Triangle of North Carolina. Its distinguished collection, park, summer performance stage, and recreational trails attract over 1 million visits per year.

The site also has a sordid history of incarceration. It was a prison farm, succession of prisons and, until recently, the site of a controversial prison for young men. For many decades, the site suffered environmental degradation by abuse and mismanagement. Today, as the Park undergoes social and ecological restoration, the history of incarceration and environmental degradation is evident in its landscape and curatorial program. An organic planning and implementation process was notably influenced by the 1989 plan called Imperfect Utopia—a framework for engagement, inclusion, and creativity.

HISTORY: FROM INCARCERATION TO CULTURE

The North Carolina Art Society was founded in the 1920s by a group of civic-minded residents in Raleigh, the quiet state capital of North Carolina in the relatively poor, agrarian South. Gilded Age wealth left few tracks in this state and, in the postwar era, it still had no major metropolitan centers. According to the 1940 US Census, Raleigh's population was just 46,879. There were few philanthropists to endow museums, yet unusually progressive leaders in the state institutionalized the North Carolina Art Society to become the first state-owned and operated art museum in the country. The North Carolina General Assembly appropriated one million dollars for art acquisition in 1947 to match an incredible gift from the Samuel H. Kress Collection, the nation's largest privately held Old Master collection—to establish the new museum. The National Gallery received the largest portion. Seven regional museums and the National Gallery were recipients of the public distribution of the Kress Collection.

With great fanfare, NCMA opened its doors to the public in 1956 in a former highway building downtown with a stunning collection of Old Master and American works under the guidance of its first director: art historian, critic, and museum director (Los Angeles and Detroit) Wilhelm Valentiner (1880–1958). The museum embraced an educational and public service mission, introducing thousands of North Carolinians to great art.

By the 1970s, museum officials were eager for a purpose-built building to house the collection and the legislature appropriated construction funds, but a vocal controversy erupted over the museum's future location: whether to stay downtown or move to a 50-acre tract of state-owned land on edge of town. The high cost of land downtown and the desire for room to expand were reasons to relocate, according to the governor-appointed State Art Museum Building Commission. Urban white-flight was occurring nationally and Raleigh was not immune to the economic and racially motivated forces driving the middle-class abandonment of cities. Many strongly advocated for the museum to remain part of the urban fabric, while others made a case that the museum could be part of a future campus near the State Fairgrounds, with room to expand. In the end, officials decided to move the museum out of downtown. The Art Museum Building Commission brought on the well-known, international-style architect Edward Durrell Stone to design a new building and selected a truly strange site behind a still-active youth prison in west Raleigh. The land, on Blue Ridge Road, had a crazy-quilt history of military and incarceration functions.

According to the NC Department of Public Safety's website,

> the original Polk facility acquired its name in 1920 from Col. William Polk, a decorated officer in the Revolutionary War. It was built on the grounds of Camp Polk, a U.S. Army tank base during World War I. Initially, inmates farmed the site.

The last prison to operate on the site was Polk Youth Center. The term "Youth Center" suggests it was a recreation hall for kids, but in reality, it was a medium-security prison for young male offenders. When it opened, Polk Youth Center's objective was "to give many young men a chance of a lifetime to participate in a real rehabilitation program—to learn a trade—so they may become community assets instead of a threat to the public and a drain upon society" (Daniels, 2001). In February 1964, Prison Commission Chairman Linn D. Garibaldi stated, "the Polk Youth Center is going to be a model for the nation" (Daniels, 2001). But by the 1990s, Polk was described as "a hellhole where prisoners can't escape sexual assaults, razor slashings, and attacks by homemade blackjacks" (Daniels, 2001).

As the prison continued to degrade, the museum architect designed a sprawling 400,000 square-foot building replete with roof gardens and reflecting pools (Figure 7.1). Stone's design was fantastically over budget and was then scaled back to 40% of its original ambition. Most of the galleries, gardens, and landscaping were removed. Stone died before the building opened in 1983 behind the still-operating Polk prison, whose double barbed-wire fences made a singularly unwelcoming foreground. The newly opened building was widely ridiculed by press and public alike, some commenting it looked more like a bunker or prison expansion than a landmark civic building for the state's distinguished collection.

After decades of public outcry, the Polk Youth Center (Figure 7.2) finally closed on Blue Ridge Road and relocated to Butner, North Carolina, joining a complex of state institutions. And in 2000, with the help of outgoing Governor Jim Hunt, the museum's director, Lawrence Wheeler (1994–2018), steered the departmental transfer of 114 acres of former Polk Youth Center property from the Department

Figure 7.1 Rendering by architect Edward Durrell Stone, new museum in Raleigh, North Carolina, 1976. The building was over-budget and ultimately only 40% completed. Image: NCMA.

Figure 7.2 View of newly opened museum located behind the Polk Youth Center, Raleigh, North Carolina, 1983. The stripped-down building was widely criticized. Photographer unknown; NCMA archive.

of Corrections to the to the art museum. With it came "the promise of turning a blight on the Raleigh landscape into a place of beauty and culture" (Daniels, 2001).

Critical questions to consider with respect to the art museum and its site: What, exactly, is it to do with 164 acres? As a public institution, what ethical responsibilities should the museum own as its custodian? How can this particular site, with its sordid history, constructively relate to the museum's mission of art and public service?

NCMA developed the land into an art park based on foundational *stewardship* obligations of art museums to be keepers of cultural assets using best practices to preserve and share those assets with constituents. Employing traditional collection stewardship standards to natural assets the museum is preserving and restoring it to a healthy state for art and public use. It also developed into a strategic part of its mission to attract and retain an expanded audience. This reasoning is supported by observational data and studies like La Placa Cohen's annual *The Culture Track, 17* survey that noted, "In 2014 we discovered that the cultural landscape had fundamentally transformed. The narrow niche of culture had expanded to include public parks alongside art museums, food and drink experiences alongside dramatic theater, and street art alongside classical dance" (LaPlaca Cohen, 2017).

Today's cultural consumers are less content to be routed through rigidly defined spaces that provide ready-made experiences; instead they are drawn to places that offer a rich menu of interactive activities that allow them to control what they see and do. NCMA's staff, in fact, were considering ideas much like these long before the additional land had even passed from corrections to the museum.

ART AND LANDSCAPE

In 1987, NCMA received a large grant from the National Endowment for the Arts (NEA) to organize a national competition to study the museum and its site. The NEA application stated that the interior and exterior of the museum building are partners in the total museum experience:

> It is the contention of the Museum that the site itself can be an outdoor museum, and thus a complement to the interior galleries. Indeed, it should be an active and effective setting for the exhibition of a wide variety of sculpture as well as the enjoyment of a broad range of art experiences within a park-like environment…The open, natural barrier-free environment will pose fewer impediments and invite a broader range of use …

The selected design team included artist Barbara Kruger, architects Smith-Miller + Hawkinson, and landscape architect Nicholas Quennell, who proposed a plan for a new park and preserve, titled "Imperfect Utopia: A Park for the New World" (Kruger et al., 1988). The plan suggested a "flexible structure that has the ability to grow with the Museum and the Community." And "in an attempt to anticipate change and allow for alteration," it considered "a strategy based on the idea of a non-finite zoning regulation." The plan described dense, active program zones close to the museum building where educational programs and festivals would be held, and more distant zones set aside for environmental protection and restoration. It proposed a flexible framework to allow management strategies to evolve over time.

The design team posited in Imperfect Utopia's program "to disperse the univocality of a 'Master Plan' into an aerosol of imaginary conversations and inclusionary tactics." Long before diversity was widely discussed as a cultural imperative, the team challenged NCMA officials to invite a wider community to participate in the life of this public institution and to share a conversation about art and culture. It envisioned "a landscape that would not exclude but would admit all possibilities, especially the possibility of change" (Coffey, 1990). While today's NCMA campus only faintly resembles Imperfect Utopia's physical *design*, or its imagined elements including a vehicular drive, sunken sculpture garden, or artist colony, the plan's

Figure 7.3 Imperfect Utopia master plan, by Barbara Kruger, Smith-Miller + Hawkinson, and Nicholas Quennell, 1989. The plan imagined an expansive idea of a multi-faceted museum. Image: NCMA.

then-radical idea of museum engagement through the landscape—with zones of formal and informal experiences, environmental restoration, and art—remain guiding principles (Figure 7.3).

Eight years after conceiving Imperfect Utopia, the first major project in the landscape was completed in 1997: an amphitheater imagined as a large-scale work of land art (Figures 7.4 and 7.5). This writer, then chief designer, frustrated by a lack of institutional support for the park, invited Kruger, Smith-Miller, Hawkinson, and Quennell back to catalyze the project. They proposed an outdoor stage and screen set within a framework of a site-specific artwork that Kruger termed the *textualized landscape*, thoroughly integrating art, architecture, and landscape design, and bending the boundaries of their creative disciplines. It was the first expression of figuratively turning the museum inside out, with its large film screen literally hanging outside the museum's contemporary galleries. The Joseph M. Bryan Museum Park Theater was indeed the catalyst that set the park's development in motion. In 2019, the amphitheater celebrated its 22nd summer season of popular performing arts in the park.

DESIGN FOR CITIZENSHIP 125

Figure 7.4 PICTURE THIS, an aerial view of NCMA, 1997, Raleigh North Carolina. Kruger's "texualized landscape" is readable from 1000 feet. Photograph: the author for NCMA.

Figure 7.5 Performance in the amphitheater, 2012. Summer concerts draw up to 50,000 visitors annually. Photograph: the author for NCMA.

The museum's acquisition of additional land, consolidating the 164-acre site, was complemented by an agreement between NCMA and the North Carolina Office of Bicycle and Pedestrian Transportation to expand the region's extensive Capital Area Greenway system through the old Polk Farm fields to Blue Ridge Road (Figure 7.6). The Greenway development was critical to the future park's development. Today a 750 foot-long pedestrian bridge stretches across Interstate 440 connecting the museum to area universities, neighborhoods, and downtown, bringing tens of thousands of recreational users to the museum. The greenway also established the spine of what would later become a network of trails through the park. With funding from the City of Raleigh, NCMA commissioned artist Thomas Sayer to make the iconic artwork *Gyre* in 2000 (Figure 7.7), the first of many site-specific works in the landscape.

An early commissioned artist, Martha Jackson-Jarvis scouted the site to prepare for a project in 2005. I showed her a pile of old bricks, set aside from prison demolition, made by inmates for prison construction in about 1920. Excited to connect to the past, she created *Crossroads*, a 20-foot column that marks a place where inmates worked the fields. Today a smokestack is the sole intact remnant of the prison, preserved in the park for a future commission to honor and connect with the site's troubled history (Figure 7.8).

The NCMA campus' overall organization is straightforward, connecting formal and informal experiences of art and programs (north-south axis) with urban

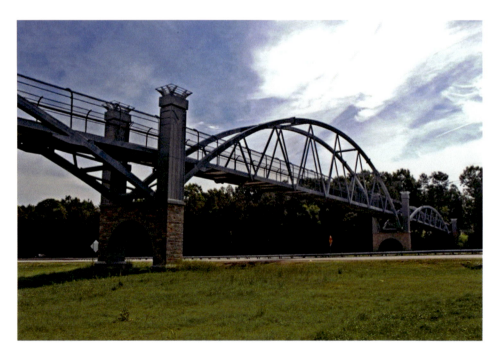

Figure 7.6 Pedestrian bridge linking NCMA to universities and 100 plus-mile regional greenway system, 2002. Photograph: the author for NCMA.

DESIGN FOR CITIZENSHIP 127

Figure 7.7 Thomas Sayer's *Gyre* integrated with the bike path, 2002, Raleigh, North Carolina. Photograph: the author, 2017 for NCMA.

Figure 7.8 *Crossroads*, by Martha Jackson-Jarvis, 2005. Photograph: the author for NCMA.

to pastoral experiences in landscapes experiences (east-west axis). The curatorial program follows suit: art in the landscape is generally more site-specific and temporary farther into the informal landscape. The Rodin collection is in a formal courtyard outside the West Building while the newly commissioned 300-foot-long work of emerging artist Daniel Johnston digs through the Upper Meadow (Figure 7.9).

In 2010, NCMA opened the elegant and minimal West Building, designed to connect the permanent collection to nature—most importantly natural light. Architect Thomas Phifer used advanced engineering to create daylit galleries throughout the one-story building, inviting visitors to experience nature's dynamic light, each passing cloud, change in season, and time of day. The enfilade of galleries connect ancient, Old Master, and modern works of art by visitor choice. Gardens and courtyards, set deep into the building's core, are prominent, further scaling connections to the Museum Park—connecting art and nature. The West Building landscape, designed by Surface 678, transitions the rigorous architectural grid to sinuously curved paths, tall-grass mounds and the park's and informality (Figure 7.10).

Figure 7.9
Organization of site functions, from formal to informal.
Diagram: Walter Havener, 2018, for NCMA.

ART AND ENVIRONMENTALISM

The prison land, as previously mentioned, was in a highly degraded state: stripped of topsoil; choked with invasive, non-native plants; and rife with badly eroding streams that sent silt downstream and trees giving way to undercut banks. In the years that followed the land transfer, I established criteria that each new development must incorporate environmental restoration. Collaborating with North Carolina State University's (NCSU) College of Natural Resources, we founded the Partnership for Art and Ecology:

> to bring together expertise and enthusiasm to create a new public destination and to offer programs that achieve both art appreciation and ecological understanding for the citizens of North Carolina, as well as ecological sustainability for the Museum's campus …This opportunity is unique among art and natural resource programs in the United States, with enormous potential to enhance ecological sustainability, art literacy, and the connections between them.
>
> (Shear and Gottlieb, 2005)

Figure 7.10 West Building, designed by architect Thomas Phifer and landscape architect Walter Havener, 2012, Raleigh, North Carolina. Both building and landscape won awards for excellence from AIA and ASLA respectively.

The partnership collaborates on issues of environmental restoration and health through scholarship and applied projects. Faculty and students contribute expertise to water management projects that handle runoff and raise public awareness of storm water's global impact. A pond, completed with the 2010 gallery building, absorbs North Carolina's frequent major storm events and reduces downstream erosion. Its sweeping curves, designed by landscape architects and environmental scientists, are a large-scale work of functional land art. A 2016 park expansion

Figure 7.11 Storm water demonstration pond, designed by Walter Havener and Steven Blake, 2010. Planted terraces clean water by removing pollutants and sediments. Photograph: the author for NCMA.

extended the pond's capacity with a thousand-foot-long water-quality band that reads like a contemporary garden. Currently, the Partnership for Art and Ecology collaboration is planning its most ambitious project to date: a climate-responsive design for the restoration of the park's 40-acre House Creek riparian environment integrated with reforestation, recreation, and art (Figure 7.11).

The museum campus embodies a wide range of landscape types, bound by a shared appreciation of nature, and our innate desire to organize its elements for human activity. The importance of preserving green infrastructure in a rapidly developing region cannot be overstated. The Research Triangle (Raleigh, Durham, and Chapel Hill) has experienced an alarming decline in protected open spaces. The Triangle Land Conservancy's State of Open Space 2000 reported that fewer than 150,000 acres are protected in the Triangle, while nearly 200,000 acres were consumed by suburbanization in a decade (Triangle Land Conservancy, 2000). NCMA is only 164 acres, but its obligation to foster environmental health and awareness may be act of ethical necessity and citizenship as a public institution.

BECOMING A CAMPUS

By 2015, the new West Building was a critical and popular success and park attendance grew to over 150,000 annual visits, expanded by non-traditional museum users who are less likely to attend exhibitions and traditional museum programs. Recreational users walk dogs, ride bikes, jog on the network of trails, picnic, and enjoy the informal pleasures of the park. In 2015, public perceptions persisted that site had two distinct identities: museum and park, disconnected by the abandoned prison landscape along Blue Ridge Road. When a donor offered to fund improvements, I targeted two objectives: to connect "museum" and "park" and to transform the still-rough edge of the former prison site into a welcoming arrival to the museum campus.

Landscape architect and urban planner Mark Johnson fulfilled the two-part program beautifully with a design that had a positive and immediate effect on public perception. Seeing the museum campus as a canvas for future experimentation, Johnson stated to the NCMA Board of Trustees in 2016, "We are purposefully putting design interventions into a space—high-quality, beautifully proportioned gardens, and promenades designed with a level of care to stimulate the thoughts and feelings, the sense of connection and wonder." The new landscape features a promenade to connect the galleries with the park, an elliptical lawn, and flanking arrival gardens that unify the identity of NCMA as a single destination (Figures 7.12, 7.13, and 7.14).

Figure 7.12 *Intrude*, by Amanda Parer on the Ellipse, celebrating the Park's completed expansion, 2016, Raleigh, North Carolina. Photograph: the author for NCMA.

Figure 7.13 Prison smokestack foregrounded by gardens, landscape architect Mark Johnson, 2016, Raleigh, North Carolina. The 100-year-old stack is what remains of the former prison. Photograph: the author for NCMA.

Figure 7.14 Visitors in the Museum Park, 2018, Raleigh, North Carolina. Photograph: the author for NCMA.

NCMA celebrated completion of the park expansion with Australian artist Amanda Parer's installation of *Intrude*. The five enormous, illuminated bunnies drew record-breaking crowds. Sculptures in the new landscape, including work by Mark di Suvero, Jaume Plensa, Hank Willis Thomas, and Giuseppe Penone, frame views to the long rolling meadow, woodlans, and trails. Taking advantage of new audiences, NCMA now experiments with new programs to strengthen connections to exhibitions, the collection, and the site's history.

TOWARD CITIZENSHIP

Once an institutional outlier, the Ann and Jim Goodnight Museum Park is now integral to NCMA's identity and its future. The combination of art and recreation in the Museum Park now attracts approximately 700,000 annual visits, eclipsing gallery visitation. Surveys conducted with NCSU's Center for Geospacial Analytics indicate growth will be sustained. Far from complete, the Museum Park will continue to mature. Guided by Imperfect Utopia's durable framework for engagement, inclusion, and creativity, I have been careful to avoid over-prescriptive design. Tastes change and future curators, artists, designers, and collaborators will shape its natural and yet-to-be-imagined built environments for years to come. Great buildings endure as relatively static settings for curated experiences. Great landscapes are in a perpetual state of change.

NCMA's identity has shifted from one that collects, preserves, and presents great art to one that offers a collage of experiences—a platform for art, health, and community interaction. The museum itself has embraced the role of public citizen.

REFERENCES

Coffey, J.W. 1990. *Imperfect Utopia, Art + Landscape*. internal report. Raleigh: NCMA.
Daniels, F. 2001. *Historical Research Report, Polk Prison Property*. Raleigh: NC State Archive.
Kruger, B., Nicholas Quennell, Henry Smith-Miller, and Laurie Hawkinson. 1988. *Imperfect Utopia: A Park for the New World*. Raleigh: NCMA.
Shear, T., and Daniel Gottlieb. 2005. "NCMA, NCSU Museum Preserve Memorandum of Understanding". Unpublished MOU.
Triangle Land Conservancy. 2000. *State of Open Space 2000*. Durham, NC: Triangle Land Conservancy.

PART 3

EXPERIENCES

Understanding and Reimagining Design Inside

The architecture of the gallery space can enhance the experience of the museum, drawing visitors through to see more of the collections, providing spaces of quiet and contemplation, inspiring engagement with ideas, supporting technology, and requiring creativity on the part of the curators. Smart offers insights on the future of gallery design, calling for architecture that creates diverse experiences and opens the workings of the museum to the public. Patterson reflects on how changing museum architecture reflects changing notions of civic identity. Norrie uses analytical diagrams of museum architecture to illustrate differences in choreographed sequences through museum space, demonstrating the development of museum ideas across time. Rohloff is a designer who has worked with museums in planning for change and offers an analysis of museum using space syntax as a basis for creating galleries that prioritizes visitor experiences. Finally, Polizzi celebrates the engaging galleries in a unique museum, while offering a commentary to understand how the design helped foster a deep connection to the material. Taken together, these five chapters offer new analytical frames for understanding gallery design and the experiences architecture offers to museum visitors.

CHAPTER 8

The Open and Integrated Museum

William Smart

I am an architecture tourist: I visit buildings that I have studied regularly and I particularly enjoy public buildings you can experience from both the outside and the inside. Of the last 20 museums around the world that I have visited, about three quarters have been partly closed due to refitting of the exhibition spaces. Even though there may have been a warning, I still went to visit these buildings so I could experience their architecture. Last year, I was berated by a gallery guard for peeking through gaps in the doors of the main room at the Fondazione Prada in Milan (Figure 8.1). I was curious to see the space and feel the light in that room, especially as the building has become a destination in itself. I asked myself the question, what would happen if we could see into the galleries during an installation? On a recent visit to the White Rabbit Gallery in Sydney (Figure 8.2), I walked through the process of the exhibition installation. It was invigorating.

These anecdotal experiences raise a series of questions which I intend to unfold through this essay, including how open could a museum become? What are some of the political, economic and societal challenges facing museums today, and what design strategies could overcome these challenges?

I am interested in the future of museums as the cultural cornerstones of our communities and the architecture that supports them. This essay is concerned with exploring a new paradigm in museum design, developed with a concept of openness. Unfolding this concept over the past two years, I have interviewed 20 directors, curators, and museum specialists from Australia and around the world. Throughout these interviews we speculated on what museums of the future might be like. The purpose of these interviews was not to conduct a survey or create an

Figure 8.1 *The Crouching Venus*, Exhibition view of 'Serial Classic', co-curated by Salvatore Settis and Anna Anguissola, Fondazione Prada Milano, 2015. Photograph: Attilio Maranzano courtesy Fondazione Prada.

Figure 8.2 White Rabbit Gallery, Installation of Xu Zhen, *Thousand-Armed European Classical Sculpture*, 2014, GFRC, marble grains, marble, metal. Photograph by David Roche. Courtesy White Rabbit Gallery, Sydney, Australia.

average of opinions. Rather, it was to enable these experts to elaborate on what the problems with existing and new museums might be, and whether these could be overcome with an architectural solution.

THE CONCEPT OF OPENNESS

The fascination of the modern architecture movement with glass and its transparent materiality might seem at odds with the curatorial, conservation and security agenda of a museum. The desire for transparent 'skin and bones' buildings developed in parallel with evolving technology, changing connotations of privacy and security, and an intent to engage with a building's surrounding environment (Colomina 2015, 96). In the design of museums, transparency is often achieved by revealing circulation or providing architectural frames of a context. This is evident in Jørgen Bo and Vilhem Wohlert's 1958 transformation of the Louisiana Museum of Modern Art in Denmark, Mies van der Rohe's 1968 Neue Nationalgalerie in Berlin, Germany, and even OMA's 1992 Kunsthal in Rotterdam, Netherlands. However, in this essay transparency and openness are understood as two distinct, but interrelated, concepts. The concept of openness goes beyond visual transparency, it embraces how a museum can engage with its community to form a social and cultural hub. This draws from the notion that museums are the cathedrals of today, revealing culture, and gathering people to reflect, feel, and contemplate; asking questions that are not normally part of our daily working lives. For many people in our secular society, the sense of belonging and fellowship that churches provided for in the past has been replaced, not by a single institution; rather in the ways we explore our hobbies and interests. Museums and their architecture, designed with an open and inclusive perspective, have an opportunity to expand their audiences to a wider range of people and groups.

An 'open and integrated' museum extends the traditional model of a museum from a place that displays art or hosts object exhibitions, into a place where the process of its creation is part of the show's content. This openness includes revealing areas like storage, conservation, design studios, office areas, and the installations of new shows. The essence of the idea is not simply to expose these transparencies, but to foresee a building that expresses these functions explicitly.

With each person I interviewed, I asked how open and integrated they believe a museum could be and whether that would bring another dimension to these buildings or not. This question was closely tied to how commercial the museums of the future might become. We discussed the need to address budget cuts, and the difficulty in raising funds from donors and sponsors. As might be expected, opinions range from those who are more conservative and believe in protecting the public nature of the institution, to those that feel that many institutions are out of touch with current culture and society, and that there is a need for change.

In an interview with the National Gallery of Australia director, Nick Mitzevich, he argued that just as Renzo Piano's Centre Pompidou design in 1970 expressed the building's mechanics to reveal how art museums are far from passive buildings, the 21st Century museum is calling for another level of openness (Mitzevich 2017). Rather than expressing the structure and services of the building, this openness would show the operations of the institution as a kind of theater to enrich the visitors' experience and give the audience more understanding of the processes behind an institution's operation. Conversely, it also connects those who work for a public institution with the broader community.

CONTENT AND PROCESS

To provide more information on their collection, many museums are making their collections available online. MoMA in New York has over 79,000 works from their collection available to view online. Mostly this is through image catalogues, however virtual tours are also now offered by some museums. Google has even created 'street-view' style tours of museums such as the State Hermitage Museum in St Petersburg, the J Getty Museum in LA, and the British Museum in London. Neil MacGregor, director of the British Museum 2002–2015, narrated 'A History of the World in 100 Objects' through 100 podcasts (MacGregor 2010). This immensely popular series boosted attendance and gave greater insight into the objects on display. It created free information, which helps to democratize the world of art, just like the internet has democratized information more broadly. Not only does it make the information easily accessible to all, but it links this into open-source forums such as Wikipedia. We can already see how many museums are embracing the concept of openness in their social media profiles. Platforms such as Instagram are being used to reveal the theater of the museum and behind the scenes with great reach (Figure 8.3).

The virtual as well as the electronically-augmented museum experience is common now, and will no doubt continue to develop, providing more detail to better connect audiences to an institution's content. The opportunity here for museums and their architects is to design a visitors' experience as active engagement with the physical institution and its architecture as an experience entirely different from what they encounter online.

When a visitor is immersed in an exhibitions' process of curation and behind the scenes operations, they gain a deeper and broader appreciation for the individual works on display and museum as a whole. In discussion with Simon Rochowski

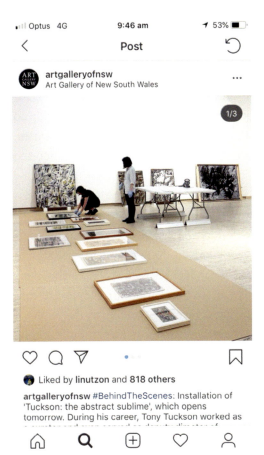

Figure 8.3 Art Gallery of New South Wales, Sydney, Australia. Installing and preparation of artworks for Tuckson – the abstract sublime exhibition, Contemporary Galleries, Lower Level 2, Art Gallery of New South Wales, November, 17 2018–February 17, 2019. Photograph by Diana Panuccio, courtesy AGNSW.

and Julin Ang of studioplusthree, an emerging architecture and exhibition design practice in Sydney, they see this starting with a more engaged and interactive experience, especially when displaying objects (Rochowski and Ang 2017). They pointed out that museums often act as a window display to view works. Arranged to suit a curator's narrative, the museum asserts authority over an object, defining its meaning. Where originally the object may have had pluralistic or ambiguous meanings, the museum frames the work in a new context. While an exhibition installation may appear to be a simple backdrop to a visitor, there is much behind the scene work done and this additional information can be equally informative to the audience. *The First Monday in May*, a documentary directed by Andrew Rossi in 2016 revealed the dramatic and exciting process of realizing a large fashion exhibition at New York's Metropolitan Museum of Art. The documentary made apparent the many layers, intricacies, and politics of mounting an exhibition, a brief glimpse behind the scenes. This trend, and the apparent interest from the community, begs the question, how can the architecture of these institutions support these activities?

REFITTING OF THE GALLERIES

The interviews I conducted with 20 directors, curators, and museum specialists centered on a conversation about allowing the museum visitor to watch the refitting of the galleries and the installation of the art. This type of openness, where the visitor has access to all parts of the museum in its various modes, would arguably help to address the perception of a 'partly closed' museum and improve visitor engagement. A few of those interviewed strongly opposed this idea, while the majority supported the concept, only if various obstacles could be overcome. The opponents thought that the dramatic reveal of the new exhibition would be marred by watching the installation and anticipated that the installation team would not appreciate being part of the 'show'. Many of those interviewed raised potential security risks here from two perspectives: visitors witnessing how valuable artworks have been secured to the wall; and having visitors enter a potentially hazardous work zone. There may also be situations where the loaning museums prohibit display of an installation. In addition to this, there is a risk that accidental damage to an artwork be caught on film by the public.

Typically, the installation of the actual artwork occupies a short amount of time compared to the construction of walls, plinths, and stands. A visitor is likely to mainly witness basic construction with ladders, scissor lifts, and timber framing, etc. Together with the visual aspects of construction, there will be smells, vapors and sounds which all need to be managed. Construction of museum props is not a smooth and uniform process. One busy period is followed by a slow period, such as waiting for paint to dry. Therefore, many directors have questioned how interesting this could be, and I believe that it would really only be interesting if coupled with spatially interesting rooms, and viewed with other back-of-house areas, such as open storage, exhibition design, and conservation activities. At the Science Gallery Melbourne, the open, flexible and modular gallery floor is highly visible in its surrounds, and the design has embraced the refitting process of an exhibition as a part of the visitors' experience (Figure 8.4). An ideal architectural solution would create a favorable vantage point, such as a mezzanine, from which to overlook the room. This physical separation would help to address security, and reduce the feeling that the staff are being scrutinized by the general public, as well as allowing several construction events to be witnessed at the same time.

OPEN STORAGE FACILITIES

Most museums only display a small fraction of their collection. The remaining portion is held in storage on racks, in file drawers, and in crates. Over the course of these interviews, I have visited several of these storage areas and found them fascinating, though I often feel overwhelmed by their scale. These facilities provide

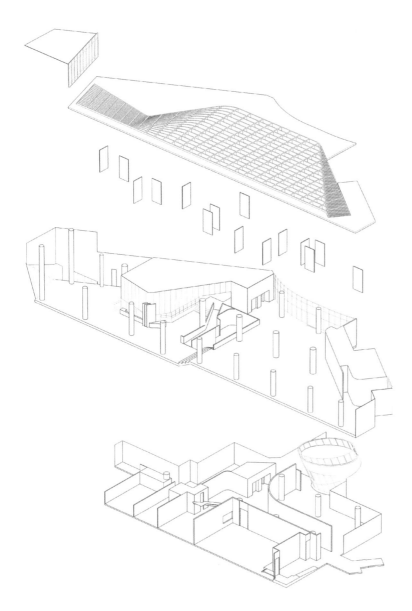

Figure 8.4 Science Gallery in Melbourne, Australia designed by Smart Design Studio, Sydney, Australia, 2019. Image: the author.

another perspective to the dynamic of a museum that goes beyond the provision of information about the works. I found a recent tour of Sydney's Museums Discovery Centre (MDC, Figure 8.5) an unforgettable experience, enhanced by the passionate tour guide who explained the history and arrangement of this collaboration between the Museum of Applied Arts and Sciences (MAAS), Australian Museum (AM), and Sydney Living Museums (SLM). There is an abundance of stories about the collected artworks and objects, which are dramatic when viewed as a whole. Similar to the proposal for viewing the refitting of the galleries, an open-storage facility would be ideal when viewed from afar, such as from a mezzanine (Figure 8.6). This allows a visitor to understand the scale of the operation and makes functional racks,

Figure 8.5 Museums Discovery Centre at Castle Hill, Sydney, Australia. Photograph by Marinco Kojdanvoski. Reproduced: courtesy of the Museum of Applied Arts and Sciences.

Figure 8.6 Louvre-Lens Museum. Image: le Musee du Louvre-Lens © SANAA/Kazuyo Sejima et Ryue Nishizawa - IMREY CULBERT/Celia Imrey et Tim Culbert - MOSBACH PAYSAGISTE/Catherine Mosbach - Photo © Iwan Baan, 2013, Lens, France

drawers, and crates interesting. Whilst it is unlikely that most project budgets would afford architecturally exciting storage spaces, their design would need consideration if forming part of a 'content-exposé' tour.

DESIGN AND CONSERVATION

When interviewing Michael Brand, the director of the Art Gallery of New South Wales, I walked into his offices only to come upon about three times the number of staff that I had expected, working on computers, in meetings, or with mock-ups and models of upcoming shows (Brand 2017). That energetic work environment excited my curiosity, and offered a rare authentic back-of-house experience. Museums seldom reveal their operational areas, even though as a cursory review of published plans reveals, this often accounts for about half of the floor area. The New Whitney Museum of American Art provides glimpses into museum offices, meeting rooms, art handling areas and the top-floor cafe kitchen. Glass doors and windows are used, allowing the visitor to see a portion of the functions behind, without over-exposing the operations or personnel. This visual connection not only provides visitors insight into how a museum operates, but also connects the staff to the visitors of the building.

Similarly, art conservation is fascinating to see in action, though difficult to witness progress as conservators work patiently and slowly to clean and restore paintings. The scale is often surprising, and large paintings frequently require ladders, or a harness to provide the conservators with close proximity for detailed work. It reminds one that these artworks are created by hands.

One comment that interviewees repeated, was concern that the staff being watched in back-of-house areas might feel uncomfortable. Although adding to the 'theater' of the museum, it offers an unedited insight rather than a rehearsed activity. Looking down over these spaces is the best way to overcome this issue, removing the proximity, so that visitors become discreet or invisible from within each room. As conservation and design can be slow and tedious, a back-of-house tour path would require careful design, and ideally be augmented by video or supplementary visual content. This kind of exposé also becomes more interesting when combined with other back-of-house events.

EDUCATION

Peter Denham, Director of Curatorial, Collections and Exhibitions at Sydney's Museum of Applied Arts and Sciences (MAAS), explains their multi-faceted approach to education (Denham 2017). As with many museums, they include classrooms, open spaces, and programs to cater for school children. They also have alliances with universities, focusing on digital and research projects, as well as opportunities to exhibit within the museum. For example, MAAS presents an annual Student Fashion Exhibition that is selected from the city's four fashion schools.

As many universities pursue private-public partnerships, and public funding to museums becomes more restricted, many foresee closer alliances between tertiary education and museums. Museums as 'Centers of Excellence' will become better connected to schools, universities and other education programs. Stronger integration of education into the museum, with facilities specifically designed to accommodate different groups of people, will invigorate it with vibrant activity, and simultaneously build a culture and community within the building. This arrangement uses the actual content and environment of the museum, and allows employed experts to remain within the building, enhancing financial efficiency.

Björn Dahlström, director of the Berber Museum and Musée Yves Saint Laurent at the Jardin Majorelle in Marrakech, emphasized that the 21st century museum should have spaces serving many different functions (Dahlström 2017). For example, a multi-functional auditorium can be used for films, talks and education, and to increase the flexibility of these types of spaces, they should have independent access. In this example of an auditorium, some functions can be income generating, and others integrated with exhibitions or the education program. A lecture theater in the day, could double up as a cinema at night. The École du Louvre, which resides within The Louvre, teaches courses in the history of art, archaeology, epigraphy, anthropology, and museology. It offers students diplomas, amongst other qualifications. In parallel with this training, the École du Louvre allows occasional enrolled students to attend various courses and organizes evening, summer, regional, and Ville de Paris courses, which are open to the general public. All courses are accessible as part of a lifelong learning program. This highly integrated approach, without much additional overhead cost, enriches the citizens of the community and produces a more purposeful institution and provides an income stream.

This 'Center of Excellence' concept also works in reverse, where universities and their respective programs assist research and design. For example, students could assist with digital content that complements an exhibition, or prepare short documentaries about the design, production and background of an upcoming exhibition. These integrated projects could be displayed as material prepared in conjunction with a university, and become an inexpensive way to prepare supplementary content.

COMMUNITY AND GATHERING

Serge Belet, Senior Exhibitions Manager at the National Gallery of Canada in Ottawa points to libraries procured in the past 20 years as good examples of buildings that connect with the public and the neighborhood (Belet 2017). Instead of succumbing to obsolescence due to the impact of the internet, libraries have adapted to integrate programs and spaces that complement access to books. Similarly, a new museum should focus on community and creativity, and develop all the areas that cannot be replicated in an online experience, exploring the light, sound, smell, materials or volume of the works and the building. A new open and integrated museum then becomes a place designed for gathering, interaction and social inclusion.

Tony Ellwood, director of the National Gallery of Victoria in Melbourne, sees the opportunity for social interaction as the most important development for museum design in the future (Ellwood 2017). He views the museum as a place where people acquire and hold memories; as artworks can make a huge emotional impression on us, and revisiting these is often a contemplative, thought provoking experience. He mentioned that, interestingly, two days after the 9/11 tragedy, there was a sharp increase in visitor numbers to museums, as people felt safe in such places, revisiting old memories. This sentiment is also echoed by Erlend Høyersten, director of ARoS in Aarhus Denmark, where they have initiated 'ARoS Public' as a mental fitness center for the community (Figure 8.7; Høyersten 2016).

Figure 8.7 The Portrait Machine, at ARoS Public. Photo: ARoS Aarhus Art Museum, Denmark.

In our interview, Jess Scully, a City of Sydney Councilor, reinforced the notion that all museum projects should be led by what the local community needs, to create an institution that is connected to and represents society (Scully 2017). She sees an opportunity for a two-way exchange between the community and the institution, and each party is treated as equal. Her concern is that the public museum is too isolated from the community (naturally, this will depend on the size of the city and its constituents). The CEO for the City of Sydney, Monica Barone, considers the local government's role as reinforcing the benefits of a creative city and encouraging this to be developed on many different levels (Barone 2017). Large public museums form part of this offering, as do small exhibition spaces, markets, and on-street events. At all scales, they help to build the culture of a city, keep people living in that city and attract tourism.

The open and integrated museum needs to extend beyond its façade to engage with the public domain. Similarly, each external surface of the building has the potential to contribute to place-making, or an external activity. A museum that is integrated and focused on creativity, rather than just art, should seek to create an inclusive environment that welcomes people of all different ages (Figure 8.8), and from different backgrounds, and they should feel comfortable in that environment, whether as an expert or a novice.

Figure 8.8 The Eyetracker, ARoS Public. Photo: ARoS Aarhus Art Museum, Denmark.

FINANCIAL MODELS AND POTENTIAL

Every museum director shared the view that maintaining sufficient funding to operate the facility is always a challenge. In Australia, most state-funded museums have experienced a steady reduction in annual funding, yet they are maintaining free entry in most exhibition areas. To cover the difference between the state funding and operating costs, museums actively seek sponsorship, donations, memberships, and ticket sales to temporary exhibitions, though the latter tend to only partially cover the expense of these costly 'blockbuster' shows. All directors interviewed were aware of the risks, and potential missed revenue, from not integrating independent income generating functions tuned to the profile of their institution. In all cases their institutions raise revenue through other non-governmental forms, such as retail offerings, hiring function rooms, cafe restaurant rental, or using their facilities for other functions such as weddings, parties, and lectures. The future museum will need to integrate these functions and provide them with independent patron and service access. This independent access allows longer hours of operation, noting that staff hours are always greater than opening hours, and helps to control the labor costs of the facility by keeping staff numbers, including security, to a minimum. It is also important to balance, not overwhelm, the museum experience with these supporting facilities, which could dilute the museum experience. Chris Saines, the director of Queensland Art Gallery & Gallery of Modern Art believes that the public nature of the public museum must be clearly legible, and that too much emphasis on retail will confuse this message (Saines 2016). The purpose is to create a public place that is distinct from a commercial operation. Evening events are great fundraisers across many museums, and usually sell. Art must remain the focus of these events, both so people feel engaged with the museum, and also so that these offerings remain consistent with the institution's core mission.

The Museum of Contemporary Art in Sydney raises a third of its income through its function rooms and venues that remain very popular, partly as a result of the museum's iconic location in Circular Quay. Their separate entrances, and isolated back-of-house servicing is essential to this operation, noting that security of the art is paramount, and costly to secure via security staff. A well-designed museum also looks to integrate the function rooms into the operation of the building, for education classes, training, etc. And there are naturally different times of the day that these facilities are used. MoMA in New York, for example, has an excellent design and book store, which offers much more than exhibition books and merchandise. The strong emphasis on clothing, designed objects, and posters as well as books, makes it a destination in its own right. MoMA also has a fine dining restaurant and cafe, exploiting its great location and outlook. At the

Science Gallery Melbourne, the open foyer and cafe is a destination within the surrounding context (Figure 8.9), separate to the galleries, with longer opening times, enabling an alternative revenue source for the museum.

In city centers, retail tenancies often dominate the ground floor of a building, without defining the nature of that building. Office and apartment buildings, for example, integrate retail to activate the public domain and serve the general public, not just the occupants of the building. Railway stations, sports arenas and airports designed in the past ten years, have also focused on integrating retail to serve those that use them, and also raise revenue for the facility. The new museum should seek to integrate secondary opportunities, such as those above, to supplement its income. Where possible, function rooms and auditoriums should be integrated into the operation of the building, including use for education and training as well as seeking opportunities for revenue. A museum conceived as a community hub, appealing to a diverse audience and with facilities accessible outside normal business hours – while not compromising the primary purpose of exhibiting art or objects – would create an expectation that the museum is always a stimulating and dynamic place. The argument here is that a museum open all the time, even while

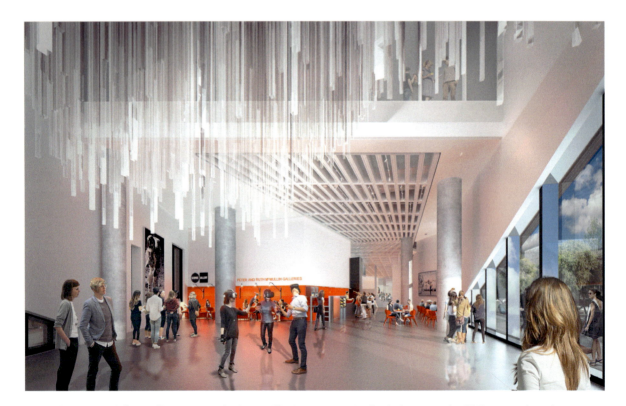

Figure 8.9 Science Gallery Melbourne, Australia designed by Smart Design Studio, Sydney, Australia, 2019. Image: the author.

an exhibition is under construction, will reinforce the relevance of that institution to the everyday life of the community it is embedded within. It builds an expectation that the museum is always stimulating.

In addition to seeking revenue opportunities, the new museum should also seek to minimize running costs. Physically, this could be done through durable materials and galleries that are easy to access and build within. The design of the building should consider how to minimize staff costs generally, especially at shoulder periods such as early mornings or evenings, when the museum may be partially open for events or functions. The services of the buildings should be designed to minimize energy and water consumption through sustainable design and long-life, efficient fittings.

THE GALLERY: UNIQUE SPACE OR 'WHITE BOX' FUNCTIONALIST

The primary activity of a museum involves exhibiting art or objects in a specific spatial situation: the gallery. The galleries in which an artwork or object is exhibited are fundamental to the capabilities, visitors' experience, and operations of that institution. I detect two main ways of approaching the design of a gallery: as a unique spatial proposition or as a functionalist white box. A museum designed as a unique spatial proposition is characterized by a building specific to its place and often with expressive circulation, material and spatial dynamics. While the 'whitebox' functionalist museum is characterized by buildings where the exterior architecture and context beyond does not interact with the galleries themselves. They have supposedly infinitely flexible gallery interiors defined by limited natural light, column-free, orthogonal, and large-scale rooms that accommodate a wide variety of arrangements. The first two Guggenheim Museums (the Solomon R. Guggenheim Museum in New York, 1959 and the Peggy Guggenheim Collection in Venice, 1980) are great examples of buildings with unique spatial dynamics distinctly different to functional white-box galleries. Richard Armstrong, the director of the Solomon R. Guggenheim Museum and Foundation noted that that 'it worked well for them', as they have continued this strategy with the Guggenheim Museum Bilbao (Armstrong 2017). These buildings attract international attention and have visitation rates that significantly exceed museums of comparable size and collections. Armstrong added that they had found ways to work with the irregular spaces and acknowledged that the Solomon R. Guggenheim Museum in New York had a number of other museums with which it shares exhibitions, so larger-scaled pieces in their collection could be housed in other museums. It is interesting to observe how museums tuned to the specifics of a place and designed with distinct and memorable material and spatial dynamics do in fact impact on visitation numbers precisely because the visitors experience something more than just an interesting exhibition or beautiful artwork.

Elizabeth Ann Macgregor, director of Sydney's Museum of Contemporary Art strongly champions the 'white-box' gallery type (Macgregor 2017). This creates a museum where art is the focus, and the cost of refitting galleries is reduced by foregoing the cost of blocking the skylights and windows (Figure 8.10). Windows to the outdoors are located in the circulation areas so that visitors experience a sense of relief from the enclosed gallery rooms. This is different from the new Whitney Museum of American Art, which, in contrast to the old, is highly engaged with the city, and has windows on every floor offering views of, and a strong connection to, its neighborhood. Generally, a space that is enclosed and disconnected from its external environment facilitates a more immersive experience than one with a glass facade, such as SANAA's new outward-looking proposal for Sydney Modern. Michael Brand, director of the Art Gallery of New South Wales., sees the heroic architecture that was common in the 1990s being replaced by this type of restrained, porous, and integrated approach.

These contrasting perspectives on museum design however remind me of a key fact: that the design of a new museum should be based on the collection of

Figure 8.10 Museum of Contemporary Art Australia in Sydney hosts an installation by Anish Kapoor courtesy the Museum of Contemporary Art Australia.

art or objects to be exhibited and the purpose of its operation. For example, in Bilbao where an objective of building the Guggenheim was to reinvigorate the city, a restrained white box museum would not have drawn a significant international audience. Richard Armstrong reminded me that most people had not heard of Bilbao until the Guggenheim commissioned the new Gehry building there. The construction of this building was part of a strategy to reinvigorate the city, and was coupled with significant infrastructure improvements, and the rejuvenation of its more downtrodden areas. People now travel the world to see the Guggenheim Bilbao, with attendance reaching its highest point in 2017 during its 20th anniversary year. The design of a new museum is often imbued with curatorial, political and economic aspirations that exceed simply designing empty vessels to display art. The provocation I put to the directors and curators interviewed is that designing a museum that is open and integrated with its place, exciting for visitors and embedded with unique spatial dynamics is more relevant than designing galleries of infinite flexibility.

CONCLUSION

I have described throughout this chapter very real aspirations of many museums in the 21st century as being integrated and deeply connected with a diverse community of active visitors. One aspiration includes the creation of museums as open cultural hubs where visitors return time and time again and gain new and exciting experiences while they reflect, feel and contemplate questions and events not normally part of their daily lives. The current situation for many museums is that they have struggled to keep up with changes in society, and, expectations of many visitors, often creating a disappointing experience. The closure of galleries for refitting gives the visitor the impression of an institution half closed. Only accessing 10% of the art collection at one time, while 90% remains in storage, is also clearly a missed opportunity. In a time when funding is being reduced, poor integration of fee-generating aspects such as retail, auditorium and function rooms is becoming a missed opportunity to supplement the museum's income. Often the design of museum buildings has not focused on social engagement beyond the walls of the institution, and they have not been designed to optimally accommodate for events within their spaces. The general public impression of art museums is that these institutions are hard to penetrate and not places for everyone.

Museum design needs to be re-conceptualized to successfully accommodate new functions and community expectations while supporting its core operations as executed by its operational team. The benefits will be to create an open, vibrant, sustainable community where the focus is concerned with building creativity, rather than individual art pieces or objects. I have promoted the concept of openness as the natural evolution of transparency in museum design. Museums should allow access to back of house areas, as well as address the expectations for the 21st century museum to be social hubs and integrated with the functions housed within. The full potential for a visitor having an actively engaged experience, which is entirely different from an online experience, should be exploited. Furthermore, as museums transition into cultural hubs they should actively connect with their local community and education sectors. A museum's design should concurrently focus on how to attract more visitors, reduce operating costs, and create supplementary income. These aspirations are all generated and supported actively by the architecture of the museum. This less passive more active direction will attract wider audiences and help their understanding of the process of creating exhibitions, as well as a deeper understanding of their content.

REFERENCES

Armstrong, R. Interview by William Smart. October 06, 2017.

Barone, M. Interview by William Smart. June 29, 2017.

Belet, S. Interview by William Smart. April 05, 2017.

Brand, M. Interview by William Smart. February 01, 2017.

Colomina, B. 2015. 'Blurred Visions: architectures of Surveillance from Philip Johnson and Mies van der Rohe to SANAA'. In *Questions of Representation*, edited by Toft, A. E. and C. Capetilo, 96–109. Aarhus: Arkitektskolens Forlag.

Dahlström, B. Interview by William Smart. March 15, 2017.

Denham, P. Interview by William Smart. June 01, 2017.

Ellwood, T. Interview by William Smart. June 09, 2017.

Høyersten, E. 2016. 'The Art Museum is a Mental Fitness Center'. Filmed October 2016 at TEDxAarhus, Aarhus, Denmark. Video, 19: 26. www.youtube.com/watch?v=p2yOH_lJlmM.

Macgregor, E.A. Interview by William Smart. May 25, 2017.

MacGregor, N. 2010. 'A History of the World in 100 Objects presented by The British Museum's Neil MacGregor', *The British Museum, podcast audio*, www.bbc.co.uk/programmes/b00nrtf5.

Mitzevich, N. Interview by William Smart. February 09 and July 19, 2017.

Rochowski, S., Ang, J. Interview by William Smart. July 05, 2017.

Saines, C. Interview by William Smart. September 30, 2016.

Scully, J. Interview by William Smart. June 15, 2017.

CHAPTER 9

Building Citizens by Building Museums

Royal Ontario Museum & Art Gallery of Ontario

Matt Patterson

Museums are instruments of nation building in that they reflect and promote certain notions of civic identity. Through their collecting practices, museums establish a category of publicly significant objects that privilege certain modes of cultural production and consumption (and, by extension, certain producers and consumers) over others (Bourdieu, Darbel, and Schnapper 1997; DiMaggio 1982). Through their curatorial practices they create narratives that tell us who we are as a political community (Aronczyk and Brady 2015; Levitt 2015). And, as tightly regulated public spaces, they enforce certain performative modes of being in (and being a) public (Bennett 1995; Duncan 1995).

Standing silently behind these institutional functions is the museum building itself. While most analyses of museums and civic identity have focused on their internal functions (e.g. collection and curation), less is understood about the role played by their external architecture. Yet, buildings are not neutral boxes within which social life takes place; they are a constitutive element of social life (Gieryn 2002). Thus, understanding the role of museum architecture in reflecting and producing civic identity is essential to fully accounting for the role of museums in nation building.

The purpose of this chapter is to develop a framework for understanding how museum architecture shapes and is shaped by notions of civic identity and public life more generally. In doing so, I draw on Thomas Gieryn's (2002) sociology of buildings, focusing on (1) how existing social forces influence the design and development of architecture, (2) how the architecture, once built, structures the ways in which civic identity is expressed within the museum, and (3) how architecture can become reinterpreted and redeveloped over time to express new identities.

The empirical focus of the analysis is the changing architecture of two museums in Toronto: the Art Gallery of Ontario (AGO), a fine arts museum, and the Royal Ontario Museum (ROM), a museum of natural and cultural history. Since their founding in the early twentieth century, both museums have undergone several renovations and expansions, incorporating a diversity of architectural styles. I analyze how both buildings were constructed and modified across three distinct political eras: imperial (1867–1945), postwar (1945–1988), and neoliberal (1988–present). Each era represents distinct understandings of civic identity and the public role of museums. By focusing on two museums in the same city, we are able to observe how institutions subject to the same contextual factors typically produce similar buildings, while also examining how contingencies and variation in their architecture relate in different ways to civic identity.

I conclude the chapter by discussing how architecture, as a concrete manifestation of otherwise abstract political and cultural logics, serves as a useful lens through which to understand larger socio-historical trends.

THE MUSEUM AS AN INSTITUTION AND AS ARCHITECTURE

The notion of a museum is perhaps more strongly tied to a physical building than any other public institution. Indeed, scholars of museums have argued that it is precisely the materiality of museums – the fact that they situate people within particular physical spaces and among arrangements of physical objects – that gives them their social power (Bennett 1995; Duncan 1995). Understanding how museums create citizens, therefore, requires us to examine the close interrelationship between the museum as a social institution and as architecture.

Social institutions are defined by two basic characteristics. First, they encompass a set of social practices that are oriented toward some underlying "logic" (Friedland and Alford 1991). At its core, the institutional logic of museums contains the idea that there is a class of physical objects that possess special social significance. This logic informs and is sustained through a set of social practices that includes collection, research, preservation, and public presentation. Exactly how museums identify and present this class of objects is influenced by other institutional logics, particularly within the political sphere (Aronczyk and Brady 2015).

Second, an institution is established only when this set of practices is reproduced across space and time. In reproducing social practices, the built environment is key. Buildings, according to Gieryn (2002), "stabilize social life" (p.35). "Brick and mortar", he argues, "resist intervention and permutation, as they accomplish a measure of stasis" (ibid). However, buildings accomplish this stabilization "imperfectly" (ibid). Some change is inevitable. Buildings themselves are in a constant process of flux and disintegration, continually being reinterpreted and repurposed by their users.

Gieryn theorizes the relationship between institutions and buildings as a three-step process. First, through the design and development process buildings *materialize* certain abstract logics, typically in ways that reflect the values, ideas, and interests of dominant actors or groups to the exclusion of others. Second, once constructed, buildings *enforce* certain institutional arrangements, including inequalities and hierarchies, and steer "social action in ways not always meaningfully apprehended by actors or necessarily congruent with their interests or values" (p.43). Finally, over time, buildings are themselves subject to material and discursive "reconfiguration" (p.44). Actors attempt to impose new ideas and uses on buildings. However, in doing so they must always compromise and adapt to what can feasibly be accomplished with the existing building.

To this framework, it is useful to add a further insight from Brand (1995) who argues that buildings are made up of various "layers" that change and adapt to social life in different ways and at different rates. With regard to museums and civic identity, I posit four distinct "layers" that span a continuum from stable to plastic and external to internal. First, *location* refers to where the building is situated. Second, *external interface* refers to the way in which the building relates to its immediate surroundings. Third, *aesthetic surface* refers to the various visual cues that the building conveys. Finally, the *internal layout* refers to the organization of interior spaces.

TWO MUSEUMS, THREE ERAS

During the century-long history of the AGO and ROM, political institutions in Toronto and Canada have change dramatically. Focusing on three distinct political eras, in this section I describe dominant understandings of civic identity, the role of cultural institutions in public life, and how the museum architecture was transformed. For visual reference, Figures 9.1 and 9.2 diagram the architectural history of each museum.

Figure 9.1 The architectural history of the Art Gallery of Ontario, Toronto, Canada, 2018. Image: the author.

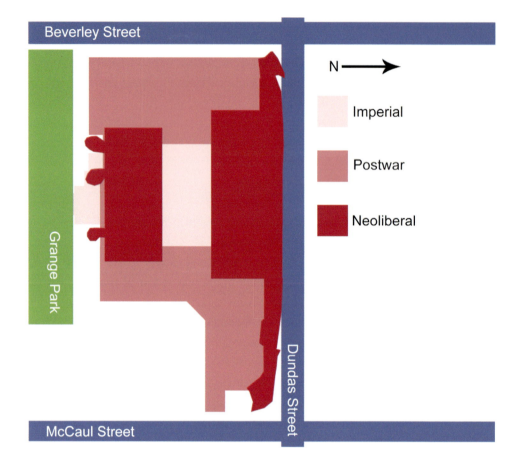

The Imperial Era (1867–1945)

From Canada's confederation in 1867 until the mid-twentieth century, Canadian elites promoted strong cultural and political ties to the British Empire in combination with domestic industrialization and westward expansion. To accomplish this, the National Policy of 1879 imposed steep tariffs on American-made goods and led to the construction of a transcontinental railway.[1] Toronto benefited greatly from this policy, becoming (along with Montreal) the industrial and financial centre of the nation, in addition to already being the capital city of Canada's largest province, Ontario (Hiller 2014, 24–25).

"Toronto, the Good," as it was known (Clark 1898), aspired to be a beacon of Victorian puritanism in North America and enforced this image through strict morality laws that outlawed, among other things, streetcar service on Sundays. The founding in the early-twentieth century of the ROM and AGO was another way in which Toronto's elite attempted to make the city into a jewel within the British Empire. Both museums were seen as necessary for the cultural improvement of the

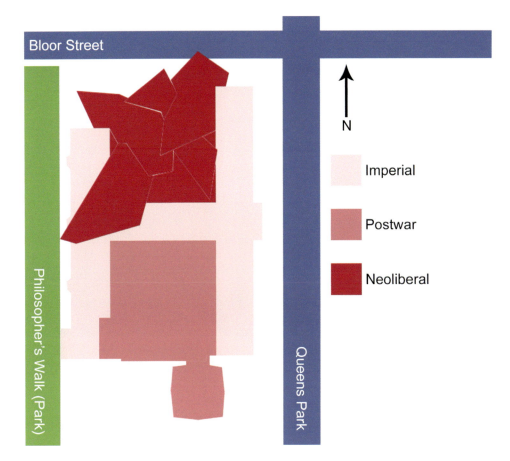

Figure 9.2 The architectural history of the Royal Ontario Museum, Toronto, Canada, 2018. Image: the author.

public and to elevate Toronto's imperial standing. The need for a museum seemed particularly urgent as artefacts and art were being snatched up by other cities in the late nineteenth century (Dickson 1986; Teather 2005).

The AGO was founded as the "Art Museum of Toronto" in 1900. In 1910 it was relocated to "The Grange," an 1817 Georgian manor house that had been built by one of colonial Toronto's elite families (Figure 9.3). When it converted to a gallery, the Grange's sprawling front lawn became a public park while the north side of the property became the location of a larger Beaux-Arts building that would be built in stages over the next three decades (Figure 9.4). Designed by local firm Darling & Pearson, the new building became the main gallery, and the main entrance moved from the Grange to Dundas Street.

The ROM was founded in 1912 through a partnership between the Ontario Government and the University of Toronto. In 1914, it opened its first purpose-built building in the northeast corner of the University's campus. Also designed by Darling & Pearson, the building is a three-storey rectangle clad in brick and

Figure 9.3 The Grange, architect unknown, 1817, Toronto, Canada. Image: the Public Domain.

Figure 9.4 The Art Gallery of Ontario by architects Darling & Pearson, Toronto, Canada, 1926. Image: of Bob Olson and the Toronto Star.

terracotta and decorated with Italianate and Byzantine elements (Figure 9.5). In 1933, serving in part as a depression-era make-work program, the ROM expanded eastward creating an H-shaped building with a new grand entrance along Queens Park (Figure 9.6). This wing, designed by new architects, retained Byzantine elements from the original building.

Figure 9.5 The 1914 Wing in The Royal Ontario Museum by architects Darling & Pearson, Toronto, Canada, 1914. Image: Alfred Pearson and the City of Toronto.

Figure 9.6 The 1933 Wing of The Royal Ontario Museum by architects Chapman & Oxley, Toronto, Canada, 1933. Image: the City of Toronto.

The Postwar Era (1945–1988)

With the disintegration of the British Empire at the end of the Second World War, Canada began to pursue a post-British identity, adopting a new flag (1965), national anthem (1980), and constitution (1982). Liberalization of immigration laws and official policies of bilingualism and multiculturalism further helped to create a new notion of civic identity detached from British ancestry. Also changing were ideas about the role of government, with massive expansions of the federal and provincial welfare states.

Toronto grew dramatically during this period, surpassing Montreal to become Canada's largest city in the 1970s. Changing patterns of immigration meant that by 1980 Protestants and people of British ancestry were minorities in Toronto. Immigrants made up almost half the population, with most born outside Western and Northern Europe. A third of Torontonians spoke a language other than English. Rather than "Toronto, the Good," the city increasingly promoted itself as the most "multicultural" city in the world.

During this era, cultural institutions across the country benefited from the expanded welfare state. In 1951 a federally-appointed commission laid out the roadmap for this investment, arguing that "it is in the national interest to give encouragement to institutions which express national feeling, promote common understanding and add to the variety and richness of Canadian life" (Government of Canada 1951, xi). It is not surprising, therefore, that the AGO and ROM saw their largest architectural expansions within this era.

In 1966 the "Art Museum of Toronto" became a provincial organization (renamed the Art Gallery of Ontario) and received an expanded mandate in public education. To fulfil this mandate, the AGO undertook a three-stage architectural expansion process designed by local architect John Parkin who planned to absorb the existing Beaux-Arts building within a larger modernist-brutalist complex (Reid 2006, 24–25). The first and second stages opened in 1974 and 1977 respectively (Figure 9.7). By the mid-1980s, community opposition, new institutional needs and changing architectural trends led to a new architect (Barton Myers) and design for stage three. Myers adopted postmodernism, replacing much of Parkin's pre-cast concrete façade with brown brick walls and a metallic roof somewhat reminiscent of the original Beaux-Art building (Figure 9.8). The Myers building opened in 1993.

At the ROM, the modernist McLaughlin Planetarium was completed at the height of the space race in 1968 (Figure 9.9). This was followed by the museum's most ambitious expansion, which filled in the empty spaces of the existing H-shaped building with two brutalist wings designed by Gene Kinoshita. To the south, the Curatorial Centre opened in 1981, consolidating the museum's backstage operations. To the north, the Queen Elizabeth II Terrace Galleries opened in 1984 (Figure 9.10).

The Neoliberal Era (1988–Present)

The 1988 signing of the Canada-US Free Trade Agreement dealt a final blow to Canada's imperial era protectionism and signaled the arrival of neoliberal deregulation. By the mid-1990s, governments across Canada had embraced austerity and

Figure 9.7 The Art Gallery of Ontario by architect Frank Parkin, Toronto, Canada, 1974. Image: Boris Spremo and the Toronto Star.

Figure 9.8 The Art Gallery of Ontario by architect Barton Myers, Toronto, Canada, 1993. Image: the City of Toronto. [on-page credit City of Toronto Archives, Fonds 200, Series 1465, File 413, Item 9].

Figure 9.9 The McLaughlin Planetarium by architects Allward and Gouinlock, Toronto, Ontario, 1968.
Image: Boris Spremo and the Toronto Star.

Figure 9.10 The Queen Elizabeth II Terrace Galleries (foreground) and Curatorial Centre (behind) at the Royal Ontario Museum by architect Gene Kinoshita, Toronto, Canada, 1984.
Image: of the City of Toronto. [on-page credit City of Toronto Archives, Fonds 200, Series 1465, File 280, Item 23].

debt reduction. The federal government cut costs by downloading responsibilities onto the provinces who, in turn, downloaded them onto municipalities.

In an effort to cut costs, the Ontario government forced Toronto to amalgamate with its five surrounding suburbs in 1998, and greatly reduced subsidies to municipal services such as housing and transportation. These changes plunged Toronto into a period of political and financial turmoil as urbanites and suburbanites struggled over how to govern a city with limited resources. Seeking new revenue, the city sought to transform itself into to center for culture and lifestyle-oriented development (Kipfer and Keil 2002).

The ROM and AGO saw significant cutbacks to their operational funding during the late-1990s (Jenkins 2009, 334), which led to the permanent closure of the ROM's McLaughlin Planetarium. However, neoliberalism provided new opportunities as well. Museums and other cultural institutions were increasingly viewed not as public services, but as economic development tools that could draw tourists and investment to the city (Patterson and Silver 2015, 272) and attract members of the "creative class" (Florida 2002). These ideas eventually motivated the Federal and Ontario governments to jointly fund the architectural expansions and renovations of seven major cultural institutions in Toronto, including the ROM and AGO (Jenkins 2005).

As a result of this funding package, the ROM and AGO expanded yet again. Adopting the spectacular deconstructivist style of internationally-renowned "starchitects," which contrasted with the institutions' history of more conservative, locally-designed architecture, both projects were designed to create "hard brands" (Evans 2003) that could sell Toronto to tourists, investors, and the creative class. For the ROM, the 1984 Terrace Galleries were demolished to make way for an aluminium-clad, crystalline-shaped wing designed by Daniel Libeskind. The "Michael Lee-Chin Crystal" opened in 2007.

The AGO, meanwhile, turned to Frank Gehry. To the north, Gehry replaced Myers' postmodern façade with a sprawling glass visor. To the south, he added a bright blue titanium box that towered over the Grange and featured external staircases that spiraled out into midair. This expansion opened in 2008.

CIVIC IDENTITY AND THE "LAYERS" OF MUSEUM ARCHITECTURE

As we can see from the previous section, through their various expansions, the architecture of the ROM and AGO has been made and remade in ways that reflect changing political climates. To better understand this relationship, I turn now to the four aforementioned architectural "layers": location, external interface, aesthetic surface, and internal layout. As the basis for this analysis, I recorded how each of these layers was established within a particular political era and then how it was subsequently sustained or modified (Table 9.1).

Location

Establishing major museums requires power and resources. Their locations, therefore, gives us a window into the political-economic dynamics at the time of their founding. However, museums also *change* the places in which they are located. Once built they become social centres of gravity that draw in resources, people, and status or "buzz" (Silver and Clark 2013). Thus, museums elevate the public significance of the places in which they are located and make those places more central to civic identity.

We can see both of these dynamics with the ROM and AGO. While major European museums are typically established by strong central states for the purposes of governance (Bennett 1995) and American museums are often founded by bourgeois elites for the purposes of distinction (DiMaggio 1982), Toronto and Canada characteristically fall somewhere in between these two models. During the imperial era, neither the state nor Canada's upper class were independently capable of amassing the collection and constructing the building necessary to establish a major museum. The ROM and AGO exist because of a network of provincial government officials, wealthy bourgeoisie, artists (particularly members of the Ontario Society of Artists), and intellectuals (particularly those associated with the University of Toronto) that existed in Toronto at the turn of the century (Teather 2005).

The influence of this group also explains the neighborhood locations of these museums. Both the ROM and the AGO are located in what were, in the nineteenth century, suburban bourgeois enclaves outside the city's downtown core that were home to many of the museums' founders. As the city grew, the core expanded and absorbed these areas. However, the institutions themselves were not passive in this expansion. Their establishment greatly changed how people thought about these previously sleepy residential areas. For example, when Toronto began aggressively building its subway system in the 1950s and 1960s, stations were built next to both museums, driving additional densification in the area.

In addition to the subway, the museums each influenced how their surrounding neighbourhoods would be rezoned and eventually redeveloped. For example, shortly after the Gehry expansion of the AGO was completed, the city decided to redevelop the nearby John Street (to which the AGO serves as the northern terminus) as a "cultural corridor." After the Michael Lee-Chin Crystal opened in 2007, a high-rise condominium called "Exhibit" was built across the street using architecture that mimicked the crystalline shape.

Table 9.1 The ROM and AGO's architectural "layers" over three political eras

Museum	Layer	Imperial	Post-War	Neoliberal
Royal Ontario Museum	Location	Outskirts/Residential----- Core/Institutional---------------Core/Commercial---->		
	External Interface	Pedestrian oriented ---Bloor (Commercial)---->		
		Entrance: Queens Park (Institutional)		
	Aesthetic Surface: • External	Historicism (Italianate, Byzantine) --->		
			Brutalism -------------------------->	
				Deconstructivism---->
	• Internal	Minimalist ----------------- Edutainment ----------------------- Minimalist---->		
	Internal Layout	Academic Disciplines ----------- Conceptual "Clusters" ----------------------->		
Art Gallery of Ontario	Location	Outskirts/Residential------ Core --------------- Core ----------------- Core/Cultural District--->		
	External Interface	Pedestrian oriented--->		
		Entrance: Grange Park (south)----Dundas Street (north)		
		------------------------->		
	Aesthetic Surface: • External	Neo-classical (Georgian, Beaux-Arts) ------------------------------------>		
			Brutalism ---------------------->	
				Post-modernism------->
				Deconstructivism------>
	• Internal	Minimalist (Modern eye)--->		
	External Interface	Genre/geography/chronology-------------------------------->		
				Thematic/Critical------>

External Interface

The external interface refers to the way that the building relates and interacts with its immediate surroundings. This interaction tells us a lot about the intended users of the museum and shapes how they access the institution. For example, many postwar cultural buildings are "solipsistic" in that they are designed to be "isolated from their surrounding neighborhoods physically, economically and culturally" (Hannigan 1998, 4). Exemplified by the Gehry-designed Goldwin Library in Los Angeles (Davis 2006, 239–241), these buildings are characterized by blank walls and other barriers that create a sense of hostile separation between their interior and the outside neighborhood. In doing so they create and physically segregate two classes of citizens: locals and outside visitors (who often arrive by car).

By contrast, their pre-automobile origins and well-to-do locations have meant that the ROM and AGO have never been particularly solipsistic. Rather, they have a more democratic external interface that is easily accessible to anyone passing by on the streets.

Political Protest

For this reason, both museums serve as effective sites for public protests. Indeed, throughout their history, both institutions have witnessed a variety of demonstrations occurring right outside their front doors. Of particular importance were protests in response to the ROM's 1989 exhibit *Into the Heart of Africa* which presented objects from the museum's African collection. Protestors, led by members of Toronto's Black community, contended that the exhibit presented celebratory images of colonialism and argued that the ROM had not adequately consulted Black Canadians in deciding how Africa should be represented (Butler 2007).

The protests demonstrate how the democratic architectural interface that was inherited from the imperial era could be used effectively to challenge notions of civic identity also inherited from that era. Non-European cultures were exhibited within the ROM, but traditionally represented by white curators to an (assumed) white audience. By occupying the physical space in front of the museum, black Canadians asserted their membership in Toronto's civil sphere and, by extension, their claim as citizens to the museum and its collection.

A decade later, as ROM curators began to plan the new galleries that would fill the Michael Lee-Chin Crystal, these protests weighed heavily. As one curator told me in an interview:

> *Into the Heart of Africa* … was this kind of startling wake up call to museums in general but also to the ROM about voice and authority … With the [new] suite of galleries, not just Africa, but also Oceana, Asia-Pacific, we would go out and

find people from those communities who would consult with us. First Nations communities as well. We all do this. It's just second nature to us now. So yes, [the protest] did make an enormous difference to us.

(ROM Curator, personal communication, 2010)

The ROM even sought to signal its embrace of the new multicultural Toronto by specifically seeking out Michael Lee-Chin, a biracial, Jamaican-born billionaire, to be the headline donor for the project. With these strategies, the ROM attempted to reposition and align itself with new perceptions of civic identity in Toronto. While the strategies are not architectural themselves, the architectural expansion gave the ROM an opportunity to implement them.

The Citizen-Consumer

Though important, protests are still a rare occurrence in front of the museums. Increasingly common, however, are consumer activities. The most recent expansions of the ROM and AGO incorporated significantly more commercial services into the external interface of the buildings. Whereas in the past, restaurants and gift shops were located within the buildings, many of these functions are now prominently situated at, and directly accessible from, the street. In this sense these new commercial spaces differ significantly from the established practice of having museum visitors "exit through the gift shop" so that they are enticed to buy representations of the artworks or artefacts that they have just experienced in person. Instead, new commercial spaces cater to visitors and non-visitors alike, selling products that may have little if any relationship to the objects inside the museum galleries.[2]

Such changes reflect the realities of the neoliberalism. Government funding cuts have forced museums to become "entrepreneurial" in a search for self-generated income (Jenkins 2009). As a result, the ROM and AGO increasingly relate to the public through shopping and dining experiences alongside their more traditional role as museums, reinforcing the neoliberal notion of the "citizen-consumer" (Johnston 2008). This consumer-oriented shift was accentuated at the ROM when the Michael Lee-Chin Crystal moved the museum's front entrance from Queen's Park, a sleepy institutional avenue home to the University of Toronto and Ontario Legislature, to Bloor Street, a busy high-end commercial street known as the "Mink Mile" (see Figure 9.2).

Aesthetic Surface

The "aesthetic surface" of a museum refers to the visual cues that the building conveys. While a seemingly superficial aspect of the building, aesthetic surfaces are actually deeply related to citizenship, particularly when they achieve "iconic power," defined as the "ability to articulate and intensify cultural meanings, narratives and myths into an aesthetically striking, easily recognizable, emotionally rich and symbolically relevant visual-material entity" (Solaroli 2015, 1; Bartmanski and Alexander 2012). To understand the meanings communicated by the ROM and AGO's aesthetic surfaces I begin by considering their external appearances and then focus on their interiors.

External Appearance
Much of the iconic power of the museum comes from its external appearance, since the outside of the building is more permanent and more public. What notions of citizenship are represented in the external appearances of the ROM and AGO? According to Teather (2005), prior to its formal founding, there was debate over what kind of museum the ROM would become and what kinds of stories it would tell. Eventually a sense of cosmopolitanism won out over more locally and nationally oriented visions and this was reinforced through the museum's architecture. In words that were written in stone around the grand entrance to the 1933 wing, the ROM would present "the record of nature through countless ages" and "the arts of man through all the years."

Additional cosmopolitan elements can be traced through all of the ROM's expansions in spite of the diverse eras and architectural genres that those expansions represent. When the museum was first built in 1914, critics noted the contrast between its Italianate and Byzantine ornamentation with the Gothic and Neoclassical architecture that dominated the University of Toronto Campus (Dickson 1986, 38). Such appeals to the exotic and the global can be further observed in the Terrace Galleries (styled after the Babylonian Hanging Gardens) and the deconstructivist "starchitecture" of the Crystal.

At the time of its founding, the AGO was more locally oriented than the ROM, with a mission to display the works being produced by Canadian artists, as well as displaying examples of European masters to inspire local artists. To this day, Canadian galleries occupy significantly more space within the AGO than within the ROM. This local-orientation is evident in the AGO's architecture as well. Until the 1970s, the AGO's expansions showed extreme deference to the original Grange house, which was seen as an essential link to Toronto's pre-industrial, colonial past. The new galleries were limited to one storey so that they could be "hidden" behind the Grange. As well, their neo-classical Beaux-Arts architecture established continuity with the Grange's neo-classical Georgian architecture.

When the AGO became a provincial organization like the ROM, it also began to resemble the ROM architecturally. As mentioned, both museums undertook ambitious expansions in the postwar era to accommodate larger public education mandates. These serious, technocratic intensions are reflected in the conservative, locally-designed brutalist architecture of the postwar expansions (described as "austere" in the *Globe and Mail* (Cameron 1974, 27)). When the political role of the museums shifted from public service to "hard brand" in the neoliberal era, their postwar façades were torn down to make way for the playful and spectacular deconstructivist designs of the global "starchitects" Daniel Libeskind and Frank Gehry.

Internal Appearance

While less public and more plastic than exteriors, museum interiors nonetheless communicate significant meanings, particularly about the intended audiences. When the ROM first opened, the galleries were minimalist rooms filled with simple (if cluttered) display cases (Figure 9.11). Such designs were based on the imperial era idea of the self-motivated visitor. The museum was there for any members of the public who wished to better themselves by looking upon the wonders of the natural world and human civilization. In other words, the museum was a place to muse.

By the postwar era, ideas about museum visitors changed significantly. Their new funding and public education mandate motivated the AGO and ROM to aspire toward serving a broader public. The ROM, urged University of Toronto

Figure 9.11 Interior gallery of the Royal Ontario Museum, Toronto, Canada, 1928. Image: the City of Toronto.

professor Marshall McLuhan (Dickson 1986, 152), also felt the need to adjust to a media-saturated world, competing for public attention with the shopping malls and multiplexes that filled the rapidly expanding suburbs.

To address these problems, the ROM exchanged minimalism for multimedia technologies, special effects, and interactive displays. Architectural elements such as windows and columns were hidden behind immersive set designs that took visitors through bat caves, cretaceous jungles, and Persian streetscapes. Rather than wandering freely between display cases, "the visitor was to be taken firmly by the hand and conducted through what has come to be called a 'learning experience' [with a] 'story-line'" (Dickson 1986, 172). These galleries ushered in the era of "edutainment" (Hannigan 1998, 92).

While many ROM staff resented what they saw as the dumbing down of the collection in these "discotheque galleries" (Dickson 1986, 153), it was not until the twenty-first century that ROM leadership abandoned edutainment. By this point, cultural institutions around the world had fixated on a new group of visitors: the creative class. According to Florida (2002), creatives reject phony, theme park-like spectacle in favour of authentic and inspiring cultural experiences. In this sense, creatives represent a return to the self-motivated visitor who muses over the artefacts. Reflecting this fact, the ROM used the Libeskind expansion to bring back minimalism. Gone were the special effects and set designs. Galleries were stripped down to their basic architectural structure and filled with glass display cases once again.

In contrast to the ROM, the AGO's minimalist galleries have changed little since the imperial era (Figure 9.12). Such continuity reflects the dominance of the "modern eye": a way of viewing and interacting with cultural objects that emphasizes formality, disinterestedness, and "art-for-art's-sake" (Peterson 2003, 462–3). Since the nineteenth century, the modern eye has provided the core logic that distinguishes art from the profane objects of everyday life and privileges those whose class background allows them to suspend worldly concerns and indulge in "art-for-art's-sake" (Bourdieu 1996). Minimalist galleries are the aesthetic embodiment of the modern eye, providing the illusion that one is really experiencing these objects in an abstracted, context-free environment. While the AGO has adopted many strategies aimed at attracting larger audiences, these strategies have never fundamentally altered the aesthetic dominance of the modern eye.

Internal Layout

The internal layout of the museum refers to the way in which the architecture organizes the spaces, functions, activities, and people inside. This is the most plastic layer of museum architecture and the area where curators have the most

Figure 9.12 Interior gallery of the Art Museum of Toronto, Canada, 1928. Image: the City of Toronto.

autonomy. Nonetheless, it is worth briefly considering how the internal layout of architecture influences curatorial practices and, by extension, notions of civic identity communicated through the galleries. While this influence exerts itself in many ways, I focus specifically on how different types of layouts can influence how social differences and hierarchies are represented in the galleries.

Long Halls versus Open Spaces

In the nineteenth century, the architects of the Beaux-Arts school embraced long halls connected in a grid pattern as the ideal museum architecture. This tradition informed Darling & Pearson, the Toronto firm that designed the original plans for both the AGO and ROM (Browne 2008, 28). Though their plans were never fully realized for either museum, the galleries that were built are long halls joined at right angles.

The curatorial implication of the long hall is that visitors encounter the collection in single, linear succession. As a result, there is an affinity between this layout and the well-established tradition in museums of assembling objects into linear narratives of "progress" wherein each object encountered is presented as advancement over the object that came before. Such narratives include biological evolution, national history, and rise of western civilization. In fact, linear galleries may even lead us to see linearity in a collection when it does not exist. For example, within museums that purport to represent the history of North America, placing indigenous galleries before colonial galleries implicitly (or explicitly) suggests that indigenous culture has been superseded by settler society when in reality the two have (uneasily) coexisted and co-developed for centuries.

By the postwar era, galleries were increasingly designed as large, open spaces that could be internally divided and continually rearranged with movable internal partitions. While the linear experience is often maintained, such flexibility affords curators the ability to create non-linear experiences as well, including the ability to present artwork or artefacts in thematic groupings rather than hierarchy or chronology. Indeed, during this period, the AGO increasingly shifted to a thematic presentation in which artwork is clustered around particular social and political issues. Such curatorial practices have led the AGO to bring indigenous and non-indigenous art into dialogue within the same galleries rather than keeping them separated or hierarchically linked in a linear narrative.[3]

For the ROM, the slanted walls and irregular spaces within the Michael Lee-Chin Crystal disrupt curators' ability to present the artefacts linearly. Instead, the artefacts are grouped into a series of islands in the middle of the gallery which can be encountered in multiple directions and different orders. As a result, the Crystal galleries are largely thematic.

Wings

The distinct wings of museums allow sets of objects to be displayed as distinct but of commensurate value (e.g. European and American Art). To illustrate, consider the ROM's 1933 wing. At its founding, the ROM consisted of several semi-autonomous galleries that corresponded to different academic departments at the University of Toronto (Geology, Paleontology, Archaeology, etc.), each with its own director and control over its own collection. The 1933 wing of the museum enshrined this egalitarian organizational structure. From its grand entrance, visitors could reach almost every gallery directly without having to go through another (Oxley 1982, 11). Even the offices of each gallery were located at the end of their respective wings.

The autonomy of these galleries eventually diminished and, during the postwar expansions, the ROM rearranged its galleries around a set of visitor-intuitive "conceptual clusters" that did not correspond neatly to academic disciplines. However, the implicit egalitarian layout of the 1933 wing remains in place. Today, the ROM has used this architectural feature to present the First People's gallery (containing indigenous art and culture) and the Gallery of Canada (representing the history of Canadian settler society) as two distinct traditions that are of equal cultural value. Previously, indigenous artefacts from Canada were relegated to the basement as part of a larger cluster of "ethnology" galleries that included all of the Americas and Africa (a common curatorial decision that implicitly devalues the work (e.g. Levitt 2015, 59)).

CONCLUSION

Civic identity refers to the way in which a political community understands its meaningful commonalities and the boundaries that separates it from outsiders. Ideas about civic identity are abstract, contested, and often implicitly held, but they are nonetheless powerful social forces. While most people do not think about civic identity much in their daily lives, these notions have significant consequences for citizenship laws, government programs, prejudice and discrimination, and other important social issues.

Museum architecture both *emplaces* and *displaces* civic identity. In *emplacing* civic identity, museums create concrete manifestations of otherwise abstract ideas and ideologies (inevitably privileging some over others). Their buildings become locations where people go to learn about who they are as a public and to experience being in public and performing as a public. Through the architecture, the ideas of one era achieve a level of stability and are carried into the future even as they may fall out of favour more generally.

However, as public spaces, museums also offer the opportunity for new and spontaneous expressions of civic identity. When this occurs, the museum becomes the battleground where different notions of civic identity are contested and where new identities may succeed in *displacing* old ones. The changing architecture of museums makes visible broader historical changes such as the shifting boundaries between the public and private, and state and market associated with neoliberalism. As well, groups who have traditionally been excluded from dominant notions of civic identity can use the physical space of the museum to demand inclusion. For example, as Canada and other countries attempt to reconcile their civic identity with a history of genocide against indigenous peoples (Truth and Reconciliation Commission of Canada 2015), museums have become a key location for the re-evaluation of this history and of indigenous-settler relations in the future.

It is precisely the *materiality* of museums that explains their ability to emplace and displace notions of civic identity; they provide people with immediate, sensory experiences of encountering each other within elaborate assemblages of significant cultural objects (Griswold, Mangione, and McDonnell 2013). Indeed, even as public life increasingly plays out in the digital world, the importance of materiality likely means museums other forms of public architecture will continue to play a consequential role in nation building.

NOTES

1. While this embrace of British identity was in part motivated by a fear of encroaching American influence, it was also driven by white supremacy. Canada attempted to impose its "British" identity through state-enforced racism, including an official campaign of "cultural genocide" waged against indigenous peoples (Truth and Reconciliation Commission 2015:1) and a head tax imposed on all immigrants from China.
2. With several retail locations scattered throughout Manhattan and even in Japan, selling everything from kitchenware to office supplies, the Museum of Modern Art (MoMA) exemplifies the trend of museum retail gaining an autonomous existence that is separate from the experience of visiting the museum.
3. The inclusion of indigenous art in general at the AGO represents a larger, ongoing trend in which these works have been re-categorized from objects of scientific inquiry to objects of artistic value.

REFERENCES

Aronczyk, Melissa, Miranda J. Brady. 2015. "Branding History at the Canadian Museum of Civilization." *Canadian Journal of Communication* 40(2): 165–184.

Bartmanski, Dominik, Jeffrey C. Alexander. 2012. "Materiality and Meaning in Social Life: toward an Iconic Turn in Cultural Sociology," In *Iconic Power*. (edited by) Alexander, Jeffrey C., Dominik Bartmanski, Bernhard Giesen, 1–12. New York: Palgrave MacMillan.

Bennett, Tony. 1995. *The Birth of the Museum*. New York: Routledge.

Bourdieu, Pierre. 1996. *The Rules of Art*. Stanford: Stanford University Press.

Bourdieu, Pierre., A. Darbel, D. Schnapper. 1997. *The Love of Art*. Cambridge: Polity Press.

Brand, Stewart. 1995. *How Buildings Learn*. New York: Penguin.

Browne, Kevine. 2008. *Bold Visions*. Toronto: Royal Ontario Museum.

Butler, Shelley Ruth. 2007. *Contested Representations*. Toronto: University of Toronto Press.

Cameron, Duncan. 1974. "The Coming of Age of the Art Gallery of Ontario." *The Globe and Mail*. Toronto: Oct. 19, 1974: 27.

Clark, Christopher, S. George. 1898. *Of Toronto the Good, a Social Study*. Montreal: Toronto Publishing Company.

Davis, Mike. 2006. *City of Quartz*. London: Verso.

Dickson, Lovat. 1986. *The Museum Makers: the Story of the Royal Ontario Museum*. Toronto: Royal Ontario Museum.

DiMaggio, Paul J. 1982. "Cultural Entrepreneurship in Nineteenth-Century Boston: the Creation of an Organizational Base for High Culture in America." *Media, Culture, and Society* 4(1): 33–50.

Duncan, Carol. 1995. *Civilizing Rituals*. New York: Routledge.

Evans, Graeme. 2003. "Hard-Branding the Cultural City – from Prado to Prada." *International Journal of Urban and Regional Research* 27(2): 417–440.

Florida, Richard. 2002. *The Rise of the Creative Class*. New York: Basic Books.

Friedland, Roger, Robert R. Alford. 1991. "Bringing Society Back in: symbols, Practices, and Institutional Contradictions," In *The New Institutionalism in Organizational Analysis*. (edited by) Powell, Walter W., Paul J. DiMaggio, 232–266. Chicago: University of Chicago Press.

Gieryn, Thomas. 2002. "What Buildings Do." *Theory & Society* 31(1): 35–74.

Government of Canada. 1951. *Royal Commission on National Development in the Arts, Letters, and Sciences*. Ottawa: King's Printer.

Griswold, Wendy, Gemma Mangione, Terence E. McDonnell. (2013) "Objects, Words, and Bodies in Space: bringing Materiality into Cultural Analysis." *Qualitative Sociology* 36(4): 343–364.

Hannigan, John. 1998. *Fantasy City*. London: Routledge.

Hiller, Harry. 2014. "The Dynamics of Canadian Urbanization," In *Urban Canada*. (edited by) Harry Hiller, 20–42. Toronto: Oxford University Press.

Jenkins, Barbara. 2005. "Toronto's Cultural Renaissance." *Canadian Journal of Communication* 30(2): 169–186.

Jenkins, Barbara. 2009. "Cultural Spending in Ontario, Canada: trends in Public and Private Funding." *International Journal of Cultural Policy* 15(3): 329–342.

Johnston, Josée. 2008. "The Citizen-Consumer Hybrid: ideological Tensions and the Case of Whole Foods Market." *Theory & Society* 37(3): 229–270.

Kipfer, Stefan, Roger Keil. 2002. "Toronto Inc? Planning the Competitive City in the New Toronto." *Antipode* 34(2): 227–264.

Levitt, Peggy. 2015. *Artifacts and Allegiances*. Berkeley: University of California Press.

Oxley, Loren A. 1982. "Retrospect – the First 75 Years." *Rotunda* 15(2): 6–13.

Patterson, Matt, Daniel Silver. 2015. "Turning the Postindustrial City into the Cultural City: the Case of Toronto's Waterfront," In *The Routledge Companion to the Cultural Industries*. (edited by) Kate Oakley, Justin O'Connor, 268–280. New York: Routledge.

Peterson, Karin Elizabeth. 2003. "Discourse and Display: the Modern Eye, Entrepreneurship, and the Cultural Transformation of the Patchwork Quilt." *Sociological Perspectives* 46(4): 461–490.

Reid, D. (ed.). 2006. "A Century of Building the Art Gallery of Ontario," In *Frank Gehry Toronto*. 22–35. Toronto: Art Gallery of Ontario.

Silver, Dennis, Terry Nichols Clark. 2013. "Buzz as an Urban Resource." *Canadian Journal of Sociology* 38(1): 1–32.

Solaroli, Marco. 2015. "Iconicity: A Category for Social and Cultural theory." *Sociologica* 9(1): 1–52.

Teather, J. Lynne. 2005. *The Royal Ontario Museum: A Prehistory, 1830-1914*. Toronto: Canada University Press.

Truth and Reconciliation Commission of Canada. 2015. *Honouring the Truth, Reconciling for the Future*. Ottawa: Truth and Reconciliation Commission of Canada.

CHAPTER **10**

Experience and Meaning in Museums

Helen Norrie

Throughout its history, the museum has oscillated from a storehouse to a site of display and a place of research, variously promoting agendas of entertainment and education. The museum can be understood as a "product of Renaissance humanism, eighteenth-century enlightenment and nineteenth-century democracy" (Alexander, 1979, 8), but it is also firmly rooted in a practice of collecting and scholarship that has existed since antiquity. Museum buildings are sites of engagement, variously passive and active, that are influenced by overlapping and sometimes competing sets of functional and symbolic agendas. From the cloistered spaces of medieval churches to the dark windowless rooms of the Renaissance *studiolo* to the grand "temples of culture," the visitors' experience was influenced by the formal and spatial order of the museum's architecture.

Pere Alberch (1994) suggests that the development of the museum occurred in three distinct stages, each reflecting the dominant values of its era. This was mirrored in changing museum architecture, which orchestrated itineraries of movement and spectacle that influenced experience and meaning. Alberch describes the first phase of the museum as that of a storehouse for the safekeeping and display of objects, which was arranged to create a sense of awe and wonder. He suggests that the second phase was influenced by the development of scientific disciplines, with a particular focus on the "observable aspects" of objects. Collections began to be utilized for research, and were essentially tools for gathering knowledge and understanding the world. Initially access was limited to scholars, but this was subsequently extended and developed into a broader agenda of public education. Alberch observes a third phase in which a concern for concepts began to take precedence over a specific interest in objects, and this was articulated as a difference between "display" and "communication" (1994, 194–7). Throughout these stages, there was an increasing curatorial shift from passive to active engagement, and the architecture of museums was orchestrated to establish dynamic relationships that were central to the construction of meaning and lived experience. This can be understood through an analysis of a range of museums from different eras to demonstrate the agency of architecture to influence visitor experience.

EXAMINING THE ARCHITECTURAL TYPOLOGY OF MUSEUMS

From classical antiquity to the Renaissance and into the present, the practice of assembling objects into collections has served both secular and sacred agendas. Egyptian tombs, ancient temples and medieval churches were storehouses for objects that were appreciated for their iconic or symbolic value, rather than their material use or artistic value. In ancient Greece, the Athenian Treasure Chamber was used to exhibit statues of victors of battles, weapons and loot acquired from wars, and other gifts dedicated to the gods. In contrast, Roman villas were furnished with statues and paintings that were esteemed for their artistic value (Naredi-Rainer, 2004, 13). Some early collections were also part of wider complexes that included libraries and gardens, notably collections established by Ptolemy Soter in Alexandria in the third century B.C and Roman Emperor Hadrian, in the expansive garden setting of his villa near Tivoli. The religious military crusades of the eleventh to thirteenth centuries resulted in the collection of spoils of war, which were valued as both trophies and art objects. Many of these collections were incorporated into the treasuries of princely palaces, which formed the precursor of the public museum (Alexander, 1979, 6.).

During the Renaissance, private collections developed through the Italian tradition of the *studiolo*, a room for study and a space that one could "withdraw into secluded creativity," which Paul von Naredi-Rainer suggests reflected a move from the authority of church to the individualism of private study (2004, 13). Throughout the fifteenth century the *studiolo* and "cabinets of curiosity" became a place for the display of diverse collections of objects, juxtaposing science and art in a manner that was intended to entertain and amuse rather than to address any didactic or devotional agenda (Olmi, 2001, 8). Olmi notes that the *studiolo* and cabinets were often richly decorated with symbolic imagery, and although there was there was generally no attempt at categorization or specialization, in Germany collections were separated into *Kunstskammern* for art and "curiosities" in *Wunderkammer*.

During the sixteenth century an alternative model of *studiolo* developed that signaled a shift from curiosity and wonder to a more scientific approach. Early naturalists gathered collections that were used as reference tools for the exploration of nature. Giuseppe Olmi observes that the space of the *studiolo* began to be arranged in a more encyclopedic fashion, mirroring the appearance and function of a laboratory or a "well-furnished medical repository" (2001, 6). Most were private collections, which allowed access to artist and professional scholars. The *studiolo* also played an important role in the promotion of Renaissance art, with patrons commissioning art for their collections (Olmi, 2001, 5). Collectors became preoccupied with the "attractive presentation" of collections, focusing on a "desire for symmetry and a pleasing appearance" (Olmi, 2001, 8). Similarly, from the early sixteenth century English country houses and French castles displayed collections of paintings in wide passageways, which were referred to as galleries. Victoria Newhouse suggests that owners and their visitors would "take exercise" by wandering through these spaces in which the art acted as scenery, or as a "distraction," similar to the way people on treadmills use televisions in contemporary gymnasiums (Newhouse, 1998, 14). Gardens were developed as settings for art structures, including loggias, pavilions, and grottos. Donato Bramante's Belvedere sculpture court in the Vatican (1508) typifies this tradition, and is attributed as the first architectural space designed specifically for the display of artworks (Naredi-Rainer, 2004, 19).

The term *museum*, in its modern sense, can be dated to this era. The Italian collector Paolo Giovio (who was a painter, biographer, and physician to Cardinal Giulio de Medici) built a villa on the shores of Lake Como in 1539 to house his collection of portraits of famous people, which he called his *Musaeum*. This was the first reference to the ancient Greek temple, to which the modern museum would aspire (Pevsner, 1979, 111). The development of spaces designed for collections continued in 1584, when the Grand Duke of Tuscany, Francesco de Medici, moved his private collection to a new architectural setting in a series interconnecting rooms of an existing building that was adapted by Bernardo Buontalenti. The Uffizi Gallery provided a strong contrast to the secret and nocturnal origins of the *studiolo*, establishing a ritual procession through the well-lit series of spaces, with rare and precious objects placed on clear view (Olmi, 2001, 10). A series of *gallerie* could be traversed *enfilade*, or accessed via a corridor that allowed the linear sequence to be subverted to visit to specific parts of the collection. The interior spaces overlooked the courtyard below, and out to the River Arno beyond.

From the seventeenth century, collections displayed evidence of the "ever-advancing progress of human rationale and man's control over the environment" (Melhuish, 1997, 22). The development of the scientific discipline of Natural History produced systematic ways of describing nature, and this influenced the way that objects were stored or displayed. As the scientific understanding of the world developed, botanic gardens and libraries also provided sites for the categorization, and ordering of knowledge (Alberch, 1994, 196). The *Musaeum Tradescantianum*, which was opened to the public in London in 1634, was the first reference to the term "museum" in an English context (Newhouse, 1998, 14). Also known as "The Ark," the collection included curiosities amassed on voyages by John Tradescant the elder, and his son of the same name. This collection of botanical, geological, and zoological items was subsequently acquired by English antiquary and politician, Elias Ashmole, and gifted to the University of Oxford in 1682 (Ashmolean, 2015). It was housed in a two-story building that also contained a laboratory in the basement with spaces for lectures and demonstration on the middle floor, firmly establishing the educational role of the museum (Markus, 1993, 192).

Throughout the second half of the eighteenth century, private collections across Europe were progressively opened to the public. The Palais Luxembourg in Paris allowed public access in 1750 (Naredi-Rainer, 2004, 14). The Medici's Uffizi Gallery in Florence, which had been opened by special request to visitors since the sixteenth century, extended access to the general public in 1780 (Ritchie, 1994, 10). The royal collections of the Louvre Palace were appropriated to form the Musée Louvre in 1793, echoing the "democratization of luxury" engendered by the French revolution (Alexander, 1979, 8). In England, the British Museum was formed in 1759, following public lobbying and the bequest of private collections. These were housed in an existing building, and visits were generally supervised tours in which the visitors' movement through the museum was a carefully controlled sequence.

The first autonomous museum building was constructed in Kassel in Germany between 1769 and 1779. The Museum Fridericianum included a library and a collection of art, antiques, weaponry, natural history, and astronomy. The geometrically symmetrical two-story, three-winged, building with a classical-style portico contained a series of enfilade spaces that mirrored the movement sequence of buildings that housed earlier collections (Naredi-Rainder, 2004, 21). This pattern came to typify museum design, and became the basis of an institutional architectural typology, as formalized by Jean-Nicolas-Louis Durand in 1802 to 1805 (Figure 10.1). Durand's speculative, paradigmatic model drew on the form and experience of museum precursors that created linear sequences, and also embraced Beaux Arts traditions of formalized ritualistic movement. Durand's model was characterized by three key elements: a central rotunda which provided a grand orienting space; a series of long, interconnected, vaulted galleries organized *enfilade* that created a sense of ritual movement; and the galleries arranged around courtyards that provided a secondary gathering space and allowed daylight to illuminate the exhibition spaces (Newhouse, 1998, 46).

The principles of Durand's paradigmatic museum model underpinned many purpose-built museums in the nineteenth century. In Britain, the Dulwich Picture Gallery (1811–14), the British Museum (1823), the Royal Museum of Scotland (1881–88), the Natural History Museum (1864–73) and in Germany the Altes

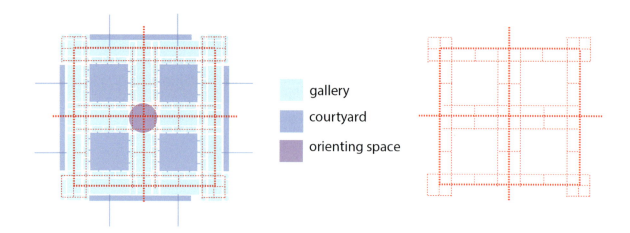

Figure 10.1 Diagram of Durand's paradigmatic museum, showing museum spaces and circulation patters. Image by author.

Museum (1823) and the Glyptothek (1816) each drew on and expanded Durand's model, employing neo-classical architecture that reinforced associative connections to the "temple of culture" (Searing, 1986, 15).

Throughout the nineteenth century, the public museum began to develop in the context of a broad agenda to "inform, instruct, improve and to a degree control" the populace, and the form and order of the museum's architecture reflected this agenda (Fleming, 2005, 56). Like public libraries, museums became "tools of Victorian pedagogy," which visitors frequented for recreation and pleasure, as well as instruction (Brawne, 1965, 8). Barbara Black observes that the display of collections underpinned a "nationalist commitment of improving public taste through mass education" (2000, 9). Museums were well ordered, beautiful, and quiet, a place where citizens could develop an "appetite for novelty, as well as nostalgia" (Black, 2000, 24.) Tony Bennett suggests that the museum's instructive and didactic agenda was underpinned by the formal arrangement of the museum's architecture, creating an itinerary of "organized walking through evolutionary time" (Bennett, 1995, 67)

Michael Levin identifies three spatial types that emerged, each characterized by different levels of spatial flexibility. An *enfilade* or "continuous flow" arrangement created a fixed linear sequence of galleries, in which spaces were traversed in an unalterable sequential progression. The "gallery and corridor" model provided more flexibility, with a secondary path that allowed visitors to bypass some of the galleries, creating more diverse itineraries. The "basilica model" or "nave and aisle" arrangement featured a central orienting space that opened to a series of adjacent smaller galleries (Levin, 1983, 62). A fixed sequence reinforced temporal "continuity and linearity," and was employed to underpin evolutionary thought and the idea of progression (Brawne, 1982, 13). The linear sequence produced a closed circuit in which the visitor's journey became a carefully prescribed tour on the "cultural conveyor belt" (Brawne, 1965, 13), while more flexible arrangements created radial

EXPERIENCE AND MEANING IN MUSEUMS   183

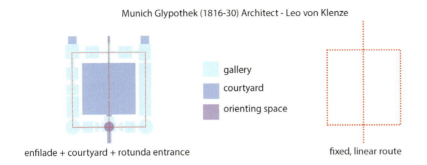

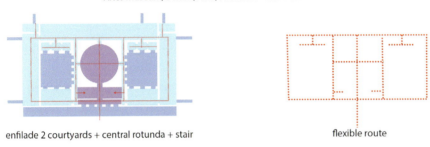

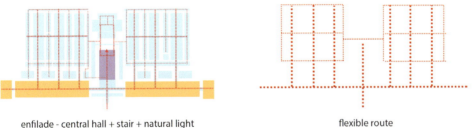

Figure 10.2 Diagram of the spatial structure of early museums, showing circulating patterns to indicate flexibility of movement. Image by author.

or "branched" circulation patterns, allowing visitors to construct undertake a range of itineraries of movement (Psarra, 2009, 145).

These patterns can be observed through analysis of the examples cited above, as demonstrated in the diagrams below (Figure 10.2). The Glyptothek in Munich and the Dulwich Picture Gallery in London offer examples of the "continuous flow" model, which produced a fixed linear sequence. In both the Munich Pinokothek and the Altes Museum the enfilade around the perimeter galleries could be subverted by a secondary path that passed through the central rotunda. In contrast, the spatial composition of the both the Kelvingrove Art Gallery and Museum in Glasgow and the Natural History Museum in London allowed direct access into galleries via a pair of naturally lit spaces on either side of the entrance, which then lead into a set of parallel galleries that flanked the main hall. The main hall formed a gathering space at the center of the museum, providing a secondary circulation sequence.

FROM TEMPLE TO FORUM

By the turn of the twentieth century, the museum's cultural and civic role was firmly established and new institutions were developed across the world as key buildings in rapidly urbanizing cities. As the twentieth century unfolded, museums came under increasing pressure to counteract the perception of their status as elite institutions, and to engage with the economic, cultural, and social life of the city. Museums developed a more diverse agenda, both educationally and socially, accommodating new visitor facilities and new types and scales of exhibitions in an effort to compete with the other forms of metropolitan entertainment. Increasingly interactive exhibitions created a shift from exhibiting (display) to communicating, which Eilean Hooper-Greenhill describes as a "form of secular ritual … a process of sharing, participation, fellowship, and association," that promotes the museum as a site of active engagement, both physically and intellectually (2001, 5).

As the museum institution transformed, museum architecture began to challenge and subvert classical associations, producing new patterns of formal and spatial order. The ideal of the museum as a "temple of culture" that reinforced ritual and rendered the visitor a passive agent was transformed through new conceptual approaches that influenced the physical form of museum buildings. Many museums became less formally structured in terms of the prescribed visitor itinerary, and more spatially open towards the physical setting in which they were located.

MUSEUMS STAGING EXPERIENCE

A significant shift in museum architecture was developed through speculative and built projects by Le Corbusier, who was commissioned in 1929 by Belgian educator Paul Otlet to design the Cité Mondial, a cultural complex at the center of a new "world city." Le Corbusier's design for the Musée Mondial within the Cité Mondial drew on the classical geometry and ordered sequence of Schinkel's Altes Museum, and was also inspired by the Outlook Tower in Edinburgh (1853–92) design by Patrick Geddes, which orchestrated both movement and visual connections that connected to the broader setting.

Geddes' Outlook Tower was conceived as an observation space that aimed to re-situate the individual in the world and to transform the entire city into a "museum of itself" (Vidler, 2003, 166). A constructed relationship between movement, visual connections, and conceptual ideas was central to the Outlook Tower, which placed the visitor "inside the bellows of a huge photographic apparatus" (Geddes quoted in Vidler, 2003, 165). The visitors' path was intertwined with specially constructed visual connections, driven by Geddes's interest in the "processes of observation and movement, the living gaze that joins a locality to its region" (Vidler, 2003, 166).

Movement through the Outlook Tower was instructive; a strict linear sequence revealed a thematic (rather than chronological) itinerary, with each space establishing the conceptual context for the next (Stephen, 2004, 87).

Visitors entered the building from the street level of Edinburgh's Royal Mile, and proceeded directly up to the roof terrace, which offered a panoramic view over the city and out to the landscape of the broader region. Moving images of the street below could also be viewed through a *camera obscura* on the roof terrace (Vidler, 2003, 165). As visitors progressed through the building, the exhibition presented "ever-widening geographical and cultural zones," which aimed to position the understanding of the city within a broader context (Welter, 2002, 78). The floor below the terrace contained information about Edinburgh, the next presented the broader context of Scotland, and subsequent floors contained exhibits about countries in which English was spoken, providing an ever-increasing context for the specific site of Edinburgh. Astronomical charts and an epidiascope (an opaque projector used to project images of books and specimens) provided a way of viewing and understanding local, regional, Scottish, and world history (Vidler, 2003, 165) (Figure 10.3).

Geddes reinforced the relationship between the museum content, the visitor experience and the broader physical and cultural context, creating an itinerary of

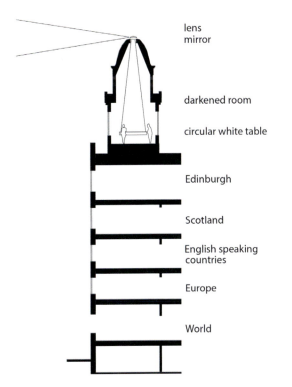

Figure 10.3 Outlook Tower, by Patrick Geddes, 1853–92, Edinburgh, Scotland. Section showing thematic arrangement of exhibitions, and photo of building exterior. Images by author.

movement, spectacle and meaning that actively engaged visitors as they moved through the thematically organized exhibition spaces. Volker Welter suggests that from within the Outlook Tower the city became an open-air museum in which the "city of the future [became] rooted in the past" (Welter, 2003, 158). The experience of the Outlook Tower extended beyond its physical location on Edinburgh's Royal Mile—out to the visual limits of the Scottish countryside that could be viewed from the roof, and connected with the rest of Britain and its colonies, Europe, and beyond—through the specifically ordered layers of exhibits on the floors below.

Inspired by Geddes, Paul Otlet developed the idea of a "useum" or "idearium" that contained objects that were not necessarily precious, but referred to specific ideas (Vidler, 2003, 162). Otlet commissioned Le Corbusier to develop ideas for the Musée Mondial. Le Corbusier drew on Geddes' strategy of orchestrating the sequence of movement, proposing that the museum would be entered via a long linear ramp that spiraled around the outside of a pyramid. The path of movement continually shifted through 90 degrees as it progressed to the summit, culminating in a panoramic view of the city, before the visitor descended into the interior. The gallery space inside was a continuous wrapping spiral, with partitions that could be erected within each of the layers of the spiral to create a more complex labyrinthine sequence.

Le Corbusier explored these ideas in his speculative proposition for the Museum of Unlimited Extension (1939) and his realized design for the Museum of Tokyo (1959), which focused on the internal experience of the museum, rather than the monumentality of the exterior. In contrast to the traditional sequence of passing through a classical façade and across a series of accentuated thresholds, visitors enter the museum via an undercroft, moving directly into the functional spaces of the museum that contain ticketing and cloakrooms. The journey into the gallery commences at the base of a double height, top-lit void, via a ramp that scissors backwards and forwards three times before arriving at the main gallery space on the first floor. The entry void, which contains the switch-back ramp, provides and orienting space, similar to the central rotunda of Durand's paradigmatic model. A spiral path of movement is embedded within the open-plan of the galleries, and this is overlaid with visual axes that provide vistas beyond the building. The spiral *parti* produces a linear sequence, but the open-plan arrangement with free-standing screens also allows visitors to also navigate a flexible, meandering route. This idea of orchestrating the building from the point of view of a mobile observer was central to Le Corbusier's exploration of *promenade architecturale,* and this notion of staging experience became central to modernist architectural thinking, and underpins the development of the architecture of museums.

In the Castelvecchio Museum (1959–73) Carlo Scarpa employed architecture as a staging device, creating a dialogue with the existing context that is central to

EXPERIENCE AND MEANING IN MUSEUMS   **187**

both the spatial experience and the interpretative narrative of the museum. The old Castelvecchio was built in a series of stages from the fourteenth to eighteenth centuries. Scarpa's intervention involves both demolition of parts of the old building and the insertion of new elements to reconfigure the complex formally and experientially. Many of the original features of the medieval castle were restored by removing more recent additions, and new insertions were overlaid to create an alternative spatial logic.

Central to the new order is the placement of the equestrian sculpture of Cangrande II della Scala, an Italian nobleman who built the original Castel in 1354–76. This sculpture was relocated from the family tomb, and is used as a key exhibit and orienting device within the museum. The visitors' path winds around the Cangrande sculpture, which acts as a landmark within the journey and icon that represents a specific associative reference, celebrating the family who ruled Verona between 1277 and 1387 (Figure 10.4).

Visitors enter the compound through a gate in the southern boundary wall, where the first glimpse of the Cangrande is revealed in the gap between two buildings, across the courtyard to the west. The position of the Cangrande at the pivot between two wings of the building is central to the spatial legibility of the museum sequence (Beltraimi and Zannier, 2006, 144). The visitor can gauge their location relative to the statue, which continually reappears en route, constantly viewed from different angles. The journey through the building presents a range of vantage

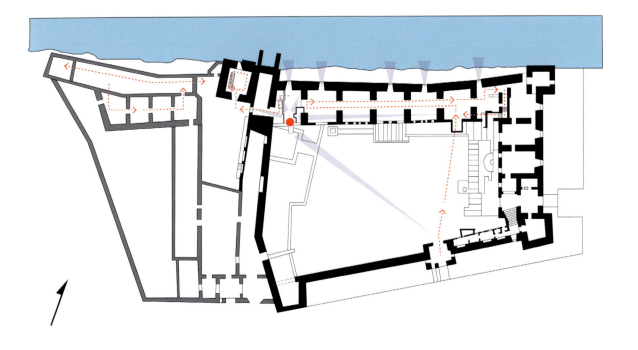

Figure 10.4
Castelvecchio Museum, by architect Carlo Scarpa, 1959–73, Verona, Italy. Diagram indicating vistas towards the Cangrande sculpture. Image by author.

points that create shifting perspectives on the Castel, across the city and out to the landscape beyond through windows in the northern wall of the compound.

The Cangrande is situated beyond the building, and Scarpa reconfigured both the entry sequence and the interior of the old building to give stronger definition and order to the series of spaces. As visitors move from the gate towards the building entrance, the Cangrande disappears from sight and then reappears further along the journey. It is experientially, but not physically, central to the museum; the relationship between the visitor and the Cangrande is deliberately orchestrated to create a spatial narrative of memory. Guido Beltraimi and Italo Zannier suggest that Scarpa's architecture has the effect of "provok(ing) a profound reflection on the relationship between ancient and modern" (2006, 144). The placing of the monument (Cangrande) was a fine example of one of the basic principles of the architect's museological work: the inseparable nature of the architecture and the staging (Beltraimi and Zannier, 2006, 144).

Norwegian architect Sverre Fehn also explored the potential of museum architecture to become an interpretative tool through the staging of experience in a series of museum projects, both speculative and realized. Fehn considered the museum is a "dance around dead things," in which the artifact and its relation to human movement is important (Fehn et al., 1992, 16). He orchestrated form and movement to establish experiential sequences that are both emotive and instructive. Fehn believed that:

> You have to integrate yourself precisely and voluntarily in the site. Never consider nature in a romantic way. Always try to create a tension between nature and your intervention. This is how architecture gains readability and architects discover the story they have to tell.
>
> (quoted in Lavalou, 1993, 85)

This idea is central to the Fehn's Archbishopric Museum in Hamar (1967–79), where the whole site is an artifact that contains physical fragments of five centuries of inhabitation. Fehn conceptualized this museum "as a kind of theatre, where the movement is in specific routes around smaller objects, around bigger objects, and around the whole space" (Fehn et al., 1992, 48). The new structure steps over the archaeological remains, allowing the visitor to traverse the site in a new sequence. A specifically ordered *promenade architecturale* is created by the insertion of ramps and bridges that establish a linear sequence, which Christian Norberg-Schulz describes as "a journey through time and space" (Norberg-Schulz and Postiglione, 1997, 28). Apertures create visual connections across the courtyard and to the lake beyond, reinforcing the historical connection to the broader landscape (Figure 10.5).

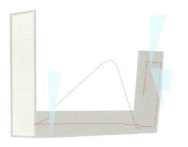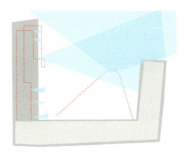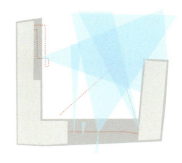

Figure 10.5 Archbishopric Museum, by architect Sverre Fehn, 1967–79, Hamar, Norway. Diagram and images showing views along showing visitors' path. Images by author.

In the Glacier Museum in Fjærland (1991) Fehn established a specific sense of order, in which the relationship between museum, visitor, and artefacts is inverted, acknowledging that the key exhibit—the largest glacier in Europe—is outside the building. Fehn describes the museum's location:

> The whole Fjærland with its fjord lies like a floor in a natural space, with the mountains as gigantic walls. In this space with the plain as a plinth, the museum rises like an instrument in which the visitors become the focal point in the total panorama and provides the peace to sense its own dimension.
>
> (Fehn, 1999, 75)

The building creates a viewing platform that orients the visitor towards this spectacular setting. The location of the museum within an expansive open plain is exploited by orchestrating movement towards the building, with the glacier as a backdrop. The building form expresses the dual ideas of mountain and cave. Approaching the building, the visitor can take one of two routes: climbing the stairs (a metaphorical mountain) to a platform from which to survey the glacier landscape; or progressing through the fissure-like "cave" into the exhibition hall, which provides a shelter from the frequently wild weather. Inside the museum the exhibition presents information about the glacier from both a scientific and descriptive point of view, with views back out to the landscape highlighted from the cafe and en route to the auditorium.

Juhani Pallasmaa's addition (1990–98) to the Sámi Museum and Northern Lapland Nature Centre (SIIDA) in Inari, Finland (established 1959), explores how the sequence through the building can provide an instructive narrative that influences the visitor's experience and understanding of the physical and cultural context of the museum. Pallasmaa is interested in the associations that architecture seeks to articulate, particularly how buildings and places can evoke emotional responses, triggering memory and sensory recall. Pallasmaa believes that, "embodied memory has an essential role as the basis of remembering a space or a place" (2012, 76). He contests that,

> Architecture is the art of reconciliation between ourselves and the world, and this mediation takes place through the senses.
>
> (Pallasmaa, 2012, 52)

SIIDA presents information about the indigenous Sámi people and the natural environment of Lapland, and it also functions as a community center and gathering place for the nomadic Sámi. The building creates a gateway to a pre-existing open-air museum that was established in 1960. It contains exhibits, administrative and commercial facilities, including a cafe and gift shop, and an auditorium on the ground level that is used for meetings of the Sámi parliament. The architecture highlights the importance of the natural landscape to the Sámi, staging movement and visual connections to emphasize this culturally significant context.

The museum sequence begins at the carpark, where a timber screen veils the adjacent lake. As visitors move towards the building, the lake is glimpsed through the gaps between the screen's horizontal slats. A canopy over the entry extends the threshold between outside and inside, accentuating the transition between the expansive landscape and the relatively small, dark space of the foyer. Upon entering, the visitor's path continues up a long ramp that projects out into the landscape, with the landing at the midway point of the ramp providing a direct visual connection to the original outdoor museum beyond. The visitor then turns 180 degrees, ascending a ramp to the main exhibition level. From here a cafe looks back out over the front entry to the lake in one direction and connects directly to an external deck and the outdoor museum to the rear (Figure 10.6).

The entry sequence encompasses a series of twists and turns, which heighten the sense of separation, with the specifically constructed views re-establishing the connection to the outdoor museum and the lake. Arriving at the upper level, the visitor is presented with a choice of three galleries: an introductory gallery to the left provides an overview of the prehistory of Lapland; an adjacent temporary exhibition space houses a series of companion displays; and the main exhibition space is located at the end of the corridor. From main gallery, visitors can exit the building and proceed down an external ramp to a path that circulates around the outdoor museum; arriving back at the cafe, where they re-enter the warm interior.

EXPERIENCE AND MEANING IN MUSEUMS 191

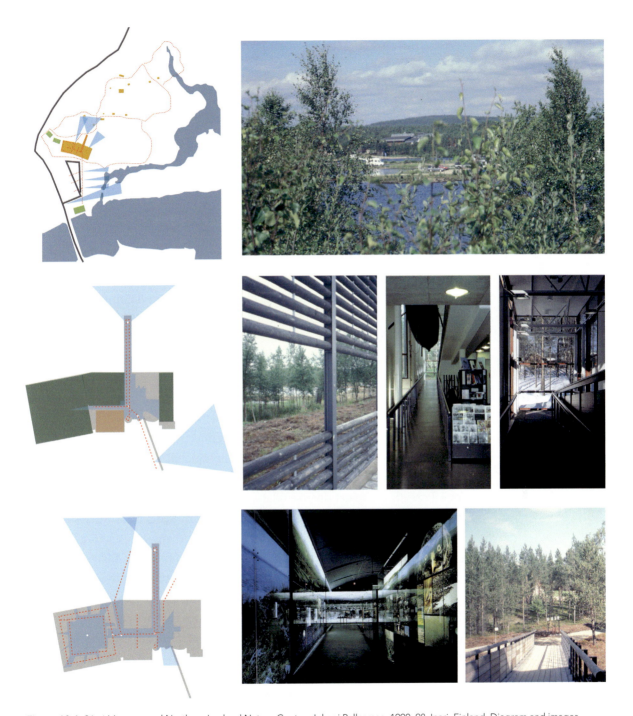

Figure 10.6 Sámi Museum and Northern Lapland Nature Center, Juhani Pallasmaa, 1990–98, Inari, Finland. Diagram and images showing views along showing visitors' path. Images by author.

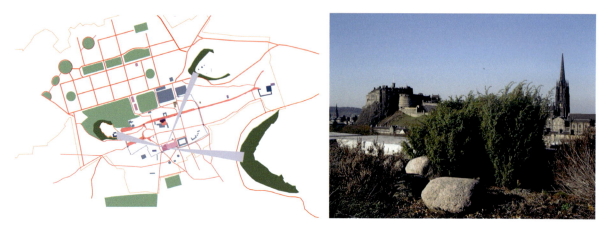

Figure 10.7 Museum of Scotland, by architects Benson + Forsyth, 1998, Edinburgh, Scotland. Visual connections to city from museum. Images by author.

Connections between a museum and its physical and cultural context is explored by Benson + Forsyth in the Museum of Scotland (Allan, 1999) in Edinburgh (Figure 10.7). The museum's architecture elicits dynamic relationships between the past, present and future, which John Allan suggests offer "new perspectives on the city itself" (Allan et al., 1999, 31). Benson + Forsyth recognize that Edinburgh was shaped by a series of visual agendas, from the pragmatic requirements of outlook and surveillance of the defensible Iron Age settlement, to symbolic ideals of the eighteenth century in which Edinburgh was reconceptualized the "Athens of the North," the cultural capital of Britain (Glendenning et al., 1997, 193). The history of Scotland is evidenced in the physical and cultural landscape of the city, and Benson + Forsyth construct diverse relationships to this context.

The building is orchestrated around a movement sequence and visual connections, which Martin Pawley suggests transform the museum from a symbolic monument to an "instrument" of active engagement (quoted in Allan et al., 1999, 128). Benson + Forsyth utilize the visual dimension of architecture in three ways: as an essential part of the movement sequence that assists orientation; as a series of orchestrated views within and beyond the museum that are contrived to evoke associative relationships; and through the use of metaphorical associations in the building form. The museum is arranged around two top-lit voids, with vistas through and beyond the building. The sequence through the building follows a chronological order, from the "Beginnings" in the basement, to the formation of the "Kingdom of the Scots" and the development of "Industry and Empire" on floors above. The journey through the building culminates on the roof terrace, which affords a panorama of the city, highlighting the three rocky outcrops on which the city was settled: the Edinburgh Castle, Calton Hill, and Salisbury Crags. At each stage of the visitor's journey, visual connections elicit associative relationships, creating a sequence that mirrors the instructive itinerary of Geddes' Outlook Tower.

Associative references also underpin the formal architectural composition; references to Scottish building traditions merge with modern and contemporary precedents. The idea of the museum as a defensible space is implicit in Benson + Forsyth's original drawings that reference Dunstaffnage Castle as an inspiration for the overall massing. Richard Murphy observes that the free-standing round entrance tower also alludes to the Pictish *broch*, a double-walled cylindrical tower built in the first millennium in the highlands and islands as a castle gatehouse (Murphy, 1999, 30). The composition of the two main street façades recalls the asymmetry of Scottish Renaissance buildings and the architecture of Charles Rennie Mackintosh, particularly the Glasgow School of Art. The blank rear wall to the south resembles the *harled* (rendered) surfaces of the Scottish domestic vernacular, as exemplified in Mackintosh's Hill House. Associations to Le Corbusier's monastery at La Tourette and chapel at Ronchamp are also embedded, which Duncan Macmillan suggests reference the way modern architecture "balanced sociability and individualism" and that we might "learn from the humanity of this historical situation" (1998, 23).

These examples demonstrate the diversity of ways that museum buildings orchestrate movement and stage experience in a manner that supports particular museological agendas, orchestrating relationships to the context in physical, visual, and conceptual ways to construct narratives of experience and meaning. Examining the evolution of museum architecture demonstrates the diversity of ways that museum buildings orchestrate movement and stage experience in a manner that supports particular museological agendas.

REFERENCES

Alberch, Pere. 1994. "The Identity Crisis of Natural History Museums at the End of the Twentieth Century." *Towards the Museum of the Future: New European Perspectives*, eds R. Miles and L. Zavala. 193–198. London: Routledge.

Alexander, Edward Porter. 1979. *Museums in Motion: An Introduction to the History and Functions of Museums*. Nashville: American Association for State and Local History.

Allan, John. 1999. "In Search of Meaning: An Architectural Appreciation of the Museum of Scotland." *Museum of Scotland*, ed. Benson + Forsyth. 120–129. London: August Media with Benson + Forsyth.

Allan, John, Patrick Hodgkinson, Paul Clarke and Neave Brown. 1999. "Museum of Memory." In *Architecture Today Vol*. 100, 28–45.

Ashmolean Museum. 2015. "History of the Ashmolean." Accessed 30 July. https://ashmolean.web.ox.ac.uk/history-ashmolean.

Beltraimi, Guido and Italo Zannier. 2006. *Carlo Scarpa: Architecture and Design*. New York: Rizzoli.

Bennett, Tony. 1995. *The Birth of the Museum*. London: Routledge.

Black, Barbara J. 2000. *On Exhibit: Victorians and Their Museums*. Charlottesville and London: University Press of Virginia.

Brawne, Michael. 1965. *The New Museum: Architecture and Display*. London: The Architectural Press.

Brawne, Michael. 1982. *The Museum Interior: Temporary and Permanent Display Techniques*. London: Thames and Hudson.

Fehn, Sverre. 1999, "Glacier Museum, Fjaerland, Norway 1981-1991." *A + U: Architecture and Urbanism* 1, no. 340, 74–91.

Fehn, Sverre, Maija Karkkainen, Marja-Riitta Norri, and Suomen Rakennustaiteen Museo. 1992. *The Poetry of the Straight Line*. Helsinki: Museum of Finnish Architecture.

Fleming, David. 2005. "Creative Space." *Reshaping Museum Space: Architecture, Design, Exhibition*, ed. Suzanne McLeod.. 53–61. London: Routledge.

Glendenning, Miles, Ranald MacInnes and Aongus MacKechnie. 1997. *A History of Scottish Architecture: From the Renaissance to the Present Day*. Edinburgh: Edinburgh University Press.

Hooper-Greenhill, Eilean. 2001. "Communication and Communities in the Post-Museum - from Metanarratives to Constructed Knowledge." Paper presented at the Nordic Museums Leadership Programme, Copenhagen.

Lavalou, Armelle. 1993, "Interview with Sverre Fehn." *Architecture D'audjourd'hui* no. 287 (June), 85.

Levin, Michael D. 1983. *The Modern Museum: Temple or Showroom*. Te Aviv: Dvir Publishing House.

Macmillan, Duncan, "Welcome Home." *The Scotsman*, St Andrews Day 1998, 23.

Markus, Thomas A. 1993. *Buildings and Power: Freedom and Control in the Origin of Modern Building Types*. London and New York: Routledge.

Melhuish, Clare. 1997, "The Museum as a Mirror of Society." *Architectural Design* 67, no. 11/12 ((November/December)), 22–25.

Murphy, Richard. 1999, "Edinburgh Tour De Force at Benson and Forsyth's Museum of Scotland, the Monumental Architecture Proves the Most Powerful Exhibit [Edinburgh]." *Architects' Journal* 209, no. 8 (February 25), 26–35.

Naredi-Rainer, Paul von. 2004. *Museum Buildings: A Design Manual*. Basel, Berlin, Boston: Birkhäuser.

Newhouse, Victoria. 1998. *Towards a New Museum*. New York: The Monacelli Press.

Norberg-Schulz, Christian and Gennaro Postiglione. 1997. *Sverre Fehn: works, projects, writings, 1949-1996*. New York: Monacelli Press, 28.

Olmi, Giuseppe. 2001. "Science - Honour - Metaphor: Italian Cabinets of the Sixteenth and Seventeenth Centuries." In *The Origins of Museums: The Cabinet of Curiosities in Sixteenth- and Seventeenth-Century Europe*, eds Oliver Impey and Arthur Macgregor. North Yorkshire: House of Stratus.

Pallasmaa, Juhani. 2012. *Eyes of the Skin: Architecture of the Senses*. West Sussex: John Wiley & Sons.

Pevsner, Nikolaus. 1979. *A History of Building Types*. Princeton. NJ.: Princeton University Press.

Psarra, Sophia. 2009. *Architecture and Narrative: The Formation of Space and Cultural Meaning*. London and New York: Routledge.

Ritchie, Ian. 1994. "An Architect's View of the Recent Developments in European Museums." In *Towards the Museum of the Future: New European Perspectives*, eds Roger Miles and Lauro Zavala. London: Routledge.

Searing, Helen. 1986. "The Development of a Museum Typology." In *Building the New Museum*, ed. Suzanne Stephens. New York: Princeton Architectural Press.

Stephen, Walter. 2004. *Think Global, Act Local: The Life and Legacy of Patrick Geddes*. Livingston: Digisource.

Vidler, Anthony. 2003. "The Space of History: Modern Museums from Patrick Geddes to Le Corbusier." *The Architecture of the Museum: Symbolic Structures, Urban Contexts*, ed. Michaela Giebelhausen. 160–182. Manchester: Manchester University Press.

Welter, Volker. 2002. *Biopolis: Patrick Geddes and the City of Life*. Cambridge, Massachusetts and London, England: The MIT Press, 2002.

Welter, Volker M. 2003. "The Return of the Muses: Edinburgh as a *Museion*." *The Architecture of the Museum: Symbolic Structures, Urban Contexts*, ed. Michaela Giebelhausen. 144–159. Manchester: Manchester University Press.

CHAPTER 11

Planning Art Museums from Inside-out

Design for Visitor Experiences

İpek Kaynar Rohloff

Today's art museums strive to reach ever-broader audiences and to attract and sustain interest in their exhibitions. A new building or an expansion can be desirable for art museums, because its design presents opportunities for curators to explore new and interesting ways of exhibiting art. However, planning a new setting can be challenging for art museums because the process needs to be guided by clear objectives, ones that can be fulfilled within the architectural design. Yet, too often, the objectives are instead quite complex due to competing requirements for extensive curatorial interpretation and wide audience appeal. On the one hand, art museums seek spatial variety to showcase new exhibitions, accommodate individualized visitor itineraries, and house new services and programs. On the other hand, a larger and more complex building may compromise the legibility and coherence of the museum setting, which could prove detrimental to visitor experiences (Kaplan et al., 1993). These competing requirements can be addressed in a planning model which integrates an empathic understanding of visitor experiences in space with implementation of the institutional goals.

In an effort to outline a planning model with an empathic approach, this chapter offers a bottom-up and inside-out formulation of museum architecture for new and expanding art museums. The discussion examines the ways in which visitors' patterns of exploring art are influenced by gallery design. It also explores how to integrate visitor-centered insights into the space programing phase of museum planning. To this end, the first part of this chapter presents a part of a case study from the author's previous research that examined the spatial properties of galleries in comparison with visitors' behavioral patterns and exhibition narratives in art museums. The results reveal the ways in which visitor experiences are influenced by gallery design, and allow us to examine whether these results align with the museum's goals. The second part of the chapter draws upon the author's work in museum consultancy practice. This section focuses on a pragmatic space programing model that determines size, access, and circulation, and adjacency requirements of museum spaces based on institutional objectives, and explores how to integrate gallery design and visitor experience objectives with the top-down process of space programing.

SPATIAL ORGANIZATION PROPERTIES OF MUSEUM GALLERIES AND BUILDINGS

The earliest gallery space formations in the Greek and medieval periods appeared in residential arrangements where collected artifacts were brought together for the purpose of "studying" them as sources of knowledge representing the universe. It was in Renaissance Europe that collecting and exhibiting gained an interpretive purpose, and the sixteenth-century gallery was indeed an "interior room mostly lighted by windows placed along the long sides, which suitably provided wall space for displaying paintings and sculptures" (Naredi-Rainer, 2004b). Variations of this "architectural motif" are noted as "a long corridor with arcades on both sides," and "a museum with a central room surrounded by galleries" (Naredi-Rainer, 2004a, 19). As these first galleries were "constituents" of royal palaces or residences, the displays were placed opportunistically, adhering to the stylistic forms of those buildings. Once museums became autonomous institutions (with public access to collections, governing administration, and a role in public education and arts studies), gallery hallways were designed for the systematic organization and placement of displays (Naredi-Rainer, 2004a, 20–21). The gallery hallways were also combined with entrances, exits, and often a central courtyard. A notable example of neo-classical museums in the eighteenth century was the Glyptothek (1816–30) in Munich by architect Leo van Klenze. He had planned the museum by coordinating the number and form of the galleries with chronological arrangements of the collection objects, while combining the galleries with banquet halls and vestibules to serve client's needs. The centrally located square courtyard provided the opportunity for a circular tour leading through differently shaped and furnished rooms, through which the "observer clearly sees the trajectory of art, its rise and fall" (Naredi-Rainer, 2004a, 22).

A number of studies in design theory examine museums in the context of the nineteenth century institutions and with respect to "classifying notion" their buildings bring to social practices. Accordingly, the cultural significance of museum buildings lies in classifying the spaces according to what objects are contained within and which users are allowed for access (Markus, 1987, 1993). Hillier (1991), furthermore, proposes two models that describe the ways in which buildings organize user spatial activity: *strong program* and *weak program*. In "strong program" buildings connections among the spaces are determined by sociocultural norms; thus the design of these buildings renders expression of existing relationships in the society; in contrast, in "weak-program buildings connections among the spaces is an interpretation, thus the design is generative of new relationships" (Hillier and Hanson, 1984; Hillier and Penn, 1991). In this framework, museum galleries can be a *strong program* or *weak program* setting based on the degree to which the spatial organization is an expression of the content. For example, the museum galleries that are formed to organize displays based on chronological categories and to present them in a strictly linear trajectory demonstrate a *strong program* serving "didactic presentation of the narratives" (Pradinuk, 1986). In contrast, the galleries that provide visual connections and multi-directional sequences can support varying interpretations of the content and thus serve to generate narratives (Psarra, 2009b).[1]

The art museum galleries of the twentieth century have been liberated from the purpose of placing displays in chronological categories or presenting in strictly controlled viewing. This change has been motivated by a few factors: one is the increasing belief that modern works of art can be understood independently of their historical context; another factor is the notion that interchangeable arrangements highlight the aesthetic qualities of the works and create greater appeal for diverse audiences (Noordegraaf, 2004; Serota, 1997; Staniszewski, 1998). As a result, the physical qualities of gallery spaces have appeared in greater variety and thus acted as active components of the exhibition design (Newhouse, 2005). Moreover, gallery design with open- or semi-open layouts has become popular to facilitate the comparative reading of displays and to promote visitors' self-directed explorations.

For today's art museums, there is still need for the purposefully formulated design in concert of the educational and cultural objectives. The research presented below contributes to understanding how to formulate gallery spaces by examining the potential impact of gallery design on visitor experience.

THE EFFECTS OF THE SPATIAL ORGANIZATION OF GALLERIES ON VISITOR EXPERIENCES

This study concentrates on analyses of three art museums: The Yale Center for British Art (1977) in New Haven, Connecticut, the Museum of Modern Art (2004) in New York, and the High Museum of Art (1983, 2005) in Atlanta, Georgia

(Figure 11.1). The author chose to analyze these museums due to their comparable architectural characteristics: gallery and atrium void connections that allow itinerary choices and vistas through space (Figures 11.1b, 11.1d, and 11.1f). The analysis was designed to explore the links between the spatial properties of galleries and visitors' patterns of explorative behavior (Rohloff, 2009b, 2009a).[2]

In this study, the spatial properties of galleries in the three museums are defined in terms of visibility relations and are expressed with techniques of "space syntax" methodology (Turner, 2001; Turner et al., 2001). This methodology describes visibility relations in two levels: local visibility—or visual connectivity—which is about how much one can see from any point in a space and describes how open that space is to its surroundings; and Global visibility—visual centrality—which addresses through how many different visual fields an entire setting unfolds to an observer and describes how easily that space can be seen from everywhere else as well as how easily one can grasp the entire layout from that space. In museum gallery layouts, spaces with low degrees of visual connectivity are those secluded from their surroundings, whereas spaces with low degrees of visual centrality are those segregated due to being positioned at the deeper end of a layout and thus accessed only after passing many other spaces.

The analysis discussed here describes visitors' patterns of explorative behavior in terms of movement paths and points of pause to view displays. The data of movement and pause were gathered by observing visitors in the three museum's galleries (Figures 11.3c, 11.3d, 11.5c, 11.5d, 11.7c, and 11.7d). Additionally, exhibition narratives presented in those galleries were decoded by examining the placement of the collection objects in the galleries and by gathering curatorial intentions from open-ended interviews with curators. The analysis then investigated correlations between visibility relations in the gallery layouts and visitors' movement and pause rates; predominant movement paths of the visitors were also compared to decoded exhibition narratives in the galleries. The results were interpreted in the light of each museum's interpretive goals as set out in publications or gleaned from the interviews. The results summarized below reveal the peculiar ways in which the architecture of these museums influenced visitors' movement and exhibit viewing behavior.

The Yale Center for British Art (YCBA) was founded in 1966 with the goal of presenting Paul Mellon's private collection of British art which dates from the 1650s to the 1850s. The collection represents British art and cultural legacy beyond borders of the Commonwealth (Meyers, 2007). As such, the YCBA addresses an audience with a primarily scholarly interest in British art and focuses on the ways in which British art and culture is studied and appreciated. The permanent collection galleries located on the fourth floor, which were analyzed for this study, present "the development of British art, life and world-view with selected portraiture

PLANNING ART MUSEUMS FROM INSIDE-OUT   199

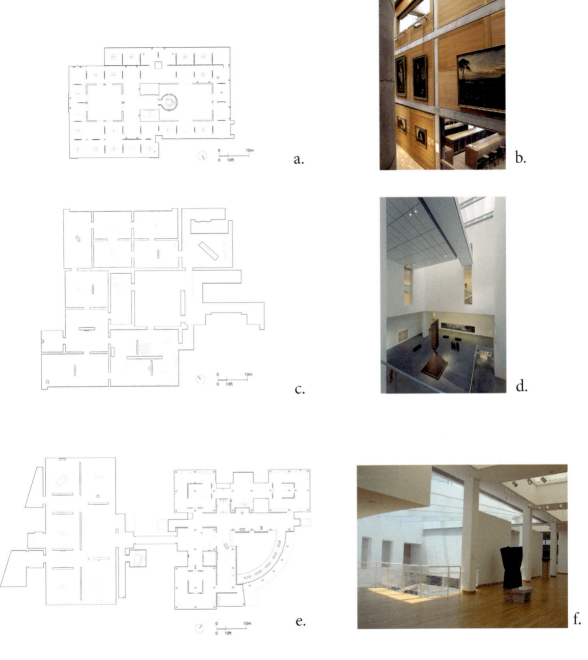

Figure 11.1 a) The Yale Center for British Art (YCBA), by architect Louis I. Kahn, 1977, New Haven, Connecticut; The Permanent Collection Galleries (fourth floor) plan: YCBA, 2005; b) Main courtyard view from third floor. Photograph: Richard Caspole; c) The Museum of Modern Art (MoMA), by architect Yoshio Taniguchi, 2004, New York, New York; the Painting and Sculpture Galleries (fourth floor) plan: MoMA, 2005; d) Atrium view from fourth floor. Photograph: Timothy Hursley; e) The High Museum of Art (HMA), by architects Richard Meier, 1983, and Renzo Piano, 2005. Atlanta, Georgia; the Skyway (fourth floor) galleries plan: HMA, 2006; f) Atrium view from the fourth floor. Photograph: author.

200 İPEK KAYNAR ROHLOFF

and landscape paintings with sculpture from Elizabethan period onward "(Meyers, 2005). The YCBA's building (1977), designed by Louis I. Kahn, was commissioned with visitor-oriented objectives in mind; the design was intended to facilitate an enjoyable experience without causing fatigue; the design should ideally offer "legibility choices in navigation" and "evoke interest and curiosity," possibly with variety of scales and depth of vision (Prown, 1977, 1983).

The YCBA's fourth floor gallery layout was composed of square-shaped bays positioned in a grid and enfilades around two courtyards within the building's rectangular volume (Figure 11.1a). The square bays were separated by partitions that were positioned to leave corners of the bays open (Figure 11.2b). This allowed for an uninterrupted gaze to farther ends of the gallery floor along with continuous circulation through the bays (Figure 11.2c).

The visibility graphs generated on the YCBA's fourth floor layout shows that the courtyard openings and corners of the bays brought high degrees of visual centrality and connectivity by visually linking remote locations and making adjacent spaces visible (Figures 11.3a and 11.3b). Correlations with visitor data indicated

Figure 11.2
Permanent Collection Galleries of the YCBA:
a) View through the main courtyard;
b) View towards adjacent spaces;
c) View towards far side of the galleries.
Photographs: author.

a.

b.

c.

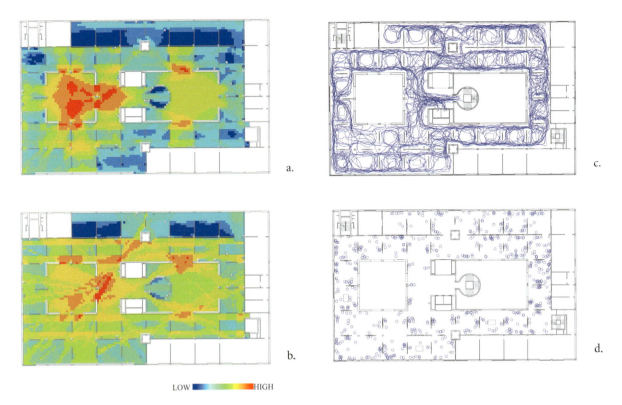

Figure 11.3 Visibility graphs and visitor behavior data at the YCBA's permanent exhibition galleries: a) Visual connectivity graph; b) Visual integration/centrality graph; c) Transcribed data of visitor movement; d) Transcribed data of visitors' stops at displays. The graphs and the line work representing the data by the author based on the floor plan provided by the YCBA.

that visual centrality and local visual connectivity were linked to the frequency of visitors' movements and pauses for viewing exhibits. More interestingly, these metrics of the movement and exhibit viewing patterns were also linked to depths of visual field, a feature of local visibility. The result suggests that visitors were drawn to spaces that are visible with the least effort from adjacent and all other spaces. Gallery and courtyard openings allowing vistas to and from those spaces had a significant effect. This link between high degrees of visibility and both movement and exhibit viewing behavior indicate that works of art were given attention by visitors as they navigate the space.

The same analysis process at the Museum of Modern Art (MoMA) and the High Museum of Art in Atlanta yielded different results.

Since its foundation 1922, the MoMA promoted works of art which it considers "experimental, progressive, original and challenging" (Elderfield, 2004, 10–12) with its mission having been "to preserve, collect and display the best works of Modern and Contemporary art and to serve as a laboratory for understanding visual art manifested by modernity" (Lowry, 2005, 24). The MoMA's galleries aimed to present a complex trajectory of modern and contemporary styles

Figure 11.4 Painting and Sculpture (Fourth Floor) Galleries of the MoMA: a) View from one of the gallery rooms to the adjacent spaces; b) View from another gallery room towards the atrium. Photographs: Timothy Hursley.

PLANNING ART MUSEUMS FROM INSIDE-OUT   **203**

within interconnected "chapter rooms," each in a well-defined rectilinear form. The museum's 2004 expansion building designed by Yoshio Taniguchi offered increased fluidity in connecting the enlarged "chapter rooms" in order to offer greater variationin viewing sequences and to afford multiple narratives (Psarra, 2009a).[3] As a result, the fourth and fifth floor galleries in the MoMA's 2004 expansion wing were characterized by rectilinear gallery rooms and enfilade around a large atrium space that remained visually separated from the galleries except for a few openings. The gallery rooms connected to each other through gateways in opposing and staggered positions and the itineraries allowed visitors to branch out towards multiple directions.

Visibility graphs generated in the fourth layouts show that, despite visibility of each room from adjacent spaces, the visitors' capacity to grasp entire layout from all other spaces remained confined in a few spaces located the end of the suggested itinerary (Figures 11.5a and 11.5b). Correlations of visibility with visitors' data indicated

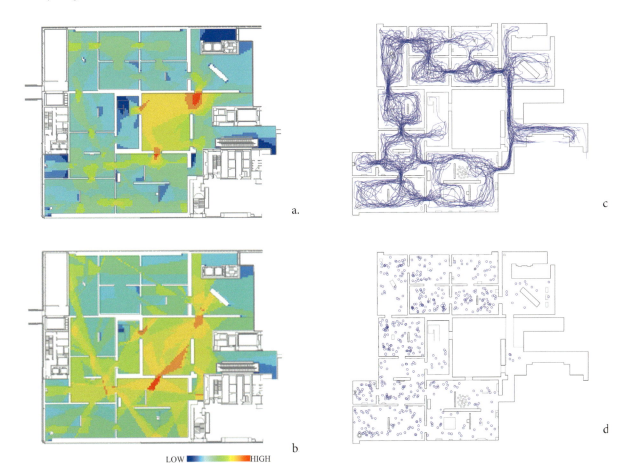

Figure 11.5 Visibility graphs and visitor behavior data at MoMA's permanent exhibition galleries: a) Visual connectivity graph; b) Visual integration/centrality graph; c) Transcribed data of visitor movement; d) Transcribed data of visitors' stops at displays. The graphs and the line work by the author based on the floor plan provided by the MoMA.

that the frequency of visitors' movements was significantly linked with local visibility; this means visitors were guided by vistas to adjacent spaces (Figure 11.4a). Contrarily, the results showed visitors' pauses for exhibit viewing were inversely linked to visual centrality, meaning visitors tended to stop to view art in visually segregated galleries. This prediction of visitor movement and exhibit viewing behavior with contrasting aspects of visibility implies that the MoMA's fourth floor layout dissociated visitors' navigation and exhibit viewing, and visitors gravitated toward more focused experiences with art apart from navigating through galleries.

The High Museum of Art (HMA) was opened to public in 1983 in Richard Meier's iconic building. Since then the museum has extended its collection from American decorative arts to modern and contemporary paintings. The latest addition of large-scale late modern and contemporary pieces to the collection motivated the expansion project with Renzo Piano's design completed in 2005 (Brenneman, 2006; Cove, 2006). The HMA's fourth floor layout, analyzed here, comprises top-floor spaces of the original building and the expansion wing connected with a bridge structure. The original wing's gallery spaces are housed in an L-shape volume that delineates an atrium in a quarter-circle shape (Figure 11.1e). The galleries adjacent to the atrium are larger and spaciously open, and yet branch into galleries featuring room-within-a-room organization with smaller and secluded rooms (Figure 11.6c). The expansion wing is a rectilinear volume partitioned by symmetrically situated walls to form a matrix of rooms. Within these characteristics, the HMA's entire fourth floor layout presented the works of American late modern, contemporary, and self-taught art. The works of modern art were in smaller rooms; while the works of self-taught art and late modern art were brought together in the larger galleries of the original wing (Figure 11.6b) by highlighting visual affinities between the genres (Brenneman, 2006). The works of contemporary art were kept in spacious galleries of the expansion wing (Figure 11.6d).

An interesting aspect of the HMA's fourth floor layout was the visual centrality along the longitudinal axis, in particular in the core space extending from the original wing's atrium area to the expansion wing's entrance (Figure 11.7b). This longitudinal core also offered spaces with increased local visibility towards smaller galleries away from the atrium (Figure 11.7a). Correlations of visibility with visitors' data indicated that the frequency of visitor movement was significantly linked with both visual centrality and connectivity. The results show visitor's pauses for exhibit viewing were inversely linked to these global and local visibility measures, meaning that visitors most likely pause to view art in secluded galleries. This result again implies that visitor's exploratory movement and exhibit viewing behavior were dissociated. As one examines visibility distribution in spatial properties of the layout, visitors tended to move around along with the core longitudinal area

PLANNING ART MUSEUMS FROM INSIDE-OUT   205

a.

b.

c.

d.

whereas focus on exhibit viewing in smaller and contained spaces that were mostly in the room-within-a-room galleries of the original wing. This result was similar to the analysis results obtained from the MoMA galleries, however the HMA's layout provided views to exhibits located in different parts of the layout, and supported comparative reading of the late modern and self-taught art in parts. The space extending along the core longitudinal axis performs as an alley where visitors move around and view casually placed works of art while being cognizant of exhibits in secluded parts of the gallery floor (Figure 11.6a).

A comparative interpretation of findings from the three museums suggest that the YCBA's gallery design supported the scholarly interpretation of British art through the linear progression along the bays, while facilitating a holistic reading of the exhibition by bringing into view displays placed in various parts of the layout. Vistas to the portraiture framed through atria openings rendered an aesthetic presentation of art within the architecture, while maintaining the legibility of the layout for a comfortable and enjoyable visit. The spatial organization of the MoMA galleries seemed to have fulfilled the museum's aim for focused visits to the modern

Figure 11.6 The Skyway (the fourth floor) Galleries of the HMA: a) View from the gallery hall by the atrium in the original building; b) View from the gallery hall before entering the expansion wing; c) Galleries in room-within-a-room organization in the original building; d) Galleries in the expansion wing. Photographs: the author.

Figure 11.7 Visibility graphs and visitor behavior data at the HMA's Skyway galleries: a) Visual connectivity graph; b) Visual integration/centrality graph; c) Transcribed data of visitor movement; d) Transcribed data of visitors' stops at displays. The graphs and the line work by the author based on the floor plan provided by the HMA.

works of art, yet the layout presented a challenge in spatial orientation and legibility as visitors were guided by visual information of one room ahead. The spatial organization of the HMA's fourth floor had the greatest diversity in architectural character as well as the exhibits, while the layout has been well utilized for the museum's intentional incorporation of casual versus more curated presentations of the art, as well as visitors' comfortable navigation.

These findings reveal that museum architecture may shape visitor experiences in peculiar ways based on how design unfolds environmental information to the observer. These insights could yield useful lessons for museum planning once the effects of gallery design are understood within each museum's programatic and spatial complexity. Indeed, the YCBA's building program focuses on the appreciation of the British art and thus brings together scholarly and popular exhibitions, conservation, research, and education functions. The main gallery floor analyzed here is characterized within compact form of a modestly scaled building. The HMA's gallery floor holds exhibitions of modern, contemporary, and self-taught art in an architecturally diverse setting. Besides exhibitions of modern and decorative arts, the museum is highly invested in community outreach and thus the building program highlights family education programs and after-hour events. The MoMA's gallery floors serve to help visitors explore the story of modern art within the most extensive building program and with numerous temporary exhibitions, performing arts events, education programs, and commercial services. Among the three, the MoMA presents the most ambitious but also challenging case for planning around visitor experiences due to its ever-expanding building size, growing collection, and programatic complexity.

SPACE PROGRAMING AND PLANNING WITH VISITOR EXPERIENCES IN MIND

In large museums, cultural content is supported by exhibitions in galleries along with education and research programs in other spaces. This role of galleries in a museum's entire program can be understood within a diagram of museum building functions and corresponding spatial categories.

Spaces in museums can be classified by levels of access, separating public access (front-of-the-house) spaces and private access (back-of-the-house) areas, or by whether or not spaces hold collections. The *Four-Zone Diagram* devised by Lord (2012) positions museum spaces based on these criteria: whether the space is assigned to hold collections or not and whether the space is open to the public (visitors) or not (Lord, 2012b) (Table 11.1).

The *Four-Zone Diagram* provides guidance for determining how much space should be allocated for each spatial category in order to support a museum's

Table 11.1 Four-Zone Diagram with Spatial Categories in a Typical Museum (concept: Lord Cultural Resources)

	Public (A)	Private (B)
Non-collections (0)	A-0: Public/Non-collections Entrance hall, restaurants, auditorium, and other visitor services	B-0: Private/Non-collections Staff rooms, education halls, and security rooms (20%)
Collections (1)	A-1: Public-Collections Galleries, temporary exhibition spaces, and museum library (40%)	B-1: Private/Collections Storage areas, conservation labs, and curatorial workrooms (20%)

cultural program successfully. This diagram has been used in planning practice to assess and articulate how much space may be required for each spatial category to accommodate a museum's upgraded programs in expansions. Some cases utilized a normative distribution of building space for functional zones as a benchmark: 40% for A-1 zone (public/collection), and 20% for each of A-0 (public/non-collections), B-1 (private/collections), and B-0% (private/non-collection) zones (Lord, 2012b, 466–467). This normative distribution has presented an assumption that, in a typical museum, 60% of the building would be allocated with front-of-the-house (A) spaces, whereas 40% of the building space would accommodate back-of-the-house (B) functions. In particular, one assumption is that A-1 zones (gallery spaces) would require twice as much area than B-1 (storage areas) where the works are in compact placement. The normative distribution could serve as a guide to understanding the reasons why a specific museum may deviate from it, i.e., why they would choose to invest in certain functions more or less than the typical models? (Lord, 2012b, 467). The spatial categories in the *Four-Zone Diagram* can also be utilized to outline access, circulation, and adjacency relationships among museum spaces.

The *Four-Zone Diagram* provides a robust and systematic framework to articulate size, access-circulation-adjacency, and materiality features of the museum spaces. Therefore, it can be useful for top-down implementation of institutional goals. On the other hand, this planning model can be advanced by taking visitor experiences into consideration and thus utilizing a bottom-up articulation of museum spaces. Next, I explore how to develop a model by thinking of visitor experiences in museum galleries.

Gallery Spaces and Size Requirements

The benchmark on a normative distribution just discussed implies that the front-of the house areas, especially exhibition galleries, require the largest square footage of a typical museum building. One factor driving the size of galleries in support of collection interpretation is how much of the collections are placed in galleries or are to be stored—in other words, the ratio of the works on display versus those kept in storage (Lord, 2012a, 213).[4] The growing trend for art museums is to show as many of the popular collection pieces as possible in galleries. For example, in the last two decades MoMA aimed to exhibit a greater number of the works from their collection in order to continue exploring story of the modern art dynamically, so the recent expansion projects (2005 and 2019) have increased the gallery space dramatically. The second factor that determines size of gallery spaces is about the exhibition strategies. One of the most used exhibition strategies that drive gallery size requirement is the *display density*, or how many works of art can be seen in a unit gallery space (Lord, 2012a, 214). Placed in modestly sized galleries, dense displays representing a certain genre or period support a comparative reading in context, and thus usually imply a scholarly layer of interpretation to the art. For example, in compact form of the YCBA galleries, a secluded part reserved as a "focus gallery" (Figure 11.8a) exhibits the period portraiture and landscape paintings in very dense arrays on its walls, supporting the museum's research studies (Trumble, 2005). Displays in low density placement, on the other hand, require generously sized galleries, and may facilitate appreciation of unique qualities of masterpieces through vistas in space. The average size of the works also plays a role in determining the required gallery area; works of contemporary art, whether large murals, video, or sculpture installations, usually require spacious galleries in order for them to be experienced from multiple viewpoints. In addition to these exhibition strategies, another factor that calibrates the required amount of gallery space is the projected number of simultaneous visitors. Indeed, this factor can be rather hard to plan for because some museums receive a high volume of attendance immediately after their re-opening. A higher volume of expected attendees may call for managing visitor flows through larger and more legibly arranged spaces in entrance lobbies, ticketing, circulation, and other service areas.

The amount of space dedicated to exhibition galleries can drive the overall size of the museum building. The size of a museum building, on the other hand, has a direct impact on visitor experiences; for example, visitors may have a very different experience when navigating in large gallery spaces and visiting exhibits one after another. In large museum complexes, the information overload and physical fatigue of visitors may be remedied by adding points of pause and vistas. This relates to access, circulation, and adjacency requirements, the planning of which should also incorporate the consideration of visitor experiences.

Gallery Spaces with Access, Circulation, and Adjacency Requirements
A number of planning models in museum practice have used access, circulation, and adjacency diagrams to plan the access-circulation relationships among museums' spatial categories with consideration of amount of space planned for them

Figure 11.8 a) Focus Gallery section at the YCBA's Permanent Collection Galleries; b) Expansion wing section of the Skyway Galleries at the HMA. Photographs: the author.

(Martin, 2012). Further articulation of these spatial categories presents opportunities to envision visitor itineraries in detail and in concert with museum goals.

Good museum design can direct visitors to required areas, such as ticketing and security check, and then guide them to exhibition galleries, or towards optional destinations, such as education rooms, performance halls, or other service areas. Gallery areas are positioned for direct access after the entrance hall and are separated from non-collection spaces in order to maintain visitors' focused interest on the exhibitions. In large and complex museums, visitors' navigation may need to be directed effectively towards the gallery areas as intended, because visitors' attention plummets after the first 30–50 minutes of their visit (Falk, 2000; Falk and Dierking, 1992). This can be achieved by managing the flow at entrances and providing views to reference areas as well as points for pause and restorative breaks (Kaplan et al., 1993; Kaplan and Kaplan, 1982). The author's analyses of on the YCBA, the MoMA, and the HMA (Rohloff, 2009a, 2011) suggests that visitors tend to pause to visually scan the museum setting when the layout offers vistas to other points of reference within the building. Furthermore, gallery layouts of the MoMA's 2004 wing had few vistas to the atrium. This confinement within homogenously sized gallery rooms and their openings resulted in a missing sense of hierarchy in navigation paths (Figure 11.9). This issue seems to be remedied with the MoMA's latest expansion project (2019) with the new layout designed to highlight a primary navigation path (Figure 11.10) while providing vistas from galleries to performance and workshop spaces (Diller, 2017).

Figure 11.9 View from the MoMA's Painting and Sculpture (fifth floor) galleries, 2005. Photograph: Sophia Psarra.

Figure 11.10 The MoMA Expansion and Renovation, by Diller Scofidio+Renfro in collaboration with Gensler, 2019, New York: a) Stacked gallery floor plans highlighting the new and renovated spaces at MoMA; b) Diagram of the planned flow connecting the existing and extended galleries. Images: Diller Scofidio + Renfro.

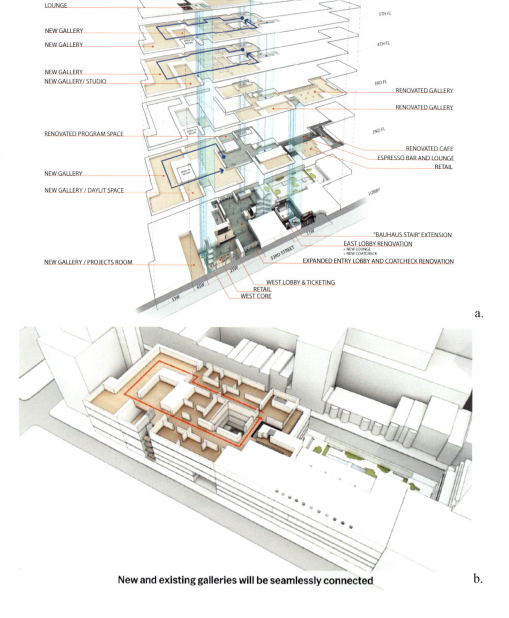

CONCLUSION

This chapter suggests that the profound role of architecture for art museums can be understood when the architectural design is evaluated in terms of spatial organization and its effects on visitor experience. Understanding this role of architecture in the scope of gallery design can be vital to implementing new museum settings in concert with the goals of an institution. The visitor experiences can then be envisioned in detail and gallery areas can be purposefully designed to facilitate intense and focused reading of exhibits or holistic viewing or else leisurely appreciation the works of art. Moreover, gallery spaces also often need to be formulated in coherence with other spaces in museum building, supporting the cultural program. For large and complex art museums, the planning phase benefits from a systematic model overseeing space requirements for museum programs in relationship with each other. Within this systematic model, space requirements for gallery spaces could be articulated with visitor experiences in mind, in particular when specifying size of space, or access, and adjacency requirements. A key strategy for institutional growth lies in envisioning visitor itineraries in support of visitors' comfort, satisfaction, and intended interactions with the art. With a thoughtful attention to design, planning for the architecture of the new art museum should incorporate an empathic understanding of visitor journeys in galleries with systematic formulation of space programing requirements.

NOTES

1. S. Psarra (2009b) examines this contrast in comparison of a science and an art museum.
2. The analysis presented here is part of the author's PhD thesis (2009) co-chaired by Jean D. Wineman and Sophia Psarra.
3. S. Psarra (2009a) provides a detailed discussion on the narrative structure and viewing sequences at MoMA (2005)'s galleries, drawing upon the research project performed by a team she supervised as a principal investigator.
4. B. Lord (2012a) discusses planning techniques with the term *display/storage ratio*.

REFERENCES

Brenneman, David. 2006. "High Museum of Art's Collections and Exhibition Programs." Atlanta, GA.

Cove, Jeffrey. 2006. "Curatorial Intent in the High Museum of Art's Skyway Floor." Atlanta, GA.

Diller, Elizabeth. 2017. "The Museum of Modern Art: Renovation and Expansion." www.dsrny.com: DillerScofidio+Renfro (in collaboration with Gensler).

Elderfield, John. 2004. "The Front Door to Understanding". In *Modern Painting and Sculpture: 1880 to the Present at the Museum of Modern Art*, ed. John Elderfield, 8–59. New York: The Museum of Modern Art, New York.

Falk, John. H. 2000. "The Physical Context". In *Learning from Museums: Visitor Experiences and the Making of Meaning*, John. H. Falk, 53–67. Walnut Creek, CA: Altamira Press.

Falk, John. H., and Lynn D. Dierking. 1992. *The Museum Experience*. Washington, D.C: Whalesaleback Books.

Hillier, Bill, and Jullienne Hanson. 1984. *The Social Logic of Space*. New York: Cambridge University Press.

Hillier, Bill, and Alan Penn. 1991. "Visible Colleges: Structure and Randomness in the Place of Discovery". *Science in Context* 4(1): 23–49.

Kaplan, Stephen, Lisa V. Bardwell, and Deborah B. Slakter. 1993. "The Museum as a Restorative Environment". *Environment and Behavior* 25(6): 725–742.

Kaplan, Stephen, and Rachel Kaplan. 1982. *Cognition and Environment: Functioning in an Uncertain World*. New York: Praeger.

Lord, Barry. 2012a. "Modes of Display". In *Manual of Museum Planning*, eds Barry Lord, Gail Dexter Lord and Lindsay Martin, 212–219. Plymouth, UK: Alta Mira Press.

Lord, Barry. 2012b. "Museum Building Zones and Functional Areas". In *Manual of Museum Planning*, eds Barry Lord, Gail Dexter Lord and Lindsay Martin, 457–467. Plymouth, UK: Alta Mira Press.

Lowry, Glenn D. 2005. *The New Musuem of Modern Art*. Worldwide: Thames and Hudson.

Markus, Thomas A. 1987. "Buildings as classifying devices". *Environment and Planning B: Planning and Design* 14: 467–484.

Markus, Thomas A. 1993. *Buildings and Power*. New York, NY: Routledge.

Martin, Lindsay. 2012. "Facility Strategies and Functional Programs". In *Manual of Museum Planning*, eds Barry Lord, Gail Dexter Lord and Lindsay Martin, 473–483. Plymouth, UK: Alta Mira Press.

Meyers, Amy. 2005. *Reinstallation of the Permanent Collection*. New Haven, CT: The Yale Center for British Art.

Meyers, Amy. 2007. "About the Center." [Web page]. *The Yale Center for British Art*, accessed March.

Naredi-Rainer, Paul von. 2004a. "The Museum as a Building Type - a Historical Survey". In *A Design Manual: Museum Buildings*, Paul von Naredi-Rainer, 19–28. Basel: Birkhauser.

Naredi-Rainer, Paul von. 2004b. "The Museum as Institution". In *A Design Manual: Museum Buildings*, Paul von Naredi-Rainer, 13–18. Basel: Birkhauser.

Newhouse, Victoria. 2005. *Art and the Power of Placement*. New York, NY: Monacelli Press.

Noordegraaf, Julia. 2004. *Strategies of Display*. Rotterdam. Museum Boijmans Van Beuningen: NAi Publishers.

Pradinuk, Ray. 1986. *Art Gallery Room Sequences: Pedagogic, Social, Categoric and Mnemonic Effects*. Master of Philosophy thesis. London, UK: University College London (UCL).

Prown, Jules David. 1977. *The Architecture of the Yale Center for British Art*. New Haven, CT: Yale University Press.

Prown, Jules David. 1983. "On Being a Client". *The Journal of Society of Architectural Historians* 42((March 1983)): 11–14.

Psarra, Sophia. 2009a. "Tracing the Modern: space, display and exploration in the Museum of Modern Art". In *Architecture and Narrative*, Sophia Psarra, 185–210. New York: Routledge.

Psarra, Sophia. 2009b. "Victorian knowledge: the Natural History Museum, London and the Art Gallery and Museum, Kelvingrove, Glasgow". In *Architecture and Narrative*, Sophia Psarra, 137–160. New York: Routledge.

Rohloff, Kaynar İpek. 2009a "Experiencing Museum Gallery Layouts through Local and Global Visibility Properties." 7th International Space Syntax Symposium, Stockholm, June 8-11, 2009.

Rohloff, Kaynar İpek. 2009b. "Museum Gallery Layouts and Their Interactions with Exhibition Narratives and Space Use Patterns." Ph.D Dissertation, University of Michigan.

Rohloff, Kaynar İpek. 2011. "Aligning Museum Building Projects with Institutional Goals", *Working Papers in Museum Studies*, No. 6, 1–25. Ann Arbor, MI, University of Michigan.

Serota, Nicholas. 1997. *Experience or Interpretation: The Dilemma of Museums of Modern Art*. New York, NY: Thames and Hudson.

Staniszewski, Mary Anne. 1998. *The Power Of Display*. Cambridge, MA: MIT Press.

Trumble, Angus. 2005. "The YCBA's Permanent Collection Display." New Haven, CT, Summer 2005.

Turner, Alasdair. 2001. "Depthmap: A Program to Perform Visibility Graph Analysis." 3rd International Space Syntax Symposium, Atlanta, GA: The Georgia Institute of Technology.

Turner, Alasdair, Maria Doxa, David O'Sullivan, and Alan Penn. 2001. "From 'Isovist' to Visibility Graph: Amethodology for Analyzing the Architectural Space". *Environment and Planning B: Planning an Design* 28(1): 103–121.

CHAPTER 12

Illuminating History

The Mosegaard Museum, in Aarhus Denmark

Jade Polizzi

The building emerges from the ground, peeking out, as an artifact that has become exposed to the elements after decades of being buried (Figure 12.1). The visitor's eye catches the white of the concrete protruding from the sea of green grass and notes that the structure seems to be revealing itself, rising from the ground and intended to be discovered and enjoyed. In a country known for originality, for clean and beautiful design, and the world's happiest people, this museum reflects the characteristics that define the Danish experience. The Moesgaard Museum, in Aarhus Denmark is a place where visitors are exposed to full sensory experience that can spark an interest in human evolution in one brief visit. Using state of the art technology the Moesgaard Museum immerses its visitors with the story of our ancestors through beautifully curated exhibits that tell of the perilous and often tragic upward climb that humankind has made in developing our civilizations.

Many of today's contemporary museums are vast in size: Zaha Hadid's MAXXI is almost 300,000 square feet, the Tate Modern complex by Herzog and de Meuron is over 370,000 square feet, Renzo Piano's California Academy of Sciences is 400,000 square feet, and Mexico's National Museum of Anthropology designed in 1964 by Pedro Ramírez Vázquez is an astounding 857,890 square feet. At 172,000 square feet, the Moesgaard Museum is average-to-small in size compared to other museums, yet it is large in stature for a building in the city of Aarhus with a population of less than 350,000. And yet, for a small city, Aarhus has many high-quality attractions. Visitors can tour the rainbow panorama in the ARoS art museum in the morning

Figure 12.1 Exterior of the Moesgaard Museum designed by Henning Larsen Architects. Aarhus, Denmark, 2014. Photo: Media Department-Moesgaard Museum.

and dine in one of the four Michelin-star restaurants in the evening. Modern architecture abounds with attractions such as the Iceberg, a series of jagged structures containing apartments located on the harbor, Dokk1: the public library and cultural center opened in 2015, or the Harbor Bath: a public swimming platform designed by the noteworthy Danish architecture firm Bjarke Ingels Group. With this variety of cultural attractions, it's clear that Aarhus, a vibrant and walkable university town, feels like a good fit for an internationally renowned archeological museum.

The original Moesgaard Museum began in the early 1970's, in a manor house on the Jutland peninsula. The former museum structure is located nearby the new building and is currently used by the archeology and anthropology department of Aarhus University. The museum artifacts are primarily Danish in origin.

The concept for the new Moesgaard Museum, designed by Henning Larsen Architects, was to integrate the landscape into the natural surroundings of the Skåde district. The new structure opened in 2014 and is known for the slanted and publicly accessible roof structure. The building is triangular, rising from the ground and roofed in grass (Figure 12.2). Visitors can be seen walking up the structure to catch views of the surrounding landscape, delighting in a mid-afternoon picnic, and children are fond of running up the grassy structure to then roll down the incline. During the winter the roof is open and enjoyed for sledding.

Having a stepped floor plan has an additional benefit to the design: it creates a series of internal layers which in turn creates exhibit space similar to that of earth's stratum (Figure 12.3). Entering on level 0 and descending either upward or downward the visitor inside of the museum becomes a temporary archeologist, unearthing and discovering artifacts belonging to our ancestors.

Upon entering the building, the visitor is exposed to the grand foyer, where ticket sales, gift shop, and cafe are located. This expansive space runs the full width of the building and contains the grand staircase, showcasing each of the structure's levels. A

ILLUMINATING HISTORY 217

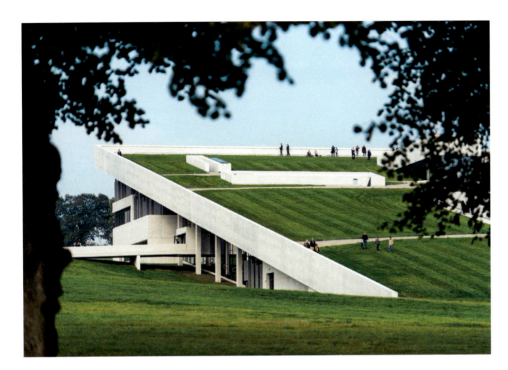

Figure 12.2 The occupiable green roof. Photo: Media Department-Moesgaard Museum.

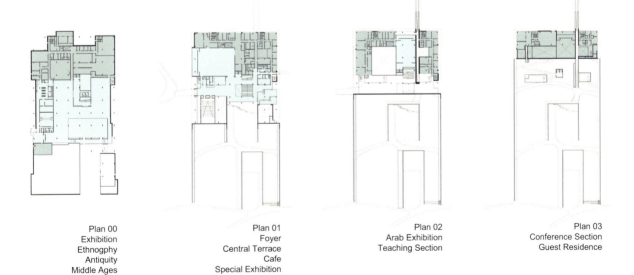

Plan 00
Exhibition
Ethnogphy
Antiquity
Middle Ages

Plan 01
Foyer
Central Terrace
Cafe
Special Exhibition

Plan 02
Arab Exhibition
Teaching Section

Plan 03
Conference Section
Guest Residence

Figure 12.3 Floor plans showing Levels 00–03 of the Moesgaard Museum. Henning Larsen Architects.

simple material palette of wooden slats, concrete, and glass harmonize together to give a clean and sophisticated atmosphere (Figure 12.4). From the foyer one can exit onto the grassy roof or begin to enjoy the archeological displays dotting the grand staircase.

The upstairs portion of the museum is devoted primarily to ethnography and also includes temporary exhibitions, while the downstairs, or belowground, section of the museum contains the permanent exhibitions. The exhibits are divided

Figure 12.4 Entrance foyer and the grand staircase exhibiting The Evolution Stairs. Photo: Media Department-Moesgaard Museum.

into four parts: Stone Age, Bronze Age, Iron Age, and Viking Age, relating primarily to the region of Scandinavia and more specifically Denmark. A feature of the Moesgaard Museum that is uncommon in many other museums is that their exhibitions are designed by an in-house design studio created through a collaboration of set designers, user-experience designers, archaeologists, photographers, and game designers (Madsen 2017).

At the center of the grand staircase directing the user either upstairs or downstairs are two sets of wax figures transcending time to create The Evolution Stairs and Origin Stairs. The Evolution Stairs contain a group of seven anatomically correct figures occupying the staircase bringing the visitor into the past to when

Figure 12.5 Interacting with historical figures on The Origin Stairs. Photo: Media Department-Moesgaard Museum.

Lucy, the infamous Australopithecus, walked the planet. The other group of mannequins located at the top of the staircase are people from our present time: Paul Gurrumurruwuy, an Aboriginal Australian, Galina Ainatgual, a Chukchi from northern Siberia, and Stephen Hawking, Britain's most well-known theoretical physicist. These three characters are engaged in a recorded conversation explaining their diverse opinions on the evolution of humankind and the afterlife. The visitor traveling on the staircase becomes a part of the display either by mingling with our ancestors or as a witness to the philosophical debate revolving around spiritual beliefs and their cultural context (Figure 12.5).

Historically, museums have displayed their artifacts by showcasing these precious individual objects in a linear fashion with a corresponding small label which defines and gives general information on the given object including the location of discovery and the estimated date of creation. This method of teaching through display does little to engage the public as the context and content is often only factual with information that is typically overly scientific. The Moesgaard Museum creates a user experience where the audience feels that they are part of an excavation: this transmedial experience tells a story, mostly fictional based on cultural theories, about the people who used the artifacts. Tosca writes that, "a transmedial museum experience is the aesthetic encounter of a user with the complex object that is the conjunction of historical artefact, informative label and fictional stories on different media platforms" (Tosca 2016). These stories, which are largely historical fiction, give life to the museum artifacts, they create an atmosphere that connects today's user to the past. Who were the people who produced these tools, weapons, and objects of beauty? One exhibit tells a story about a boy's rite of passage into adulthood through the gift of a razor for shaving his facial hair. The discovery shows that ancient man may not be so different than the people we are today.

The display exhibits include more than just singular objects cherished independently and without context. The designers choose to showcase multiples objects in many of their displays to strengthen the effect. Approximately 20 hair combs are piled onto each other reinforcing that this common tool was constructed thousands upon thousands of times with the primary purpose of untangling hair. When observing the armor used by soldiers the display contains each of the tools and weapons a soldier may use presented in a collection and repeated in rows: a helmet, stones for throwing, awl, and multiple spears. The repetition of this armor over 40 times results in the effect of a small army pressing an attack (Figure 12.6).

Figure 12.6 Artifact Display: a figurative army. Photograph: the Author.

Voyaging through the historical exhibits of the Moesgaard museum is a full sensory experience. The exhibit design blends sound, sight, texture, and technology seamlessly together to create an interactive atmosphere of storytelling and exploration.

The exhibits have a soundtrack of sorts, a faint background music playing an avantgarde electronic undersong that gives a glittering or somber mood to the space based on each display. Many of the displays communicate directly with museumgoers – some through the use of headphones answering questions by today's specialists displayed on a screen. Other auditory communications are in the form of a videotaped lecture by a life-size and present-day expert. In the day of the dead exhibit a camera scans your body and projects your moving form as a skeleton dancing along with a mariachi band of skeletons. These techniques create a personal experience for the visitor (Price 2015). An auditory and an engaged visual experience with the exhibit provides an opportunity to share the experience with others and allows for a dialog amongst visitors. In sharing and discussing museum experiences, knowledge about the exhibit becomes further embedded in our minds creating a longer-lasting memory.

To better create a contemplative mood most of the exhibits are dark with minimal lighting, allowing the participant to feel that they are on a path of discovery, unearthing humankind's ancient treasures. Because most of the peripheral space is dark and the objects are spot lit, the viewer feels an intimacy with the artifacts. Other times lighting is used to create an experiential atmosphere. Rippling light is projected on the floor while walking by a canoe making the visitor feel that they themselves are wading through water. In the Stone Age exhibit the night sky appears, highlighting the cosmos and challenging us to marvel at the process of human evolution (Figure 12.7). And later, thunder and lightning set the stage for a pending storm while fishermen are out at sea attempting to trap fish and hunt porpoise (Modegaard Museum no date).

Materiality and color play a strong role in how the museum exhibit is experienced. Rough stone, aged wood, and smooth metal work together to create a dialog with each artifact. In one Stone Age exhibit golden shafts of wheat laser cut from brass plates can be seen bending and swaying at the visitor's touch. Materials spill from the exhibits and cascade to the viewers feet in the case of a display that shows a young girl and her child collecting food amidst a mountain of oyster shells. In a prehistory exhibit two red walls are pierced through with spears representing blood spilled over the years through war.

Other ways to engage the audience is through the use of digital technology. The museum designers used animation and film to communicate stories creating a scenographic environment for the visitor. Some screens are small, where individual viewers touch a question to watch archeologists, scholars, and historians explain

Figure 12.7 The cosmos illuminates the Stone Age exhibit. Photo: Media Department-Moesgaard Museum.

a theory or discuss an object's significance in time. Other screens are large, taking up the whole room. A museumgoer watches an animated battle projected onto the wall or looks in plan as dots, representing soldiers, from different tribes converge into war. Another exhibit is a video depiction of a muted watercolor cartoon with two troops of soldiers advancing towards each other in preparation for battle. The exhibit designers make a stronger impact by placing the visitor in the center of these two concave screens, each approximately 25 feet wide, where you are now in the center of the battle (Figure 12.8).

At the Moesgaard Museum exhibits talk, music plays, lights twinkle, and a mechanical breeze is created to heighten the mood. This sensory experience affects the way that the visitors explore the museum exhibits. Kali Tzortzi (2017) noted in *Museum Architecture for Embodied Experience,* that because the viewer is drawn into the exhibits they tend to spend a longer time viewing and give more attention to displays than in a typical museum. The display is akin to installation art. While this makes for a more powerful experience it is possible to feel a sensory overload. To help relieve that overload, each exhibition room has a corresponding break room. The break rooms give views to the surrounding landscape and provide a place to sit and relax while digesting all that has been seen. Some of these spaces

Figure 12.8
Animated narratives communicate proposed stories of historic times. Photo: Media Department-Moesgaard Museum.

exit out onto the large grass rooftop and others are windows looking onto Aarhus Bay and the surrounding forests and meadows (Figure 12.9).

The best-known artifacts in the museum are the human remains from prehistoric people; the Bronze Age Borum Eshøj bodies and the Grauballe Man, also known as the bog body. The Borum Eshøj bodies are a series of three family members dating back over three thousand years found in oak coffins (Figure 12.10). They are displayed next to each other placed in their individual log coffins inside of a full-size barrow. Neil Price (2015) comments that,

> What (is experienced) is the manner of the telling, which is stunning. Without wanting to give too much away, visitors encounter an immersive theatre of the night sky set against solar motifs and the looming image of the burial mound; this culminates in the log coffins of the Borum Eshøj grave actually situated inside a full-size barrow, lit by a subterranean sun. Here, the contemplative music really works; one stands alone with the dead in an earthen chamber and a sense of a genuine resting place with a dignity and respect far, far beyond what is common. Long after leaving, I found myself thinking of the Borum people down there in the dark, in what is quite truly a new grave, in the silence of the museum's night-time closure.

When entering the exhibit for the Grauballe Man the surface of the ground shifts from hard stone to a spongy material, as if one were walking through a wetland

Figure 12.9 Visitors can refresh themselves by quickly escaping to outdoor space. Photo: Media Department-Moesgaard Museum.

marsh. As this bog was a place of sacrifice the viewer is exposed to the multitudes of weapons and artifacts that were discovered in the Danish marsh, culminating in the Grauballe Man, the world's best-preserved bog body. It is thought that this man was a religious sacrifice thrown into a bog, yet the climate preserved him so that his hair, skin and even the slit in his throat can be witnessed (Figure 12.11). The body is accompanied by a descriptive story, written by the museum archeologists:

> On a cold winter's day, a small group of people gathers on the edge of the bog where they have been cutting peat last summer. Amongst the villagers are a priest and a young man, who, despite the cold, is not wearing anything but a thin cloak. He is shivering as the priest prays to the gods to accept the offering the villagers are about to give them … When the priest is done, someone steps forward and takes the cloak of the shoulders of the young man. He stands in front of the naked man, and without looking him in the eye, swings a heavy wooden club, breaking the young man's left leg so he is forced to his knees. As he shouts out in pain, the priest grabs his hair, draws back his head and quickly

Figure 12.10 The Borum Eshøj family in their burial chamber underneath a full-size barrow. Photo: Media Department-Moesgaard Museum.

cuts his throat from left to right with a sharp knife, instantly silencing the man's moaning. Bleeding heavily, the man loses consciousness within minutes and then dies. The villagers watch in silence as his life's blood flows into the waters of the bog. Then, two men lift the naked body and place it in one of the summer's peat cuttings. They cover it with turfs to stop it from floating up and step back as the priest raises his arms in prayer once more, beseeching the gods to be merciful and provide for their people. The villagers join him in prayer and then head back to their homes in the village, leaving the bog, where nothing stirs anymore besides the birds and the wind rustling in the branches of the trees.

(Mosegaard Museum, MOMU)

This story is contrived of historical assumptions and we will never know the truth of what happened. However, providing a descriptive story relating to the exhibit enhances the viewers understanding of the lives of our ancestors and creates a stronger emotional experience.

Architecture is not solely about structure and materiality. The architecture of a building inside and out should create an atmosphere (Tzortzi 2017). A building must do more than contain space, it has the potential to create an emotional experience. This can be done by simply changing the temperature in a space from warm and embracing to cool and mysterious. Lighting in a space, whether daylit or mechanically lit, can create tension, it can encourage a user to pause or to move

Figure 12.11
Grauballe Man. Photo: Media Department-Moesgaard Museum.

through a space. Sound draws upon past experiences, reminding one of happy times or stirring primordial emotions by resonating with our rhythmic cycle. Texture is a tool that most designers use frequently in the selection of materials, yet it is often done based on color or for the purpose of assembly. Selecting materials based on the surface and user experience elevates the character of the environment from just a space to a place of memory. At the Moesgaard Museum the building and exhibits, produce a multisensory experience. The use of film, animation, music, lighting, written descriptions in the form of narratives, and textural displays all work together with the artifacts of the museum to stir the visitor's imagination allowing the museumgoer to travel through time to a historic world. The stone and metal used to construct the building speak to a permanence but the way the building sinks into the land reminds us that permanence is an illusion and that one day we will not be a part of this landscape.

The combination of architecture and exhibit design creates a multi-dimensional setting for the viewer to represent a synthesis that blends modern architecture and the latest technology with historical and archeological artifacts. The form of the museum works in conjunction with the exhibit design to create a historical continuum. Former museum director, Jan Skamby Madsen says of the process,

"[Designing the museum] was about creating the opportunity to facilitate our knowledge in a way that is interesting to children, parents, and grandparents. There should be something for everyone in spite of their prerequisites" (Jensen 2014). A visitor at the Moesgaard museum is likely to feel that they are part of an excavation, unearthing artifacts that link the past and the present. As Travel + Leisure described the museum, "the Moesgaard is what you'd get if PBS's Nova documentaries stepped off the screen to mix with science experiments and the fashion runway—and then marched outside to an exquisitely landscaped lawn" (Heller 2016). The architects drew strength in the design by creating a series of juxtapositions: a place for indoor education and outdoor pastoral experiences, of darkness and light, warm and cold atmospheres, environments that are energetic such as a bustling cafe or somber and subdued in the tombs of the Garubaelle man. These juxtapositions create shifts in our senses that make the physical experience of visiting the museum an experience of lasting memory.

REFERENCES

Heller, Nathan. 2016. "Travel + Leisure." *Move Over, Copenhagen: In Denmark, It's All About Aarhus*, April 17.

Jensen, Josefine Lykke, Marie Abidhauge Oleson, Morten Schjodt-Pedersen, Camilla Bengtsen. 2014. *Mosegaard Museum-Part of the Landscape*. Issuu. November 24. Accessed October 2018. https://issuu.com/henninglarsenarchitects/docs/moesgaard_museum_magazine_web.

Madsen, Kristina Maria. May 30-June 2, 2017. "REDOing the Museum Exhibition Design." Kolding, Denmark: Proceedings from the Cumulus REDO Conference.*Mosegaard Museum, MOMU*. www.moesgaardmuseum.dk/en.

Price, Neil. 2015. "The New MOMU: Meeting the Family at Denmark's Flagship Museum of Prehistory and Ethnography." *Antiquity Publications Ltd, Issue 343, Vol. 89, (February 2015)* (Cambridge University Press) 478–484.

Tosca, Susana. 2016. "Transmedial Museum Experiences: The Case of Moesgaard." *Artnodes* (No. 18).

Tzortzi, Kali. 2017. "Museum Architecture for Embodied Experience." *Museum Management and Curatorship*, Vol. 32, No. 5, 491–508.

PART 4

BODIES AND MINDS

Designing for Inclusion

Differences in body type and brain structure subtly but powerfully change how people experience space, and while the architecture of museums has profound effects on all visitors, those with cognitive or physical differences are especially aware of spatial realities. While public buildings are usually required to be minimally accessible to people with impairments, this section explores how museum architecture can go beyond accessibility to including and celebrating the diversity of embodied experiences. Banasiak discusses museum architecture from the perspective of differing cognitive experiences, while Van Doren, Heylighen, and Vermeersch offer an analysis of museum space from differing physical abilities. Cranz closes the section with a call for body-conscious design in museums to account for difference and support health. Taken together, these chapters represent a challenge to museum designers for architecture that is more inclusive.

CHAPTER **13**

A Sensory Place for All

Meredith Banasiak

Drums, gongs, banjos, and even an electronic buzzing instrument called a theremin were being played by more than a dozen children in the Experience Gallery at the Musical Instrument Museum in Scottsdale, Arizona. "Does the noise ever get to you?," I yelled to the museum volunteer. She gave me an embarrassed grin and replied, "Yes – sometimes I get headaches."

"Do you have any floorplans of the museum for sale?," I asked the gift shop staff at the Denver Art Museum's Hamilton Building. "No," she replied, "though that would be a helpful thing to have. The building is very confusing. Even I have a hard time finding my way."

As illustrated in these vignettes, discordant sensory stimuli are often an underlying cause of undesirable outcomes for museum users ranging from headaches to disorientation. By examining the perceptual impacts created by interrelationships among user, museum, and exhibits, we can better understand how sensory variables impact a museum user's holistic experience, both positively and negatively. While all types of buildings should aim to optimize the relationship between user and environment, museums have an added challenge of integrating a third variable: the exhibit material, i.e., the contents. In museums, a user's holistic sensory experience consists of interrelationships between user-environment, user-contents, and environment-contents. Any discordancy within or between these components can disrupt the overall homeostatic experience. By cultivating an understanding of how stimuli are perceived by users, designers can better choreograph appropriate sense interactions which support and enrich an integrated museum experience.

SUPPORTING INCLUSIVITY ACROSS PERCEPTUAL ABILITIES

Civically-minded museums aim to serve and educate the public. Such a mission implies that museums would thereby adopt an inclusive approach to the design of their environments, learning programs, and aesthetic experiences to best serve a diversity of public visitors. Universal Design describes an ethical orientation that supports inclusivity across age, physical mobility, cognitive and perceptual ability, language and literacy, and gender identification. Seven Principles of Universal Design were developed by The Center for Universal Design to address the spectrum of physical, sensory and informational user experience (Table 13.1). The aim to optimize perceptible information (Principle Four) states that, "The design communicates necessary information effectively to the user, regardless of ambient conditions or the user's sensory abilities" (The Center for Universal Design 1997). This principle is particularly important to achieve an integrated experience for the user by reconciling conflicting information between environment and exhibit information, i.e., container-contents, for users of all perceptual abilities. Inclusivity associated with neurodiversity, including diversity among cognitive and sensory experience, is a consideration most absent from universal design dialogs in museum architecture. With recent advances in cognitive science, evidence

Table 13.1 The Principles of Universal Design, Version 2.0. Copyright © 1997 North Carolina State University, The Center for Universal Design

PRINCIPLE ONE: Equitable Use
The design is useful and marketable to people with diverse abilities.

PRINCIPLE TWO: Flexibility in Use
The design accommodates a wide range of individual preferences and abilities.

PRINCIPLE THREE: Simple and Intuitive Use
Use of the design is easy to understand, regardless of the user's experience, knowledge, language skills, or current concentration level.

PRINCIPLE FOUR: Perceptible Information
The design communicates necessary information effectively to the user, regardless of ambient conditions or the user's sensory abilities.

PRINCIPLE FIVE: Tolerance for Error
The design minimizes hazards and the adverse consequences of accidental or unintended actions.

PRINCIPLE SIX: Low Physical Effort
The design can be used efficiently and comfortably and with a minimum of fatigue.

PRINCIPLE SEVEN: Size and Space for Approach and Use
Appropriate size and space is provided for approach, reach, manipulation, and use regardless of user's body size, posture, or mobility.

is increasingly available to inform how interactions among brain, body, and environment can optimize the perceptibility of information. Thus, all museums have the ability and imperative to design for cognitive and perceptual inclusivity.

PERCEPTIBLE INFORMATION: NOT ENOUGH, TOO MUCH, AND JUST RIGHT

A landmark event occurred in 2004 when a complaint was filed against the International Spy Museum in Washington, D.C. for being inaccessible to those with visual impairments. It was a case of "not enough" perceptible information to support the sensory needs of all users. The Department of Justice reached a settlement agreement with the museum in 2008 requiring significant facility revisions to ensure access citing Title III of the Americans with Disabilities Act (ADA) which, "prohibits discrimination on the basis of disability in the activities of places of public accommodations" (Department of Justice 2008). This cautionary precedent prompted American museums to evolve from exhibits that were largely unisensory, i.e., exclusively visual, to exhibits which provided multisensory experiences. These updates were made with respect to both informational and artifactual accessibility. As a result, many museums provide print and electronic informational materials across multiple formats such as audio, large print, braille, and languages, and many exhibits themselves often include sensory material such as tactile, smell, sound, and even taste experiences to supplement and enhance visual content.

The 2015 Tate Sensorium at Tate Britain was groundbreaking in both design and research aims to advance multisensory access to exhibits. This temporary exhibit enabled visitors to experience a small collection of visual art works through all senses, including through the use of a novel haptic technology using ultrasound pressure-induced tactile patterns congruent with the visual paintings (Vi et al. 2017). It was anticipated that the orchestrated multisensory engagement would offer visitors greater stimulation and emotional engagement with the art when compared to a purely visual engagement with the art. To evaluate whether these aims were met, select visitors volunteered to participate in a study sharing their liking and arousal experience for the art. In addition, study participants were asked to comment on whether their non-visual, haptic perceptual experience matched their visual experience of the painting. Results indicated that the multisensory correlation embedded in the exhibit experience for each painting supported greater stimulation, immersion, opportunity to focus, and emotional connection. Researchers also tested tactile patterns incongruent with the visual paintings with the result that users reported feeling "distraction" created by the sensory conflict (Vi et al. 2017).

Another milestone advancing integrative sensory exhibit design was Cooper Hewitt's 2018 "The Senses: Design Beyond Vision" whose explicit goal was to

Figure 13.1 Installation photo of "The Senses: Design Beyond Vision" at Cooper Hewitt, Smithsonian Design Museum, April 13 through October 28, 2018. Visitors experience a multisensory interaction with falling snow in the exhibit, "Snow Storm" by Christopher Brosius, by touching and smelling suspended balls of felted wool infused with a winter-inspired scent. Photograph by Scott Rudd Associates, courtesy Cooper Hewitt, Smithsonian Design Museum.

Figure 13.2 Installation photo of "The Senses: Design Beyond Vision." Visitors can experience over 100 sensations such as "A bag of microwave popcorn" through immersive tactile vibrations and audio narratives in the exhibit, "Seated Catalog of Feelings" by Sosolimited. Photograph by Scott Rudd Associates, courtesy Cooper Hewitt, Smithsonian Design Museum.

"expand the discourse on inclusive design" (Baumann 2018, 6) by including multisensory information embedded within art (Figure 13.1, Figure 13.2). The exhibit also provided information about the art accessible across multiple means of communication (text, braille, and audio). As curators Ellen Lupton and Andrea Lipps explained, "When designers address multiple senses, products and services reach a greater diversity of users" (Baumann 2018, 6), and support the changing sensory abilities of individual users over a lifetime (Lupton and Lipps 2018, 14).

The Tate Britain's and Cooper Hewitt's innovation in sensory exhibit design demonstrates the important role of sensory stimuli in effectively communicating information. This integration approach is necessary for achieving a "just-right" state of perceptible information. Access to perceptible information is a fundamental need pervasive across all perceptual abilities, and most acute among persons with sensory processing differences. For example, during a study about museum design for persons with autism, one visitor compared her experience of incompatible sensations as equivalent to "bleach and coffee" (Tuckett, Marchant, and Jones 2004, 4.3). While providing an experience that relies on one sense, such as purely visual information, is not enough to communicate perceptible information, there is a complementary danger of having too much multi-sensory information, which can create an overwhelming experience for many users. Neither situation results in a perceptible nor inclusive experience. A possible litmus test is, "Does the museum need to provide alternative, and hence segregated and therefore inequitable, experiences for users with different sensory abilities and needs such as supplementary museum tours or visit times?" Such accommodations suggest that the typical museum experience as designed is somehow not supporting perceptible information on its own. As accessibility consultant and 2012 White House Champion of Change, Sina Bahram advocates, meeting the universal design principle of perceptible information includes: 1) providing equal access despite a sensory ability, and 2) eliminating disturbances – conflicting sensory stimuli such as noise – in the environment (Bahram 2018, 30).

The Tate Sensorium utilized a blank, black box to effectively tune out environmental stimuli so focus could be directed to the exhibit material, the contents. Intentionally embedding objects, buildings and exhibits with congruent multisensory information, so that the information perceived is complementary and redundant across the senses, can eliminate unintentional sensory disturbances and support everyone's ability to integrate information. Howes's approach to supporting the interrelationships of multisensory design (Howes 2013, Howes 2003) is captured in Upali Nanda's sensthetic model (Nanda 2005, 156) (Figure 13.3) where there is an emphasis on connections, or correspondences, between senses. Multisensory information redundant across the senses supports sensemaking, while conflicting

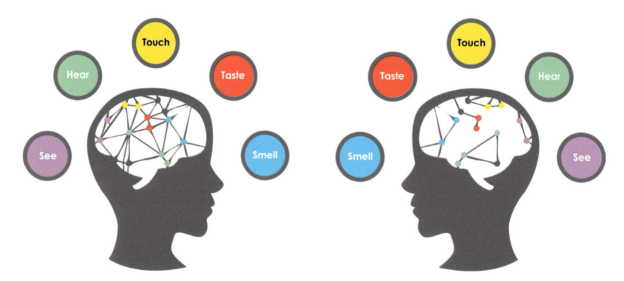

Figure 13.3 Node connection model (adapted from Nanda 2005, 158). The node-connection model illustrates Nanda's sensthetic framework describing how connections between sensory node modalities contribute to the overall experience of an environment. In the first diagram, the environment activates multiple senses which are complementary and correlated. The sense nodes have established, existing neuronal connections between them, and the information perceived is redundant across the senses, with the result that there is a coherent experience of place supporting sensemaking. In the second diagram, the environment activates multiple senses simultaneously, but there are no connections between the sense nodes. The senses may be perceiving conflicting information with the result that the overall experience of place is fragmented and perceptibility of it is confusing. Brain infographic adapted from design by Freepik.

sensory information such as visual and sound disconnect, can cause confusion or stress. Integrating sense information and maintaining sensory connections is a key strategy which can support sensemaking for all museum visitors.

Chronic detrimental effects of multisensory conflict caused by abundant and disconnected sensory information have been documented in long-term residents of urban environments where it is believed that psychotic symptoms and psychiatric disorders are triggered by an inability to inhibit the constant multitude of attention-demanding dissonant stimuli in the environment (Golembiewski 2017). The acute, short term effects of sensory conflict commensurate with museum visits are less understood.

WHEN SENSES ARE IN CONFLICT: AN IMPERCEPTIBLE EXPERIENCE

Daniel Libeskind's Frederic C. Hamilton Building at the Denver Art Museum opened in 2006; it was the first Libeskind building for the United States. Intended to be a statement piece for the city of Denver, its earliest concept drawings (Figure 13.4) referenced angled shapes inherent in the rocky mountain landscapes west of the city. However, the Hamilton building's form strongly contrasts other buildings in the immediate surrounding urban context.

Figure 13.4 Daniel Libeskind, Sketch for Form and Character (Panel 3), 2000. Libeskind's earliest concept for the Hamilton Building referenced angled shapes inherent in the rocky mountain landscapes. Image: the Denver Art Museum.

Libeskind was among the first to experiment with emerging 3D design, modeling, and digital-fabrication technology including using automated control for positioning the angles of the titanium and steel building elements (Johnson 2016). Prior to the emergence of these digital generation and fabrication tools, such non-orthogonal forms were largely cost prohibitive. Advances in technology supported the creation of new building forms. Users interacting with these new forms had new perceptual experiences with some unanticipated results.

The angled interior (Figure 13.5) of the Hamilton building is consistent with its exterior (Figure 13.6, see p. 239). Some users have reported experiencing a sense of dizziness in response to the angles, particularly on the main staircase where not only the walls and ceiling converge and diverge at angles, but also the floor plane inclines to provide the intended vertical circulation. The likely source of dizziness is a visitor's brain struggling to orient itself in space. Orientation relies on input from multiple sources. The brain attempts to integrate converging inputs from vestibular, visual, and proprioceptive systems to adjust posture and movement and maintain desired orientation. One source of input comes from vestibular structures in the inner ear. A layer of gravel-like crystals presses down on a dense bed of sensory cells in response to gravity (Baloh, Honrubia, and Kerber 2010) signaling whether the head (and by association, the body) is upright or tilted. Standing on the stairs, the message from these inner ear cells to the brain is, "upright!" Meanwhile, the visual system also contributes information about body position (Witkin and

238 MEREDITH BANASIAK

Figure 13.5 The four-story El Pomar Grand Atrium in the Denver Art Museum's Frederic C. Hamilton Building, 2006, Denver, Colorado. Some have reported experiencing dizziness while ascending on the museum's stair where the walls, ceiling and floors converge and diverge altering one's visual sense of being upright. Photograph © by Jeff Goldberg/Esto.: courtesy of the Denver Art Museum.

Asch 1948). The disorienting visual cues from the angled planes defining the stairway signal that the body is "*not* upright!" The result can be an imperceptible experience, "Am I upright? Am I not upright?," as the brain struggles to make sense of the competing messages and adjust body position. The result is that some users report experiencing a sense of dizziness. Similar disorienting experiences have been documented by users of Frank Gehry's buildings such as in MIT's Strata Center where the spatial complexity of the undulating planes in the conference room reportedly cause one third of visitors to feel dizzy (Smith 2007). Such dizziness effects not only create sensory discomfort, but also physical mobility concerns potentially increasing the risk of falls for visitors who miscalculate movements

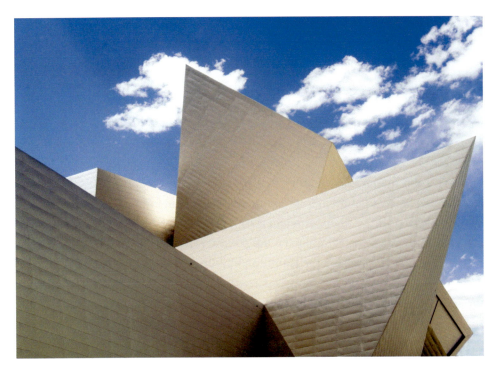

Figure 13.6 Titanium exterior of the Frederic C. Hamilton Building, 2006, Denver, Colorado. Emerging technology made it possible to construct new, angled building forms such as the Hamilton Building. Photograph by Jeff Wells, courtesy the Denver Art Museum.

resulting from conflicting sensory information. Libeskind's Contemporary Jewish Museum in San Francisco completed in 2008 also utilizes his characteristic angled forms; however, the stairs at the Contemporary Jewish Museum offer visitors one orthogonal side wall plane which helps orient visitors in space potentially reducing sensations of dizziness and subsequent falls.

Does the building emotionally bias or confuse what the experience of that same painting might be in a different physical environment? The architecture of the Hamilton building primes the user for an experience which may not be consistent with some of its visual art works and temporary exhibit themes. Studies have shown that context influences a user's ratings of beauty and preference for an artwork, and thus a museum can induce a certain way of viewing an object (van Paasschen, Bacci and Melcher 2015). According to Chatterjee and Vartanian's model of neuroaesthetic experience that illustrates the interaction between sensory–motor, emotion–valuation, and meaning–knowledge neural systems, (Chatterjee and Vartanian 2014) building geometries can influence a user's aesthetic experience and contribute to differences in perceived emotion and meaning (Banaei et al. 2017). Hence, the container-contents relationship, described as how the exhibit space and art legitimize each other (Joy 1998), is at odds in cases where there is a conflict between the perceptual responses generated by the building and by the art. For example, neuroscience studies have shown that a fear response is triggered in the brain by sharp objects and sharply angled spaces because sharpness signals threat (Bar and Neta 2007; Vartanian et al. 2013). The perceptual experience of the Hamilton building's sharp contours, as well as the stairwell experience which may predispose a user to sensations of dizziness, likely support a state of high physiological arousal. Yet, this architectural experience could be in conflict with visual art pieces which aim to support contemplative states more closely associated with calmness.

Tuning the interaction effect so that there is not a disconnect between building and art, between container and contents, means including or commissioning exhibit material which aligns with and is supported by the building itself. Certainly, not all art intends to be calming. To the contrary, highly arousing art forms exist and can be created for which the Hamilton building is an ideal resonator. The novel architectural form and resulting new perceptual experiences have been an impetus for artists and curators to inspire new art and exhibit installations created for this specific building (Lindsay 2016). Art with themes more aligned with the building's perceptual and emotional experience have emerged such as Matthew Brannon's large-scale vinyl wall mural "Last to Know" (2009) (Figure 13.7) commissioned for the angled wall of the Newman Overlook in a space adjacent to the stairs in

Figure 13.7 Matthew Brannon, *Last to Know*, 2009 Denver Art Museum Collection: Museum purchase with funds from Baryn, Daniel and Jonathan Futa, 2010.391. The sharpness of the symbolic content in this artwork complements the sloping walls and stairs of the Newman Overlook in the Frederic C. Hamilton Building. ©: of the artist and David Kordansky Gallery, Los Angeles, CA. Photograph courtesy the Denver Art Museum.

the Hamilton Building, amplifying sensations of sharpness. In addition, immersive exhibits including interactive animations projected on angled walls in cave-like spaces gives users realistic sensations of being on Arctic icebergs. In such cases, the museum's architecture and art comingle and is experienced by the whole body and multiple senses interacting.

Because the Denver Art Museum includes many temporary and rotating exhibits, exhibits which must fit into many different museum buildings along their tour, the museum faces a greater challenge in aligning perceptual experiences between container and contents than museums which house permanent collections where interactions can be better anticipated and choreographed from design inception.

A PERCEPTIBLE MUSEUM EXPERIENCE INTEGRATING USER, ENVIRONMENT, AND CONTENTS

The Holocaust Museum in Washington D.C. completed in 1993 designed by architect James Ingo Freed directs visitors through three floors of densely packed, emotionally charged permanent exhibition material detailing the history of the Holocaust and remembering its victims. Visitors start at the top of the building and descend floor by floor to the exit. After completing the exhibit material on one floor, and before beginning the content on the subsequent floor, visitors are brought into a lounge transition space (Figure 13.8). The entire museum experience culminates in a grand, awe-inspiring space: the empty Hall of Remembrance designed to be a

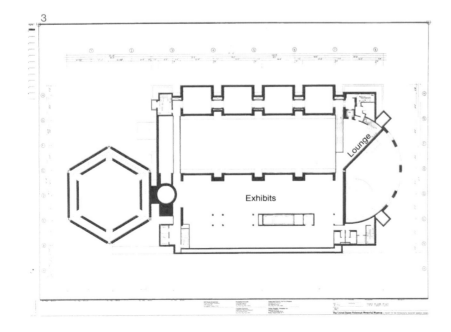

Figure 13.8
Exhibitions Division: Museum Floor Plan Drawings Used in the Visitor Brochure, ca. 1992, 3rd floor plan, United States Holocaust Memorial Museum, Washington, D.C. Visitors descend from the sensory dense 4th floor exhibit to the third-floor lounge before entering the dense 3rd floor exhibit space. USHMM Institutional Archives Accession No. 2002.107. Courtesy the United States Holocaust Memorial Museum.

"point of release for contemplation" (Giovanni 1993). The Hall of Remembrance and the lounges are a stark counterbalance to the sensory dense, highly stimulating exhibit spaces containing thousands of original objects from the Holocaust. These exhibit spaces with immersive, multisensory stimuli are intended to engage the body (Giovanni 1993). Even visual materials are so highly textured as to be tactile and cross-modally stimulate a visitor's sense of touch (Spence and Gallace 2011). Content alluding to horrors, and spaces eliciting a sense of being trapped activate a visitor's instinct to flee through motor neuron sensations and physiological stress response (Chatterjee 2014, Freedberg and Gallese 2007). As Freed explained, " … if you don't understand (the building) with your body, it's a failure … It must be intestinal, visceral; it must take you in its grip" (Giovanni 1993).

The lounges and Great Hall offer a sensory and emotional reprieve to strategically limit arousal at key intervals along the journey. Absent of attention-grabbing stimuli, the spaces optimize internal contemplation. It is the third-floor lounge which parallels the spatial vocabulary of the Libeskind buildings. Light bounces off the white angled planes, punctuated by Ellsworth Kelly's four white-wall sculptures, appropriately titled *Memorial* given its role in supporting memory creation

Figure 13.9 Third floor lounge in the United States Holocaust Memorial Museum. A stark contrast from the dark, and sensory dense exhibit spaces, light bounces off white angled planes in the 3rd floor lounge, punctuated by Ellsworth Kelly's four white wall sculptures, titled *Memorial*. Photograph by Timothy Hursley. Courtesy the United States Holocaust Memorial Museum.

and recall. (Figure 13.9). For memorial museums in particular, supporting memory is a key performance goal. This sculptural third floor lounge might be described as a *liminal space*, a space devoid of external attention demands to support internal mind wandering, "allowing the neural mechanisms of memory consolidation to activate" (Hoffman 2018). This design strategy to include liminal spaces in long routes of travel such as the museum visitor experience is supported by studies which suggest that having a few minutes of rest after learning can boost associative memory and support information retention, as compared to when attention is focused on additional new information (Craig et al. 2015). Thus, Freed's intent to create a "resonator of memory" (United States Holocaust Memorial Museum n.d.) is realized with much credit to his thoughtful inclusion of liminal spaces. In addition, because of the muted sensory stimuli in the lounges, they also serve as a de-escalation refuge for visitors across competencies including those who experience challenges with sensory processing (Whitby 2017). Providing spaces which offer an escape allows visitors more control over their sensory experience along the journey. As described on the museum website, this museum "is not a neutral shell" but rather a case where container and contents are strategically integrated to maximize the perceptual, and hence memory experience for all visitors.

CONCLUSION

With respect to the role of museum architecture's relationship to exhibit material, emerging scientific evidence suggests the building container does not have a neutral effect on its contents. The degree to which the sensory experience is aligned between container and contents can positively or negatively impact users' perceptual experience, and therefore their emotional and cognitive sense-making ability with respect to both art and environment.

While the angled white spaces within Libeskind's Hamilton Building and Freed's third floor lounge are superficially similar, their impacts on visitors are dissimilar based on their relationships to the art contents. In the case of the Hamilton building, the disorienting stair experience primes visitors for how they engage with subsequent artworks which may not always be consistent with the dizzying stair experience. Yet, in galleries where art has been specifically commissioned to be compatible with the angled space, there is an object-environment congruency reinforcing the holistic perceptual experience through consistent sensory messaging. In Freed's Holocaust Museum, the lounge spaces on each floor offer a rhythmic, complementary contrast by minimizing sensory information during key transition points along a sensory and emotionally demanding journey throughout the museum.

It is easier to align these disparate elements, container and contents, when the art content is a known and fixed quantity – as in the case of a permanent versus rotating exhibit. There is, however, an opportunity to use the building container to inspire new art forms and provoke experiences driven by the perceptual nature of the container itself as the curators and artists of the Denver Art Museum are exploring. No matter what the intended emotive or sensorial message, optimizing multisensory information and reducing sensory conflict between the art and the environment supports greater perceptibility of the messaging. Such a strategy not only promotes good design, but also ethical design by providing an experience supporting diverse perceptual abilities so that the museum can remain an accessible place for all.

REFERENCES

Bahram, Sina. 2018. "The Inclusive Museum." In *The Senses: Design beyond vision*, edited by Lupton, Ellen, Andrea Lipps, 24–35. New York: Princeton Architectural Press.

Baloh, Robert., Vicente. Honrubia, Kevin Kerber. 2010. *Clinical Neurophysiology of the Vestibular System, 4th Edition*. Philadelphia: Oxford University Press.

Banaei, Maryam, Javad Hatami, Abbas Yazdanfar, Klaus Gramann. 2017. "Walking through Architectural Spaces: The Impact of Interior Forms on Human Brain Dynamics." *Frontiers in Human Neuroscience* 11, no. 477 (September): 1–14.

Bar, Moshe, Maital Neta. 2007. "Visual Elements of Subjective Preference Modulate Amygdala Activation." *Neuropsychologia* 45: 2191–2200.

Baumann, Caroline 2018. "Foreword." In *The Senses: Design Beyond Vision*, edited by Lupton, E., A. Lipps, Vol 6, 6. New York: Princeton Architectural Press.

The Center for Universal Design. 1997. *The Principles of Universal Design, Version 2.0*. Raleigh: North Carolina State University.

Charles, Spence, Alberto Gallace. 2011. "Multisensory design: Reaching Out to Touch the Consumer." *Psychology & Marketing* 28: 267–308.

Chatterjee, Anjan, Oshin Vartanian. 2014. "Neuroaesthetics." *Trends in Cognitive Sciences* 18, no. 7: 370–375.

Craig, Michael, Michaela Dewar, Sergio Della Sala, Thomas Wolbers. 2015. "Rest Boosts the Long-Term Retention of Spatial Associative and Temporal Order Information." *Hippocampus* 25, no. 9: 1017–1027.

Department of Justice. 2008. "United States of America and the International Spy Museum under Title III of the Americans with Disabilities Act," DJ No. 202-16-130, June 3, 2008, *Americans with Disabilities Act*. Accessed 8 May 2018. www.ada.gov/spymuseum.htm.

Freedberg, David, Vittorio Gallese. 2007. "Motion, Emotion, and Empathy in Esthetic Experience." *Trends in Cognitive Sciences* 11: 197–203.

Giovanni, Joseph 1993. "The Architecture of Death: to Design the U.S. Holocaust Museum, James Freed Had to Challenge the Values that had Guided His Work–and Confront Old Horrors." *Los Angeles Times*, April 18, 1993.

Golembiewski, Jan 2017. "Architecture, the Urban Environment and Severe Psychosis: Aetiology." *Journal of Urban Design and Mental Health* 2, no. 1.

Hoffman, Miriam 2018. "Places of Pause: the Cognitive Impact of Wakeful Rest." *Conscious Cities Journal*, no. 5.

Howes, David. 2003. *Sensual Relations: Engaging the Senses in Culture and Social Theory*, Ann Arbor, MI: University of Michigan Press.

Howes, David. 2013. "The Social Life of the Senses." *Ars Vivendi Journal*, no. 3 (February 2013): 4–23.

Johnson, Brian R. 2016. *Design Computing: An Overview of an Emergent Field*. New York: Routledge.

Joy, Annamma. 1998. "The Framing Process: The Role of Galleries in the Circulation of Art." In *Servicescapes: The Concept of Place in Contemporary Markets*, edited by Sherry, J. F. Jr., 259–304. Lincolnwood, IL: Nike Town Chicago Business Books.

Lindsay, Georgia. 2016. "Chapter 6: Denver Art Museum's Hamilton Building." In *The User Perspective on Twenty-First-Century Art Museums*, edited by Lindsay, G., 96–112. New York: Routledge.

Lupton, Ellen, Andrea Lipps. 2018. "Why Sensory Design?" In *The Senses: Design beyond vision*, edited by Lupton, E., A. Lipps, 8–19. New York: Princeton Architectural Press.

Nanda, Upali 2005. "Senstethics: A Crossmodal Approach to the Perception, and Conception, of Our Environments." PhD diss., Texas A&M University.

Smith, Kyle. 2007. "Frank Lloyd Wrong." *New York Post*, November 11, 2007. https://nypost.com/2007/11/11/frank-lloyd-wrong/.

Tuckett, Polly, Ruth Marchant, Mary Jones. 2004. "Cognitive Impairment, Access and the Built Environment." *Project Art Works*. http://projectartworks.org/wp-content/uploads/2015/08/close-to-the-wall.pdf.

United States Holocaust Museum. N.d. "About the Museum: Architecture and Art — United States Holocaust Memorial Museum." Accessed: April 6, 2018, www.ushmm.org/information/about-the-museum/architecture-and-art.

van Paasschen, Jorein, Fransesca Bacci, David Melcher. 2015. "The Influence of Art Expertise and Training on Emotion and Preference Ratings for Representational and Abstract Artworks." *PLoS One* 10, no. 8: e0134241.

Vartanian, Oshin, Gorka Navarrete, Anjan Chatterjee, Lars Brorson Fich, Helmur Leder, Cristian Modroño, Martin Skov. 2013. "Impact of Contour on Aesthetic Judgments and Approach-Avoidance Decisions in Architecture." *Proceedings of the National Academy of Sciences USA* 110: 10446–10453.

Vi, Chi Thanh, Damien Ablart, E. Gatti, C. Velasco, Mariann Obrist. 2017. "Not Just Seeing, but also Feeling Art: Mid-Air Haptic Experiences Integrated in a Multisensory Art Exhibition." *International Journal of Human-Computer Studies* 108: 1–14.

Whitby, Maximilienne. 2017. "Scoping of Shared Spatial Needs During Public Building Use: Autism Spectrum Disorder (Sensory Overload) and Borderline Personality Disorder (Dissociation)." *Journal of Urban Design and Mental Health* 3: 9.

Witkin, Herman, S. Asch. 1948. "Studies in Space Orientation. IV. Further Experiments on Perception of the Upright with Displaced Visual Fields." *Journal of Experimental Psychology* 38, no. 6: 762–782.

CHAPTER **14**

Understanding Museum Architecture from Disability Experience

Pavilion of Knowledge in Lisbon, Portugal

Caroline Van Doren, Peter-Willem Vermeersch, and Ann Heylighen

INTRODUCTION

Anticipating how a building or space will be experienced is a major challenge for architects and other designers. They are expected to conceive environments with an eye to offering people a future experience, often without having direct access to these future users' motivations, values, or prior experiences. Moreover, because architecture is experienced in an embodied way, it can be thought of as 'communication from the body of the architect directly to the body of the persons who encounter the work, perhaps centuries later' (Pallasmaa 2005, 67). This encounter may correspond to the designers' intentions – but also may not (Crilly et al., 2008, 15). That is, architects can have specific intentions in mind, but users may not experience them (Heylighen et al., 2013, 7).

Anticipating users' experience of a building or space is particularly challenging for architects when clients do not coincide with the end-user or the end-user is unknown, as is the case in the design of public buildings. Even more challenging are design assignments where a building's future function is unknown during the design process, as was the case for the Pavilion of Knowledge discussed here. To our knowledge, no legal or professional obligation exists to compare the architects' intentions with people's actual experience of the resulting environment. A more consistent feedback learning mechanism in architecture would be particularly valuable for public buildings, which should be accessible to all people. For museums this applies not only to the physical accessibility of the building, but also to how the museum and its exhibitions are experienced.

The case study presented in this chapter seeks to contribute to understanding the embodied experience of museums from the perspective of disabled persons.[1] Previous research has shown how they can appreciate spatial qualities that architects may not be attuned to (e.g. Heylighen 2015, 78; Vermeersch and Heylighen 2015, 20). Elaine Ostroff (1997) introduced the term 'user/expert' to denote

> anyone who has developed natural experience in dealing with the challenges of our built environment. User/experts include parents managing with toddlers, older people with changing vision or stamina, people of short stature, limited grasp or who use wheelchairs. These diverse people have developed strategies for coping with the barriers and hazards they encounter every day. The experience of the user/expert is usually in strong contrast to the life experience of most designers and is invaluable in evaluating both existing products and places as well as new designs in development.

Attending to the experiences of user/experts, and comparing these with the architects' intentions, provides a richer understanding of architecture. In this chapter we focus on one case of museum architecture, the Pavilion of Knowledge, originally built for Expo '98 in Lisbon, Portugal.

THE PAVILION OF KNOWLEDGE

Great events often require specialized structures (Ferreira et al., 1996, 28). For a world exhibition new spaces are needed which are appropriate for the event but which can be re-used immediately afterwards. The Lisbon World Exposition took place between May 21 and September 30, 1998 in the eastern part of the capital of Portugal (Machado 2006, 125). The Portuguese architect João Luis Carrilho da Graça was commissioned to design one of the five major buildings of the Exposition. During the World Exposition, the Pavilion accommodated an exhibition about the seas, showing the process of discovering knowledge about and appropriating the oceans by humankind (Pereira 1998, 41). Visiting the exhibition was a voyage of discovery itself: in every room, visitors discovered a new aspect of the theme. One year later, the pavilion would become a museum of sciences called Centro Ciência Viva, hosting permanent and temporary exhibitions (Pavilhão do Conhecimento 2010, 5). Initially, the stages created for Expo '98 were used without alteration for the exhibitions of the science museum (Fonseca 2008, 81). In May 2006 a new program was formulated for the building's renovation. In 2010 the foyer and the entrance were thoroughly transformed following a design by Carrilho da Graça and his team. However, at the time of design, the architect had little knowledge of the detailed contents for either the expo or the museum.

We chose the Pavilion of Knowledge for this case study for multiple reasons. First, the building is a well-known contemporary building that attracts a large volume of visitors every year. Second, the architect paid explicit attention to persons with an impairment from the beginning. He described his intentions as follows: 'My objective, in a certain way, is making people happy. Creating spaces that support the life of people' (Pimenta 2010, 27). Third, the building's conversion from Pavilion to Museum was planned from the beginning. Finally, the pavilion is currently a museum of science with activities for children between 9 and 14 years old; they are invited to touch and experience the space and exhibits, which influences their perception and impression of the museum.

In 2010 when these data were collected, the museum presented three permanent exhibitions – 'Vê, Faz, Aprende!' (See, Do and Learn!), 'Explora,' and 'A Casa Inacabada' (The Unfinished House) – and two temporary exhibitions – 'Sexo … e então?!' (about sex and love for 9 to 14 year-olds) and 'Expedição Amazónia' (about the Amazon rainforest). The temporary exhibitions are often collaborations between two or more science centers, with exhibits on loan from other institutions. Since the research took place the museum building has undergone changes, which are not covered in this chapter.

COMPARING INTENTIONS AND EXPERIENCES

To fully understand the architect's concept, we studied published information about the building, then interviewed Carrilho da Graça and an accessibility employee of the museum. To understand how the building is experienced, Caroline worked with two user/experts, Tiago and Sofia (pseudonyms). Tiago lost his sight at age 36, a few years before the study. He usually makes use of a white cane to feel the built environment. Sofia was born without legs and is very skilful at moving around with her manual wheelchair. Caroline accompanied each of them during their visits to the building. For Tiago, it was not his first visit. For this analysis, we focus on the arrival and main entrance, the space where visitors gather, and the actual exhibition spaces.

Figure 14.1 The main entrance consists of a ramp that surrounds the patio and brings the visitor to the first floor. In the middle of this patio there is a fountain. The steel banister on the left side of the ramp has been added later for safety. Photograph: Pavilion of Knowledge.

A Megalithic Cross

Fernandes and Cannatà (2001, 299) describe the pavilion as consisting of a vertical and horizontal volume which together form a megalithic cross in white concrete finished with wooden elements (Cannatà and Fernandes 2000, 114). A square hollowed out from within the horizontal mass serves as the access patio (Figure 14.1). The entrance consists of a ramp that surrounds this patio.

The main material of the entrance is white 'lioz.' This limestone, which contains a variety of maritime fossils, is the same material as is used in the old areas of Lisbon. Its use refers to Oceans, the original exhibition theme. One side of the ramp floor is rough while the other side is polished (Figure 14.2), a difference that Tiago was aware of: he mentioned that there are different types of stone and not all stones feel cold like people generally think. He says that even the same type of stone can feel different depending on the surface finish. Touching the materials can provide an interesting experience.

Tiago likes the fact that the ramp is made of stone because it provides excellent grip, but he worries about the grip when it is raining. Sofia notices the difference in finish too (Figure 14.2). She tries to ride up the ramp on the side with the rough finish, but this is not easy. She thinks that the ramp will be slippery when wet. The accessibility employee confirms that several persons have fallen in rainy conditions. As the ramp is too steep for Sofia, she enters through what is intended as the exit, takes the interior elevator, and crosses the building to the entrance on the first floor.

Tiago thinks it is important for a ramp to have a banister. He walks up the ramp by touching the inner banister with his cane; all he has to do is follow it. The accessibility employee agrees that banisters are very important, and highlights that the

Figure 14.2 The entrance ramp is made of a white limestone with maritime fossils. This material is a direct reference to the main theme of the exhibition during Expo '98 – the oceans – and to the old city center of Lisbon where this material is frequently applied. One side of the limestone is polished, the other side is rough. Different finishing can provide another tactile experience. Photograph: Caroline Van Doren.

outer banister made of steel is absolutely necessary. Originally, there was no outer banister, and several visitors fell over the edge because there was no distinction in material or color between the edge of the ramp and the rest of the space. Tiago suggests adding another one in the middle of the wide ramp, although he admits that it would probably not be very beautiful.

From the original design for the Exposition, there has been a fountain in the center of the patio, an important feature for sound. As Fernandes and Cannatà (2001, 299) describe: 'We are then in the square and we have the water whisper.' Tiago recognizes the sound of the water from a distance, making it useful to help locate the pavilion. However, he does not use it to navigate within the patio; he uses his cane to find the ramp.

The architect says that he intended for the materials to communicate a kind of tranquillity; with the Pavilion of Knowledge, he did not want to create a dazzling building but a building that provides a kind of serenity before you enter it. An architecture critic sums up his response to the building: 'With minimal constructive means and materials a strong expression is reached' (Tilman 1998, 42).

The tranquillity the architect had in mind is not entirely experienced by the user/experts. For Sofia knowing she will have problems leaving the building makes

MUSEUM ARCHITECTURE AND DISABILITY EXPERIENCE   251

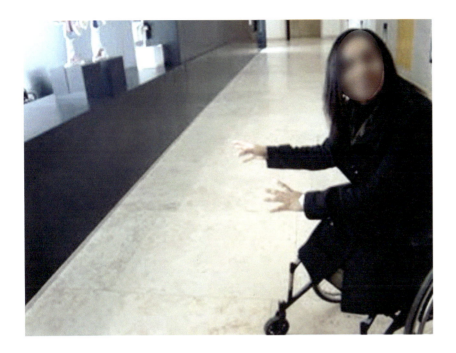

Figure 14.3 During the 2006 renovation the architect inserted a black box on the first floor for all the entrance functions. The lower part of the design of the ticket office is useful for wheelchair users and contributes to a pro-children policy. Photograph: Caroline Van Doren.

her feel uncomfortable while visiting the exhibitions. Later on, inside the pavilion she makes another striking comment: 'If an exhibition is interesting, the access and exit of the space don't really matter to me. Although if the exhibition is boring or uninteresting, I feel even worse because of the ramp.'

Diving into the Water

During the renovation of 2006 a black box was placed on the first floor to gather all the entrance functions, including the ticket office (Fonseca 2008, 81). In this new ticket office, one side of the desk is lower than the other (Figure 14.3), which Sofia appreciates. Besides being useful for persons with a physical impairment, it contributes to a pro-children policy. She finds it odd that the organization thinks about such details but not about the accessible entrance.

Coming from the entrance hall the visitors then pass through a black corridor to visit the exhibitions (Figure 14.4). During the Exposition, the visitors were supposed to feel like they were under water while crossing this corridor (Mateus and Mateus 1998, 31), and it also drew the attention of vision impaired persons. Tiago points out that the sound inside this corridor is totally different from that in the entrance hall; he claps his hands to demonstrate the echo. The accessibility employee indicates that the corridor served as an orientation point for a vision impaired person who used to work in the pavilion: while walking in front of this corridor she was able to experience a float of air.

Figure 14.4 From the entrance hall, visitors are guided to a black corridor serving as a starting point. During Expo '98 they were supposed to feel like diving into the water while crossing this corridor. Tiago points out the interesting sound and float of air. Photograph: Pavilion of Knowledge.

A Ship in A Ship

The central vertical volume of the building is a two-story-space (Figure 14.5); at the time of the World Exposition it was called 'the ship' ('Nave' in Portuguese) (Fernandes and Cannatà 2001, 300). The immensity of this volume serves the function of exhibiting large elements (Ferreira et al., 1996, 60). During Expo '98, it displayed pieces of a ship: 'The large room contained in the pavilion's vertical volume of the megalithic cross perceived from the outside creates a spectacular centerpoint, where allusion of shipyard is made by structures resembling naval architecture, and where natural light entering from high above introduces the reality of Nature's elements' (Toussaint 1999, 304). This space provided the visitor a feeling: 'It is the confrontation between the man and his relatively unimportant scale comparing to the largeness of the sea' (Mateus and Mateus, 1998, 38).

Tiago notices the acoustic and thermal conditions of the tall space, which help him know he has entered the Nave. It feels cooler than the two smaller exhibition spaces inside the pavilion he visited before, and the acoustic qualities are totally different from the previous exhibition spaces. Both help visitors to get an impression of the size of this expansive space.

Additionally, the space has a strong visual effect. Through dramatic lighting, the tallness of the space is emphasized: 'It is in this area that, maybe in a more evident way, we feel the scale of the building is hard to define' (Fernandes and Cannatà 2001, 300). It is the only exhibition space where natural lighting, in this case zenithal lighting, was present from the beginning (Escolano 1998, 144).

MUSEUM ARCHITECTURE AND DISABILITY EXPERIENCE   253

Boarding

For Expo '98, the curators planned a coherent exhibition track: 'The route through the diverse exhibition sectors is a journey and the building is the paralytic ship that transports us' (Dias 2005, 32). There is no typical exhibition track anymore, though. The accessibility employee explained that, although the pavilion contains smaller spaces and sometimes the building layout may seem chaotic, the activities do not require a set track.

To locate different exhibitions, visitors can follow colored lines on the floor (Figure 14.6). In Tiago's opinion, a tactile guide path on the floor is not a good option for this museum because the building is too small. Although he is not able to follow the colored lines on the floor, he likes the approach of the exhibitions. In his opinion the building layout is clear. He does not like an exhibition track at all because he prefers to decide himself where to go. Sofia thought that, unlike the outside of the building, the layout inside was very clear.

A banister on the mezzanine of the Nave protects the visitor from falling. Sofia does not understand why one side of the banister is made of transparent glass and the other side, facing the foyer, of frosted glass. In her opinion one of the qualities of this tall space is that it gives an overview of the temporary exhibition on

Figure 14.5 The central area of the Pavilion of Knowledge is the called the 'Nave' (Portuguese for ship). This vertical volume served during Expo '98 for showing large elements like pieces of a ship, it was 'a ship in a ship.' Now the first floor provides an overview of the temporary exhibition. Photograph: Pavilion of Knowledge.

Figure 14.6 Colored lines on the floor mark the way to the exhibition spaces. For Tiago these lines are not helpful, but he follows the banister for moving inside the building. Coming from the Foyer Sofia cannot get an overview of the ground floor because the banister is made of frosted glass. At the other side transparent glass is used, allowing her to observe the activities of the lower floor. Photograph: Pavilion of Knowledge.

the ground floor. Regrettably, because of the frosted glass, this overview cannot be enjoyed by children, persons small in stature, or wheelchair users. At the other side of the Nave she notices the transparent banisters and over there she is able to look downstairs. In her opinion it is not really a problem that the glass is opaque on one side, on the other sides she is able to perceive activity on the ground floor. However, she does not understand why opaque glass is applied on the side of the foyer, which gives visitors a first impression of the exhibition spaces. When the architect is asked about this issue, he does not remember the distinction was made. It must have had 'an architectural reason,' he thinks, but he understands the difficulties certain visitors face.

Inside the foyer, Tiago asks for guidance. In the Nave, by contrast, he wants to walk by himself. Here he has the possibility to follow the banister with his hand. Handrails throughout the building are a tactile aspect that Tiago generally appreciates in public buildings. On spots in the pavilion where a banister was provided, he preferred to follow it. At the end of the visit, however, he mentions that he is not able to visit the pavilion by himself because the museum is not designed for disabled persons visiting it on their own.

Blank Slate

The content of the original exhibition about the knowledge of the seas was designed not by Carrilho da Graça, but by ARX Architects (Mateus and Mateus 1998, 31). Since the architect had no knowledge of the contents of the exposition, he created empty spaces with a height of seven meters each. He compares this design process to designing a theater: he was responsible for conceiving the empty stage – a blank slate – but not for the lighting, decoration, etc.

As mentioned, the most striking difference Tiago notices between the Nave and the other exhibition spaces, is the difference in acoustic conditions and temperature. This difference becomes particularly apparent during a visit to the permanent exhibition 'Explora.' While the accessibility employee is explaining something, many children are testing activities; the sound of the children makes the conversation almost unintelligible. Because it is an activity museum, the accessibility employee points out, there are almost no calm spaces. Tiago admits these acoustic conditions would be ideal for a museum with works of art, but for this kind of museum he finds them rather unsuitable. In the exhibition space of 'A Casa Inacabada,' white acoustic panels hang from the ceiling and the walls, but the space is still loud. The acoustic conditions of 'Expedição Amazónia' are more or less the same for Tiago, although it is quieter. The quietness is deceptive in his opinion, because the current exhibition focuses on the visual experience and does not involve hands-on activities.

The 'blank slates' of the permanent exhibitions 'Explora' and 'A Casa Inacabada' are organized as a garden in which the activities are positioned at random, spread over the whole exhibition space (Figure 14.7). Sofia appreciates this layout because

Figure 14.7 The layout of the activities is spacious, which feels comfortable. Moreover, activities at child's height offer advantages for Sofia. Vision impaired persons sometimes face difficulties because they cannot follow a guideline or a banister and therefore feel kind of lost in the space. Photograph: Pavilion of Knowledge.

of the spaciousness. She likes the fact that she immediately has an overview of the space; in this way she knows what to expect. While the accessibility employee knows this layout is valued by physically impaired persons, she admits it could be difficult for vision impaired visitors. Tiago does not comment on its setup, possibly because he is guided. The activities of 'Sexo … e então?!' are placed more closely to each other. Sometimes Sofia meets with little obstacles – like a small step – but in general she appreciates this layout too.

Both user/experts are pleased with the design of the exhibitions 'Explora,' 'A Casa Inacabada,' and 'Sexo … e então?!' These exhibitions are adapted to children's heights and seem to be comfortable for the user/experts too. When trying out an activity with a table, Sofia can smoothly move her wheelchair underneath it. For another activity visitors have to stand up at a distance. Her perception differs from that of a standing adult, but is similar to a child's.

They both appreciate the finishes in the exhibitions. Tiago likes the round finishes of the tables of 'Explora', the working surfaces of 'A Casa Inacabada,' and the separations inside the space 'A Casa Inacabada' and of 'Sexo … e então?!' In the latter sometimes soft material is used in accordance with the subject (Figure 14.8). He likes different kinds of materials; the variety offers him an interesting tactile experience.

The issues mentioned in these last paragraphs are not the responsibility of the architect. Nevertheless, they influence the experience of the user/experts. Visitors do not distinguish between the movable and the immovable characteristics of a building.

Figure 14.8 The design of the exhibitions is not the responsibility of the architect, but it strongly influences the experience of the visitors. The round shapes and the soft materials of the exhibitions directed to children offer an interesting and comfortable tactile experience for the user/experts. Photograph: Pavilion of Knowledge.

DISCUSSION AND CONCLUSION

When comparing the architect's design intentions with disabled visitors' experiences of the built museum, we identified a number of themes that illustrate challenges or opportunities for museum design.

First, the notion of aesthetics acquires a broader meaning. When architects design a certain space or building, they mostly have visual aesthetics in mind and want to provoke a certain feeling. However, there could be other approaches, such as auditory or tactile-haptic aesthetics can strengthen or weaken the architectural concept. A well-balanced succession of different kinds of spaces and related acoustic conditions is considered comfortable, i.e., the equivalent of 'beautiful' in a visual approach (Heylighen et al., 2013, 17–18). This case study underscores that architecture is not only seen, but experienced by the whole body (Pallasmaa 2005, 41).

Second, many architects still seem to have troubles to integrate accessibility measures with the architectural concept in an elegant way. As Malik (2006) points out, 'Most buildings are first designed and then these "special requirements" are merely pasted on.' In the interview the architect said he always wants to do better than regulations prescribe. Architects need to realize there is a distinction between accessibility and the experience of the building.

Architectural solutions that enrich the experiences of all visitors fit in with the concept of Inclusive Design, Universal Design, or Design for All. Mace, Hardie, and Place (1991, 1) defined Universal Design as "designing all products, buildings and exterior spaces to be usable by all people to the greatest extent possible." Judging from the case study, persons with impairment themselves may suggest only partial solutions, while the purpose of Universal Design is to serve as many people as possible. In reality, one situation may be ideal for a person with vision impairment, but not liked by a wheelchair user.

Carrilho de Graça explains the concept of exhibition spaces conceived as blank slates: 'If it's for other people, or even for people we don't know, we have to build extremely simple spaces' (Pimenta 2010, 27). By contrast, characteristics like acoustic qualities and temperature betray that the spaces are not as blank as the architect had intended. There obviously is a distinction between the architect's conception of use and the observed use.

Architects may have specific intentions in mind, but sometimes users do not experience them. Paying attention to the experiences of persons with impairment, and combining these insights with the architect's objectives, provides a richer understanding of a building. The building might provide unforeseen challenges to specific (disabled) users, but may as well turn out to exhibit unforeseen qualities.

ACKNOWLEDGMENTS

This research received funding from the European Research Council under the European Community's Seventh Framework Programme (FP7/2007-2013)/ERC grant agreement n° 201,673, and from the Research Fund KU Leuven (Grant No. C14/16/047). The authors would like to express their special thanks to everybody who has contributed to the study reported in this article, especially to Sofia and Tiago, the architect, and the accessibility employee.

NOTE

1 Any language used to describe issues related to disability is understandably politically charged. In writing this chapter, we have tried to adopt the most widely acceptable conventions. Yet, conventions vary between countries and cultures, and evolve over time. Moreover, controversies about language use exist even among disabled people themselves. In a society that takes little account of impairment, people's activities can be limited and their social participation restricted. They therefore become disabled by the society they live in, not directly by their impairment, which is an argument for using disabled people, rather than people with disabilities. Yet, since each has its advocates, readers are asked to be patient with any inaccurate or inadvertently insensitive language that may be found.

REFERENCES

Cannatà, Michele and Fatima Fernandes 2000. 'Pavilhão do Conhecimento dos Mares.' In *A tecnologia na arquitectura contemporânea*, 114–127. Lisbon: Estar.

Crilly, Nathan, Anja Maier, and John P. Clarkson 2008. 'Representing artefacts as media.' *International Journal of Design* 2, no. 3: 15–27.

Dias, Manuel Graça. 2005. 'Pavilhão do Conhecimento dos Mares.' In *Candidaturas aos Prémios UIA 2005: Prémio Auguste Perret*, ed. Luiz Trigueiros, 32–35. Lisbon: Ordem dos Arquitectos.

Escolano, Victor Perez. 1998. 'Pavilhão do Conhecimento dos Mares.' In *Exposição mundial de Lisboa*, 141–144. Lisbon: Blau.

Fernandes, Fátima, and Michele Cannatà. 2001. 'Pavilhão do Conhecimento dos Mares.' In *Arquitectura portuguesa contemporânea 1999-2001*, 299–303. Porto: Asa.

Ferreira, Mega, Jorge Gaspar, Bruno Soares, Francesco Indovina, Vassalo Rosa, and Michel Toussaint 1996. *Lisbon World Expo '98: Projects*. Lisbon: Blau.

Fonseca, João Carlos. 2008. "Remodelação do Pavilhão do Conhecimento/Ciência Viva." *Archinews* 10: 78–81.

Heylighen, Ann. 2015. 'Enacting the Socio-material: Matter and Meaning Reconfigured through Disability Experience.' In *Revisiting 'Social Factors'. Advancing Research into People and Place*, eds Georgia Lindsay and Lusi Morhayim, 72–90. Newcastle upon Tyne: Cambridge Scholars Publishing.

Heylighen, Ann, Caroline Van Doren, and Peter-Willem Vermeersch 2013. 'Enriching Our Understanding of Architecture through Disability Experience.' *Open House International* 38: 7–19.

Mace, Ronald L., Greame J. Hardie, and Jaine P. Place 1991. *Accessible Environments. Towards Universal Design*. Raleigh: North Carolina State University.

Machado, Aquilino. 2006. 'A Exposição Mundial de Lisboa – Expo '98.' In *Os espaços públicos de exposição do mundo português da Expo '98*, 85–149. Lisboa: Parque Expo '98.

Malik, Seema. 2006. 'More Than Meets the Eye.' In *Blindness and the Multi-Sensorial City*, eds Patrick Devlieger, Frank Renders, Hubert Froyen, and Kristel Wildiers, 177–201. Antwerp: Garant.

Mateus, José and Nuno Mateus 1998. 'O Projecto Expositivo.' In *Pavilhão do Conhecimento dos Mares: Exposição Mundial de Lisboa 1998: catálogo oficial*, ed Reis, A. Estacio dos, 31–40. Lisbon: Parque Expo '98.

Ostroff, Elaine. 1997. 'Mining our Natural Resources: The User as Expert.' *Innovation* 1: 33.

Pallasmaa, Juhani. 2005. *The Eyes of the Skin. Architecture and the Senses*. West Sussex: Wiley-Academy.

Pavilhão do Conhecimento. 2010. *Pavilhão do Conhecimento – Ciência Viva*. Lisbon: Pavilhão do Conhecimento.

Pereira, Mário. 1998. 'O Pavilhão do Conhecimento dos Mares.' In *Pavilhão do Conhecimento dos Mares: Exposição Mundial de Lisboa 1998: catálogo oficial*, ed Reis, A.Estacio dos, 41–50. Lisbon: Parque Expo '98.

Pimenta, Joana. 2010. 'Interview to Joāl Luís Carrilho da Graça.' *Arquitectura Ibérica* 7, no. 34 (April): 16-27.

Tilman, Harm. 1998. 'Tentoonstelling in beweging: Expo '98 succesvol geïntegreerd in Lissabon.' *De Architect* 29, juli-augustus: 34–45.

Toussaint, Michel. 1999. 'Expo '98 has ended. What about the new Lisbon neighbourhood?' In *Anuario Arquitectura* Vol. 4, 298–315. Lisbon: Blau.

Vermeersch, Peter-Willem and Ann Heylighen 2015. 'Mobilizing Disability Experience to Inform Architectural Practice: Lessons Learned from a Field Study.' *Journal of Research Practice* 11: 2.

CHAPTER 15

Body Conscious Design in Museums

Galen Cranz and Chelsea Rushton

WHAT IS BODY CONSCIOUS DESIGN AND HOW IS IT RELEVANT TO MUSEUMS?

The welfare of our bodies is not what one usually thinks about when considering the design of museums. Although buildings shelter the body from weather and predators, designers often forget that the body is the center of human experience of the world. Design researchers think about the person in person-environment relations as a psychological being rather than a physical one (Bell et al. 1996; Gifford 2007; Ittelson et al. 1974; Steg et al. 2019). The authors of this chapter propose taking persons into account, not as either conscious beings or physical entities, but as both. The integrated body-mind point of view, sometimes called mindful, sometimes somatic, here called Body Conscious,[1] has implications for environmental design in general. Here we will explore those implications for museums.

Body Conscious Design acknowledges the cultural constraints on our bodies even as it advances the cause of freely moving, emancipated bodies. A body conscious designer does accept the power of cultural constraints like fashion, style, and propriety, and chooses to take a stand and challenge cultural norms to create innovation and transformation. Body Conscious Design embraces the importance of alignment and movement by acknowledging that design influences physical alignment including the feet, spine, and head, as well as desires, feelings, and thoughts. Accordingly, Body Conscious Design gives people choice in postures and thereby legitimates the idea of making oneself comfortable. To date, discussions about visitor comfort have first been defined socially and intellectually rather than physically. For example, Nina Simon, Executive Director of the Santa Cruz Museum of Art and History, discusses museum visitor comfort in a post on her blog (2007).

This post identifies four kinds of visitor comfort: content, interaction, programatic, and creature. However, even creature comfort is defined by social-behavioral limits, rather than physical affordances.

Ideally, Body Conscious Design means that rooms in all domestic and institutional buildings should offer at least five of these eight postures—sit, stand, kneel, squat, sit cross-legged, lounge, lie down, or perch half way between sitting and standing. Moreover, movement is essential. Body Conscious Design has elements of ergonomics (humans in their work environments) and anthropometrics (anatomical differences amongst people who vary by size, gender, and genetic differences), and is influenced by the newer field of somatics that defines humans as bodies that are shaped by emotional, social, and cultural preferences. Through Body Conscious Design, architects and designers use their creative problem solving skills to envision and implement alternatives to straightjacket environments, including but not limited to shoes, chairs, desks, classrooms, and offices.[2]

Body Conscious Design is relevant to and necessary for all institutions—any environment that builds and furnishes its structure and directs people's actions according to an industrial standard. Schools, universities, hospitals, prisons, offices, housing, and museums can all benefit from a Body Conscious Design perspective. Museums will benefit by being designed from the point of view that visitors are both physical and conscious beings, neither cattle to be herded through a circulation pattern, nor etheric souls who only commune with the soul of the artists whose work is on display.

Globally, museums are becoming increasingly numerous, and popular as visitor attractions. Many urban centers are investing in major art museums to maintain relevance in global art conversations and to draw locals, tourists, and their disposable income into their city's economy (Lindsay 2016). People go to museums on field trips and days off to enjoy leisure time with families and friends, to learn, to increase social status, and to have fun (Dilenschneider 2009; Falk and Dierking 1992, 2016).

In addition to growing in number and popularity, museums are growing in size—and in cost. Well known examples of behemoth museums in the US include (but are not limited to) New York's Metropolitan Museum of Art, which covers over 2,000,000 square feet of floor space; the Museum of Modern Art in New York (MoMA), occupying 630,000 square feet with 165,000 square feet of gallery space as of 2004, with an expansion completed on October 21, 2019 that adds 40,000 square feet of exhibition space to the campus; the San Francisco Museum of Modern Art (SFMOMA), newly renovated to include 170,000 square feet of exhibition space; and San Francisco's de Young Museum, housing 74,309 square feet of exhibition space. As of October 2019, the Metropolitan Museum of Art has 21 current exhibitions, MoMA has 14, SFMOMA has 18, and the de Young Museum has six. In 2019, the average museum admission fee for one adult ranged from approximately $20–25 in local currency. General admission is often supplemented by additional fees to view special exhibitions that have travelled to a museum from other institutions, which could increase admission for one adult to as much as $50.[3]

Museum collections and exhibitions promote viewers' perceptual, emotional, and intellectual growth. However, they do not consider—and sometimes even oppress—their visitors' physical well being. As a result, visitors almost inevitably leave museums exhausted and worn out—a phenomenon commonly referred to as *museum fatigue* (Gilman 1916; Melton 1935; Falk, Koran Jr., Dierking, and Dreblow 1985; Falk and Dierking 1992, 2016; Bitgood 2009).[4] Why?

This chapter can help readers understand the nature of museum fatigue, some of the physical problems associated with museum fatigue, and some potential individual and institutional methods to resolve them. We include in our discussion primiarily American museums that we think will be familiar to readers and also in which we have had direct experiences. We write from the dual perspectives of museum-goers and advocates of Body Conscious Design.

WHAT IS MUSEUM FATIGUE? SOME COMMON CAUSES AND SOME PROPOSED SOLUTIONS

Despite motivations for going to a museum and the costs to get in, once inside, visitors tire surprisingly quickly. Johan Idema (2014) writes about a kind of museum fatigue that has intellectual, emotional, and physical components. Intellectual fatigue arises because viewers are being presented with ideas often beyond our knowledge frameworks; we learn new things, we measure those things against our systems of knowing, and, whether we respond favorably or critically to the new information, our brains are being exercised and expanded. Artworks can also stir strong emotional responses, particularly when people know (or do not know) what the works communicate. Viewers might relate to or react against the subject or content of what we see. The physical fatigue arises from *museum shuffle* or *museum feet*: walking a few steps and then stopping to look at an artwork, then walking a few more steps, then stopping again. Human bodies evolved to walk for long periods to cover distances, and the stopping and starting takes a lot more energy than just starting and keeping on going.

In this section, we discuss several common design problems that cause museum fatigue:

1. Bad standing
2. Not enough places to sit: in pairs, groups, solo
3. No places or permission to recline
4. Fixed movement circuits with no alternative movement choreography
5. No way out of the experience

Following each problem, we propose possible solutions based on our own experiences as Body Conscious museum visitors—of what is not working, but also, in some cases, of what is working.

Bad Standing

Some of the physical fatigue that results from museum shuffle comes directly from how artworks are hung and what positions visitors take when looking at them. The museum standard for hanging artwork puts the center of a piece 4'10" up from the floor, to accommodate the standard eye-height and neutral viewing position of a person measuring 5'6" (Lindsey Sharman, Curator of Art, Art Gallery of Alberta, Facebook message to Rushton, August 16, 2018). But what about children, or people in wheelchairs, basketball players, or anyone else who is not 5'6"? How much straining up or down is involved in viewing a painting? Should the average height of works be raised or lowered to make them more accessible to different audiences? What about reading labels—do viewers have to bend over to read them? Are their typefaces large enough and dark enough to see clearly? The short answer to all these questions is that it is very difficult to mount artworks at a height that can accommodate every viewer, which makes it that much more important to offer visitors a variety of positions in which to view works, both for short and long looks.

According to a study conducted by Smith and Smith (2017), people spend an average of 28.63 seconds looking at a work of art. A viewer is not likely to sit down for a work they look at for 28 seconds or less; they will probably stand in place to do so. Standing with alignment in mind (such as the Alexander Technique principles of head, neck, and shoulders free, the spine upright and lengthened) can greatly reduce the physical fatigue of standing. One way for museums to facilitate reduced-fatigue or supported standing could be to install pub-style viewing partitions at which people lean some of their upper body weight on the counter and use the foot rail to shift lower and full body weight from one leg to the other as they view the work in front of them.

For those works attracting longer interest, sitting may be an appropriate alternative to standing. A 2001 study by Smith and Smith determined that the longest look a work of art received (within their sample group) was three minutes and 48 seconds. With digital technologies, curators may eventually learn which works will get the longest looks by which visitors and plan exhibition seating accordingly, but individuals will always have their own preferences. Rushton once sat on the floor in front of an Emily Carr painting in the Vancouver Art Gallery because no bench was placed in front of it, and she was almost immediately approached by a guard who told her sitting on the floor was not permissible. Failing the addition of extra fixed seating, museums could also provide portable perching stools, such as the MOGO by Focal Upright Furniture, for visitors to use wherever they want to pause and take a longer look.[5] These could be available for check-out or rental, for instance, at the admission kiosks, coat check, or an audio guide counter.

Not Enough Places to Sit: In Pairs, Groups, Solo

As we discussed in the previous section, museums would improve user experience by offering more seating—but not only as a relief from standing and the museum shuffle. Seating also serves as designated space for individuals, pairs, and groups to think and talk about what they have seen without interfering with other viewers. The most common location for seating is the center of a gallery room to invite sitting in front of particular works of art. However, other opportunities abound: sometimes in a transition space between galleries, in a special corner, in a reading room, or in a foyer or lobby. Discussing works on view with friends, museum staff, or other visitors adds depth to the experience by integrating our thoughts and feelings into our social selves. Yet, talking might interrupt others who want a more private relationship to the work. Galleries could vary—some silent, some conversational. Or, upholstered seating with sound baffling suspended overhead from the ceiling could signal the areas where conversation is appropriate.

More seating and a variety of spaces also affords visitors an opportunity to meditate or contemplate work either during or after a viewing experience. Some galleries or nooks could be dedicated for meditation—whether standing, seated on a chair or bench, sitting cross-legged, or kneeling. Is art a subject of meditation? It can be. Several modern and contemporary art institutions have been designed especially to facilitate a meditative experience while viewing artwork: the Rothko Chapel (Houston TX 1971), which is furnished with simple, movable benches and floor cushions (*zafus*) for meditative sitting; the Agnes Martin Gallery at the Harwood Museum of Art (Taos NM 1997), built to house seven paintings Martin created in 1993 that visitors are encouraged to view seated on the four yellow benches designed specifically for the gallery by Donald Judd; and "Austin," Ellsworth Kelly's gift to the Blanton Museum of Art (Austin, TX 2015), which contains a stationary bench to facilitate immersive experiences in the changing light of the space (Figure 15.1).[6]

Even museums not specifically designed for meditative art viewing host special events that promote meditation and contemplation of artworks during less trafficked time in their spaces. For instance, New York's Museum of Modern Art hosts an ongoing series called Quiet Mornings. On the first Wednesday of each month, visitors are invited to the museum from 7:30–9:00 am at a special admission rate to "take time to look slowly, clear your head, silence your phones, and get inspiration for the day and week ahead" (MoMA n.d). On these mornings, the museum provides a drop-in meditation space and offers guided meditations from 8:30–9:00 am.

BODY CONSCIOUS DESIGN IN MUSEUMS   265

Figure 15.1 Kelly, Ellsworth, "Austin," 2015, Artist-designed building with installation of colored glass windows, marble panels, and redwood totem, 60 ft. x 73 ft. x 26 ft. 4 in. Blanton Museum of Art, The University of Texas at Austin, Gift of the artist, with funding generously provided by Jeanne and Michael Klein, Judy and Charles Tate, the Scurlock Foundation, Suzanne Deal Booth and David G. Booth, the Longhorn Network, and other donors. © Ellsworth Kelly Foundation.

Although sitting can often provide much-needed relief from standing and shuffling, sitting in the right angle seated posture involves its own musculoskeletal strains to the pelvis, back, torso, neck, and head. Yet, most Westerners are accustomed to this position and want to rest in this way. Stools are a useful compromise between right angle sitting and standing because without a back they require that people use their torso strength. Tall stools invite a perch position, which places less strain on the joints and promotes optimal spinal alignment in what NASA calls *neutral body posture,* the position the human body naturally assumes when no gravitational force pushes or pulls on it (Figure 15.2).

Museums could consider using stools as much as or more than conventional chairs. Further, museums have an opportunity to *set a precedent* for designing galleries to invite both the perch position and its partner position, rotated 90 degrees in space: the lounge.

No Places or Permission to Recline

The spine and legs tire from the stand/walk shuffle and the chair-sit; the eyes tire from seeing; the brain tires from learning; the nervous system tires from processing emotions. Having a place—and permission—to recline, either by lying down or lounging, would offer much relief and respite for weary museum visitors. Imagine Rushton's surprise when she awoke from an undisturbed 45-minute nap on a bench in the Egyptian Wing of the Brooklyn Museum, having been scolded by museum

Figure 15.2 Neutral Body Posture. Diagram by NASA (1986).

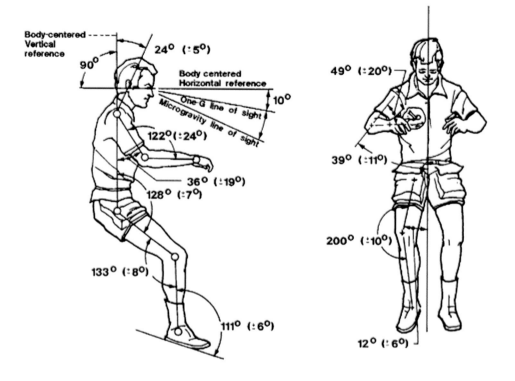

guards across the continent for lying on empty benches that "must be kept available for other patrons"—even when the galleries are unpopulated and the benches otherwise unused. Cranz has fared better, being of a certain age; at the 2016 Venice Biennale she took constructive rest position, on the back with the soles of the feet on the floor, knees bent, with support under the head (Figure 15.3), at the edge of a brick and mortar arch entitled *Breaking the Siege* designed by Gabinete de Arquitectura in the Central Pavillion. Within two minutes she was approached by security personnel who, rather than telling her to get up, asked her if she felt unwell and offered to bring her a drink of water. Museum staff are apparently instructed to ensure that those who lie down are brought upright again as soon as possible.

Although the consequences of our actions have varied, both of us have learned through experience that lying down in an exhibition space is not okay. Why is lying down in an exhibition space not okay? Perhaps because museum and gallery officials are worried that those who lie down will interrupt the experience for other visitors? Exhibition spaces could be appropriated by people who have no other place to sleep? Lying down suggests sexual invitation? Lying down could be a signal that someone has passed out, is in distress, or needs medical attention? But lying down—particularly in constructive rest position—helps the spine lengthen and widen, and restores tired bodies. How can museum personnel differentiate between distress and rest?[7]

BODY CONSCIOUS DESIGN IN MUSEUMS   267

Figure 15.3 Galen Cranz in Constructive Rest Position (2019). Photograph: Chelsea Rushton.

If museums and galleries would provide space for visitors to recline, their exhibition designers would have to think carefully about how opportunities for reclining could be integrated into their exhibitions and galleries. That said, they would also likely avoid (or at least contain) many of the worries that afflict their governing bodies. Visitors may currently experience opportunities to lie down—either subversively or with permission—in museums' video and multimedia galleries.

Additionally, many non-video works lend themselves to being viewed either flat or recumbent. Recumbent viewing rests the spine, while the head and eyes are raised so that viewing objects and making social contact are both easy. A circle of benches or couches or, better yet, lounge chairs, that puts heads or feet together could become popular in a gallery with work hung on the ceiling. An excellent candidate for reclined viewing is "The Lawrence Tree" by Georgia O'Keeffe.[8] She painted this New Mexican ponderosa pine looking up from the base of the tree "so it could be hung in any direction" (Harris and Zucker 2011). Another example of a painting suitable for reclined viewing is "Portrait of My Heart and All Its Protectors" by Chelsea Rushton (Figure 15.4).

Some contemporary artworks encourage viewers to lie down, such as Ernesto Neto's "Water Falls from my Breast to the Sky," an ongoing soft sculptural installation on display on the first floor of Chicago's Museum of Contemporary Art

Figure 15.4 Chelsea Rushton, "Portrait of My Heart and All Its Protectors," gouache and acrylic on paper, 14 × 18 inches, 2019. Photograph: Chelsea Rushton.

(MCA) (Figure 15.5). This site-specific installation evoking a cocoon "offers visitors a multisensory place for rest, camaraderie, and reflection […] [V]isitors are invited to enter the installation and sit on cushions, which are filled with scented organic materials like seeds and herbs … " (MCA n.d).

What if people fall asleep? What's wrong with falling asleep? Can museums let people sleep? How can museums designate space among their galleries for sleeping during regular or special hours? The Rubin Museum, for instance, hosts an annual Dream-Over, most recently from December 7–8, 2019. Dream-Over is a programmed event that not only permits visitors to sleep among gallery exhibitions, but also pairs participants with a piece of art based on a questionnaire they fill out at the time of registration. Dreamers learn about dreaming in the Tibetan Buddhist tradition, and participate in bedtime stories, lullabies, and dream discussion groups. A midnight snack and light breakfast are served. In 2019, registration for non-members was $140 for a single ticket and $280 for a couple's ticket; registration for members was $112 for a single ticket and $224 for a couple's ticket (The Rubin n.d).

The high fees of general admission to museums and their special events mean that museums are not likely to take on the problems of public libraries becoming homes for the homeless. In the case of nappers napping during regular gallery hours, someone else might want to experience the furniture that a napper has

BODY CONSCIOUS DESIGN IN MUSEUMS   269

Figure 15.5 Ernesto Neto, "Water Falls from my Breast to the Sky," Museum of Contemporary Art, Chicago, Illinois, 2017. Made with cotton voile crochet, cotton knit fabric, cotton rope, stones, polyamide stockings, lavender, wood, polyurethane foam, and painted bowls; overall dimensions variable. Commissioned by the Museum of Contemporary Art Chicago, NC2017.3. Photograph: Nathan Keay, © MCA Chicago.

hogged. In that case, waking people up when there are many visitors might make sense, but not on slow days or times. This kind of discernment on the part of the guards is as much a managerial as a material design decision.

Fixed Movement Circuits, No Alternative Movement Choreography

Humans are designed for movement; holding still in any position (standing, sitting, lying down) is fatiguing. We have ball and socket joints, so holding any one position requires work on one side of a joint, which becomes tiring. Moving allows each muscle to have its movement and rest, and thus distributes muscular work over a sequence of muscles. Because each posture other than sleeping involves work, no one posture is ideal. As the Norwegian architect Peter Opsvik (2009) has quipped, "The best posture is the next posture." Beyond the shuffle, museums need to offer movement repertoires to visitors.

Thinking about the sequence of movement from one resting position to another is a design opportunity. In high-traffic museums and/or during high volume hours or times of year, visitors are sometimes directed to move through galleries in a set sequence with little choice of going against the flow. During lower-traffic times, curators, exhibition designers, public engagement coordinators, and museum guides can and do offer alternative pathways through museum galleries that require less sequential and more random looking, such as guided or self-guided tours. Museums can partner with businesses like Watson Adventures to give visitors the option of exploring their galleries via a thematic scavenger hunt. Also, museum staff or text panels can suggest walking backwards or sideways or sitting or squatting mid-way or turning around twice or raising one's arms through a particular gallery simply as a movement repertoire to progress visitors through galleries and between resting poses, or based on the content of the work being shown. For instance, paintings of dance and dancers might invite dance moves; images of people in contemplation could be paired with suggestions to rest or lounge; images of warriors might be paired with suggestions to assume those stances. Still-life paintings, color-field paintings, and abstract paintings could ask viewers how they would express those objects, colors, and forms. The authors noted on a trip to the Auckland Art Gallery in January 2019 that text accompanying paintings in a corridor invites viewers to move in different ways relating to the brush strokes of the works. These simple changes to movement patterns stimulate the brain, improve blood and lymph flow, and thereby enliven visitors' experiences.

Some museums get visitors moving by hosting art and yoga events, in which participants can practice yoga and meditation in or adjacent to museum galleries. "Adidas: Art & Yoga" at the Brooklyn Museum includes museum admission in the $16 event fee. Following a session of "yoga and mindfulness meditation led by local instructors," visitors are encouraged to "explore our galleries on a self-guided tour of specially selected contemplative objects" (Brooklyn Museum n.d.).[9] These kinds of events promote physical and mental wellness, and alternative viewing experiences.

No Way Out of the Experience
Our bodies can be annoying. In addition to moving and resting, they also need to eat, drink, and eliminate—often on schedules that do not correlate with our day planners or with the design of our built environments. For instance, immediately

after admission into Rome's Sistine Chapel, Rushton found herself in need of some Advil to alleviate a sudden onset of menstrual cramps. She did not have any painkillers with her and no guards could help her find any, so her visit to the museum was painful because if she left early she would not be allowed back in.

Do museums' designs adequately account for our bodily needs? Are there bathrooms and water fountains on every floor or in every wing? Do museum floor plans provide shortcuts to a main entrance/exit so visitors do not have to backtrack through a labyrinth of galleries to get out? Museums now frequently offer visitors opportunities to have a snack, eat a meal, or go outside without leaving the building. The newly renovated six-floor SFMOMA designed by Snøhetta responds well to the potential of their myriad galleries and exhibitions to overwhelm and tire visitors, because in addition to two main entrances/exits, it provides indoor/outdoor experiences in which folks can refuel and recenter (Figure 15.6).

On the third floor, coffee and pastries are served by Sight Glass, a cafe located adjacent to the Photography Interpretive Gallery. Cafe 5 on the fifth floor serves seasonal family-friendly California-fusion fare both indoors and on a terrace, and Michelin-starred In-Situ on the first floor has created a fine dining menu of over 90 dishes contributed by international chefs (SFMOMA n.d). If one function of museum

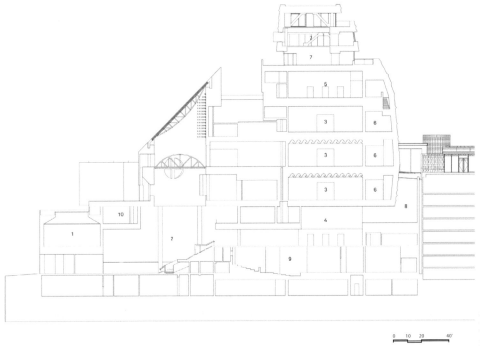

Figure 15.6 East-West section drawing of the San Francisco Museum of Modern Art, by architecture firm Snøhetta, 2010–2016, San Francisco, California, © Snøhetta.

1. Painting and Sculpture Galleries
2. Atrium
3. Fisher Collection Gallery
4. Schwab Hall
5. Contemporary Galleries
6. City Gallery
7. Offices
8. Sculpture Terrace and Living Wall
9. Theater
10. Photo Collection Galleries

cafes and restaurants is to facilitate conversation about the work in the galleries, then locating cafes at several spots in a museum, as SFMOMA has done, makes it easier for visitors to stop for conversation, rest, or contemplate than if there is only one cafe or restaurant at the entrance. SFMOMA's variety of dining options also speaks to the needs and tastes of different demographics of people who visit the museum.

SFMOMA's design does not insist that people buy refreshments in order to take a break from viewing art, however. The press release issued in advance of the museum's 2016 grand re-opening detailed the unique architectural features that allow visitors to rest their brains, eyes, and bodies from art-viewing:

> Terraces adjacent to many galleries extend exhibitions into the city, displaying outdoor sculptures and offering unparalleled views of San Francisco. The new third-floor Pat and Bill Wilson Sculpture Terrace is home to the largest public living wall in the United States with more than 19,000 plants and 21 native species. This curated sequence of spaces allows visitors to move between incredible artworks to broad overlooks, and enjoy views of the city as they circulate through and up the museum.
>
> (SFMOMA 2016)

That SFMOMA currently houses the largest public living wall in the United States shows that museums can be leaders in innovative, human-centered, body-friendly architecture, and make such advancements easier for other kinds of buildings. Designed by David Brenner of Habitat Horticulture, "The Living Wall" (Ibid.) does much more than give visitors an outdoor photo op with a cool background (Figure 15.7).

Deputy Director Ruth Berson describes the wall as an "orienting feature" that can be seen from select locations on all six floors of the museum—"a way to know exactly where you are in the expanded building" (Westbrook n.d). The designer cites recent scientific research that proves the stress-relieving, restorative effects of spending time with plants:

> When you take a break from whatever you're doing, at work or otherwise, and look at some greenery—specifically shades of green, it's been found—you return to what you were doing more efficiently. It lowers your heart rate, makes you feel connected to nature .
>
> (Ibid.)

We encourage designers to envision additional ways to give respite from the intense focus of viewing art works. Views, movement, food, and rest allow visitors a way

BODY CONSCIOUS DESIGN IN MUSEUMS 273

Figure 15.7 Rushton and Cranz interacting with "The Living Wall," designed by David Brenner of Habitat Horticulture, SFMOMA, San Francisco, California, April 2016. Photograph: Aaron Marcus.

"out" without leaving. And also, allowing people back in once they have literally exited the building is a people-friendly policy.

CONCLUSIONS

Contemporary developments in museums show support in the application of Body Conscious Design principles, which, in review, are to take the body's need for structural alignment seriously, take its need for changing postures and movement seriously, while at the same time acknowledge that the body includes a conscious mind that needs to be engaged in understanding why postural variety and movement are important. If museums continue to prioritize the application of Body Conscious Design, they could catalyze a paradigm shift toward being more inclusive, human-centered, and embracing of multiple perspectives, voices, and needs. Body Conscious Design could be a framework through which museums implement the claims they make regarding their inclusion and accommodation of broad audiences. We propose that museum boards, directors and administrators, architects, and designers start out by thinking carefully and consciously about posture and movement in conjunction with other forms of intellectual and social engagement. We have discussed many examples that support the human need for food and water and the social preference for sharing experience by talking, as well as the individual desire for independence from others. We would like to see even more experimentation in museums regarding the physical need for variety in posture and movement.

Because Body Conscious Design for museums is a new field of programatic and physical design, there are no quantitative studies of its effects as yet; for example, no visitor accounts or documented attendance rates. We hope to inspire museum management to create Body Conscious programing, and scholars and researchers to follow up with empirical assessments. The examples we have offered can be used by museums undergoing development or renovation to improve visitor experiences. They can also be used by museum visitors to improve their own experiences even where institutional accommodations have not been made for them. Broadly, Body Conscious Design features in museums can serve as an inspiring example for other institutions of urban life. If we experience body-friendly routines in museums, we might want them everywhere.

NOTES

1. Body Conscious Design is a concept and field of research defined and developed by Galen Cranz, both in teaching at the University of California at Berkeley, and in publication (*The Chair: Rethinking Culture, Body and Design*, New York: W.W. Norton & Company, 1998, paperback 2000). She and other researchers, practitioners, and parties interested in this field created the Association for Body Conscious Design online: www.bodyconsciousdesign.com/contact/network/abcd.
2. For example, an empathetic librarian, Anthony Bernier, designed a teen space in an Oakland library to accommodate teens lying down and leaning on one another. Cranz, Galen and Eunah Cha. "Body Conscious Design in a Teen Space: Post Occupancy Evaluation of an Innovative Public Library." *Public Libraries* 45, no. 6 (Nov/Dec., 2006): 48–56.
3. For example, the special exhibitions *Gauguin: A Spiritual Journey* and *Monet: The Late Years* at the de Young Museum (2019) cost $28 per adult and $35 per adult, respectively, in addition to the $15 general admission fee. The tickets to *Monet* grant entrance to *Gauguin*, subject to availability.
4. Thanks to Ipek Kaynar Rohloff for directing us to references on the history of research on museum fatigue.
5. The MOGO can be viewed and purchased at: www.fully.com/mogo-by-focal.html; www.safcoproducts.com/focal%E2%84%A2-mogo-seat
6. All of these galleries can be viewed online at their respective websites: www.rothkochapel.org; www.harwoodmuseum.org/collections/agnes; www.blantonmuseum.org/ellsworth-kellys-austin/
7. Raquel Meseguer, a U.K. based theatre maker with chronic pain, promotes the inclusion of resting places in public spaces. In her keynote address at Agenda's 2018 Communicating the Museum Conference in Brussels, BE (May 28–31), she offered some guidelines that can help museums find ways to include places for reclined rest in their galleries, and to assist guards in recognizing the needs of people who need to rest but do not pose

a security threat or require medical attention. Those guidelines can be viewed here: www.agendacom.com/wp-content/uploads/sites/38/2018/06/WED-PM-DREAMS-RESTNG-SPACES.pdf.
8   This painting is held in the collection of the Wadsworth Atheneum Museum of Art in Hartford, Connecticut.
9   Not every museum's conservation practices will accommodate such activity. The Brooklyn Museum's large central space in which visitors practice yoga minimizes changes to the temperature and humidity of the art spaces at its periphery and does not disturb the galleries elsewhere in the building.

REFERENCES

Bell, Paul, Thomas Greene, Jeffrey Fisher, and Andrew Baum. 1996. *Environmental Psychology*. 4th ed. Orlando: Harcourt College Publishers.

Bitgood, Stephen. 2009. "Museum Fatigue: A Critical Review." *Visitor Studies* 12, no. 2: 93–111. https://doi.org/10.1080/10645570903203406.

Cranz, Galen. 1998. *The Chair: Rethinking Culture, Body and Design*. New York: W.W. Norton & Company.

Cranz, Galen and Eunah Cha. 2006. "Body Conscious Design in a Teen Space: Post Occupancy Evaluation of an Innovative Public Library." *Public Libraries*, 45 no. 6 (Nov/Dec): 48–56.

Dilenschneider, Colleen. 2009. "10 Reasons to Visit a Museum." *Colleen Dilenschneider: Know Your Own Bone*. Published July 31, 2009. www.colleendilen.com/2009/07/31/10-reasons-to-visit-a-museum/

Falk, John H. and Lynn D. Dierking. 1992, 2016. *The Museum Experience Revisited*. New York: Routledge.

Falk, John H., John J. Koran Jr., Lynn D. Dierking and Lewis Dreblow. 1985. "Predicting Visitor Behavior." *Curator: The Museum Journal* 28, no. 4 (December): 249–258. doi: 10.1111/j.2151-6952.1985.tb01753.x.

Gifford, Robert. 2007. *Environmental Psychology: Principles and Practice*. 4th ed. Colville: Optimal Books.

Gilman, Benjamin Ives. 1916. "Museum Fatigue." *The Scientific Monthly* 2, no. 1: 62–74. www.jstor.org/stable/6127.

Harris, Beth and Steven Zucker. 2011. "O'Keeffe: The Lawrence Tree." *Smarthistory. art. history. conversation*. Published October 1, 2011 on YouTube. Video, 2:13. www.youtube.com/watch?v=wQq2xOs2BYU

Idema, Johan. 2014. *How to Visit an Art Museum: Tips for a Truly Rewarding Experience*. Amsterdam: BIS Publishers.

Ittelson, William H., Harold M. Proshansky, Leanne G. Rivlin, and Gary H. Winkel. 1974. *An Introduction to Environmental Psychology*. Oxford: Holt, Rinehart & Winston.

Lindsay, Georgia. 2016. *The User Perspective on Twenty-First-Century Art Museums*. New York: Routledge.

MCA. n.d. "Ernesto Neto: Water Falls from my Breast to the Sky." Exhibitions. Accessed January 30, 2019.

Melton, Arthur W. 1935. *Problems of Installation in Museums of Art*. Washington, DC: American Association of Museums.

Meseguer, Raquel. 2018. "Dreams of Resting Spaces." Keynote Presented at the Communicating the Museum Conference, Brussels, BE, May 2018. www.agendacom.com/wp-content/uploads/sites/38/2018/06/WED-PM-DREAMS-RESTNG-SPACES.pdf

MoMA. n.d. "Quiet Mornings." Accessed January 29, 2019. www.moma.org/calendar/programs/77?locale=en.

Brooklyn Museum. n.d. "Adidas: Art & Yoga." Calendar. Accessed October 30, 2019. https://www.brooklynmuseum.org/calendar/event/art_yoga_october_2019.

Opsvik, Peter. 2009. *Rethinking Sitting*. New York: W. W. Norton & Company.

The Rubin. n.d. "Dream-Over: A Sleepover for Adults." Events. Accessed October 30, 2019. https://rubinmuseum.org/events/event/dream-over-12-07-2019.

SFMOMA. 2016. "The New San Francisco Museum of Modern Art Opens to the Public on Saturday, May 14, 2016." News. Accessed August 17, 2018. https://www.sfmoma.org/press/release/new-san-francisco-museum-modern-art-opens-public/.

SFMOMA. n.d. "Dining at SFMOMA." Accessed January 30, 2019. https://www.sfmoma.org/visit/dining-sfmoma/?gclid=EAIaIQobChMIjeGRy6r-3AIVDnF-Ch18qwVvEAAYASAAEgJvLvD_BwE.

Simon, Nina. 2007. "Straddling the Comfort Zone." Museum 2.0. Published December 13, 2007. http://museumtwo.blogspot.com/2007/12/straddling-comfort-zone.html.

Smith, Lisa F. and Jeffrey K. Smith. 2001. "Spending Time on Art." *Empirical Studies of the Arts* 19, no. 2: 229–236.

Smith, Lisa F., Jeffrey K. Smith, and Pablo P. L. Tinio. 2017. "Time spent viewing art and reading labels." *Psychology of Aesthetics, Creativity, and the Arts* 11, no. 1: 77–85. http://dx.doi.org/10.1037/aca0000049.

Steg, Linda, Agnes E. van Den Berg, and Judith I. M. de Groot. 2019. *Environmental Psychology: An Introduction*. 2nd ed. Hoboken: John Wiley & Sons Ltd.

Westbrook, Lindsey. n.d. "The Living Wall." SFMOMA. Accessed August 17, 2018. www.sfmoma.org/watch/the-living-wall/.

PART 5
SUSTAINABILITIES
Green Design for New Museums

Long concerned with protecting objects inside their buildings, some museums are looking outward to contemplate how they might view their natural surroundings as part of their collection and are striving to nurture and protect the larger ecosystem beyond their walls. The chapters in this section articulate this connection beyond the building, exploring how architecture can enhance an ethic of ecological awareness. Moss and Alt offer a case study explicating the triple bottom line: the commitment to ensure financial stability and sustainable building practices in a way that simultaneously enhances the community. Bean offers a glimpse into the technical side of sustainable design, proposing that Passive House techniques be brought to museum architecture as a way to simultaneously protect collections and the environment. Finally, Loder advocates for museums to build stronger connections using landscape and green roofs. Taken together, these chapters offer a framework for expanding the scope of museum architecture to include attention to larger ecosystems.

CHAPTER **16**

Triple Bottom Line Sustainable Design

Western Spirit: Scottsdale's Museum of the West in Arizona, US

Christiana Moss and Christopher Alt

Western Spirit: Scottsdale's Museum of the West upends common assumptions about museum buildings (Figure 16.1). It sets a new benchmark for museum development, one that integrates economic and social sustainability with better-known standards for resource-efficient building systems and materials. This evolution sprang from the quest of the City of Scottsdale and local arts and cultural leaders to establish an institution that would expound the importance of the American West. The museum would address the historical forces that have made the region mythic by using its art and cultural objects to tell its stories (Western Spirit: Scottsdale's Museum of the West, n.d.). Founding a museum dedicated to the American West would cement Scottsdale's identity as the "West's most Western town," the city's slogan (City of Scottsdale, 2019), and enhance its stature as one of the great arts centers in the United States (Covert, 2015).

Too often, the founders of cultural organizations assume that a significant institution must be housed in a costly building, and they lavish money on expensive construction materials because they believe that their mission of edification calls for building an edifice. The phenomenon has been described in Deyan Sudjic's *Edifice Complex: How the Rich and Powerful Shape the World* (Sudjic, 2005). But while remarkable architecture draws attention, a costly building can sink the institution's mission by upping a museum's operating costs to levels that are unsustainable without external funding. The Newseum (McGlone and Roig-Franzia, 2019), and

Figure 16.1 Western Spirit: Scottsdale's Museum of the West, designed by Studio Ma, in Scottsdale, Arizona. This community touchstone reinforces the arts district's new center. It is centrally located, a short walk to downtown districts, and easily reached by public transit, which helps moderate transportation carbon emissions. Image: Bill Timmerman Photography, 2015.

the recently expanded Corcoran Museum (Cain, 2016), both in Washington, DC, are two recent examples that have occurred in large cities.

The founders of Western Spirit: Scottsdale's Museum of the West made financial success their highest priority. This caused hard choices about the museum's business plan and construction. Ultimately, the team was able to deliver a building of superior architectural quality that was constructed inexpensively yet meets stringent museum collections standards for environmental controls and security. The museum has been financially successful from its opening, something rarely accomplished by institutions with similar resources. It has also freed the museum to expand its mission of immersing visitors in the story of the greater Western region by throwing light on its past to shape its future.

MUSEUM ORIGINS

From its inception, Scottsdale has been a center for arts and crafts celebrating the American West. Arts and tourism comprise roughly one third of the City of Scottsdale's economy. Old Town, the earliest settled portion of Scottsdale's downtown, is its arts and cultural district. Many well-known Western artists and craftspeople have studios in Old Town, and local galleries feature both historic and contemporary Western arts. Scottsdale has been an intellectual center for artists who examine the West in their work, with both European-American and Native American artists bringing their perspectives on its history, politics, and the surrounding country.

Scottsdale was a village of about 1,000 people in 1920, and its population has grown rapidly to approximately 250,000 in the late 2010s. At its peak, more than one hundred art galleries and arts businesses thrived in Old Town. As Scottsdale urbanized, it expanded outward, and its downtown declined as an economic center (Wikipedia, 2019). By the 1980s, the City's arts and civic leaders recognized the importance of establishing a museum that would showcase regional arts and culture. Organizations approached the City of Scottsdale on three separate occasions with plans to open a museum celebrating the West's history, culture, and arts, but failed to agree upon financial terms. Herb Drinkwater, Scottsdale's mayor at the time, continued to press for a museum, and he approached Mike Fox, then director of the Heard Museum, the highly regarded Native American museum, to help lead its formation (Michael Fox, 2018). By 2012, the city issued a call for proposals from cultural organizations to develop and operate a museum of the West (City of Scottsdale. 2012). After an open competition, Fox's team was selected to establish the museum.

City leaders had chosen a site adjoining a bus transit center in Old Town for its museum of the West after evaluating many possible locations. It was selected for its proximity to other arts venues, which they hoped would guarantee an ample visitor base. The property was part of a superblock that stood at the western end of Old Town, along North Marshall Way between East Main Street and East Second Street. Art studios and galleries line the neighborhood's streets. The city's premier cultural institutions are immediately east: the Scottsdale Museum of Contemporary Art, the Scottsdale Historical Museum, and the Scottsdale Center for the Performing Arts are a short walk away. Slightly farther east are Scottsdale City Hall and the main library.

CREATING ECONOMIC AND SOCIAL SUSTAINABILITY

As part of the development agreement, the City of Scottsdale offered the museum both the site and $7.5 million towards construction. The City would own and maintain the museum building's structure and grounds. Western Spirit: Scottsdale's Museum of the West would be responsible for the museum's design, construction and ongoing operations.

An earlier feasibility study had called for a 42,700 square-foot facility, a size that was eventually reduced as project development progressed. While the money offered by the City was generous, it amounted to less than one-third of what most museum buildings cost at the time. According to Oliver Fox of the firm MGAC, which offers cost consulting, project and program management for many prominent cultural institutions, costs at the time for a high-end, large, humidity-controlled museum like the African American History Museum in Washington, DC, ranged from $750 to $950 per square foot (Oliver Fox, and Tiany Galaskas, email to the author, January 11, 2019). A medium-quality museum like the International Spy Museum ranged from $550 to $650 per square foot, and costs for a low-end museum span from $375 to $525 per square foot. Brett Perkins of the cost consultancy Stuart-Lynn Company, a specialist in museum construction, corroborated that, even when factoring in Arizona's construction climate, which typically does not require union labor, the budget was less than average for the region and building type (Breck Perkins, phone interview with the author, December 21, 2018). Museum organizers launched a fundraising campaign that brought the total construction funding to $11.5 million, which was still only half of typical museum costs. Moreover, Western Spirit: Scottsdale's Museum of the West would operate with no permanent collections to use for its exhibitions, instead relying on loans from other institutions and collectors. Fox and his team were faced with the difficult challenge of how to design and construct the museum in just 32 months while resolving these issues. In contrast, the University of California, Davis selected three finalist architect-builder teams for their Jan Shrem and Maria Manetti Shrem Museum of Art in late 2013. The university had received two large donations amounting to $13 million to underwrite building costs. These teams were required to submit preliminary designs and costs as part of the selection process. The winning team was chosen in April 2013 (Nikos-Rose, 2013). The building was opened in November 2016. While design/build procurement had been used to keep costs down, the final cost of the 31,340 square-foot building was $30.5 million (Nikos-Rose, 2016), or roughly $973 per square foot (UC Davis, Office of Design and Construction Management, n.d.). Northern California has among the highest construction costs in the United States, but even accounting for the regional variances, Western Spirit: Scottsdale's Museum of the West was built quite economically for a facility that meets Smithsonian standards. The building, eventually reduced to 35,310 square feet in area, was completed in 2015 for $11.5 million (Studio. Ma, n.d) or approximately $326 per square foot. The architects began design in 2013, and the building opened in 2015.

During negotiations with the City of Scottsdale, Western Spirit: Scottsdale's Museum of the West evaluated responses from more than seventy builders and architects. They selected a team comprised of two builders, LGE Design/Build and Core Construction, and the architecture firm Studio Ma. The three would use the design/build method to construct the museum, which is unusual for museum buildings, but is emerging as an option: the University of California, Davis Jan Shrem and Maria Manetti Shrem Art Museum was also built using this method. Most cultural facilities are designed and constructed with the owner holding separate contracts with the architect and builder, because it allows the architect to advocate for high design standards throughout the process. With design/build, the general contractor and architect work as a single entity and commit to producing a building that meets the owner's criteria for functionality and performance for a predetermined price.

After reviewing the budget and schedule, LGE and Core determined that tilt-up construction was the only choice for meeting contractual requirements. For tilt-up construction, the contractor makes a building's exterior walls by pouring concrete into wooden forms laid on the ground; once the concrete is set, they pull up the wall and secure it to the foundation and adjoining walls. The method is quick and inexpensive, but the aesthetic quality of the concrete is frequently poor, because the contractor cannot see and correct pocking and clumps in the concrete aggregate as the form is filled. While the museum's founders were focused on getting the building constructed and operational as quickly and inexpensively as possible, the architects, Studio Ma, wanted to make a landmark building despite such limited funding and an accelerated construction schedule.

The Phoenix-based firm excelled at both creating striking buildings and working with modest budgets and other difficult project conditions. They had recently teamed with Core Construction to rebuild Arizona State University's primary student center at its flagship Tempe campus, which had been heavily damaged by a fire, in only five months. Studio Ma was concurrently in the process of designing a large graduate student-housing complex for Princeton University, which is known for its outstanding architecture. Princeton had wanted to test out working with a private real-estate developer to save on construction costs and they had expected Studio Ma's graduate housing to meet their architectural standards at a fraction of the university's typical construction costs. Studio Ma had also helped with the expansion of the Phoenix Art Museum, and had renovated part of the Heard Museum. Along with their credentials, Studio Ma had an ethos of designing buildings that evoke the surrounding landscape and recognize the preciousness and fragility of natural resources. This outlook was married with two operating principles: that architecture should be for everyone, not just the wealthy, and that the best buildings do the most with the least. They were a perfect complement for an organization building a museum that all hoped would be a national center for the West's arts and culture and without the time, funding or collections that more risk-averse institutions would demand.

 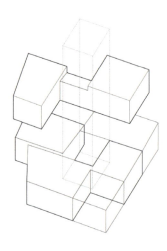

Figure 16.2 (left) Courtyard. "Old West" meets "New West" – the museum's design is inspired by regional symbols, such as the horseshoe, woven basket, and the characteristic red cliffs and mesas of the Colorado Plateau. Image: Bill Timmerman Photography, 2015. (right) Diagram of the museum. The public spaces of the museum are organized like horseshoes around a spike, with a series of U-shaped spaces clustered around a tall courtyard. Image: Studio Ma, 2015.

SUSTAINABLE BUILDING DESIGN

The team quickly determined how to build a museum within these strictures. Studio Ma proposed a design concept for the museum based on symbols of the American West. The building would be organized like horseshoes around a spike, with a series of U-shaped spaces surrounding a central sculpture courtyard (Figure 16.2). This arrangement makes it easy for visitors to travel through the galleries and other public spaces, and it shelters the courtyard from the desert heat. Surmounting the concrete structure is a perforated metal sunscreen system that refers subtly to Native American woven baskets. The sunscreen shades the building's exterior walls, as well as it glass windows and doors, to reduce air-conditioning demands. The main galleries on the second floor are linked by a bridge that looks out to Camelback Mountain, an iconic landform of the Phoenix Valley (Figure 16.3).

The architects and the museum then developed a flexible interior layout; the walls within the exhibition areas were mounted on wheels. This would allow the museum to reconfigure spaces quickly and eliminate the need to build and demolish custom-built walls with each exhibition change. Moreover, there would be no dust and fumes for visitors and staff to suffer through during exhibit construction. This design element minimized the museum's future operating costs significantly, and eliminated construction waste from exhibition changes (Figure 16.4).

TRIPLE BOTTOM LINE SUSTAINABLE DESIGN **285**

Figure 16.3 (left) Bridge linking main galleries on the second floor. (right) The two-story design brings life to western motifs, ecology, and ideas, and it connects to desert vistas with its second-level interior bridge offering northwestern views to iconic Camelback Mountain. Images: Bill Timmerman Photography, 2015.

Figure 16.4 A flexible interior gallery layout allows for permanent and travelling exhibitions. Image: Bill Timmerman Photography, 2015.

Figure 16.5 A multiuse space for gatherings and presentations with a flexible riser seating system. Image: Bill Timmerman Photography, 2015.

Studio Ma took a similar approach for the Museum's theater. They designed the room with a level floor, instead of the customary raked floor, and used a riser seating system that can be tucked against one wall. This lets the Museum convert the theater for dinners, receptions, and classroom-style education. By making the theater multipurpose, Studio Ma eliminated the need for additional space while meeting the museum's functional demands (Figure 16.5).

Studio Ma proposed other design elements that maximized the building's functionality: tall ceiling heights for its two floors, which improved their aesthetic quality while making it easy to set up and dismount exhibitions, and exposing the concrete building structure within the facility's interiors, which reduced the cost

Figure 16.6
Concrete, glass, and Western red cedar materials used throughout the museum help to reduce costs as well as refer to desert-adapted construction and Western frontier buildings. Image: Bill Timmerman Photography, 2015.

of drywall (Figure 16.6). The wooden forms used for the museum's tilt-up exterior walls were fabricated to have gaps between boards, which created interesting striations in the concrete, and the concrete became imprinted with the wood's surface texture as it settled against and cured in the mold. By taking such care with the concrete forms, Core Construction and Studio Ma were able to mimic the character of the much more expensive poured-in-place concrete construction used for many civic and cultural buildings (Figure 16.7). Moreover, the concrete's wood-imprinted surface recalls both the ribs of native saguaro cactus and the wooden buildings constructed by American and European settlers as they moved into the West. And like the saguaro, the ribbed concrete helps nourish the building: air

Figure 16.7 The tilt-up concrete panel exterior walls of the museum were made with forms constructed from worn and heavily textured wood boards. The walls are both inexpensive to build and have a high thermal mass, which regulates interior temperature. Image: Bill Timmerman Photography, 2014.

pockets between the ribs provides self-shading to the outside faces of the walls, which lower temperatures within the museum (Figure 16.8).

Studio Ma, LGE, and Core Construction limited the number of building materials to concrete, glass, and Western red cedar whenever possible. This reduced costs and created architecture that suited the Museum's urban location and referred to both desert-adapted construction and Western frontier buildings. The Museum's concrete exterior fits with contemporary art museum design; it also responds well to the heat and dryness of the Sonoran desert, providing durability and a similar visual weight to that of the vernacular adobe construction found across the desert Southwest. Within the building, cedar boards were used to clad walls in some public areas and create overhead baffles in the theater.

To meet American Alliance of Museum standards for collection loans, exhibition and storage areas are subject to strict environmental controls and security

Figure 16.8 The architects textured the concrete walls with vertical ribs, following a biophilic principle seen in saguaro cacti in the surrounding Sonoran Desert, to provide self-shading and reduce energy costs. Image: Bill Timmerman Photography, 2015.

measures. Studio Ma and the mechanical systems engineer, Syska Hennessy Group, selected conventional heating, cooling, and ventilation equipment, both for the lower initial cost and ease of maintenance by City staff. Highly energy-efficient equipment costs more and can require increased oversight to operate. Yet the Museum and Studio Ma expected the facility to meet LEED Gold standards for sustainable building design, which requires high energy and water efficiency. Summer temperatures in Scottsdale can reach to 120°F, or nearly 50°C, an ordeal for any building. Studio Ma responded by using the concrete tilt-up construction to their advantage. The designers modeled energy and daylighting levels for the various designs they considered until they arrived at a scheme that gave the museum the facility it wanted and achieved LEED Gold efficiency standards. The building's light-mass volumes shade its lower, high-mass volumes to reduce energy use. By relying primarily on passive building design elements, Western Spirit: Scottsdale's

Figure 16.9 A weeping wall on the exterior artfully directs condensate to a sunken riparian garden in the courtyard. (right) Detail. Images: Bill Timmerman Photography, 2015.

Museum of the West uses 36 Btu per square foot per year, which is a 38% reduction in energy use from baseline models for typical museum buildings (Western Spirit: Scottsdale's Museum of the West, 2016). Overall, the museum's operating costs are 35% below average for peer facilities (Mike Fox, Executive Director, Western Spirit: Scottsdale's Museum of the West, email to the author, January 14, 2018).

To reduce water usage, Studio Ma chose high-efficiency plumbing fixtures, and the building's grounds feature cacti and other desert plants. A "weeping" steel wall in the courtyard is fed by moisture that has condensed from the building's climate control systems; it flows down the face of the wall to irrigate the landscaping, reducing water use (Figure 16.9). The amount of plantings on site doubled from what had preexisted, and bioswales in the plazas and courtyard also capture storm water. Together, the Museum consumes 40% less water than baseline models for the average museum facility (Figure 16.10) (Western Spirit: Scottsdale's Museum of the West, 2016).

SOCIAL SUSTAINABILITY

The second principle of triple bottom line sustainability is social equity. This is best seen in the urban design of Western Spirit: Scottsdale's Museum of the West. The property is adjacent to a bus transit center, which has been identified as a future

Figure 16.10 Western Spirit: Scottsdale's Museum of the West integrates ecological design with sensory pleasure. The pavement holds up to heavy foot traffic and is run through with a large bioswale planted with shade trees. The swale crisscrossed with steel grates, referring to cattle guards. Image: Bill Timmerman Photography, 2015.

expansion area. Because of the site's characteristics, all four sides of the building and its roof would be visible to pedestrians and those living in neighboring residential complexes. Studio Ma designed each side of the building as a public face for the museum, and they cloaked its loading and delivery area. The Mordant Wing of the Museum of Contemporary Art in Sydney, designed by Sam Marshall Architect and the New South Wales Government Architects Office, used a similar strategy several years earlier.

A sculpture courtyard next to the Museum's theater provides spillover space for events. The building's grounds facing the transit center have been landscaped to provide shaded areas, and are used by people visiting the neighborhood or waiting for a bus (Figure 16.11).

The Museum's shop is placed at the center of the site, where East First Street terminates at North Marshall Way, to give it the most visibility to both vehicle and foot traffic (Figure 16.12). The shop's prominent location has improved street life in the area, which has struggled since the rise of internet sales and the popularity of international art fairs. Many local art dealers have shuttered their galleries, and

Figure 16.11 Visitors can sit amidst 100% native plantings and tree shade, including majestic saguaro, barrel cactus, and yucca. Image: Bill Timmerman Photography, 2015.

Old Town has only half the galleries it had in its heyday. Unlike other museums, Western Spirit: Scottsdale's Museum of the West opted not to build its own cafe, which prompts visitors to patronize local restaurants.

The Museum's commitment to social equity is also seen in its curatorial and educational programming. Western Spirit: Scottsdale's Museum of the West prominently features Native American history, arts, and crafts. Its exhibitions tell the stories of many ethnic groups who have made the West their home. It trains volunteers to serve as docents and assist with educational programs for local schools. Scottsdale residents can visit the Museum for free, and a special program offered Native Americans free admission over an extended window of time.

ECONOMIC SUSTAINABILITY

The principle of economic sustainability is perhaps the most noteworthy part of the conception of Western Spirit: Scottsdale's Museum of the West. Environmental sustainability has become mainstream for cultural buildings, and many institutions propound social justice in their missions, such as the Brooklyn Museum.

Figure 16.12 (top) Site Plan by Studio Ma. (bottom) Western Spirit: Scottsdale's Museum of the West provides a landmark, multiuse museum, meeting and retail venue to anchor an enhanced arts district. Image: Bill Timmerman Photography, 2015.

But as a class, cultural buildings often fail to live up to economic expectations, whether on the micro scale of their financial operations, or at the macro level of revitalizing their communities. For every Guggenheim Bilbao, there are numerous institutions whose attendance plummets once their novelty fades. Seph Rodney's overview in *Hyperallergenic* (Rodney, 2018) is largely based on a January 2018 article by Baltimore Sun reporter Mary Carole McCauley that describes drops in visitor attendance at local museums, even for new or recently expanded institutions (McCauley, 2018). McCauley cites studies by the National Endowment of the Arts (NEA, 2015) and the American Academy of Arts and Sciences (American Academy of Arts and Sciences, 2017), along with the 2014 National Awareness, Attitudes & Usage Study of Visitor-Serving Organizations (Dilenschneider, 2014); all remark on national declines.

Founding a museum without a permanent collection frees the institution from the staff and building costs that come from storing and conserving collections, but the museum must meet international standards for museum loans as quickly as possible, or it will have no objects to use for its curatorial programming. Two events helped Western Spirit: Scottsdale's Museum of the West. It was able to meet loan standards in a record time of less than six months from its opening, which qualified it to become a Smithsonian Museum affiliate while interest in the museum was high. This helped assure its attractiveness for future exhibitions and consequently, future visitors. And during planning and construction of the museum facility, an anonymous donor offered a painting and sculpture collection on permanent loan to Western Spirit: Scottsdale's Museum of the West. This generous donation required some modifications to the museum building while it was under construction, but Studio Ma and the Museum staff developed part of the second floor to accommodate the collection and its donor's vision. Western Spirit: Scottsdale's Museum of the West has received subsequent donations and long-term loans from other collectors who have been impressed with the museum's quality. As a result, the museum has planned on an expansion that adds collections storage and conservation areas. Because Western Spirit: Scottsdale's Museum of the West has been financially successful from its opening, the increased costs that come with permanent collections will not strain its operations (Figure 16.13).

The Museum has made the surrounding area more desirable, and the City of Scottsdale has entered into a public-private partnership to build two hotels and residential towers within the superblock where the museum is located. This is hoped to bring more tourists and residents to downtown (Trimble, 2018). Western Spirit: Scottsdale's Museum of the West enlisted Studio Ma for their planned expansion, which adds new administrative offices and reuses a portion of an underground parking garage below the museum building as collections storage. The architects

Figure 16.13 Natural light from the courtyard is a central, organizing element for the museum, reminding visitors of the colorful and dramatic quality of the Western landscape while reducing electrical lighting loads. Image: Bill Timmerman Photography, 2015.

will also adapt the building's urban design to accommodate the new hotel and residential high-rises, so that public open space continues to offer Scottsdale residents a better quality of life.

By becoming the economic catalyst civic leaders wanted the museum to be, Western Spirit: Scottsdale's Museum of the West has fulfilled its promise of triple bottom line sustainability. The museum building advances environmental sustainability through its use of passive construction and reductions to energy and water usage. Where once there was an empty lot next to an underused transit center in a neighborhood losing economic vitality, there is a thriving cultural district supporting local artists and craftspeople. And Scottsdale has shown itself to be not just the West's most western city, but an intellectual center for examining what the American West means in our cultural life.

REFERENCES

American Academy of Arts and Sciences. 2017. "Art Museum Attendance." *Humanities Indicators Project*, November 2017. https://www.humanitiesindicators.org/content/indicatordoc.aspx?i=102

Cain, Abigail. 2016. "What Happens When a Museum Closes?," *Artsy*, May 13, 2016. www.artsy.net/article/artsy-editorial-what-happens-when-a-museum-closes.

City of Scottsdale. 2012. "Western Art and History Museum Request For Proposals Pre-Proposal Meeting Summarized Meeting Minutes." City of Scottsdale, Arizona, January 25, 2012. www.scottsdaleaz.gov/AssetFactory.aspx?did=42908.

City of Scottsdale. 2019. "City of Scottsdale." Accessed on February 9, 2019. www.scottsdaleaz.gov.

Covert, Tricia. 2015. "An Interview with Mike Fox, CEO of Scottsdale Museum of the West." *Arizona School of Real Estate and Business*, January 21, 2015. www.asreb.com/2015/01/interview-mike-fox-ceo-scottsdale-museum-west/.

Dilenschneider, Colleen. 2014. "Signs of Trouble for the Museum Industry (DATA)." *Colleendilenschneider*, December 03, 2014. https://www.colleendilen.com/2014/12/03/signs-of-trouble-for-the-museum-industry-data/

Fox, Michael. 2018. Email to the author, January 14, 2018.

Fox, Michael. 2018. Phone interview with the author, July 26, 2018.

Fox, Oliver and Tiany Galaskas. 2019. Email to the author, January 11, 2019.

McCauley, Mary Carole. 2018. "In Baltimore and nationwide, art museums fight sharp declines in attendance." *Batimore Sun*, January 12, 2018. www.baltimoresun.com/entertainment/arts/bs-fe-museum-attendance-20171002-story.html.

McGlone, Peggy, and Manuel Roig-Franzia. 2019. "The Newseum was a grand tribute to the power of journalism. Here's how it failed." *Washington Post*, February 1, 2019. www.washingtonpost.com/entertainment/museums/the-newseum-was-a-grand-tribute-to-the-power-of-journalism-heres-how-it-failed/2019/02/01/aeeb2482-25a4-11e9-81fd-b7b05d5bed90_story.html?utm_term=.3e44ddcac1cd.

National Endowment for the Arts. 2015. "A decade of arts engagement: findings from the survey of public participation in the arts, 2002–2012'. NEA Research Report #58. Washington: National Endowment for the Arts, January 2015. www.arts.gov/sites/default/files/2012-sppa-feb2015.pdf.

Nikos-Rose, Karen. 2013. "UC Davis selects architectural team to create an art museum for the 21st century." *UC Davis*, May 1, 2013. www.ucdavis.edu/news/uc-davis-selects-architectural-team-create-art-museum-21st-century.

Nikos-Rose, Karen. 2016. "The UC Davis Manetti Shrem Museum Points to a New Direction in U.S. Museum Design." *UC Davis*, July 20, 2016. www.ucdavis.edu/news/uc-davis-manetti-shrem-museum-points-new-direction-us-museum-design

Perkins, Brett. 2018. Phone interview with the author, December 21, 2018.

Rodney, Seph. 2018. "Is Art Museum Attendance Declining Across the US?" *Hyperallergic*, January 18, 2018. https://hyperallergic.com/421968/is-art-museum-attendance-declining-across-the-us/.

Studio Ma. n.d. "Projects: Museum of the West." Accessed February 1, 2019. http://studioma.com/index.php?/project/museum-of-the-west.

Sudjic, Deyan. 2005. *The Edifice Complex: How the Rich and Powerful Shape the World*. New York: Penguin Press.

Trimble, Lynn. 2018. "A Museum Square Development Is in the Works for Downtown Scottsdale." *Phoenix Sun-Times*, July 13, 2018. www.phoenixnewtimes.com/arts/could-museum-square-revitalize-old-town-scottsdale-10611537.

University of California, Davis. n.d. "Jan Shrem and Maria Manetti Shrem Museum of Art." *Design and Construction Management*. Accessed February 9, 2019. https://dcm.ucdavis.edu/shrem

Western Spirit: Scottsdale's Museum of the West. www.scottsdalemuseumwest.org.

Western Spirit: Scottsdale's Museum of the West. 2016. "Western Spirit: Scottsdale's Museum of the West Awarded Prestigious LEED® Green Building Certification." Press Releases, April 15, 2016. https://scottsdalemuseumwest.org/wp-content/uploads/2016/04/FINAL_LEED-Certification-NR_website_04-15-16.pdf.

Wikipedia. "Scottsdale, Arizona." Last modified on February 5, 2019. https://en.wikipedia.org/wiki/Scottsdale,_Arizona.

CHAPTER 17

Less Energy, More Stability

Passive Building Principles for Collection- and Visitor-Friendly Net-Zero and Net-Positive Buildings, and a Proposal for the Museum of Energy

Jonathan Bean

INTRODUCTION

As the cultural role that museums play has expanded, so has the size, cost, and energy use of museum structures. While the energy impact of museums—along with its contribution to climate change—has not gone unnoticed, two prevailing perspectives are apparent. The first is that increased energy use is unavoidable. From this perspective, energy use is a necessary consequence of larger buildings, more visitors, and heightened expectations for the role of climate control in conserving museum collections. In the 1970's, Garry Thomson's book *The Museum Environment* established the 50/70 rule, which calls for conditions of 50% relative humidity at 70° F ± 2. Standards established since then by the American Society of Heating, Refrigeration, and Air-Conditioning Engineers (ASHRAE), which sets the standards that architects and mechanical engineers use when designing buildings, allows slightly more variation in both relative humidity and temperature depending on the class of control. Recently, within the museum community there has been a robust discussion about whether how rigidly to control the interior environment of the museum building (Atkinson 2014; Padfield and Borcherson (Kramer et al. 2018). The Environmental Guidelines Working Group of the American Institute for Conservation of Historic & Artistic Works (AIC), for example, suggested a range of 40–60% relative humidity and an acceptable temperature range of 59–77°F (AIC wiki 2019). While a more flexible approach has the potential to reduce energy consumption for museums with collections that are less sensitive to fluctuations in temperature and humidity, the role of standard loan agreements, which often specify a tight range of temperature and humidity levels, limits the potential for radical departures from the norm of a highly controlled building environment. A separate but equally important consideration that does not appear to have been discussed in the museum literature is the dwindling range of temperature levels that the mass public (including museum visitors) deems comfortable (Shove 2003). As many have noted, maintaining these norms carries a penalty in the form of carbon pollution because maintaining stable interior conditions within conventionally constructed buildings requires large inputs of energy. This is unintentionally reinforced by the structure of the standards in combination with expectations of professional performance. For example, ASHRAE's standard specifies only the interior conditions that the building must maintain, saying nothing about the amount of energy that can be used to achieve this goal (ASHRAE 2017). Faced with the possibility that excess variation in interior climate conditions could imperil a museum's collections, it is understandable that architects and engineers tend to make conservative decisions that reduce risk but increase energy consumption and therefore carbon pollution. While it is possible that the engineer or architect could be the subject of legal action if a building does not perform to the contracted standard, neither the architect or engineer are on the hook for the energy bill.

The idea that a building can either save energy *or* provide stable interior conditions, however, is a false dichotomy. In fact, many buildings achieve a dramatic reduction in energy consumption can be achieved while reducing risk by increasing the stability of interior conditions. This result can be achieved by using high performance building techniques in conjunction with passive design strategies. This approach offloads much of the work typically done by carbon-intensive mechanical systems to the building envelope. The purpose of this chapter is to serve as introduction for interested readers who do not have specialized knowledge of architecture or engineering to the promise of passive building for museums. The intention is to build on previous work by Rose (1994) to help the reader distinguish the contemporary Passive Building approach from the ever-growing world of green and sustainable building standards and certifications, such as LEED, Energy Star, and Green Globes, to explain the basic principles that inform cutting-edge building science, and to communicate the value of a systemic approach to creating buildings that are part of the solution to climate change. Based on the assumption that stewardship for the future should be part of every museum's mission, the conclusion builds on ideas from the anthropology of energy to speculate on how museums built this way could leverage their cultural authority to provide a transformative experiential education on the potential for the built environment, which currently accounts for almost half of all carbon emissions, to become the primary pathway to address climate change.

WHY DO MUSEUMS USE SO MUCH ENERGY?

The short answer is that they do not! Compared to the energy use of many other categories of buildings, museums use significantly less. In conjunction with the Commercial Buildings Energy Consumption Survey (CBECS), the US Energy Star program tracks the energy use of different US building types. The metric used, Energy Use Intensity, or EUI, is on the way to become the standard comparative metric. Calculating EUI is relatively simple: add up how much energy a building uses over the course of a year, and then divide by area. Obviously, the units matter; if you want to compare the EUI of a building in Europe to one in the US, you may have to convert both units of heat and area. But the idea is simple and powerful. The average museum, according to Energy Star data, use about 56.2 kBTU per square foot over the course of the year (2018). If you are unfamiliar with units used to measure energy, one BTU, or British Thermal Unit, is the amount of energy it takes to increase the temperature of one pound of water by one degree Fahrenheit at sea level. Boiling three quarts of room temperature water, which would fill a small stockpot, requires about 1000 BTUs, or 1 kBTU. This means that on an annual basis an average museum building could be operated with the same amount of energy required to boil 45 pots of water, multiplied by the number of square feet of floor area the building contains.

For comparison, a typical enclosed mall has a EUI of 65.7 kBTU/SF, while an energy-guzzling building such as a typical fast food restaurant has a EUI of 402.7 kBTU/SF (EnergyStar 2018). (In addition to the energy that goes into cooking the food, busy restaurants must also run air-conditioning year-round to remove extra heat from the kitchen as not to cook the staff.) The only building type that uses more energy than a fast food restaurant is a data center, which tops the charts at 1,821.0 kBTU/SF. This is a breathtaking amount of energy, and many large data centers consume significant percentages of the energy output of nearby power plants. That is why they tend to be located in places with very inexpensive electricity, such as near hydroelectric dams in the Pacific Northwest. This brings up one of the most important considerations when evaluating the EUI of a building: whether to measure site EUI or source EUI.

As referenced above, the average museum uses 56.2 kBTU/SF. This is a site EUI, which measures the amount of energy consumed on site. Measuring site

EUI is simple, and you can do it for your own home. Tally up your electric usage over the past 12 months, measured in kilowatt hours, then tally up your gas usage, which is typically measured in therms, then convert both to kBTU, add them together, and divide by the square footage of your house or apartment. But source EUI is more complex. It is a measurement of how much energy has to be produced at the power plant to deliver that same amount of energy to your house. No power technology is 100% efficient. Burning coal, for example, sends significant amounts of heat (along with mercury and other pollutants) up smokestacks and into our shared atmosphere. Further losses happen when the energy is sent over large distances, such as from a remote solar or wind farm. In the US, the average grid ratio is about 3:1, meaning that for each unit of power used, two more are wasted in generation and transmission. This is why understanding the source EUI is also important. For example, a typical fast food restaurant has a source EUI of 886.4 kBTU/sf, more than its site EUI. But a data center's source EUI is very close to its site EUI, largely because data centers tend to locate immediately adjacent to power that can be generated very efficiently, such as hydroelectric dams, wind, solar, or all three. Since museums tend to be located in urban or suburban areas, their source EUI is 112.0 kBTU/sf, almost exactly twice the site EUI of 56.2 kBTU/sf. Calculating a precise source EUI is complicated and more than likely to lead to arguments between experts; indeed, a new release of data between drafts of this chapter changed some of the EUI figures given above by more than 25%. Increased use of renewables and gas generation instead of coal-fired power plants is one reason for the change.

For some, the design of the power grid in the US, the interchangeability of all electrons, whether generated from dirty or reneweable energy sources, and the dynamic and time-specific use of energy suggest that the simplest solution is to use a national average to determine how much carbon pollution to attribute to a kilowatt of electricity regardless of the location of the building. Whether this makes sense, however, is an active debate. Others argue for a local or regional approach to determining the global warming potential of a specific building. This is because in regions such as the Pacific Northwest, or in other areas where energy is generated with renewable solar, wind, or hydro generation, gains in site energy efficiency do not translate to carbon reductions at a power plant. Advocates for this point of view argue that a super-efficient building in Seattle does not do much to reduce the amount of coal burned, but it does reduce the demand for renewable energy (Hershberg and Mead 2018; Johnson 2019). As Gretchen Bakke points out in *The Grid: The Fraying Wires between Americans and Our Energy Future*, a lack of investment in existing infrastructure coupled with uncertainty about future energy systems is a further complication (2016).

This perspective reflects a continuing and important debate about the meaning of net-zero. A commonly used definition of net-zero energy indicates that on an annual basis, a building uses no more energy than can be generated by renewable energy generated on-site or nearby (Peterson et al. 2015). Yet an approach that targets an annual average can generate serious problems because renewable energy is not always produced when it can be used. Imagine a sunny autumn afternoon. You've recently put a large solar-panel system on your house. It's pleasant outside, so you've thrown the windows open in your newly net-zero house, settled into your favorite chair with a nice glass of iced tea, and have become completely captivated by watching your electricity meter run backward. Now imagine an entire neighborhood of homes like this. Where does all that electricity go? Our current grid has very little ability to store excess energy, and power lines have to be sized to accommodate the peak capacity. Then the sun sets. You've left the windows open a little too long, so you turn on the heat. But since it is dark, the only way the power company can deliver energy to you is by operating a gas or coal power plant. Planning for net-zero site energy does not necessarily result in carbon reductions, whereas planning for net-zero source energy—or net-zero carbon emissions—requires architects and designers to grapple with the full complexity of energy use by taking peak load and storage into consideration. The good news is that museum energy use is, as explained above, relatively low. This makes the job of the architect and design team somewhat easier and amplifies the positive impact of getting to—or beyond—net-zero source energy.

INTRODUCING PASSIVE BUILDING

Passive building is an umbrella term for a combination of approaches that can deliver high-performance, net-zero source energy buildings at costs comparable to—or even lower than—other green standards such as LEED. The founder of the Passive House Institute United States explains (Klingenberg 2017) that there are five principles of passive building:

1. Continuous Insulation

Until recently most building codes allowed insulation to be designed and installed in such a way that severely degrades its performance. This is because of a phenomenon called thermal bridging. In conventional construction, it is not uncommon for structural elements to be in contact with both the conditioned space on the interior of the building and the outside conditions on the exterior of the building. If you are reading this in a wood-framed building, chances are that the wall you are looking at was constructed with wood studs spaced at about 16 inches on center (figure 17.1).

The exterior is covered with plywood and some sort of finish material, insulation—most often fluffy pink or yellow fiberglass—is placed between the studs, and then drywall is installed on the interior. This means that your house has a vertical thermal bridge located every 16 inches along every exterior wall, plus another thermal bridge at the top and the bottom where horizontal plates connect the studs. Wait for a cold day and place your hand along the wall—or use a thermal camera—and you will very clearly feel or see the thermal bridge. Or check your bathroom; the thermal bridges may be clearly visible, as mold and mildew grow by using the water that condenses in these cold spots. Commercial buildings are often built with elements such as window and door frames, or concrete floor slabs that extend from inside to outside, that function as thermal bridges. In a museum building, thermal bridging can amplify the detrimental effect of inadequately insulated exterior walls. Canvas paintings, for example, trap air

Figure 17.1 Many buildings are built with thermal bridges that decrease the effectiveness of insulation. The reclaimed cotton insulation in these walls has an effective R-value of 13, but the wood framing reduces the overall R-value of the wall by 15%. Thermal bridges can also attract moisture, which reduces the durability of the building assembly and promotes the growth of mold. Photo and illustration: Jonathan Bean.

when hung flush with a wall surface. This cold area attracts condensation that can damage both wall and painting (Neuhaus 2013). This is because humid air condenses when it comes into contact with a cold surface; think of the bathroom mirror after taking a long, hot shower. The typical way of addressing this problem has been to install dehumidification equipment attached to sensors. When mechanical equipment and sensors operate correctly, the dewpoint[1] can be kept out of the risk zone. But this solution is expensive in terms of equipment and energy costs, and it is also prone to failure. Sensors wear out and there is no clear indication when they are not working properly (Singer 2018). A better solution is to use an appropriate amount of continuous insulation on all exterior walls. Continuous insulation is a sheet product typically installed on the exterior of a building underneath the finished surface. It can be made of petrochemical foam, mineral wool, wood fiber, cork, or any other insulation material rated for this use. Minimum thickness varies by climate zone; in temperate climates, as little as one inch of insulation can do the trick, whereas several inches may be necessary in cold climates. Properly installed continuous insulation eliminates thermal bridging and ensures that wall temperatures, even in inside corners, which tend to be colder, can be kept out of the condensation risk zone, with a minimum of energy-intensive dehumidification.

2. Airtight Construction

William Shurcliff, a physicist and passive building pioneer, memorably made the point that we do not accept leaks in the plumbing systems we install, so it makes little sense to accept leaks in buildings (1988). Yet buildings are routinely designed and detailed in such a way that it is very difficult even for a builder with the best of intentions to construct airtight exterior assemblies. The areas most prone to leaks are where two or more materials come together: for example, where a roof meets a wall. Airtightness is further complicated by the inconvenient fact that buildings move—and sometimes a lot! Even outside of earthquake zones, daily and seasonal cycles of expansion and contraction put significant stress at the interface between different materials. Materials that the architecture and building industry have typically used to address these problem areas, such as caulk and sealant, degrade over time and require maintenance. When these materials fail, the performance and durability of the building is compromised. The failure of visible seams can detract from the aesthetic appearance of a building. But what about all the joints and junctions that are hidden from view? These cannot be maintained without costly, destructive, and disruptive disassembly of the building, so buildings tend to leak more air over time. Buildings that become leakier over time not only become less durable, but also waste energy because any air that seeps into a building displaces air that has been heated or cooled. Increased leakage also makes the interior climate of the building more difficult to control.

Air leakage causes a host of problems in buildings. First and most concerning is its impact on building durability. Air carries moisture, and when air carries more moisture than the materials around it, that moisture is transferred as the air goes by. Even a small stream of air can carry a tremendous amount of water. Assuming conditions of 70° F and 30% relative humidity, a 1 inch square hole can transport nearly 30 quarts of water over the course of a year. As with thermal bridging, the typical way of dealing with this problem has relied on the extravagant use of energy, by using lots and lots of heat or air conditioning to drive off the moisture that migrates through the envelope. But as building codes have restricted energy use, moisture problems have increased because there is less energy available to dry out damp assemblies. A better approach is taking care in design and construction to ensure that outside air, and its attendant moisture, do not end up in buildings.

The second problem with air leakage relates to indoor air quality. Air seeping through a wall assembly, especially parts of the wall assembly that may be damp or wet, does not arrive in the building clean and pure. In addition to water vapor, air carries a host of pollutants, including dust and pollen, which are irritants to people who suffer from asthma. In urban locations, outdoor air tends also to be high in particulate matter. Generally speaking, the smaller the particulate, the more harmful it is to human health. PM 2.5, which stands for Particulate Matter 2.5 microns or smaller in diameter, is a catch-all category that includes the byproducts of fossil-fuel combustion, heavy metal dust coming from vehicle brakes, biological matter, and other sources, and is generally regarded as the indoor air pollutant most deleterious to health. Leaky buildings admit more pollution from outside sources to the interior of the building than airtight buildings. Leakage also continually reintroduces PM 2.5 pollution, reducing the effectiveness and increasing the energy cost of air filtration.

For museum buildings, one additional benefit of airtightness stands out: pest resistance. Since bugs are larger than air molecules, a focus on achieving excellent airtightness will also result in a building that is resistant to pests. Further measures, such as compartmentalizing the building, or dividing it into separate zones that are themselves airtight from one another, can help contain to contain pests that might enter by hitching a ride on a visitor or a new acquisition. In fact, compartmentalization has been a somewhat surprising driver of the adoption of passive building in the affordable housing industry. Affordable housing operators learned quickly that compartmentalized airtight apartment buildings were highly resistant to systemic bedbug infestations, an expensive and intrusive problem to treat. Given the risk pests pose to collections, airtight construction makes at least as much sense for museum buildings as it does for affordable housing. No building is perfectly airtight, but it doesn't hurt to aim for perfection. Airtightness is measured by blowing air out of a building using a powerful fan and measuring the difference in pressure between the inside and the outside. One standard measurement is taken at 50 pascals, which is roughly equivalent to the pressure exerted on a building in a strong breeze. The measurement represents how much air leaks through each square foot of enclosure. Builders routinely achieve less than 0.1 cubic foot per minute per square foot of enclosure when a building is completed. The passive house standard requires less than this—a range of 0.06 CFM/minute/SF for new construction to 0.08 CFM/minute/SF, with the rationale that leakage will likely drift up slowly over time due to regular building movement. Specifying a mandatory airtightness test using a blower door, which can be done even in large buildings, is an excellent way to ensure quality design, construction, and improve indoor air quality. In large buildings with complex programs, or where uses are not compatible, for example, in archives, collections storage, and the museum cafe, compartmentalization, which means dividing the building enclosure into discrete airtight sections, can be used to ensure performance.

3. Optimized Windows

One especially apparent change in museum design and other buildings is a radical increase in the use of glass. For example, the extension to the Art Institute in Chicago designed by Renzo Piano Building Workshop Architects, completed in 2009, is almost entirely clad in glass. Architects like the aesthetic properties of the material, in particular its ability to make a building glow or shimmer. Glass also sends a powerful semiotic signal that aligns with the expressed desire of many institutions to become more open and transparent. Glass, however, can be a problematic material for museums. Too much light, of course, is not good for sensitive collections, and can severely restrict what in the collection can be exhibited, as is the case in the Milwaukee Art Museum's Quadracci Pavilion, designed by Santiago Calatrava Architects & Engineers, or require clumsy interior coverings such as those in the Crystal Bridges Museum of American Art, designed by Safdie Architects. Too much glass, the wrong kind of glass, or excessive amounts of glass, especially facing east or west, can make achieving a zero-net source energy goal difficult or impossible. This is because glass, in comparison to most other building materials, does not insulate particularly well. A standard 3.5 inch thick fiberglass batt of the kind likely stuffed between the studs in your home performs better than nearly all glass on the market, and especially the perfectly flat, extra-clear kind favored for museums and other high-profile buildings where it is congruent with a focus on aesthetics. A further problem is the amount of solar energy unshaded glass allows to enter a building. For museum buildings, the design team should seek a balance point between aesthetic considerations, the symbolic message of glass, interior lighting levels, and energy performance. Architects can also consider other ways to provide reflectivity and transparency. An excellent example is Farshid Moussavi's design for the Cleveland Museum of Contemporary Art, which uses stainless steel polished to a mirror finish to make the exterior of the building entirely reflective (see Figure 10.1).

The most important contribution of optimized windows in a passive building is thermal comfort. We tend to think about comfort as a steady-state condition, in part because of the way that our home and office thermostats are designed. Too warm at 78°? Turn down the temperature to 76°. Find that too cold? Bump it up to 77°. But air temperature, which is what the thermostat is measuring, is only one component of thermal comfort through which the human body assesses whether or not it is comfortable. Relative humidity, which is a measure of how much moisture the air can absorb before it becomes completely saturated, also impacts comfort. Humid, hot days are uncomfortable outside because the saturated air inhibits the evaporation of sweat. As noted in the introduction, museums often have levels of relative humidity that are higher than optimal for comfort in order to better preserve objects in the collection. Furthermore, conventionally built museums can have relative humidity levels that vary with height within one gallery or space; relative humidity might be too low at ground level, but too high at head height, with negative impacts to both the collection and visitors. This is because when buildings are dependent on large injections of heating or cooling energy to remain in a steady state, the added energy for conditioning does not necessarily mix evenly within a space; cold air tends to sink to the bottom of a space, while warm air rises to the top. Since warm air can hold more moisture, relative humidity increases with height. Again, the best way to address this problem is not through the provision of more intensive mechanical equipment, but instead through careful design that limits the amount of energy needed to maintain conditions in the space.

In addition to air temperature and relative humidity, an often-overlooked component of thermal comfort is radiant temperature. Think of how warm and cozy you can be outside huddled next to a roaring campfire, even when the air is very chilly. Conversely, think of how much you would like to crank up the thermostat if you were stuck sitting next to a single-pane window on a subzero day. Our bodies sense the temperature not only of the ambient air, but also of the things around us. Our sensation of comfort emerges when this input is combined with whether the air is warm or cold and whether perspiration is able to evaporate to cool the body. Windows matter, especially when there are lots of them, because they exert an outsize influence on this equation. Inadequately insulative windows have a surface that is hot in the summer and cold in the winter. A surprising quality of radiant heat transfer is that distance does not matter; if the body is in the line of sight of a hot or cold surface, it senses that temperature. So a cold bank of windows across a room or a hot strip of skylights far overhead can render a space with 72° F ambient air uncomfortable by shifting the Mean Radiant Temperature, or MRT. This is one reason why passive building standards encourage a comfort criteria for all glass areas, specifying that the temperature be kept around 7° F of the air temperature, even on the hottest and coldest days of the year. In conjunction with continuous insulation, this ensures that all building surfaces remain well within the safety zone for mold growth, protecting the museum building, the artifacts it contains, and museum workers and visitors.

4. Balanced Ventilation

While the provision of fresh air has only recently been introduced to residential building codes, most commercial and institutional buildings built in the last 20 years have included dedicated systems to provide fresh air. Much new research is focused on quantifying the health and productivity benefits of increased ventilation rates. This research may make it seem that any kind of building, including museums, simply cannot get enough fresh air. But, especially for museums, this is not the case. One problem is simple physics: from an energetic standpoint, it is expensive to heat or cool air. It takes one BTU to raise the temperature of one pound of air by 1 degree Fahrenheit. But there is a lot of air in a building, air comes in constantly in a conventional leaky building, and air is surprisingly heavy—the air in a small bedroom or office weighs about 60 pounds. Of course, one way to provide fresh air is to open a window, but that is not always comfortable, and opening windows can use a lot of energy, because the air conditioning and heating must run in overdrive. Unconditioned fresh air can also cause large swings in humidity, which can be especially problematic for sensitive artifacts.

This is especially true when it is warm and humid outside, because warm air can carry significantly larger amounts of moisture than cool air. Put another way, a small amount of 90° air at 90% relative humidity can cause a big jump in the relative humidity of 72° indoor air. When ventilation rates are increased in conventionally constructed, leaky buildings, the risk of moisture and mold problems increases. Increased visitor flows further amplify the problem. More people breathing and offgassing what building scientists politely term bioeffluent means a concomitant need for increased fresh air. Since conventionally museum buildings are typically slightly pressurized—a fan in the mechanical room continually blows extra outside air into the building, forcing conditioned air to seep out of gaps and cracks in the building—simply increasing ventilation rates has the effect of driving more moisture-laden interior air through the building enclosure, and this further increases the risk to the building and its enclosure. A better solution is to use balanced ventilation in conjunction with a carefully sealed building enclosure. Balanced ventilation systems use a mechanical device to expel stale air while using the energy from that airflow to pre-heat or pre-cool incoming outdoor air (Figure 17.2).

The design team and mechanical engineer should use modeling software to study the interaction between increased ventilation rates and interior relative humidity levels. This is especially important in hot climates where high humidity occurs during all or part of the cooling season. The amount of humidity that needs to be moved out of the building, or kept in, will inform the choice of balanced ventilation technology: either energy recovery ventilators, heat recovery ventilators, or dedicated outdoor air systems. In a low-load building, the efficiency of the air exchange device is paramount. For museums, scalability is another important factor. The design team should specify a balanced ventilation system capable of variable flow rates with the goal of bringing in just enough outside air to maintain pleasant conditions inside the building. A simple way of doing this is to use carbon dioxide sensors and increase ventilation rates when CO_2 levels exceed 1,000 PPM, which is a level generally accepted as a marker for the presence of other pollutants.

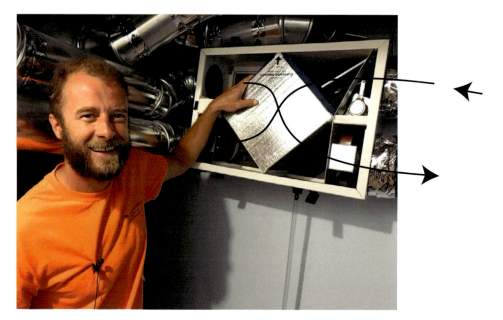

Figure 17.2 This is a residential energy recovery ventilator, but ones for commercial buildings work using the same principle. Stale air from inside the building is sent through channels a recovery core made of a fabric-like membrane material. Fresh air passes through adjacent channels in the membrane. This allows heat to transfer between the stale outgoing air and the fresh incoming air. The two air streams do not mix. Photo under illustration: "Heat Recovery Ventilation System" by Green Energy Futures is licensed under CC BY-NC-SA 2.0 https://flic.kr/p/YPikXX. Illustration: Jonathan Bean.

5. Minimal Mechanical Systems

When the previous four principles are employed and a building has continuous insulation without thermal bridging, airtight construction, optimized windows, and balanced ventilation, the whole is more than the sum of its parts. Mechanical systems can be significantly smaller than in a conventionally constructed building because loads have been reduced significantly. Smaller systems, of course, are less expensive to install, and as a rule they operate at higher efficiency levels than larger systems, meaning that they use even less energy. For museum buildings, there are three important considerations for the design team to consider when deciding just how much the mechanical system can be downsized. First is the question of capacity. If the building will be unoccupied overnight, and the collection can handle some swings in temperature and relative humidity, it may take less energy to use oversized equipment so that it is possible to idle the building overnight and heat or cool in the morning before the first occupants arrive (Kramer et al. 2015). Second is the question, raised above, of variable visitor flows and changing usage patterns. A too-small system will not be able to handle a larger-than-expected crowd on a particularly warm or cold day. Retrofitting larger systems, unless planned for in advance, can be costly and result in undesirable changes in the performance of the building enclosure, such as the accumulation of moisture. Third is the tendency of passive buildings to maintain more stable interior conditions. Since the need for large energy inputs has been designed out of the building, it is easy for many passive buildings to maintain interior temperatures of 55° F or greater in winter even if the power goes out. To date, this concept, which is generally referred to as passive survivability (Wilson 2018), has been applied to human survivability, but it would be worthwhile to extend it to the museum context with the goal of better understanding how museum buildings and their collections could ride out medium- to long-term interruptions in the power supply.

OTHER CONSIDERATIONS

As the distinction between source and site energy makes clear, there is not, and cannot be, a single prescription for carbon-neutral or carbon-positive building appropriate for every climate, every site, and every museum. An area worthy of reflection—and one the current version of passive guidelines do not take into consideration—are the intertwined issues of embodied energy, embodied carbon, and global warming potential. Given that conservation of the collection for an indefinite future period is a central goal for many museums, these already thorny issues have the potential to become even more complex for the institution client and the design team. A further wrinkle is that, just as glass in museum structures is often intended to signal transparency and openness, other material choices are made to signal permanence and solidity. Two very common materials, concrete and steel, are particularly energy intensive (Landberg and Hodges 2019). These choices, which are important to fulfil the symbolic role of the building, ironically often accelerate the cycles of extraction, depletion, and pollution that are destabilizing our climate. What are the parameters that dictate when to trade off a long-lasting, but energy-intensive material, for one that may not last as long, but has a better carbon profile? Finding workable answers to this question that do not endanger the museum's collection or the building requires a nimble and well-informed design team. Embodied energy is the amount of energy required to produce a material. Wood, such as the studs in most houses, has relatively low embodied energy, while aluminium, which requires energy-intensive mining and refining processes, has high embodied energy. Embodied carbon is calculated similarly, but the math can get fuzzy. Is wood a low- or negative-carbon material? It depends on where it comes from and how long you think it will last. (For as definitive an answer to this question as I have found, I direct the interested reader to Howard Odum's concept of "emergy," which is spelled with a "m" (2007).) Natural materials, such as cork, cellulose, or wood fiber insulation, are often, but not always, alternatives with lower embodied energy and carbon. But no matter how you do the math, concrete is one of the most energy- and carbon-intensive construction materials, so it is a worthwhile design objective to limit its use in construction. If the goal is to limit the damage wrought by the climate crisis, it is also worth considering the global warming potential, or GWP, of building materials and components. Growing awareness of its importance has driven significant change in the petrochemical foam industry, because some types of plastic foam, such as extruded polystyrene, have historically used foaming agents that contribute significantly to global warming when they eventually escape the foam. Awareness is also growing of the global warming potential of the refrigerants commonly used in air conditioning units, heat pumps, dehumidifiers, and even household refrigerators. This is a concern because systems tend to leak at low, but not insignificant, rates over time, and catastrophic losses of refrigerant are not uncommon. The most commonly used refrigerant, R410a, has 2400 times the global warming potential of carbon dioxide. Leaders in the industry have identified refrigerant management as the most important path to reducing the impact of climate change (Hawken 2017). This is yet one more reason to engage the five pillars of passive design and reduce the size of mechanical systems.

THE MUSEUM OF ENERGY: A PROVOCATIVE SPECULATION

The role of the museum in broader culture continues to emerge. Many museum institutions now consider conservation just one plank of a broader mission of community engagement. While museum buildings have long been destinations for art or history buffs and tourists, this new form of the museum aims to attract a broader public, with spaces designed to be rented for receptions, banquets, and weddings (Lindsay 2016). The increasing number of people spending time in museum buildings presents a novel opportunity for advocates of high performance, zero- and positive-net energy, and passive buildings. That opportunity is to highlight the exceptional comfort achieved when a building uses all five principles of passive building. One of the biggest problems with green and sustainable buildings is that many are indistinguishable from buildings that waste energy. Yes, some architecture firms are known for flaunting the green status of their buildings with flamboyant design moves, using organic forms or covering the building with living green material. The sociologists Simon Guy and Graham Farmer refer to this mode as the eco-aesthetic logic, which they identify as one of six competing logics that comprise sustainable architecture (2001). Other buildings, such as those covered with visible solar panels or that make a design feature of wastewater treatment systems, are designed in the eco-technic logic, one that has proved broadly compatible with the diffusion of relatively inexpensive solar power and internet-connected sensors. But these buildings do not necessarily use less energy than other buildings—indeed, with current technology it is difficult to provide enough solar panels to offset the energy consumption of most buildings over five stories or so—and so much of what the public identifies and experiences as sustainable architecture is, in fact, little more than window dressing. This gets to the crux of the matter. What is a reasonable way forward if there is no way to see energy savings, the ways we represent saving energy are not resonant with most people, and the built environment is filled with false signals that give people the sense that buildings are doing more than they actually are to reduce carbon emissions? Here is where experience matters. The anthropologists Mike Anusas and Timothy Ingold have argued that solar panels should hum (2013). While this would likely be distracting in a museum, the point is to make perceptible otherwise imperceptible processes. This would be analogous to the workings of other ways of generating power, such as the roar and belch of burning coal, and would provide an important signal that they are busy working. Extending this idea to the context of the museum suggests a different orientation toward building construction and operation. Traditionally the approach has been to hide these things from the public behind smooth white walls, dropped ceilings, and utility plenums, an understandable approach when the sheer bulk of mechanical systems gave them a grotesque quality and the amount of energy moving through them made them hazardous. But in high performance buildings that use passive building principles, this work is largely done by inert elements in the enclosure of the building. Museums might make a point out of connecting the dots for their visitors by peeling back the curtain on wall assemblies and mechanical systems and explaining how these systems keep the collection safe and visitors comfortable. Design inspiration might be taken from the Pompidou Center in Paris (though the result would be far more stripped down) or from Galen Cranz's vision of the sustainable park (Cranz and Boland 2004), where essential features of urban living, such as wastewater management, are dealt with in a way that is both aesthetically engaging and educational. But the most important role museums could play is to reset the needle for public expectations of comfort. The massive flows of energy that we use now to condition buildings make it difficult to achieve comfort, yet few have experienced buildings that work any other way. Imagine that you are taking a bath and the only way you have to raise or lower the temperature is to dump in huge buckets of water either at a rolling boil or frozen solid. It would be difficult to get the water to a comfortable temperature in the first place and even more difficult to maintain it. But this is the way most buildings work, and since it is the norm, there is little reason to question it. The Museum of Energy—and this provocation is only partially tongue-in-cheek—would bracket the lived experience of comfort with an explanation of the physical features of the built environment that contribute to reduced carbon pollution, better air quality, and increased durability. These are qualities worth pursuing not just for a hypothetical Museum of Energy, but for all museums, but for all buildings, and indeed for all people.

NOTE

1   The temperature at which moisture condenses on a cold surface.

REFERENCES

American Institute for Conservation wiki. (2019). https://conservation-wiki.com/wiki/Environmental_Guidelines.

Anusas, Mike, and Tim Ingold. 2013. "Designing Environmental Relations: From Opacity to Textility". *Design Issues* 29 (4): 58–69.

ASHRAE [American Society of Heating Refrigerating and Air-Conditioning Engineers Inc.]. 2017. *2017 ASHRAE® Handbook* (I-P Edition). Atlanta, GA: ASHRAE.

Atkinson, Jo Kirby. 2014. "Environmental Conditions for the Safeguarding of Collections: A Background to the Current Debate on the Control of Relative Humidity and Temperature." *Studies in Conservation* 59 (4): 205–212. doi: 10.1179/2047058414Y.0000000141.

Bakke, Gretchen. 2017. *The Grid: The Fraying Wires between Americans and Our Energy Future*. New York and London: Bloomsbury USA.

Cranz, Galen, and Michael Boland. 2004. "Defining the Sustainable Park: A Fifth Model for Urban Parks". *Landscape Journal* 23 (2): 102.

Energy Star Portfolio Manager Technical Reference. "U.S. Energy Use Intensity by Property Type." 2018. https://portfoliomanager.energystar.gov/pdf/reference/US%20National%20Median%20Table.pdf.

Guy, Simon, and Graham Farmer. 2001. "Reinterpreting Sustainable Architecture: The Place of Technology". *Journal of Architectural Education* 54 (3): 140–148. doi: 10.1162/10464880152632451.

Hawken, Paul, ed. 2017. *Drawdown: The Most Comprehensive Plan Ever Proposed to Reverse Global Warming.* New York: Penguin.

Hershberg, Karina, and David Mead. 2018. "Local Greenhouse Gases: A Bold New Approach to Tracking Sustainability." Living Future Conference. Portland, Oregon. https://livingfutureunconference2018.sched.com/event/CAj5/local-greenhouse-gases-a-bold-new-approach-to-tracking-sustainability.

Johnson, Lucas. 2019. "Avoid The Carbon Rebound: How Passive House Can Create Higher-Carbon Buildings Than Conventional Methods." Passive House Northwest Conference. Portland, OR. https://phnw.memberclicks.net/2019-conference-presentations?option=com_community&view=profile.

Klingenberg, Katrin. 2017. "Five Fundamental Passive Building Principles." *Builder*. August 30, 2017. https://builderonline.com/building/building-science/five-fundamental-passive-building-principles_o

Kramer, Rick, Lisje Schellen, and Henk Schellen. 2018. "Adaptive Temperature Limits for Air-Conditioned Museums in Temperate Climates". *Building Research & Information* 46 (6): 686–697. doi: 10.1080/09613218.2017.1327561.

Kramer, R.P., M.P.E. Maas, M.H.J. Martens, A.W.M. van Schijndel, and H.L. Schellen. 2015. "Energy Conservation in Museums Using Different Setpoint Strategies: A Case Study for a State-of-the-Art Museum Using Building Simulations". *Applied Energy* 158 (November): 446–458. doi: 10.1016/j.apenergy.2015.08.044.

Landberg, Reed, and Jeremy Hodges. 2019. "What's Wrong With Modern Buildings? Everything, Starting With How They're Made." *Bloomberg*, June 19, 2019, sec. Climate Changed. https://www.bloomberg.com/news/features/2019-06-20/what-s-wrong-with-modern-buildings-everything-starting-with-how-they-re-made

Lindsay, Georgia. 2016. *The User Perspective on Twenty-First-Century Art Museums.* London: Routledge.

Neuhaus, Edgar. 2013. "A Critical Look at the Use of HVAC Systems in the Museum Environment." In *Climate for Collections: Standards and Uncertainties*, edited by Jonathan Ashley-Smith, Andreas Burmester, and Melanie Eibl, 117–126. London: Archetype Publications Ltd.

Odum, Howard T. 2007. *Environment, Power, and Society for the Twenty-First Century: The Hierarchy of Energy.* New York: Columbia University Press.

Peterson, Kent, P. Torcellini, Roger Grant, C. Taylor, S. Punjabi, and R. Diamond. 2015. "A Common Definition for Zero Energy Buildings." U.S. Department of Energy, Building America, Office of Energy Efficiency and Renewable Energy.

Rose, William. 1994. "Effects of Climate Control on the Museum Building Envelope." *Journal of the American Institute for Conservation* 33 (2): 199–210. doi: 10.1179/019713694806124847.

Shove, Elizabeth. 2003. *Comfort, Cleanliness and Convenience: The Social Organization of Normality.* Oxford and New York: Berg.

Shurcliff, William A. 1988. *Super Insulated Houses and Air-to-Air Heat Exchangers.* Andover, MA: Brick House Pub. Co.

Singer, Brett. 2018. "IAQ at Home: How Are We Doing?" presented at the Twenty-Second Annual Westford Symposium on Building Science, Westford, Massachusetts, August 6.

Wilson, Alex. 2018. "Resilience as a Driver of Passive Design". In *Activism in Architecture: Bright Dreams of Passive Energy Design*, edited by Margot McDonald and Carolina Dayer, 1st ed., 132–139. New York: Routledge. 2019. | Series: Routledge research in architecture: Routledge. doi: 10.4324/9781315182858.

CHAPTER **18**

Bringing Nature into Place

Green Roofs as Place Makers in Museum Architecture

Angela Loder

INTRODUCTION

Faced with increasing competition for visitors, museums have been reinventing themselves to draw traditional and non-traditional visitors into their spaces (Plaza 2007). Following the success of iconic museums that have used famous architects to draw attention to their buildings, museums are using a multitude of strategies to entice visitors to their spaces and maintain their relevance (Patterson 2012). For example, some museums are using architecture, amenities, and even landscape architecture to blur traditional edges between formal exhibit space and public space to entice traditional and non-traditional users (Lindsay 2016). Similarly, some museums are redefining the role of the museum in cities, seen with an increasing number of museums pursuing sustainable architecture and site design strategies (American Alliance of Museums 2017; Gelles 2016; New York Real Estate Journal 2019). While the integration of at-grade garden spaces for museums is not rare, the inclusion of a green roof is: the green roof on the California Academy of Sciences in San Francisco garnered as much, if not more, attention than the museum itself (Lanks 2008; Lloyd 2007).

The relative novelty of green roofs as part of museum design makes them unusual case studies, particularly in their approach to non-traditional user engagement (Lindsay 2018). While the design, aesthetics, and intent of green roofs on museums vary, the analysis in this chapter reveals an ambiguous relationship between more traditional goals around green roof implementation—such as mitigation of the urban heat island effect—and their role as a key component of the narrative and goals of the museum. The emerging presence of green roofs as part of museum architecture means that they also reflect larger debates around the role, meaning, and value of urban nature. This chapter examines green roofs in three case studies—the Denver Museum of Modern Art, the Los Angeles Holocaust Museum, and the Canadian War Museum in Ottawa, Ontario—that reflect this tension between museum narrative, user experience, and the symbolism of urban nature.

THE CREATIVE CITY: COMPETITION, INVESTMENT, AND MUSEUMS AS PLACEMAKER

The neoliberal shift in the 1990s reduced government spending on public amenities to a more entrepreneurial model, pitting cities against one another to compete for speculative investment from private capital to make up for government cutbacks (Harvey 2005, 1989; Logan 2002). Cultural amenities such as museums, theaters, and parks with high-quality cultural programing were common to attract the so-called "creative class" as theorized by Richard Florida (Florida 2012). Enormously influential, this approach can be seen very clearly in the "age of museum madness" at the turn of the millennium. Museums competed with each other to attract so-called "starchitects"—often through highly touted international competitions—to create the splashiest or most innovative museum architecture that would entice global tourists to struggling post-industrial cities (Greenberg 2008; Newhouse 2006; West 2006). In addition to architectural design, these museums often included other cultural amenities such as dining, shopping, or public spaces (Tilden 2004).

The most successful example of the use of a museum to spur economic and cultural revitalization is often referred to as the "Bilbao effect." This refers to the enormously successful Guggenheim Museum at Bilbao (GMB), Spain, by the famous architect Frank Gehry, that put a struggling post-industrial third or fourth-tier city on the international map and which currently earns roughly $39.9 million a year for the Basque treasury (Plaza 2007; Sassen 2002). While this level of success has been hard to replicate (Plaza 2007, 2006), it has not stopped other museums from attempting to do so, such as the Denver Art Museum's use of Daniel Liebskind to "put Denver on the map" (Lindsay 2018).

This focus on branding and attracting international attention through the creation of collective cultural capital has led some to argue that the neoliberal focus has turned the city into a spectacle for consumption rather than a place that caters to the lived experience and needs of the local population (Domosh 1996; Hannigan 1998; Lefebvre 1996; Zukin 1991, 1991). Possibly in response to this criticism, the latest trend in museum architecture is moving beyond simply garnering global attention to the museums' architecture but is actively trying to integrate and engage with the surrounding communities (Lindsay 2016, 255). In her book *The User Perspective in Twenty-First Century Art Museums*, Lindsay argues that in addition to traditional museum users, such as visitors, staff, and the art itself, there are four kinds of new museum users that are being catered to: amenities-users, people who use the auxiliary spaces of a museum but not necessarily the galleries themselves; cities or regions, which use the museum as part of a revitalization or neighbourhood engagement; non-visitors, such as those who consume global architecture through media; and ecological systems, which sometimes are referenced in the museums' design (such as achieving LEED), but is impacted by it regardless (Lindsay 2016, 255). In addition to examining how they link to values around nature, the case studies below showcase different approaches to engaging three of those four types of users: the amenities users, cities or regions, and ecological systems.

GREEN ROOFS: AMENITY SPACE OR ECOLOGICAL SOLUTION?

While green roofs on museums are somewhat unusual, they reflect larger trends that see cities rethinking their approach to urban nature. Faced with the combination of increasingly volatile environmental conditions from climate change, ageing infrastructure, and prohibitive costs for continuing the "big pipe" grey infrastructure tradition (Knight 2017), cities are recognizing that urban nature can help to mitigate environmental and infrastructure challenges while also connecting cities to surrounding ecosystems. So-called "green infrastructure" (GI) such as vegetated swales, storm water catchment basins, and green roofs all help reduce extreme environmental conditions such as heat waves and flooding while reducing the impact on existing infrastructure. This framing of how nature can help cities manage their infrastructure and climate change issues has also shifted ideas about nature and the role of the city: ecology terms like corridors, patches, and habitat have begun to influence city planning (City of Toronto 2015), while so-called "socio-cultural" or "co-benefits" of GI are being discussed by planners and academics who are attempting to quantify public benefits of incorporating nature into the city (Gómez-Baggethun and Barton 2013).

The primary reasons green roofs are implemented are usually ecological, such as their ability to reduce stormwater overflow and the urban heat island effect (Bliss et al., 2009; Chih-Fang 2008; Shafique et al., 2018; Vijayaraghavan 2016) or provide habitat to birds and invertebrates. (Bliss et al., 2009; Butler et al., 2012; Chih-Fang 2008; Partridge and Clark 2018; Vijayaraghavan 2016). However more recent discussions have recognized their ability to contribute to the health and well-being of urbanites. This is through providing visual or physical access to "nature" through the green roof, which, similar to other more traditional types of nature, has been linked to improved concentration (Lee et al., 2015; Loder 2014) and psychological restoration (Lee et al., 2015; Loder 2014; Mesimäki, Hauru, and Lehvävirta 2019). While the potential for human benefit is not the main reason cities are creating policies mandating or incentivizing green roofs, their high visibility has meant that green roofs are a potent symbol of ecological commitment and attention to the aesthetics of urbanites. For this reason, many buildings are including green roofs as part of their sustainability mandate, or as amenity spaces for their tenants.

While museums are a relatively unusual and new building type for green roofs, it is an emerging trend, with museums in Cincinnati, London, Werkendam, Oakland, and San Francisco using green roofs as part of their design, image, and programming. Though they are often associated with sustainability initiatives, due to their novelty green roofs tend to lack the symbolism of more traditional forms of urban nature such as parks or trees. This means that they can provide unique insights into urbanites' values, perceptions, and feelings toward urban nature (Loder 2011). When combined with the design and user-engagement needs of museums, green roofs present an unusual opportunity to explore both how green roofs contribute to the design goals and user experience specific to museum trends, as well as insight into the human relationship with urban nature. In this chapter, I present an analysis of three case study museums chosen for their engagement with local ecology, user interface, and urban location. Data was collected via interviews, site visits, and media analysis.

MUSEUM OF CONTEMPORARY ART, DENVER

The Museum of Contemporary Art (MCA) was founded in 1996 but opened in its current location in downtown Denver in 2007 (Museum of Contemporary Art Denver). The type of museum and its design goals heavily influenced the green roof. According to John Grant—hired as the Deputy Director of the museum and the owner's representative during the architecture selection process—one of the goals of the project was to select an architect who understood the mission of a contemporary art museum, which is less about storing objects and more about "… presenting a space that is alive and ever-changing in its experience" (Grant 2019). The selection of David Adjaye of Adjaye Associates (UK) as the architect allowed them to design the building as "… an additive part of the museum experience so that the building itself could be experienced … as a … work of art or as a work of sculpture." (Grant 2019). Designed to "… minimize the boundaries between the exterior spaces of the city and the interior galleries of the museum," the museum has a central transitioning stairway, five galleries on two floors, hidden skylights that fill the interior with natural light, dedicated education spaces, a library, shop, and rooftop café (Museum of Contemporary Art Denver). The building is certified LEED Gold.

Though the museum is not a collecting museum, they envisioned having five permanent art pieces, one of which was the roof garden (Dakin 2019). As such they had a very specific goal for the green roof as a piece of art in its own right and as an amenity space on the roof next to the cafe (Figure 18.1). Hiring Karla Dakin as the landscape architect supported this dual vision, as she is both a landscape architect and artist (Grant, John (Former Deputy Director, Museum of Contemporary Art Denver) 2019). Three factors influenced the design of the green roof: the constraints of the site itself; the landscape of Colorado; and an artists' vision to mix things up and make the plant selection surprise and delight visitors (Dakin 2019). The site for the green roofs is tiny: only 15 x 30 feet, sandwiched between the triangular skylights. Riffing off skylights, Karla designed the green roofs to be a series of broken up five- or eight-sided beds that zigzagged from high to low. The upper beds represent the prairies from a macro view, so that you only see the top of the grasses but not what is growing in them, similar to some views Dakin experienced on her walks in Colorado. The lower beds represent valleys, with "… tiny little jewel plants … you have to almost get on your hands and knees or on your belly to appreciate" (Dakin 2019). Both the cascading beds and the plant selection was meant to "… incorporate these two places in Colorado that I loved and merge them together … by plant selection." Dakin also played with plant types, structure, and form to make the green roof beds "… artful and intriguing … to captivate audiences …" that would not normally seek out or look at plants (Dakin 2019). She achieved this through continuing her theme of fuzzy balls from her ceramic and print making work in the plant selection

Figure 18.1 Rooftop garden designed by Karla Dakin at the Museum of Contemporary Art in Denver, Colorado, USA. Courtesy J.C. Buck.

Figure 18.2
Globularia punctata, a plant native to Colorado, on the rooftop garden at the MCA. Courtesy J.C. Buck.

(Figure 18.2), as well as juxtaposing plants that normally would never be placed together. Lastly, she wanted to promote visitor engagement with the green roof by encouraging kids to pet the plants and making visitors aware of locally endangered plants. Partly in response to the failure of a high-profile green roof in Denver at the time Dakin did not include any traditional sedums in her green roof as an example of how to create a successful green roof in Colorado's climate (Dakin 2019).

Public response to the green roof was generally very positive, barring some negative comments about the aesthetics of the green roof before it grew in and filled out (Dakin 2019; Grant 2019). However, the museum did not seem to know how to advertise or promote the green roof in the same way it did for other permanent pieces, and it never garnered the same publicity as the iconic red heart outside the building (Dakin 2019). As of the time of publication there are discussions on the potential removal of the green roof to provide more flexible amenity space on the roof. Despite this uncertainty, the green roof serves as an interesting example of a museum using a green roof as part of its placemaking and engagement with users through a playful connection to art, sustainability, landscape, and form.

CASE STUDY: LOS ANGELES MUSEUM OF THE HOLOCAUST

Though perhaps better known for film than museums, Los Angeles nonetheless has some prestigious museums, one of which is the Los Angeles Museum of the Holocaust (LAMOTH). Like the MCA, LAMOTH also started as a smaller collection in a previous building; it is the oldest survivor-founded Holocaust museum in the United States. In addition to memorializing the dead, the museum aims to educate youth so that the events of the Holocaust will not be forgotten. Admission is always free to ensure that no one is turned away (Belzberg 2018, Los Angeles Museum of the Holocaust n.d.).

The current location, opened in 2010, is an innovative response to both the site location and purpose of the museum. Designed by Hagy Belzberg of Hagy Belzberg Architects, the museum is covered by a green roof that seamlessly links the building with the popular Pan Pacific Park in the Los Angeles Fairfax District (see Figures 18.3 and 18.4). Belzberg was able to convince the design competition jurors, the public, and the Parks District of the merit of the proposal with a design that actively juxtaposed the site with the goals of the museum. For example, Belzberg justified taking park space in an area where park space is rare by repeating the aesthetic patterns of the park as viewed from above—smooth concrete undulating paths and grass—and "… consolidating it, creating our own patterning from it, and … wrapp(ing) it up and over the museum so that the disparity between building and park were the same" (Belzberg 2018). However, Belzberg also realized that preserving open space was not an adequate justification for the museum given the gravity of the subject matter. So he used the juxtaposition of the park and the entrance as a teachable moment. Referencing the apparent ignorance of those in 1935 who visited parks or forests next to concentration camps, the docents point out the park and the people to the 30,000 to 40,000 high school kids visiting the museum every year:

> … playing in the park and picnicking but right adjacent to it unbeknownst to them … (is) a museum that unearths the horror and stories of humanity—the two coexist and it's that dichotomy that we also bring … today where the teachers say … where is this happening in our own society where horrible things happen right down the street?
>
> (Belzberg 2018)

Figure 18.3 Entrance to the Los Angeles Museum of the Holocaust (LAMOTH), in California, designed by Hagy Belzberg of Hagy Belzberg Architects, opened in 2010. Courtesy Iwan Baan.

Figure 18.4 LAMOTH sits in the Pan Pacific Park in the Los Angeles Fairfax District. Courtesy Iwan Baan.

This juxtaposition of the park, green roof, and museum thus becomes part of the narrative teaching visitors about the Holocaust.

The design of the green roof continues this narrative. Belzberg chose Lisa Lee Benjamin and Karla Dakin, the landscape architect for the MCA, reflecting the diversity and breadth that green roof designers are being asked to provide for museum projects. With a strict budget, the landscape architects worked with John Greenlee to develop a palette of three grasses that provided the "shaggy dog look" requested by Belzberg, link native Californian plants with Mediterranean bulbs to remind visitors of Israel, and be visible from both the park and entrance. The site itself was technically challenging with some slopes of 45 degrees, so they added a fast growing invasive succulent common in dry climates and on green roofs. Due to the seamless blending of the green roof and the adjacent park, a series of olive trees were planted to demarcate the transition from park to museum green roof and continue the linkages with the Mediterranean (Dakin 2019).

The green roof also helps shape user experience of the museum. Building a green roof over the space and having visitors gradually wind underground to more difficult material means that the sounds of the park gradually recede to quietness and "… the content becomes the most important aspect … you want the facts, the historical records … to play into people's consciousness … not what the architects believe" (Belzberg 2018). By subsuming the majority of the architecture under the green roof, the architect was able to "contain the narrative and ensure that the experience … helps prepare you" (Belzberg 2018). Like the MCA, the LAMOTH pursued LEED certification (and achieved LEED Gold), viewing a sustainable building as the right thing to do: " … it's our responsibility. You don't preach social justice but fail in the most primary relationship to who we are today and how we should … how we can build … the building needs to follow through with the message of the content" (Belzberg 2018). This informed other sustainability features of the museum, such as the use of non-potable water and low-water grasses on the roof (Dakin 2019).

The green roof and museum were well received with extensive media coverage and publications, and reception continues to be positive (Belzberg 2018). However, perceptions about the success of the green roof differ. While the architect and Benjamin wanted the green roof to be no-maintenance and saw the seasonal change of vegetation as true to the spirit of the roof (Belzberg 2018), Dakin felt strongly that there needed to be some maintenance. In the end the landscape architects felt it prudent to provide a detailed maintenance manual to the museum (Belzberg 2018; Dakin 2019). Current views on the success of the green roof differ as well. A 24-hour security camera had to be installed to prevent local prostitutes from using the green roof. While Belzberg views the green roof as a success, and has said that no one has complained about it (Belzberg 2018), Dakin has argued that when called upon by the new director to make the green roof look full again for a large fundraiser, she arrived to find that 90% of the grasses had died from lack of maintenance and a broken irrigation system (Belzberg 2018; Dakin 2019). As a temporary solution they planted some new grasses; it remains uncertain whether there is an ongoing budget for maintenance when most of the budget goes toward the maintenance of the interior collection (Dakin 2019). Despite these challenges, the use of the green roof as an integral part of both the local park and the narrative of the museum provides a good example of green roofs as place maker through user experience and links to ecology.

CASE STUDY: CANADIAN WAR MUSEUM, OTTAWA, ONTARIO

As the capital city of Canada Ottawa also has numerous popular museums, one of which is the Canadian War Museum (CWM). While the museum can be traced back to 1880 as a collection of militia artifacts, it opened in its new location in 2005 after an extensive public outreach and consultation process by the architecture firm Moriyama and Teshima (Larocque 2019, Canadian War Museum n.d.).

Like the LAMOTH the CWM is covered by a green roof that seamlessly rises from the surrounding parkland in the west and up and over the building toward the entrance at the eastern end (Figure 18.5). The public consultation process, the site itself, and the architect's experiences with internment during the Second World War inspired the museum design that won over the Board of Trustees (Moriyama 2019). During the consultation process, the architect insisted on hearing from Canadians (who tend to be reluctant to glorify war) how they felt about the war museum and if they wanted it in the first place. Responses from women, such as, "Going to war is like going to the depths of hell to resurrect the soul," inspired Moriyama throughout the extensive refinement process (Moriyama 2019). The second source of inspiration was the site itself, particularly grasses by the Gatineau River bordering the site and the view of the Peace Tower on Parliament Hill (Figure 18.6). Lastly Moriyama's experience as a 13-year old boy in Japanese-Canadian internment camps during the Second World War influenced the design, particularly memories of sitting in a tree house hearing the breeze and imagining the fatigue and hunger of soldiers on both sides of the war just wanting it to be over (Moriyama 2019). The combination of these experiences led to the goals of the project, which are to honor the past and those who served; highlight Remembrance Day when Canadians hold two minutes of silence at 11 o'clock on November 11th; and hope for the future (Moriyama 2019).

These goals combine in the structure of the building, which is meant to be an active part of the experience (even using rough concrete to imitate war-torn cities

Figure 18.5 The Canadian War Museum (CWM) in Ottawa, Canada, designed by Moriyama and Teshima, opened in 2005. Photograph: the Canadian Aerial Photo Corporation/PCL Constructors.

Figure 18.6 The CWA at sunset. Photograph by Harry Foster, Canadian War Museum.

in places) and the blend of nature and built form. While there are stunning examples of this in the museum, an integral and visible symbol of these goals is the green roof covering the museum (Moriyama 2019).

According to Guy Larocque, who oversaw the construction of the museum and green roof, the green roof is a living symbol of this nature-building integration and of regeneration and healing: " … war would destroy the landscape and nature over time re-hybridizes and heals and covers over the landscape with grass and plants …," a sentiment echoed by the architect (Larocque 2019). The grasses were selected to be the same grasses that grow along the river and tested in a pilot green roof plot to make sure they worked, allowing the green roof and surrounding landscape merge seamlessly. As visitors walk from the grounds—which mimic First World War trenches—up along the green roof they come to a barrier meant to imitate the barrier of the trench; they can see grass and the peace tower as a symbol of hope for future generations (Larocque 2019; Moriyama 2019) (Figures 18.7 and 18.8). Lastly the profile of the museum also blends nature and built form; the eastern end of the building is reminiscent of a bunker, while the profile of the whole building represents the landscape of Canada from the Atlantic to the Pacific (Moriyama 2019) (Figure 18.9).

The reason for implementing the green roof was as a symbolic portrayal of the regenerative power of nature over war. However, the building does boast numerous sustainability features (it could have achieved LEED Silver but chose not to

Figure 18.7 The eastern end of the CWA resembles a bunker. Courtesy Tom Arban.

Figure 18.8 The eastern end of the CWA resembles a bunker. Courtesy Tom Arban.

due to the cost) (Larocque 2019). Despite a tight budget, on-going maintenance for the green roof is part of the landscaping for both museums (the CWM shares its budget with the Museum of Canadian History), including annual grass cutting and weeding. Feedback on the museum and green roof has been very positive from the public—receiving numerous accolades and making it the number one attraction in Ottawa for visitors—and the museum itself, which sees the maintenance budget and energy efficiency features of the building as very low cost (Larocque 2019; Moriyama 2019). The use of a green roof as both a link to local landscape and to the larger narrative of the museum showcases the use of green roofs to combine ecology, narrative, and user engagement.

Green Roofs and Museums: Concluding Thoughts

Like many institutions, museums are redefining themselves and offering additional amenities to continue to attract visitors. The addition of a green roof to the museum can be an effective way to engage what Lindsay terms the other new types

Figure 18.9 The CWA entrance both leads up to the green roof and the front entrance. Courtesy Tom Arban.

of users to museums: cities and ecological systems (Lindsay 2016, 255). Though they do not always mean that a building is "green," green roofs have long been associated with green buildings and have been used by cities and buildings to signify their ecological commitment (Cole et al., 2008; Loder 2011). This is particularly true when the green roof makes a reference to regional habitat, often through native plant selection.

This engagement with different types of users can be seen clearly in our three case studies. The MCA chose to pursue LEED certification as a statement of leadership and a specific vision of what contemporary art museums should be: innovative, engaged with contemporary issues, and ecologically responsible. Placing the green roof adjacent to an amenity (the rooftop cafe) is a way to connect amenity users with the local landscape and a tactile, visual example of sustainability. The LAMOTH also pursued LEED certification, and like the MCA, this influenced many design decisions. The commitment to sustainability contributed to the renown of the museum, and the green roof is one of the largest intensive green roofs in California (Los Angeles Museum of the Holocaust). The green roof was conceptualized to connect both museum and park users, and by making visitors walk through the green roof from the park into the buried museum space, the museum and green roof become part of the experience and connection with the larger city. The CWM has many similarities with LAMOTH; while it did not pursue LEED certification, it features many sustainable components and has one of the largest green roofs in North America (Canadian War Museum). The green roof on the CWM also blends seamlessly with neighbouring parkland and, given that the museum is also partly buried under the roof, is an integral part of the design of the museum. All the case studies use the green roof to engage users and connect them to the city, and landscape, beyond the walls of the museum. While the LAMOTH and CWM are the most obvious, the MCA does this in a more abstract, playful way.

The three green roofs also engage more specifically with local ecology, the third "audience," through their use of plant selection and edges. In the case of the MCA, Dakin referenced and blended two archetypical landscapes in Colorado through plant selection and viewpoint: the high prairie grasses, and the low valley alpine plants. Both the LAMOTH and the CWM deliberately used plants to reference local ecology as well: two of the three grasses used in the LAMOTH green roof are either native to the Rockies of California or the desert, while the plants for the CWM were chosen based on the architects initial visit to the site and blend seamlessly with the surrounding park (Dakin 2019).

There are two characteristics of green roofs that make their use on museums particularly symbolic, and thus useful for narrative and engagement. Green roofs by design have some kind of edge, a symbol that the green roof is not naturally occurring but deliberately placed there by people, and fit easily into the ecology framework of corridors, nodes, and patches. Research has shown that this can confuse people's perceptions of the green roof as part of nature or not—while they know that it was created by people, it also has plants on it that have their own agency and power (Loder 2011). The three case studies above show a playful approach to this dichotomy and tension. In the case of the MCA, Dakin's use of perspective and edges to play with visitors' experiences of symbolic Colorado landscapes is an integral component to the playfulness and experimentation of the green roof boxes and the playfulness of the museum. Both the LAMOTH and the CWM use their green roof to blend seamlessly with the surrounding parkland—thus nodding to cultural and ecological integration—but also shape and constrain the green roof with the sharp concrete edges of the buildings and historical referent. This juxtaposition of edges with "wild," often native, grasses and plants, is known to be an effective strategy to let viewers know that the wildness is on purpose, and not merely a sign of neglect, called "cues to care" (Nassauer 1995). While edges can be effective in increasing public acceptance of the green roof or naturalized space, they also can align well with the goals and purposes of the museum. Edges can be places of creativity and boldness, and "wildness" in the selection of plants, combined with sharp architectural edges, can open up a dialectic between nature and human activity, a slippery place of otherness, possibility, and creativity (Brady 2006; Chapman 2004). For the

MCA this aligns with their goal of creative exploration and innovation, while for the LAMOTH and the CWM it supports the vision, or journey, back through memory and history, to revisit often painful events of the past while in a state of possibility and healing.

This knowledge of the particular power of using nature is reflected in the vision of the architects and landscape architects for each of the projects below. For the MCA, the juxtaposition of iconic Colorado landscapes and a child-like exploratory play with texture, plants, and color means that the green roof is a unique tool for rethinking the place of the contemporary art museum in the Colorado landscape, as well as our relationship with such iconic nature. By reminding us to both appreciate the distant, scenic gaze iconic to Colorado, as well as a child-like sense of wonder and possibility, the green roof at the MCA challenges our ideas and relationship with nature in the city. For the LAMOTH, the vision to both invite the visitor into a challenging, painful history through the endearing shape of a shaggy dog, as well as by blending seamlessly with a popular park and referencing nearby nature, enables the green roof to use nature to gently bring us to face painful collective memories while referencing healing and regeneration. For the CWM, Moriyama's memory of the painful realities of war, seen through the eyes of a child interned in a shameful part of Canada's history, is a vehicle to regeneration and healing not just for him but for all Canadians. The combination of the green roof with other aspects of nature, such as the sound of wind in the Regeneration hall, help to both open the visitor to painful memories while reminding them of the regenerative capacities of all.

These green roofs challenge the idea of museums as static, and antiquated, collections of art. By incorporating living, breathing nature into their designs, they gently engage the visitor and larger community in ways that are both immediate and evocative of memory and experience. Additionally, they challenge the idea of nature as a static, scenic amenity to be only "really" experienced by leaving the city (Cronon 1995). Finally, it also reveals ongoing tensions we have with urban nature and built form—while we appreciate and want nature as part of our daily lives, we struggle with the realities on daily, ongoing engagement and maintenance that it requires, seen in the disputed maintenance of the LAMOTH green roof and the inability of the MCA to fully integrate the green roof into their permanent collection and identity. Despite this last challenge, however, their incorporation into places of memory, art, and creativity are promising for future ideations of green, creative cities.

REFERENCES

American Alliance of Museums. 2017. *Four Museums Recognized for Sustainability by American Alliance of Museums*. Arlington: American Alliance of Museums.

Belzberg, Hagy (Founding Principal, Belzberg Architects), Interview by Angela Loder. 2018.

Bliss, Daniel J., Ronald D. Neufeld, and Robert J. Ries. 2009. "Storm Water Runoff Mitigation Using a Green Roof." *Environmental Engineering Science* 26 (2):407–417.

Brady, Emily. 2006. "The Aesthetics of Agricultural Landscapes and the Relationship between Humans and Nature." *Ethics, Place and the Environment* 9 (1):1–19.

Butler, Colleen, Erin Butler, and Colin M. Orians. 2012. "Native plant enthusiasm reaches new heights: Perceptions, evidence, and the future of green roofs." *Urban Forestry & Urban Greening* 11 (1):1–10. doi: 10.1016/j.ufug.2011.11.002.

Canadian War Museum. "About the Museum." *Canadian War Museum*, accessed 7/6. https://www.warmuseum.ca/about/about-the-museum/#tabs

Chapman, Robert. 2004. "Crowded Solitude: Thoreau on Wilderness." *Environmental Philosophy* 1 (1):58–72.

Chih-Fang, Fang. 2008. "Evaluating the thermal reduction effect of plant layers on rooftops." *Energy & Buildings* 40 (6):1048–1052.

City of Toronto. 2015. Toronto Official Plan. City of Toronto.

Cole, Raymond J., John Robinson, Zosia Brown, and Meg O'Shea. 2008. "Re-contextualizing the notion of comfort." *Building Research & Information* 36 (4):323–336. doi: 10.1080/09613210802076328.

Cronon, William. 1995. "The Trouble with Wilderness: or, Getting back to the Wrong Nature." In *Uncommon Ground*, edited by William Cronon, 69–90. New York: W.W. Norton & Co.

Dakin, Karla (Owner, K. Dakin Design, Inc.), Interview by Angela Loder. 2019.

Domosh, Mona. 1996. "The feminized retail landscape: gender ideology and consumer culture in nineteenth-century New York City." In *Retailing, Consumption and Capital: Towards The New Retail Geography*, edited by Michelle Lowe Neil Wrigley, 257–270. Harlow: Longman Pub Group.

Florida, Richard L. 2012. *The Rise Of The Creative Class: Revisited*. New York: Basic Books.

Gelles, David. 2016. "Art Museums Seek a Green Palette." *The New York Times*, March 15, Art & Design. www.nytimes.com/2016/03/17/arts/design/art-museums-seek-a-green-palette.html.

Gómez-Baggethun, Erik and David N. Barton. 2013. "Classifying and valuing ecosystem services for urban planning." *Ecological Economics* 86:235–245. doi: http://dx.doi.org/10.1016/j.ecolecon.2012.08.019.

Grant, John (Former Deputy Director, Museum of Contemporary Art Denver), Interview by Angela Loder. 2019.

Greenberg, Miriam. 2008. *Branding New York: How a CIty in Crisis Was Sold to the World 1st ed.* New York: Routledge.

Hannigan, John. 1998. *Fantasy City: Pleasure and Profit in the Postmodern Metropolis*. London: Routledge.

Harvey, David. 1989. "From managerialism to entrepreneurialism: the transformation in urban governance in late capitalism." *Geografiska Annaler: Series B, Human Geography* 71 (1: The Roots of Geographical Change: 1973 to the Present):3–17. doi: 10.2307/490503.

Harvey, David. 2005. *A Brief Hsitory of Neoliberalism*. New York: Oxford Unversity Press.

Knight, Sophie. 2017. "What would an entirely flood-proof city look like?" *The Guardian*, 25 Sep 2017, Resilient cities. www.theguardian.com/cities/2017/sep/25/what-flood-proof-city-china-dhaka-houston.

Lanks, Belinda. 2008. "Spotlight: The California Academy of Science's Green Roof." Metropolis, September 1.

Larocque, Guy (Former Director of Facility Management and Security Services, Canadian Museum of History), Interview by Angela Loder. 2019.

Lee, Kate E., Kathryn J.H. Williams, Leisa D. Sargent, Nicholas S.G. Williams, and Katherine A. Johnson. 2015. "40-second green roof views sustain attention: The role of micro-breaks in attention restoration." *Journal of Environmental Psychology* 42 (0):182–189. doi: http://dx.doi.org/10.1016/j.jenvp.2015.04.003.

Lefebvre, Henri. 1996. "The Right to the City." In *Writings on Cities*, edited by Henri Lefebvre, Eleonore Kofman, and Elizabeth Lebas, 63–181. Oxford: Wiley-Blackwell.

Lindsay, Georgia. 2016. *The User Perspective on Twenty-First-Century Art Museums*. New York: Routledge.

Lindsay, Georgia. 2018. "One icon, two audiences: how the Denver Art Museum used their new building to both brand the city and bolster civic pride." *Journal of Urban Design* 23 (2):193–205. doi: 10.1080/13574809.2017.1399793.

Lloyd, Carol. 2007. "The California Academy of Sciences' beautiful new living-roof may well spark a revolution." *SF Gate*, November 2. www.sfgate.com/entertainment/article/The-California-Academy-of-Sciences-beautiful-new-2532159.php.

Loder, Angela. 2011. "Greening the City: Exploring Health, Well-being, Green Roofs, and the Perception of Nature in the Workplace." Doctor of Philosophy, Geography and the Centre for Environment, University of Toronto.

Loder, Angela. 2014. "'There's a meadow outside my workplace': A phenomenological exploration of aesthetics and green roofs in Chicago and Toronto." *Landscape and Urban Planning* 126:94–106.

Logan, R.J. and Molotch, H.L. 2002. "The City as a Growth Machine." In *Readings in Urban Theory*, edited by Susan S. and Campbell Fainstein, Scott, 199–238. Oxford: Blackwell. Original edition, "The City as a Growth Machine", Urban Fortunes: The Political Economy of Place, 1987.

Los Angeles Museum of the Holocaust. "History." *Los Angeles Museum of the Holocaust*, accessed 7/6. www.lamoth.org/the-museum/history/.

Mesimäki, Marja, Kaisa Hauru, and Susanna Lehvävirta 2019. "Do small green roofs have the possibility to offer recreational and experiential benefits in a dense urban area? A case study in Helsinki, Finland." *Urban Forestry & Urban Greening* 40:114–124. doi: https://doi.org/10.1016/j.ufug.2018.10.005.

Moriyama, Raymond (Partner Emeritus, Moriyama & Tashima Architects), Interview by Angela Loder. 2019.

Nassauer, Joan. 1995. "Messy Ecosystems, Orderly Frames." *Landscape Journal* 14 (2):161–170.

New York Real Estate Journal. 2019. "American Museum of Natural History breaks ground on $383 million, 230,000 s/f Richard Gilder Center." New York Real Estate Journal, July 16. https://nyrej.com/amnh-breaks-ground-on-383-million-230-000-s-f-richard-gilder-center.

Newhouse, Victoria. 2006. *Towards a New Museum*. Expanded ed. New York: Monacelli Press.

Partridge, Dustin R., and J.Alan Clark. 2018. "Urban green roofs provide habitat for migrating and breeding birds and their arthropod prey." *PLOS ONE* 13 (8):e0202298. doi: 10.1371/journal.pone.0202298.

Patterson, Matt. 2012. "The Role of the Public Institution in Iconic Architectural Development." *Urban Studies* 49 (15):3289–3305. doi: 10.1177/0042098012443862.

Plaza, Beatriz. 2006. "The Return on Investment of the Guggenheim Museum Bilbao." *International Journal of Urban and Regional Research* 30(2):452–467.

Plaza, Beatriz. 2007. "The Bilbao effect (Guggenheim Museum Bilbao)." *Museum News* 86 (5).

Sassen, Saskia. 2002. "Cities in a World Economy." In *Readings in Urban Theory*, edited by Susan S. Fainstein and Scott Campbell, 31–56. Oxford: Blackwell. Original edition, Cities in a World Economy 2000.

Shafique, Muhammad, Reeho Kim, and Muhammad Rafiq. 2018. "Green roof benefits, opportunities and challenges—A review." *Renewable and Sustainable Energy Reviews* 90:757–773. doi: 10.1016/j.rser.2018.04.006.

Tilden, Scott J. 2004. "Preface." In *Architecture for Art: American Art Museums, 1938-2008*, edited by Paul Rochelau, 7–9. New York: Harry N. Abrams Inc.

Vijayaraghavan, K. 2016. "Green roofs: A critical review on the role of components, benefits, limitations and trends." *Renewable and Sustainable Energy Reviews* 57:740–752. doi: 10.1016/j.rser.2015.12.119.

West, Mark. 2006. "Edifice Complex: Museums Spend Fortunes on Trophy Buildings, but Are They Really worth It?" W Magazine, November.

Zukin, Sharon. 1991. *Landscapes of Power: From Detroit to Disney World*. Berkley: University of California Press.

Index

Page locators in *italics* and **bold** refer to images and tables, respectively.

access to gallery spaces 209–211, *212*, 233–235, 241, 247–257
J'accuse (Attia) *20*
ADA (Americans with Disabilities Act) 233
adaptive reuse 10–11, 13
Adidas: Art & Yoga 270
adjacency requirements of gallery spaces 209–211, *212*
advertising 29, 33
agenda setting 45–46
Agnes Martin Gallery 264
AGO (Art Gallery of Ontario) 155–177
Ai WeiWei 30, *31*
air temperature 306
airtight construction, energy conservation 303–305
Alaily-Mattar, N. 24–25
Alberch, P. 178–179
Allward and Gouinlock 162, *164*
Altes Museum, Germany 181–182
AM (Australian Museum) 143
American Society of Heating, Refrigeration, and Air-Conditioning Engineers (ASHRAE) 297–298
Americans with Disabilities Act (ADA) 233
Andersons, A. 13
Ang, J. 140–141
Anguissola, A. 137, *138*
Anna and John J. Sie Welcome Center (Denver Art Museum) 68, *69*, 73, *74*
THE ANTITHINKERS (Yitzhak) 98
Anusas, M. 311
Archbishopric Museum 188, *189*

"The Ark" 180–181
Armstrong, R. 151
ARoS 147–148
Art Gallery of New South Wales 140, *141*
Art Gallery of Ontario (AGO) 52, **53**, 155–177; aesthetic surface 169–172, *173*; architectural history 157, *158*; citizen-consumer activities 169; civic identity 165–175; external appearance 170–171; external interface 168–169; founding 159, *160*; imperial era 156, 158–160, *161*, 166, *167*; internal appearance 171–172, *173*; internal layout 172–175; layers of architecture 165–175; location 166; long halls/open spaces 173–174; main eras 157–165; neoliberal era 156, 162, 165; postwar era 156, 161–162, *163*–164; wings 174–175
Art Institute, Chicago 305
Art Museum Building Commission, North Carolina 120
ARTBAR event 15, *16*, 22
Arthur Boyd Gallery and Creative Learning Center 115–117; bunker/bridge elements 115, *116*; Riversdale visitor facilities 115, *116*; "The Bridge" 115, *116*–117, 117
ARX Architects 255
Ashmole, E. 180–181
ASHRAE (American Society of Heating, Refrigeration, and Air-Conditioning Engineers) 297–298
ASLA awards 128, *129*
Attia, K. *20*

Auckland Art Gallery 270
"Austin" (Ellsworth Kelly Foundation) 264, *265*
Australian Museum (AM) 143
awards: AIA 128, *129*; ASLA 129, 196; Dominion Community Impact 96; RIBA 11; Royal Fin Art Commission Trust Building of the Year 11

Bakke, G. 300
Barone, M. 148
Barton Myers Associates, Inc. 162, *163*
basilica model spatial types 182–183
Baxter, L. 67–68
BEC (Boyd Education Center) 115
Belet, S. 147
Bella Program 15, 19, *19*
Belzberg, H. 320, *321*, 322–323
Benjamin, L. L. 322
Bennett, T. 182
Benson + Forsyth 192
Berber Museum, Marrakech, Morocco 146–147
Bilbao effect 23–24, 26, 54–55, 153, 315
Black, B. 182
black communities of Toronto 168–169
Blake, S. *130*
Blanton Museum of Art 264, *265*
Bo, J. 139
body conscious design 260–276; definitions 260–262; museum fatigue 262–273
bog bodies 223–225, *226*
Borum Eshøj family burial chambers 223, *225*
Boyd Education Center (BEC) 115
Brand, M. 145, 152
Brand, S. 157
Brannon, M. 240–242
Breaking the Siege (brick and mortar arch) 266, *267*
Brenner, D. 272, *273*
"The Bridge", Boyd Education Center 115, *116–117*, 117
bridges: NCMA *126*; Scottsdale Museum 284, *285*

British Museum 181–182
Bronze Age exhibit, Moesgaard Museum 217–218
Brooklyn Museum 270
Brosius, C. *234*
burial chambers 223, *225*

C3West community programs 22
"cabinets of curiosity" 179
California Academy of Science 2, 215, 314
Calton Hill, Scotland 192
camera obscura 185
campuses: Monash University 105–109; NCMA 130–133
Canadian Opera Company 52, **53**
Canadian War Museum (CWM) 323–326, 327–329, *327*
Cangrande II della Scala 187–188
Cannatà, M. 249
Carrilho da Graça, J. L. 247–248
'A Casa Inacabada' exhibition (The Unfinished House) 248, 255–256
Castelvecchio Museum 186–187
CBECS (Commercial Buildings Energy Consumption Survey) 299
Center of Excellence concepts 146–147
Central Pavillion, Venice Biennale 266
Centre Pompidou, Paris, France 140, 311–312
Centro Ciência (museum of sciences) 247–248
Chatterjee, A. 239–240
circulation 14–15, 107, 109–110, 139, 151–152, 182–183, 196, 200–209, 237, 261
circulation of gallery spaces 209–211, *212*
CIS (Creative Industries Styria) 35
citizen-building 155–177
citizenship 119–134
city branding 4, 24, 26, 48–50, 54, 315
Cleveland Institute of Art (CIA) 87, 94–95, 99
clock towers 36–37
Commercial Buildings Energy Consumption Survey (CBECS) 299

Comte, C. 101, 103, *103*
concrete 309–310
conference and event spaces 33
contemporary art 10, 26, 90, 209, 267
conservation 145, 297–313; *see also* environmentalism
Constructive Rest Position 266, *267*
Contemporary Jewish Museum (Libeskind) 239
"continuous flow" spatial types 180–183
Cook, P. 26
Cooper Hewitt Smithsonian Design Museum, New York 233, *234*, 235
Le Corbusier 186
Corcoran Museum 279–280
Core Construction 283–284, 288
Cranz, G. 266, *267*, 272, *273*, 311–312
"creative class" 46–47, 315
creative community definition 73, 76
creative economy 34–35, 45–52
Creative Hub (Denver Art Museum) 67–84, *69*, *74*, *75*, *80*
Creative Industries Styria (CIS) 35
Creative Learning Center 115–117
Crossroads (Jackson-Jarvis) 126, *127*
The Crouching Venus 137, *138*
Crystal Bridges Museum of American Art 305
cultural districts 46–49
Curatorial Centre (Royal Ontario Museum) 162, *164*
CWM (Canadian War Museum) 323–326, 327–329, *327*

Dahlström, B. 146
Dakin, K. 318–320, 322–323
Darling & Pearson 159–160, *160*, *161*, 173
de Arquitectura, G. 266
de Young Museum, San Francisco, California 261–262
Denham, P. 145–146
Denver Art Museum (DAM), Colorado 2, 3, 65–85, 232, 236–237, *238*, *239*, 244, 315; Frederic C. Hamilton Building 236–237, *238*, *239*
Design Month Graz 35

Diller Scofidio+Renfro 211, *212*
disabilities 76, 233, 246–259
Dream-Over (Rubin Museum) 268
Dreher, J. 24–25
Drinkwater, H. 281
Dulwich Picture Gallery, London 181–182, 183
Durand, J.-.N.-L. 181–182

East York, Ontario 49–50
eco-aesthetic logic 311
ECOC (European Capital of Culture Year) 25–26, 29–30
École du Louvre 146
Edifice Complex: How the Rich and Powerful Shape the World (Sudjic) 279–280
Edinburgh Castle, Scotland 192
El Pomar Grand Atrium, Frederic C. Hamilton Building 237, *238*
Ellis, S. 107, *108*, 109
Ellsworth Kelly 264, *265*
Ellwood, T. 147
emergy (Odum) 310
Emperor Hadrian 179
energy: conservation 297–313; *see also* sustainabilities
Energy Star programs 299
enfilade access 180–183
environment, sensory place 241–244
environmentalism 129–130, 314–332
Enzinger, M. 30–32
Etobicoke, Ontario 49–50
EUIs (energy use intensities) 299–301
European Capital of Culture Year (ECOC) 25–26, 29–30
Evolution Stairs, Moesgaard Museum 216–219, *218*
"Exhibit" high-rise 166
experiences 135–227; citizen-building 155–177; illuminating history 215–227; inside-out planning 195–214; meaning in museums 178–194; open and integrated museums 137–154; sensory place 236–244

'Explora' exhibition (Pavilion of Knowledge) 248, 255–256
The Eyetracker (ARoS Public) 148

Fairfax District, Los Angeles 320, *321*
Farmer, G. 311
Fehn, S. 188, *189*
Fentress Architects 70, *71, 74*
Fernandes, F. 249
financial models 149–151
First Monday in May (Rossi) 141
First People's gallery 174–175
flexibility of movement of early museums 183–184
Floorscape (Picket) 94–95
Florida, R. 51, 172, 315
foaming agents 310
Fondazione Prada, Milan 137, *138*
food service 98–99
Foreign Office Architects (FOA) 89
Fournier, C. 26
Four-Zone Diagrams (Lord) 207–208
Fox, M. 281
Fox, O. 282
Frederic C. Hamilton Building *see* Denver Art Museum
Freed, J. I. 242
funding 1, 9, 11, 14, 21, 30–33, 43, 46, 50–51, 126, 146, 149, 153, 165, 169, 171, 279, 282–283
furniture 94–95, 101, *102*, 103, 264

Gabinete de Arquitectura 266
Gallery of Canada 174–175
gallery and corridor model spatial types 182–183
gallery refitting 142, *143*
Garcia, C. 15, *16*
Garibaldi, L. D. 121
Geddes, P. 184–186
Gehry, F. 165, 168, 238–239
GENEXT event 22–23, *22*
Gieryn, T. 157
Giovio, P. 180
Glacier Museum, Fjærland 189

Glasgow School of Art 193
glass 305–307; *see also* windows
global warming potentials (GWPs) 310
Globularia punctata 318–319
Glyptothek, Munich 181–182, 183, 196
GMB (Guggenheim Museum in Bilbao) 23–24, 54, 315
Goldwin Library, Los Angeles 168
Gorochow, J. 76
Gottlieb, D. P. 129
"The Grange", Art Gallery of Ontario 159, *160*
Grauballe Man exhibit, Moesgaard Museum 223–225, *226*
graves 223, *225*
green roofs 2, 121, 216–217, 314–332; *see also* sustainabilities
Greenway development, North Carolina 126, *126*
The Grid: The Fraying Wires between Americans and Our Energy Future (Gretchen) 300
Grosse, K. 97
Guggenheim Museum in Bilbao (GMB) 1, 23–24, 54, 151, 153, 254, 315
Guggenheim Museums 23–24, 54, 151–153, 315
Gund, A. 89
Gund Commons (Museum of Contemporary Art) 91–92, 97, 101, 103, *103*
Gurian, E. H. 105
Guy, S. 311
GWPs (global warming potentials) 310
Gyre (Sayer) 126, *127*

Habitat Horticulture 272, *273*
Hadrian (Emperor) 179
Hagy Belzberg Architects 320, *321*
Hall of Remembrance, Holocaust Memorial Museum 241–242
Hanson, J. 197
Harrison, F. 107, *108*, 109
Harwood Museum of Art 264
Havener, W. 128, *128*, *129*, *130*

Heard Museum 283
Heat Recovery Ventilation Systems 307, *308*
Heinrich, C. 70
Hello Big Institution (HBI) 19
Henning Larsen Architects 216, *217*
Hewitt, C. 233, *234*, 235
High Museum of Art (HMA), Atlanta, Georgia 197–212
Hillier, B. 197
'A History of the World in 100 Objects' (MacGregor) 140
Holocaust Center (JHC) 109–112
Holocaust Museums 241–242, 243, 320–323, 327–329
Hooper-Greenhill, E. 184
House Creek riparian environment (NCMA) *130*
Høyersten, E. 147
humidity 306
Hunt, J. 121–122
Hyacinth Gloria Chen Crystal Court 56
Hyperallergenic (Rodney) 294

Ian Potter Sculpture Forecourt, Monash University Museum of Art 107, *108*, 109
icons 7–62; Ikon Gallery 9–11, *12*; MCA 13–15, *14–18*, 19–22; Star Architecture 23–42; transformational architecture 43–62
"idearium" 186
Ikon Gallery, Birmingham 9–11, *12*
Imperfect Utopia program 123–124
Ingold, T. 311
inside-out planning 195–214; four-zone diagrams 207, **208**; gallery spaces/size requirements 208–209; museum galleries and buildings 196–197; space programming/planning 207–212; visitor experience 197–207
insulation 301–303; aluminium 310; carbon 310; cellulose 310; cork 310; cotton 301–302; embodied carbon 310; extruded polystyrene 310; polystyrene 310; wood fiber 310

integrated museums *see* open and integrated museums
International Spy Museum, Washington, D.C. 233
Into the Heart of Africa 168–169
Intrude (Parer) 131, 133
invitations 63–133; citizenship 119–134; place-maker 105–118; revitalization/communities 65–85; Urban Living Rooms 86–104
Iron Age exhibit, Moesgaard Museum 217–218

J Getty Museum, Los Angeles 140
J. Landis & Sharon Martin Building (Denver Art Museum) 66, 68, *69*, 70, *71*, 73, *74*
Jack, Joseph, and Morton Mandel Welcome Center (Museum of Contemporary Art) 93–94, 100–101
Jackson-Jarvis, M. 126, *127*
James Corner Field Operations 93
Jewish Holocaust Center (JHC) 109–112
J.F. Driscoll Family Gallery 55
JKURTZ Architects 100
Johnson, M. 131, *132*
Johnston, D. 128
Joseph M. Bryan Museum Park Theater 124
Judd, D. 264
Judy Crook (Steinkamp) 97

Kahn, L. I. 197–198, *199*, 200
Kapoor, A. *152*
Kelly, E. 242–243
Kelly Ellsworth Foundation 264, *265*
Kelvingrove Art Gallery and Museum, Glasgow 183
Kerstin Thompson Architects (KTA) 105–111, *108*, *111*, 114–115, *116–117*
key audience-facing staffers (VEAs) 100–101
Kinoshita, G. 162, *164*
knowledge economies 49–53
Kohl Atrium 97, 101–102

Kohl Family Monumental Staircase 88–89
Kristallnacht (night of broken glass) 110
Kruger, B. 123, 124, *124*
KTA (Kerstin Thompson Architects) 105–111, *108*, *111*, 114–115, *116–117*
Kunsthal, Rotterdam 139
Kunsthaus Graz 25–26, *27*; clock tower 36–37; effect on institution 29–33; exhibition Space 01 *27*; firm development 35; glass façade 30–31, *32*; historic center 26, *27*; as landmark 39–40; marketing brochures 37, *38*; nozzle frames 36–37; number of visitors 30, *31*; roof 36–37; Space 01/running costs 30–31, *32*; space 04 conference/event 33; UNESCO City of Design 34–35, 38–39
Kunstskammern 179

LAMOTH (Los Angeles Museum of the Holocaust) 320–323, 327–329
Landis & Sharon Martin Building (Denver Art Museum) *66*, 68, 69, 70, *71*, 73, *74*
Larocque, G. 325–326
Larsen, H. 216, *217*
Last to Know (Brannon) 240–242
"The Lawrence Tree" (O'Keefe) 267, 275
Learning and Engagement Center 68, 70, *71*, *72*, 78
Lee-Chin, M. 51–52; *see also* Michael Lee-Chin Crystal
LEED certification 96, 289–290, 322, 325–326, 327–328
Levin, M. 182
Levitt Bernstein Associates 11
LGE Design/Build 283–284, 288
Libeskind, D. 55–56, 165, 236–237, *238*, *239*, 239
libraries 168
limestone, entrance ramps 249, *250*
Lindsay, G. 315–316, 326–327
linear spatial types 182–183
Living Museums, Sydney 143
"The Living Wall" 272, *273*
logics 156–157, 311
Lord Cultural Services 89–90

Los Angeles Museum of the Holocaust (LAMOTH) 320–323, 327–329
Louisiana Museum of Modern Art, Denmark 139
Louvre Palace 181
Louvre, The 146, 181
Louvre-Lens Museum 143, *144*, 145

MAAS (Museum of Applied Arts and Science) 143, 145–146
McCauley, M. C. 294
MacGregor, N. 140
Macgregror, E. A. 152
Machado Silvetti 69, 70, *71*, *72*, *74*, *75*
Mackintosh, C. R. 193
McLaughlin Planetarium (Royal Ontario Museum) 162, *164*, 165
McLeese, D. 76
McLuhan, M. 171–172
Macmillan, D. 193
Madsen, J. S. 226–227
Mandel Welcome Center 91–94, 100–103, *102*, 103, *103*
Maritime Services Board building (MCA) 13, *14*
marketing brochures 37, *38*
Marshall, S. 15, *16–18*
Martin Building (Denver Art Museum) *66*, 68, 69, 70, *71*, 73, *74*
MCA (Museum of Contemporary Art), Australia 13–22, 149, *152*, 291
MCA (Museum of Contemporary Art), Chicago 267–268, *269*
MCA (Museum of Contemporary Art), Denver 317–320, 327–329
MDC (Museums Discovery Centre), Sydney 143, *144*
meaning in museums 178–194
mechanical systems in energy conservation 309
de Medici, F. 180, 181
Meier, R. 204
Memorial (Kelly) 242–243
Metropolitan Museum of Art, New York 141, 261–262

Michael Lee-Chin Crystal 43, *44*, 45, 55–57, 165, 168–169
Miller, D. 50–51
Milwaukee Art Museum 305
MITs Strata Center 238–239
Mitzevich, N. 140
moCa (Museum of Contemporary Art) 86–104
Moesgaard Museum, Aarhus, Denmark 215–227; animated narratives 222, *223*; artifact display 220; entrance foyer 216–217, *218*; Evolution Stairs 216–217, 218–219, *218*; exterior 215, *216*; floor plans 216, *217*; Grauballe Man exhibit 223–225, *226*; green roof 216, *217*; Origin Stairs 218–219, *219*; outdoor access 222–223, *224*; Stone Age exhibit 217–218, 221, *222*
MoMA (Museum of Modern Art), New York 140, 149–150, 197–212, 264–265
Monash University Museum of Art (MUMA) 105–109; Ian Potter Sculpture Forecourt *108*, 109; services canopy 106–107
Morgridge Creative Hub (Denver Art Museum) 67–84, *69*, *74*, *75*, *80*
Moriyama and Teshima architecture firm 323
Morton, C. 106
Moussavi, F. 88–103, 306
Multiple Streams policy frameworks 46
MUMA (Monash University Museum of Art) 105–109
municipal policymakers 43–62
Musaeum Tradescantianum 180–181
Musée Louvre 146, 181
Musée Mondiale 186
Musée Yves Saint Laurent, Marrakech, Morocco 146–147
Museum of Applied Arts and Science (MAAS) 143, 145–146
Museum Architecture for Embodied Experience (Tzortzi) 222–223
Museum of Contemporary Art (MCA), Chicago 267–268, *269*
Museum of Contemporary Art (MCA), Denver 317–320, 327–329
Museum of Contemporary Art (MCA), Sydney, Australia 13–22, 149, *152*
Museum of Contemporary Art (moCa), Cleveland 86–104, 306; cafe kiosk 98, *99*; exterior 86, *87*; furniture 101, *102*; ground floor 87–89; Gund Commons 91–92, 97, 101, 103, *103*; Kohl Family Monumental Staircase 88–89; store 91, *92*; Welcome Center 93–94, 100–101, *102*; West facing façade 93
museum fatigue 262; bad standing 263–264; definitions 262–273; exit experience 270–273; fixed movement circuits 269–270; recline position 265–269; seating 264–265
Museum Fridericianum 181
Museum of the Holocaust (LAMOTH) 320–323, 327–329
Museum of Modern Art (MoMA), New York 140, 149–150, 197–212, 264–265
Museum of Modern Art, San Francisco 261–262, 271–272, *273*
Museum of Scotland 192
Museum of Tokyo 186
Museum of Unlimited Extension 186
Museums Discovery Centre (MDC), Castle Hill, Sydney 143, *144*
Musical Instrument Museum, Phoenix, Arizona 231
Myers, B. 162, *163*

Nancy Spero: Parade 11, *13*
National Art Gallery of Australia 140
National Ballet School 52, **53**
National Centre for Creative Learning (MCA) 15, *17*, 19, *19*
National Endowment of the Arts (NEA) 123
National Gallery of Canada 147
National Gallery of Victoria, Melbourne 147
National Lotteries etc. Act 9
Natural History Museum, London 181–182, 183

nature 129–130, 314–332
nave and aisle spatial types 182–183
NCMA (North Carolina Museum of Art) 119–136
Neto, E. 267–268, *269*
net-zero/net-positive buildings 297–313
Neue Nationalgalerie, Berlin 139
neutral body posture 265, *266*
Newseum, The 279–280
night of broken glass 110
node connection model *236*
Norberg-Schulz, C. 188
North Carolina Art Society 119–120
North Carolina General Assembly 120
North Carolina Museum of Art (NCMA), Raleigh 119–136; aerial view 124, *125*; amphitheaters 124, *125*; art and environmentalism 129–130; art and landscape 123–128, *129*; campuses 130–133; Museum Park 131, *132*; pedestrian bridge 126, *126*; prisons and culture 119–123; site functions 128; smokestack 131, *132*; storm water demonstration ponds *130*; West Building 128, *129*
North Carolina State University (NCSU) 129
North York, Ontario 49–50
North/Martin Building (Denver Art Museum) 66, 68, *69*, 70, *71*, 73, *74*
nozzle frames 36–37

Odum, H. 310
OFF THE RULING CLASS (Yitzhak) 98
Office of Bicycle and Pedestrian Transportation, North Carolina 126, *126*
O'Keefe, G. 267
Old Town, Scottsdale, Arizona 279–296
Olmi, G. 179–180
open and integrated museums 137–154; community and gathering 147–148; concepts 139–140; content and process 140–141; design and conservation 145; education 145–146; financial models/ potential 149–151; gallery refitting 142, *143*; open storage facilities 142–145; unique space/white box 151–153
open storage facilities 142–145
Opera House, Sydney 13–15, *18*
operating costs 38, 149, 154, 279, 284, 290
Opsvik, P. 269–270
optimized windows 305–307
orchestras 10
Origin Stairs, Moesgaard Museum 218–219, *219*
Ostroff, E. 247
Otlet, P. 186
Outlook Towers 184–185, 186

Pakesch, P. 26, 28–29, 32–33
Pallasmaa, J. 189–190
Pan Pacific Park, LA Holocaust Museum 320, *321*
paradigmatic museum (Durand) 181–182, 186
Parer, A. 131, 133
Parkin, F. 162, *163*
parks 159–160, *161*, 169, 312, 317, 320–323, *321*, 327–329
passive building principles 297–313; airtight construction 303–305; continuous insulation 301–303; mechanical systems 309; optimized windows 305–307; other 309–310; ventilation 307–308
Pavilion of Knowledge, Lisbon, Portugal 246–259; activity layout 255–256; 'blank slates' 254–255; boarding 253–254; colored directions/aids 253, *254*; entrance functions 251, *252*; entrance hall 251, *252*; entrance ramp 249, *250*; exhibition design 256; main entrance 249; megalithic cross 249–251; the 'Nave' 252, *253*; 'the ship' 252, *253*; ticket office 251; wheelchair access 251
Pawley, M. 192
Peggy Guggenheim Collection, Venice 151
Penn, A. 197
Penone, G. 133

Perkins, B. 282
Petronick, K. 98
Phifer, T. 128, *129*
Phoenix Art Museum 283
Picket, D. 94–95
Pier Arts Centre, Orkney 11
place-makers 105–118
plastic foam 310
Playhouse Complex, Cleveland 89–90
Plensa, J. 133
political protest 168–169
Polk Youth Center, Raleigh 120–122
Pompidou Centre, Paris, France 140, 311–312
Ponti, G. 68, *69*, 70
Ponti Hall (Denver Art Creative Hub) 67–84, *69*, *74*, *75*, *80*
The Portrait Machine (ARoS Public) 147
"Portrait of My Heart and All Its Protectors" (Rushton) 267, *268*
Price, N. 223
prisons 119–123; smokestacks 131, *132*
Process Creative 101
promenade architecturale 188
Ptolemy Soter 179
public policy 45–46

Quadracci Pavilion, Milwaukee Art Museum 305
Queen Elizabeth II Terrace Galleries (Royal Ontario Museum) 162, *164*, 165
Queen's Park 160, *161*, 169
Queensland Art Gallery & Gallery of Modern Art 149
Quennell, N. 123, 124, *124*
Quiet Mornings 264–265

R410a refrigerant 310
radiant temperature 306–307
Raiffeisen Bank 32–33
Raleigh, NCMA 119–136
refitting of galleries 142, *143*
refrigerants 310
relative humidity 306
Renaissance Buildings of Scotland 193

Renzo Piano Building Workshop Architects 305
Research Triangle (Raleigh, Durham, and Chapel Hill), North Carolina 130
residential energy recovery ventilators 307, *308*
revitalization 3, 23, 36, 47–48, 50, 54, 65–85, 96, 109, 315–316
RIBA Award 1999 11
Riversdale visitor facilities 115, *116*
Rochowski, S. 140–141
Rodin, A. 98
Rodney, S. 294
roofs 36–37, 216, *217*, 314–332
Rossi, A. 141
Rothko Chapel, Houston, Texas 264
Roy Thompson Hall 52, **53**
Royal Exchange Theatre, Manchester 11
Royal Fine Art Commission Trust Building of the Year Award 11
Royal Museum of Scotland 181–182
Royal Ontario Museum (ROM) 43–62, 155–177; 1914 Wing 159–160, *161*; 1933 Wing 160, *161*; aesthetic surface 169–172, *173*; architectural history 157, *159*; citizen-consumer activities 169; civic identity 165–175; external appearance 170–171; external interface 168–169; founding 159–160; as icon 53–54; imperial era 156, 158–160, *161*, 166, *167*; institution/architecture 155–156; internal appearance 171–172, *173*; internal layout 172–175; layers of architecture 165–175; location 166; long halls/open spaces 173–174; main eras 157–165; neoliberal era 156, 162, 165; political protest 168–169; postwar era 156, 161–162, *163–164*; wings 174–175; world architecture stage 54–57
Rubin Museum 268
Rückert, L. 36
Rushton, C. 267, *268*, 270–272, *273*

Safdie Architects 305
Saines, C. 149

Salisbury Crags, Scotland 192
SAM (Shepparton Art Museum) 112–114
Sámi Museum and Northern Lapland Nature Centre, Inari, Finland (SIIDA) 189–190, *191*
Samuel H. Kress Collection 120
San Francisco Museum of Modern Art (SFMOMA) 261–262, 271–272, *273*
SANAA (Japanese studio) 14, 144, 152
Santa Cruz Museum of Art and History, Santa Cruz, California 260–261
Santiago Calatrava Architects & Engineers 305
Sauerbruch and Hutton 14, 21
Sayer, T. 126, *127*
Scarborough, Ontario 49–50
Scarpa, C. 186–187
Schnitzler, A. 26, 29, 32–33, 36
Schrempf, E. 26–28, 35
Science Gallery, Melbourne 142, *143*
Science Gallery Melbourne 149–150
Scully, J. 148
"Seated Catalog of Feelings" (Sosolimited) *234*
seating: museum fatigue 264–265; *see also* furniture
"The Senses: Design Beyond Vision" (Hewitt) 233, *234*, 235
Settis, S. 137, *138*
'Sexo… e então?!' exhibition 248, 256
SFMOMA (San Francisco Museum of Modern Art) 261–262, 271–272
Shear, - 129
Shepparton Art Museum (SAM) 112–114; building form 113, *114*; ground plane 114; site 112, *113*
Shoalhaven 115, *117*
Shoval, N. 24
Sie Welcome Center (Denver Art Museum) 68, *69*, 73, *74*
SIIDA (Sámi Museum and Northern Lapland Nature Centre) 189–190, *190*
Silverscreen (Morton) 106
Silvetti, J. *69*, 70, *71*, *72*, *74*, *75*
Simon, N. 66–67, 260–261

Sistine Chapel, Vatican Museums 180
Skyway galleries (HMA) 197–198, *199*, *205*, *206*
SLM (Sydney Living Museums) 143
Smith, L. F. & J. K. 263–264
Smith-Miller+Hawkinson 123, *124*, *124*
Smithsonian Design Museum, Cooper Hewitt 233, *234*, 235
smokestacks 126, 131, *132*
Snøhetta 271
"Snow Storm" (Brosius) *234*
solar panels 311
solipsistic architecture 168
Solomon R. Guggenheim Museum, New York 151
space syntax methodology 198
Spacelab Cook/Fournier GmbH Graz 26
spatial organization of inside-out planning 196–208
spatial structure of early museums 183
spectacle and design *see* icons
staging experience 184–193
stainless steel 306
Stair of Wonders (Royal Ontario Museum) 55
stakeholder partnerships 52, **53**
Star Architecture 23–42; effect on city 34–38; effect on institution 29–33; function/program 25–29
State Hermitage Museum, St-Petersburg, Russia 140
steel 306, 309–310
Steinkamp, J. 97
Stone Age exhibit, Moesgaard Museum 217–218, 221, *222*
Stone, E. D. 120, *121*
storm water demonstration ponds *130*
Strobl, H. 36
Strom, E. 24
strong program (inside-out planning) 197
Studio Libeskind 239
Studio Ma designs 279–296
studiolo rooms 179–180
studioplusthree 140–141
Sudjic, D. 279–280

Sudler, J. 68, *69*
Sundell, N. 89
Surface 678 128, *129*
sustainability 277–332; nature 314–332; passive building principles 297–313; triple bottom line design 279–296
di Suvero, M. 133
Sydney Living Museums (SLM) 143
Sydney Opera House 13–15, *18*, 24
Sydney's Museums Discovery Centre 143, *144*
Symphony Orchestra of Birmingham 10

Talalay, M. 89
Tate Modern 11, 13
Tate Sensorium at Tate Britain 233, 235–236
Tate's Turner Prize 10
Teather, J. L. 170
temperature 306–307
"temple of culture" 181–182, 184
Terrace Galleries (Royal Ontario Museum) 162, *164*, 165
textualized landscape 124
Thane Studios 11
"The Bridge", Boyd Education Center 115, *116–117*
thermal bridges 301–302
thermal comfort 306–307; *see also* insulation
Thierstein, A. 24–25
The Thinker (Rodin) 98
Third Man Begins Digging Through Her Pockets (Grosse) 97
Thomas, H. W. 133
Thomas Phifer and Partners 128, *129*
Title III of the Americans with Disabilities Act (ADA) 233
Toby's Plaza (moCa) 93, 95
Tokyo Museum 186
Toronto: Art Gallery of Ontario 155–177; black communities and protest 168–169; cultural policy landscape 51–52; economic development **50**; municipal cultural policy 57–58; public goods **51**; Royal Ontario Museum 43–62, 155–177; stakeholder partnerships 52, **53**; transformational architecture 43–62
Tosca, S. 219–220
Tradescant, J. 180–181
transformational architecture 43–62; agenda setting 45–46; arts and culture 46–49; knowledge economies 49–53; public policy 45–46
Trenkler, T. 28
Triangle Land Conservancy 130
triple bottom line sustainable design 279–296
Tuckson – the abstract sublime exhibition 140, *141*
Tzortzi, K. 222–223

Uffizi Gallery, Florence 181
United Nations Educational, Scientific, and Cultural Organization (UNESCO) 34–35, 38–39
United States Holocaust Memorial Museum, Washington, D.C. 241–242, *243*
universal design principles **232**
universities: California, Davis 282–283; Monash 105–109; NCMA 130–133; North Carolina State 129
University Circle, Cleveland 90
Unlimited Extension Museum 186
The User Perspective in Twenty-First Century Art Museums (Lindsay) 315–316
"useum" 186

Value Museums 39–40
van der Rohe, M. 139
van Klenze, L. 196
Vancouver Art Gallery 263–264
Vartanian, O. 239–240
Vatican Museums 180
'Vê, Faz, Aprendre!' exhibition (See, Do and Learn!) 248
VEAs (key audience-facing staffers) 100–101
ventilation 307–308
Viking Age exhibit, Moesgaard Museum 217–218

Wadsworth Atheneum Museum of Art, Hartford, Connecticut 267, 275
"Water Falls from my Breast to the Sky" 267–268, *269*
weak program (inside-out planning) 197
Weidenfeld, A. 24
welcome centers 68, *69*, 73, *74*, 91–94, 100–103, *102–103*
Welter, V. 185–186
Western Spirit: Scottsdale Museum, Arizona 279–296; bridges 284, *285*; building design 284–290, *291*; building materials 286–287; concrete texture 287–288, *289*; courtyard lighting 194, 294, *295*; ecological design 290, *291*; economic sustainability 292, 294–295; economic/social sustainability 281–283; exterior walls 287, *288*; exterior/location 279, *280*; interior gallery layout 284, *285*; meeting/retail use 291–292, *293*; native plantings/tree shade 291, *292*; origins 280–281; site plan 291–292, *293*; social sustainability 290–292, *293*; space for gatherings/presentations 286; two-story-design 284, *285*; weeping walls/riparian gardens 290

Westlake Reed Leskosky (WRL) 89
Wheeler, L. 121–122
white box gallery types 151–153
White Rabbit Gallery 137, *138*
Whitney Museum of American Art 145, 152
windows 152, 222–223, *224*, *265*, 305–307
wings 159–160, *161*, 174–175
Wohlert, W. 139
Wunderkammer 179

Xu Zhen 137, *138*

Yale Center for British Art (YCBA), New Haven, Connecticut 197–212
Yesterday Today Tomorrow MCA Collection 20–21, *21*
Yitzhak, N. 98
yoga events 270
York, Ontario 49–50
de Young Museum, San Francisco, California 261–262
Yves Saint Laurent, Marrakech, Morocco 146–147

Zigzags and Diagonals (Comte) 101, *103*